The New Politics
of Communist China

Modernization Process
of a Developing Nation

Winberg Chai
University of Redlands

GOODYEAR PUBLISHING COMPANY, INC.
Pacific Palisades, California

To Our Children: May-lee and Jeffrey

Current printing (last digit) :
10 9 8 7 6 5 4 3 2 1

Library of Congress Catalog Card Number: 78-188277

ISBN: 0-87620-619-4
Y-6194-8

Printed in the United States of America

PREFACE

The story of the modernization process of China can now be told. "The extraordinary thing about this oldest civilization in the world," wrote James Reston from Peking on 27 July 1971, "is that it seems so young. You do not have the feeling here—so depressing and oppressive in some other parts of the Orient—of weariness, sickness and death, of old men and women, spent before their time, struggling against hopeless odds. . . . The people seem not only young but enthusiastic about their changing lives."

The purpose of this book is in fact to describe and analyze the modernization process of China's political, economic, cultural, and foreign affairs from the 1950s to the 1970s. The work is thus divided into three principal parts: part one provides background information for the general reader—on Chinese land, people, recent history, the Communist Party, and the meaning of Maoism as a developing ideology; part two describes the policy and process of contemporary China, and the impact of Maoism upon Chinese society and international politics; part three includes original resource materials, documents, and biographical data of Chinese leaders. There are also many tables, charts, and maps for beginning students of Chinese history and politics.

During the preparation of this book, this author consulted hundreds of sources, original and secondary, and conducted personal interviews with scholars who had recently returned from China. Most of these sources are cited either in the footnotes or listed as suggested readings at the end of each chapter. Unavoidably a condensation of this nature may strip the researchers, learned and experienced China scholars, and China watchers of their living flesh, reducing them to bare bones, arranged in patterns of this author's choosing. Responsibility for using other men's scholarship in this cavalier fashion lies directly with the writer.

In addition, my many thanks to colleagues in the Los Angeles China Seminar and Berkeley Regional Seminar on Modern China for their very informative exchanges of views; to Al Goodyear, Clay Stratton, Ann Harris and the editorial staff of Goodyear Publishing Company, as well as the anonymous readers for their appreciation of the need for this book; to my parents, Dr. and Mrs. Ch'u Chai formerly of Nanking, now of New York City, for their guidance, devotion, and love; to my wife, Carolyn, and my children, May-lee and Jeffrey for their help, enthusiasm, and patience. Since Carolyn Chai, herself a creative journalist and painter, has reviewed the manuscript as a spokesman for the general reader, I hope I have not failed her, or the readers for whom she spoke.

Contents

List of Tables, Charts, Maps, and Illustrations

LIST OF TABLES

LIST OF CHARTS

LIST OF MAPS

LIST OF ILLUSTRATIONS

The People's Republic of China: 1949-72

A Chronology of Political, Social and Economic Development

Political

People's Liberation Army advances through China

Preparatory Commission for a new Political Consultative Conference held in Peking on June 15–19

New Chinese People's Political Consultative Conference (CPPCC) convened on September 21 with 661 delegates

First session of CPPCC adopted three important documents: The Common Program, the Organic Law of the Central People's Government, and the Organic Law of CPPCC

The People's Republic of China officially proclaimed on Oct. 1. Mao Tse-tung elected Chairman; Chu Teh, Liu Shao-chi, Kao Kang (Communists), Soong Ching-ling, Li Chi-shan (Kuomintang Revolutionary Committee), and Chang Lam (Democratic League) named Vice-chairmen. Chou En-lai becomes Premier of the State Administrative Council and Foreign Minister

Nationalists under Chiang Kai-shek establish an exile government on Taipei, Taiwan

1949

Social and Economic

Chairman Mao's writings on "New Democracy" and "On People's Democratic Dictatorship" promoted as China's blueprint for social and economic development

Mass mobilization and trials initiated throughout China

Political		Social and Economic
Sino-Soviet Treaty of Friendship and Alliance concluded after Mao Tse-tung visits Moscow from December, 1949 to February, 1950	1950	"Group Study" as means of mass mobilization promoted throughout China
People's Liberation Army occupies Tibet simultaneously with the first stage of its intervention in Korea		New Marriage Law promulgated in April by the Central Government
President Truman orders U.S. Seventh Fleet to enter into Taiwan Straits to prevent PLA's occupation of Taiwan		New Land-reform Law adopted in June
A system of "military-administrative" committees established into six areas: the Northeast, North China, East China, Central South China, Northwest China, and Southwest China	1951	Nationwide "thought reform" mass movement launched in May
		Selected Works of Mao Tse-tung published in October
Korean armistice negotiations beban		"Three anti" and "Five Anti" mass movements promoted
		"Mutual-aid" agricultural teams introduced
State Planning Commission established in Peking under Kao Kang	1952	Land reforms throughout China completed
Regional "military-administrative" committes converted into new administrative committees directly responsible to the Central Government in Peking		Private business nationalized
Provincial governments strengthened		
Provincial governments placed under direct control of the Central Government in Peking	1953	First Five Year Plan inaugurated
		First nationwide census taken
Electoral Law of The People's Republic promulgated on March 1		Agricultural producers' cooperatives in rural areas announced
China unified under Central Government in Peking; six administrative areas abolished	1954	Population increases dramatically; a higher form of collectivism implemented throughout China
First Constitution of The People's Republic of China adopted by the National People's Congress on September 20		Educational system unified with introduction of three levels of schooling
		New cultural policies adopted with purges of anti-party writers
Mao Tse-tung elected first Chairman of the Republic; Chu Teh named Vice-chairman; Liu Shao-chi, Chairman of the Standing Committee, and Chou En-lai, Premier of the State Council		New economic planning agencies established

Political   **Social and Economic**

China expands foreign contacts; Chou En-lai attends Geneva Conference; Khrushchev visits Peking; U.S. signs defense pact with Chiang Kai-shek to contain China

| | 1955 | |

New Conscription Law promulgated throughout China

Major Party purges begin with the ouster of Kao Kang

Regionalism suppressed

Chou En-lai participates in the Bandung Conference and expands contacts with lesser-developed countries

Sino-American ambassadorial talks begin in Geneva

1955

Important conferences on reforms of Chinese written languages held in Peking

Adult educational programs in rural areas intensified

State-owned trading companies expanded

Industrialization intensifies with new construction of railways, highways, improvements in irrigation and flood control projects

1956

Eighth Party Congress convenes in Peking with expansion of Party membership throughout China

Chairman Mao disagrees with Premier Khrushchev over the latter's denouncement of Stalin at the 20th Party Congress

China proposes cultural exchange program with U.S. and is rejected by U.S. at Geneva conferences

Chairman Mao announces "Hundred Flowers" campaign for "free" criticism

New China News Agency announces the adoption of a new 30-letter Latin alphabet into the Chinese language system

Central Government adopts new policy to slow down economic program

1957

Central Committee Plenum adopts Chairman Mao's new mass mobilization program

Chou En-lai travels to Moscow in January to negotiate new Sino-Soviet cooperation

Chairman Mao visits Moscow again in November to attend International Communist Party meeting

Chairman Mao announces new social policy: "On the Correct Handling of Contradictions Among the People"

Party launches new "anti-rightist rectification" drives

Chairman Mao proposes new policy of "Three Red Flags" including "Hsia Fan" movement and "Great Leap Forward"

1958

Major policy differences develop within the Party, Mao resigns as Chairman of the Republic

Central Government adopts new military program of People's Militia

Military conflicts in Taiwan Straits begin; U.S. initiates talks with Chinese in Warsaw

"Great Leap Forward" programs promoted with the establishment of "People's Communes" in rural areas

Economic and political crisis begins throughout China

Political		Social and Economic
Political realignment begins — Liu Shao-chi succeeds Mao as chairman of the Republic	1959	China continues economic crisis despite liberal programs promoted by the Government
Political purges continue during the Lushan Meeting of the Central Committee; Lin Piao named Defense Minister—replacing Peng Teh-huai		
People's Liberation Army suppresses Tibetan revolt; Dalai Lama flees to India		
China faces foreign policy crisis, including Sino-Indian border clashes and USSR's abrogation of nuclear sharing agreement		
Liu Shao-chi initiates new political program	1960	China continues economic crisis
		Party lessens ideological control
China's foreign relations with the USSR worsen; Soviet technicians withdraw in August; Party publishes "Long Live Leninism"		
China establishes diplomatic relations with Cuba and initiates new policies with respect to the "third world"		
Liu Shao-chi develops new political style; veiled criticism of Chairman Mao published for the first time in Party journals by Wu Han, Teng T'o, and Liao Mo-sha	1961	Party announces further liberalization measures in agriculture and in industry
		Government promotes "cultural renaissance" to include traditional Chinese literature
Sino-Soviet relations continues in low key; Chou En-lai attends International Conference in Geneva in May on Laos and Twenty-second Party Congress in Moscow in October; China defends Albania		
Mao Tse-tung and Liu Shao-chi begin open "power-struggle" within the Party; Liu chairs March Supreme State Conference	1962	New "Socialist Education Movement" initiated
		New "mass movement" begins with "Four Withs," "Four Clearances" and "Three Fixes and One Substitution," etc.
Sino-Soviet relations worsen; China publicly attacks Soviet "revisionism"		
Sino-Indian border clashes recur		

Political		Social and Economic
Mao Tse-tung encourages People's Liberation Army to take on more political works	1963	New intensified study of Mao's works initiated and promoted
China begins to negotiate differences with the Soviet Union		Research and development in military industries promoted
Test-ban treaty concluded; China refuses to sign		
National People's Congress meets in Peking	1964	Party launches a new rectification campaign
China initiates diplomatic offensive with Chou En-lai's extensive visits to Africa		New "Emulate the PLA" campaigns promoted
Party rejects Soviet call for world conference of Communist parties; Khrushchev falls from power in USSR		
China explodes first atomic bomb		
Lin Piao gains more power within the Chinese Army; he publishes "Long Live the Victory of People's War"	1965	Party begins purges of anti-Maoists intellectuals
Power struggle within the Party intensifies; Maoists publish critique of Wu Han's play		PLA initiates large scale study of Chairman Mao's thought
Liu Shao-chi's foreign policy fails in Indonesia; Vietnam war escalates		Crisis emerges within the cultural and educational systems throughout China
China explodes second nuclear test bomb		
Maoists emerges as victors in the power-struggle with anti-Maoists headed by Liu Shao-chi	1966	Chairman Mao swims Yangtze to generate enthusiasm
Party "adopts" resolution on the "Cultural Revolution"		Maoists introduce "big character poster" to faciliate mass communication
Massive demonstrations begin with introduction of "Red Guards" throughout China		Red Guards throughout China demand new cultural system for China
Party organization paralyzed; Central government reorganized	1967	Violence on upswing throughout China
Major purges continue throughout China; Liu Shao-chi denounced as China's Khrushchev		Cultural Revolution intensified
China's foreign relations come to a standstill; and China explodes first hydrogen bomb		

Political		Social and Economic
Chou En-lai emerges as new mediator for various factions	1968	Violence continues
Revolutionary Committees formed as new administrative organs		Mao Tse-tung criticizes the Red Guards for lack of discipline
Liu Shao-chi expelled from the Party; his followers purged		Chiang Ching reconstructs new cultural systems and value orientation for youth
PLA begins to restore order		Nationwide campaign promoted to support the Army
Cultural Revolution unofficially ends with the opening of new Ninth Party Congress	1969	New value and cultural systems promoted throughout China
Party Congress adopts new Constitution; Lin Piao named Mao's successor		Red Guards urged to return to schools
Drive to rebuild Party institutions in the provinces stepped up		Emulation of PLA heroes promoted
Kosygin visits Peking after Sino-Soviet borders wars on Ussuri River		
Reconstruction of new governmental institutions and Party structures continues throughout China	1970	Intensive re-evaluation of China's economic and cultural programs promoted throughout China
New proposed (secret) Constitution for the Republic circulated among cadres		
Central Government begins new foreign policy		
China begins a period of new politics	1971–72	Principles of revolutionary pragmatism adopted for social, economic, and cultural development
Chou En-lai emerges as China's new leader		A new "Fourth Five Year" Plan for gradual, proportional economic development adopted
Lin Piao and extreme Leftists purged		New educational system stressing egalitarian and integrative programs adopted
China moves toward reconciliation with foreign countries; admitted into U.N., negotiates a joint communiqué with President Nixon		Final goal to develop a "national, scientific, and mass culture" initiated

PART ONE

Background

CHAPTER ONE

The Humanized Landscape

No one denies the importance of the role of geography in the development of human civilization, as evidenced by the Nile valley in Egypt, the Tigris-Euphrates valleys in Babylonia, and the Ganges river valley in India. In China, the earliest civilization originated in the various alluvial tracts of land formed by the Yellow River (Hwang Ho) and its tributaries. The Yü culture (2255–2205 B.C.) for example, was on the northeast bank of the Yellow River; the Hsia culture (2205–1766 B.C.) on the south bank; and the Chou culture (1122–255 B.C.) on the west bank. Therefore, it is no accident that we begin the analysis of Chinese polity with an examination of Chinese geography.

China stands within the central position on the eastern part of the Eurasian land mass, chiefly between latitudes 30° N. to 45° N. Its east coast is washed by the waters of the Pacific Ocean. With the exception of a small tropical portion in the south, the country lies in the temperate belt with marked differences of the four seasons. China has some areas which enjoy perpetual spring, while others are covered in snow all the year round.

From south to north, the temperature decreases

in winter months, ranging from an average of 60° F. south of the Nan Ling range to about 40° F. along the middle and lower Yangtze valley, to about 30° F. and –17° F. in Central and Northern Manchuria. In the summer, the temperature is more uniform over the entire country (80° F. mean in July), with cooler nights again in the North and slightly hotter months in the South.

However, when the cold waves from the Arctic Ocean move across Siberia and Mongolia and reach northwest and northern China, they generate such strong cold air currents that they sometimes cause the temperature to drop by ten degrees or more within 24 hours, resulting in frost damage to agricultural crops.

Rainfall is essentially monsoonal or seasonal in its distribution. Most rainfall occurs in the summer when the atmospheric moisture blows gently from the Pacific toward the warm interior.

The amount of precipitation decreases from south to north, with an annual average of 60 to 80 inches in the Hsi River valley and the adjacent hilly land along the southeastern coast; 40 to 60 inches in the Yangtze valley; and about 25 inches over the northern China plain. It drops sharply northwestward to less than ten inches in the interior.

On the southeastern coast, the period between July and September is known as the typhoon season. While typhoons bring a certain measure of rainfall and are responsible for some cooling, they are usually in the form of storms which are extremely harmful to planted crops and even cause loss of human life in the coastal regions.

The wide range of temperature and humidity prevailing from one part of the country to another and the great variation in altitude provide the conditions for a great variety of soil. In general, the north region with nonacid soil represents the wheat area, and the acid-soil region of the south is the rice growing area. Because of the flat topography, low annual rainfall, and limited irrigation, the north region has unleached or slightly leached soil, rich in minerals and plant food, but with little organic matter. There is also a belt of neutral, slightly acid soil, found in western Hupeh, southern Shantung, the Yangtze Delta, and northern Szechwan. This is known as the transitional zone of the two major crops, wheat and rice.

The vegetation cover of China has been drastically altered by man as the Chinese earth is pervasively humanized through long occupation. According to a recent study by Yi-Fu Tuan,[1] about half the Chinese domain was originally wooded and the other half was covered with steppe and desert vegetation. For example, the Manchurian coniferous forest is strongly reminiscent of those in North America and Europe; but south of the Manchurian region, the land has been intensively exploited by man for some 2,000 years. The natural vegetation has been almost entirely removed, and in its place we find a deeply humanized landscape. Map I illustrates the distinctive regional features of China today.[2]

Map 1: Communist China — Distinctive Regional Features

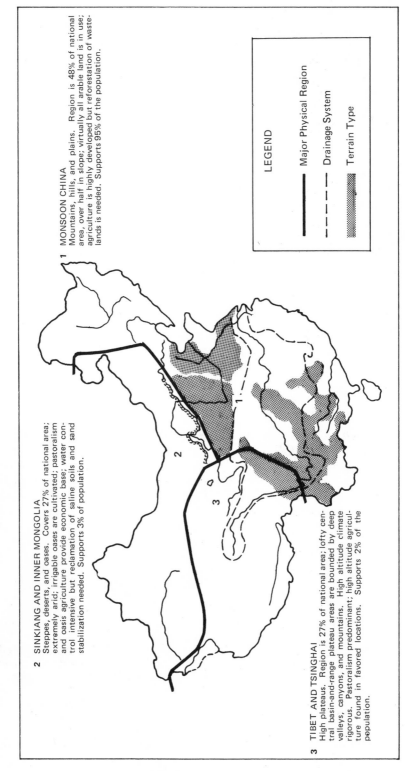

2 SINKIANG AND INNER MONGOLIA
Steppes, deserts, and oases. Covers 27% of national area; extremely arid; irrigable oases are cultivated; pastoralism and oasis agriculture provide economic base; water control intensive but reclamation of saline soils and sand stabilization needed. Supports 3% of population.

1 MONSOON CHINA
Mountains, hills, and plains. Region is 48% of national area, over half in slope; virtually all arable land is in use; agriculture is highly developed but reforestation of wastelands is needed. Supports 95% of the population.

3 TIBET AND TSINGHAI
High plateaus. Region is 27% of national area; lofty central basin-and-range plateau areas are bounded by deep valleys, canyons, and mountains. High altitude climate rigorous. Pastoralism predominant; high altitude agriculture found in favored locations. Supports 2% of the population.

LEGEND

—— Major Physical Region

‐ ‐ ‐ Drainage System

Terrain Type

THE CHANGING LANDSCAPE

China is by far the most populous nation in the world. She occupies an area of 9.6 million square kilometers (3.7 million square miles) and ranks territorially as the world's third largest nation.

Topography

The relief map of China shows that she has diverse physical features: altitudes range from 8,882 meters (25,000 feet) on Mount Jolmo Lungma (in the Himalayas), the world's highest peak on the Sino-Nepalese border, to 154 meters (928 feet) below sea level in the Turfan depression in Sinkiang. The Mongolian plateau stretches for over 2,000 miles from the Greater Khing-an range in the east to the foothills of the great mountains of Pamir, Kunlun, Tien Shan, Tannu, and Sayan in the west. The following indicates proportions of the topography:[3]

Table 1

Proportions of Topography in China

Mountainous upland	33	(percent)
Plateaus	23	"
Basins (desert)	19	"
Cultivable plains	12	"
Hills	10	"
Water areas	3	"

Lofty mountains in China have always inspired artists for their pristine beauty as illustrated in classical paintings, such as those of the T'ang and Sung dynasties. From the Pamirs of Central Asia, came four major mountain systems which form the major watersheds of all the principal rivers in China:

1. Altai system in northwest China: It has an average height of 6,000 feet and some peaks reach an altitude of 10,000 feet.
2. Tien Shan system in Sinkiang: It consists of a series of parallel chains trending east to west at an average height of 12,000 feet above sea level. The principal peak, the Tengri Khan, in the west, reaches 23,600 feet.
3. Kunlun Shan system: It divides the Tarim Basin of Sinkiang from the high plateau of Tibet, then branches into three separate chains: the Astin Tagh Nan Shan range in the north, the Tsinling Shan and Tapa Shan ranges in the center, and the Thanglha range in the south which meets the eastern end of the Himalayan system in western Szechwan and northwestern Yunnan.
4. Himalayan mountain system in Tibet: It consists of three gigantic, highly folded, parallel mountain ranges, of which the central range is the highest, with many peaks over 25,000 feet.

In addition, there are two major independent mountain systems: Sinic mountains in the northeast and Nan Ling range in the southeast, close to the Pacific coast.

Drainage Basins

China's exterior drainage basins which cover some two-thirds of the surface of the country, roughly coincide with the humid, semihumid and semiarid zones. The rivers in these basins flow into the Pacific, Indian, and Arctic oceans.

The Pacific drainage basin, which accounts for 50 percent of the country's total drainage area, includes some of China's greatest rivers, the Yangtze, the Yellow, the Pearl, and the Lantsang (upper Mekong).

The Yangtze, by far the largest river in China, is 3,237 miles long and drains an area of over 700,000 square miles. Its source is only 50 miles from that of the Yellow River, the second largest river in the country. The Yellow River is 2,980 miles long and covers an area of 600,000 square miles. In the northeast, the Armur River (Heilung or Black Dragon) drains a great part of the Manchurian basin in its winding course of over 2,500 miles.

The Arctic and the Indian drainage account for only 5 and 6 percent of the country's total. The Indian Ocean drains those rivers which have their sources in the mountainous regions of Tibet and western Szechwan, and some of the Arctic drainage is in China.

There is also inland drainage which accounts for 39 percent of the country's drainage area, roughly coinciding with the arid zone where the rivers are chiefly fed by glaciers and melting snow from the high mountains. Their flow is greatest in summer when most of the mountain glaciers and snow are melting. The principal inland rivers are the Rarim in Sinkiang, the Joshui (Edsin Gol) in Kansu and Inner Mongolia, and the Tsaidam in Chinghai.

Most of the rivers in the eastern part of the country flow from west to east. In ancient days, the lack of waterways created a big problem for communication between the north and the south. To solve this problem, many canals were dug, the largest of which is the Grand Canal. From Peking it passes through four of China's provinces, links five rivers, and finally reaches Hangchow, a distance of over 1,700 kilometers.

China's coastline is 2,500 miles long, and extends from the mouth of the Yalu River in the northeast to the mouth of the Pei-lun River in the south. If minor inlets are included, the distance amounts to nearly 7,000 miles.

The coastline forms a great arc with the peninsulas of Liaotung and Shantung in the north and Luichow in the south, protruding respectively into the Yellow Sea and the South China Sea. The coastline is separated from the Pacific Ocean by a series of islands and archipelagos, such as the Liu-chiu (Ryukyus), Taiwan, Peng-nu (Pescadores),

Hainan, Tung-sha (Pratas), Hsi-sha (Paracel), and Nan-sha (Spratly) groups. This chain of islands not only gives China a continuous series of partially enclosed coastal seas, like the Gulf of Chihli, the Yellow Sea, the East China Sea, and the South China Sea, but it also forms the two great gulfs of Liaotung in the north and Tonkin in the south.

Floods and Droughts

While water resources are adequate under normal circumstances, precipitation in most areas comes from the summer monsoon. The annual rainfall is therefore concentrated in certain seasons, and this results in big variations in the water levels of rivers and lakes. According to a scholarly study of 17 provinces for which rainfall data is available, seven provinces have their maximum rainfall in July, seven in June, and three in August. At times, rainstorms will give rise to floods and lack of rainfall will result in droughts. The seriousness of the problem may be illustrated in the following table showing the frequency of floods and droughts from 206 B.C. to A.D. 1911.[4]

Table 2

Frequency of Floods and Droughts from 206 B.C.–A.D. 1911

DYNASTIES	FLOODS	DROUGHTS
Former Han	18	28
Later Han	39	62
Three Kingdoms	8	7
West Chin	25	21
Eastern Chin	33	50
Period of Division	82	69
Sui	5	5
T'ang	151	133
Five Dynasties	8	28
Northern Sung	195	133
Southern Sung	159	130
Yuan	163	116
Ming	370	256
Ch'ing	365	354
TOTAL	1,621	1,392

Since the formation of People's Republic in 1949, considerable progress has been achieved in rural water conservation. It is claimed that the Chinese people have built more than a million small reservoirs and ponds, dug nine million wells, and developed new canals and storage basins. This increased the irrigated area by 120 million acres during the first 12-year period.[5]

One of the most ambitious undertakings by the People's Republic is the attempt to harness the Yellow River, which requires the construction of 46 dams on the main river, 24 large reservoirs along the major

Map 2: Sketch Map of the Yellow River

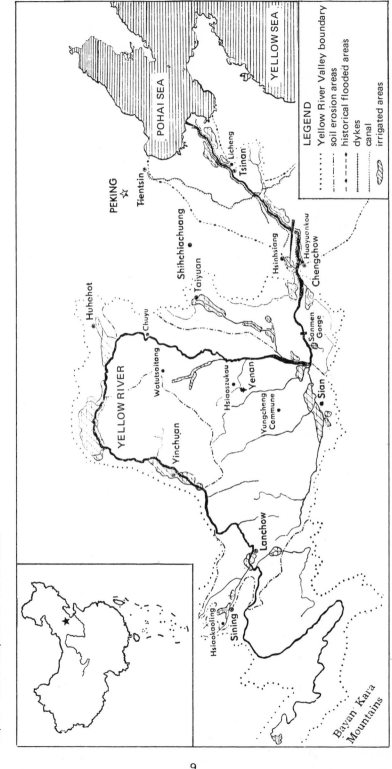

YELLOW SEA

POHAI SEA

YELLOW SEA

PEKING

Tientsin

Licheng

Tsinan

Shihchiachuang

Taiyuan

Hsinhsiang

Huoyuankou

Chengchow

Huhehot

Chuyu

Sanmen
Gorge

YELLOW RIVER

Wotutsailang

Hsiaoszukou

Yenan

Sian

Yinchuan

Yungcheng
Commune

Lanchow

Hsiaokaoling

Sining

Bayan Kara
Mountains

LEGEND
······· Yellow River Valley boundary
—·—·— soil erosion areas
—·◆·— historical flooded areas
◆———◆ dykes
———— canal
〰〰 irrigated areas

9

tributaries, and numerous small check dams on the side streams to hold back the immense amount of silt in the loose plateau. According to a 1971 report, more than 40 million *mu* of farmland on the upper and lower reaches of the river are irrigated by the Yellow River water, and electric power is supplied to industrial and agricultural production. Afforestation in this area is part of the total effort to check the movement of silt into the river. The entire project will probably take decades to complete, but a good beginning has already been made.[6]

NATURAL RESOURCES

The Chinese live very close to nature and something like 550 million Chinese, three-quarters of China's total population, are directly engaged in and supported by agriculture. On the other hand, China's arable area, concentrated in large measure on the plains and river-valley lands of humid China proper, is less than 60 percent as large as that of the United States. On the average, it provides only about half an acre of arable land per capita to the agricultural population, and only two-fifths of an acre per capita to the total population. Therefore, the problem of an adequate food supply is an old one that dates back to the ancient days of the empire.

Agriculture

Chinese agriculture has had a long and honored history. China produces good yields per acre, but such production is the result of good management and laborious use of manpower. Excessive care is bestowed upon the field, and some areas have been in use for some 2,000 years. Many crops are grown (rice and wheat are two main crops) and no one can travel more than a few hundred miles without being impressed by marked differences in crops and farm practices.

South China is a green, humid, and subtropical riceland while North China is a dry, brown wheatland under the influence of the desert. Wheat extends well into the Yangtze valley as a winter crop, but is not widespread in the south. However, China has seldom produced enough food for her own needs. Since the People's Republic was established, the Chinese government has attempted to increase agricultural production, including among other measures, water conservation, increased irrigation, afforestation, and reforestation.

China boasts more than 30,000 varieties of exogens, or seed-bearing plants. Of these, over 5,000 are woody and nearly 1,000 are timber trees. But only a tenth of China is forested and large areas are without significant vegetative cover. The total recent timber resource of the country was no more than 5.4 billion cubic meters, which would last about 35 years. As a result of this urgency, the People's Republic began a national program of afforestation at the end of 1955. It called for the planting of some 105 million hectares of land in the next 12 years to give China

a forest cover of 20 percent of its total surface. By the end of the first
Five-Year Plan (1957), the Chinese claimed to have planted more than
10 million hectares. In fact, further success was evident by the 1958
drive which resulted in the afforestation of 69 million acres that year.[8]

It is difficult to assess the results of Chinese efforts in agriculture
due to the lack of official statistics. However, some increases in food-
grain production must have been made because agricultural products
now comprise the major items for international trade and continue to
support her growing population.

Mineral Deposits

Fortunately for China, a number of important mineral deposits
were known to exist. China has very large reserves in coal and iron
ore. She is the world's leading producer of tungsten and is a sizeable
producer of manganese, tin, mercury, molybdenum, and antimony.[9]

The country's coal reserves consist largely of bituminous coal and
some anthracite, and the main producing areas are in southern Manchuria. Manganese is mined primarily in the central Yangtze region,
while tungsten, mercury, and antimony are mined in the hill country of
South China. She has small but adequate reserves of copper, lead, zinc,
and aluminum-bearing ores. Chrome, cobalt, and nickle, used in the
production of a certain type of steel, are in short supply.

Although coal is by far the major source of mechanical energy in
China, oil reserves are being developed. Oil fields include the old ones
in Yumen, the Tsaidam Basin, and Karami in the Dzungarian Basin.
Some new fields are also being opened in Taching (northern Manchuria)
and at Sengli (North China Plains). These recent discoveries have made
China virtually self-sufficient in petroleum products; however, by world
standards, she is still a minor producer.

In order that the widespread resources and scattered production
and consumer centers may be integrated into a functioning whole, the
Chinese have constructed a new transport network. With the principal
railways and the major rivers (Yangtze, Pearl, and Sungari) as the
arteries, the network is supplemented by highways, airlines, roads, and
canals built by the local population.

The principal railways running north-south are the Peking-Canton
line, the Tientsin-Pukow and Shanghai-Nanking lines, and the Chang-
chun-Harbin and Changchun-Talien lines. The main east-west railways
are the Lunghai and Lanchow-Sinkiang lines, the Peking-Paotow and
Paotow-Lanchow lines, and the Chekiang-Kiangsi and Hunan-Kwangsi
lines.

There are also important new roads into western border regions,
particularly to Tibet, where feeder routes extend to the Sino-Indian
border and to Nepal. Roads constructed to the Tsaidam Basin and in
parts of Sinkiang have permitted the Chinese to exploit the mineral
resources of those areas.[10]

THE TEEMING POPULACE

No one can travel across China without being aware of the pressure of people on the arable land, because China is the largest country of the world in population. However, the size of the Chinese population has long been in dispute. For years, Chinese Nationalists have referred to the country as the "Land of Four-hundred Million," although the population reached 430 million in 1850. There have also been temporary fluctuations because of natural and man made disasters.

In the modern period, perhaps the greatest natural calamity that the world has known took place in North China between 1876 and 1879. Four Chinese provinces, Shenhsi, Shanhsi, Hanan, and Hopei were hit by famine. Some nine to 13 million people perished from hunger, disease, or violence and the population of the region was drastically reduced. Again during the period from 1920 to 1921, some 20 million people were destitute because of famines which brought about the death of half a million people.

During the Sino-Japanese War, the bank of the Yellow River was deliberately breached at a point a few miles east of the crossing of the river by the Peking-Hankou railway. The breach was made so that the floodwater could block the advance of the invading Japanese army. The river swung south and meandered over a broad strip of good farmland and some 800,000 people perished either directly or indirectly through this deliberately induced flood.

Statistical Survey

In the spring of 1953, the People's Republic began one of the greatest statistical projects in history, and for the first time the population of the world's largest country was to be enumerated by modern census methods. The net result was announced on 30 June 1953 with a figure of 582,603,417 including a male-female sex ration of 107:100. In 1957, the only other time China announced an official population statistic, the census showed that the population had increased to 646,530,000.

It may be of interest to note that there are minority nationalities in China—in fact, they have been residing in China for many centuries. These minority nationalities, constitute about 6 percent of China's total population, and are situated mainly in seven border regions: (1) Manchuria; (2) Inner Mongolia; (3) Sinkiang, Tsinghai, and Kansu; (4) Tibet; (5) Szechwan, Yunnan, and Kweichow; (6) Kwangtung and Kwangsi; and (7) Taiwan.

The majority of Chinese are known as the Han people, and account for 94 percent of China's population. The remaining six percent or 40 million (1957 figure) are made up of more than 50 national minority groups. Maps 3 and 4 illustrate China's population grouping patterns and population density.[11] The large minority

Map 3: Communist China —
Population Groupings

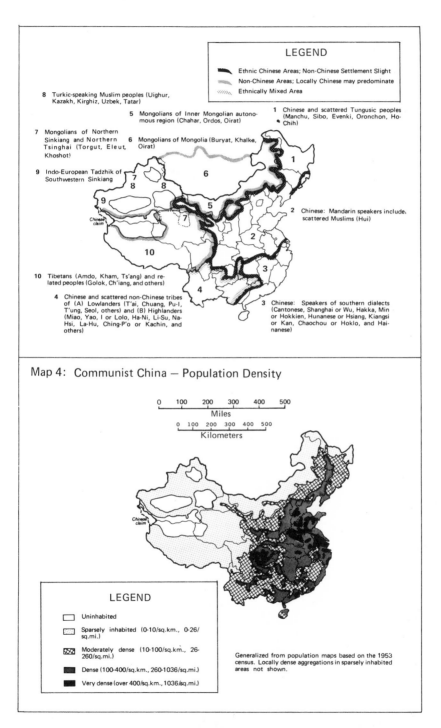

LEGEND

Ethnic Chinese Areas; Non-Chinese Settlement Slight

Non-Chinese Areas; Locally Chinese may predominate

Ethnically Mixed Area

8 Turkic-speaking Muslim peoples (Uighur, Kazakh, Kirghiz, Uzbek, Tatar)

5 Mongolians of Inner Mongolian autonomous region (Chahar, Ordos, Oirat)

7 Mongolians of Northern Sinkiang and Northern Tsinghai (Torgut, Eleut, Khoshot)

6 Mongolians of Mongolia (Buryat, Khalka, Oirat)

9 Indo-European Tadzhik of Southwestern Sinkiang

1 Chinese and scattered Tungusic peoples (Manchu, Sibo, Evenki, Oronchon, Ho-Chih)

2 Chinese: Mandarin speakers include scattered Muslims (Hui)

10 Tibetans (Amdo, Kham, Ts'ang) and related peoples (Golok, Ch'iang, and others)

4 Chinese and scattered non-Chinese tribes of (A) Lowlanders (T'ai, Chuang, Pu-I, T'ung, Seol, others) and (B) Highlanders (Miao, Yao, I or Lolo, Ha-Ni, Li-Su, Na-Hsi, La-Hu, Ching-P'o or Kachin, and others)

3 Chinese: Speakers of southern dialects (Cantonese, Shanghai or Wu, Hakka, Min or Hokkien, Hunanese or Hsiang, Kiangsi or Kan, Chaochou or Hoklo, and Hainanese)

Map 4: Communist China — Population Density

0   100   200   300   400   500
Miles

0   100   200   300   400   500
Kilometers

LEGEND

☐ Uninhabited

▨ Sparsely inhabited (0-10/sq.km., 0-26/sq.mi.)

▨ Moderately dense (10-100/sq.km., 26-260/sq.mi.)

■ Dense (100-400/sq.km., 260-1036/sq.mi.)

■ Very dense (over 400/sq.km., 1036/sq.mi.)

Generalized from population maps based on the 1953 census. Locally dense aggregations in sparsely inhabited areas not shown.

nationality groups include: (1) the Mongols of Inner Mongolia and Manchuria; (2) the Koreans or Manchus who were of Tungus origin in Manchuria; (3) the Uigurs or eastern Turks of Sinkiang or northwest China; (4) the Tibetans of Tibet, Tsinghai, and Kansu; (5) the Miao and Yao of south and southwest China; (6) the Chuang, a Thai-speaking group of western Kwangsi; (7) the Yi or Lolo, of the borders of Szechwan and Yunnan; and (8) the Puyi or Chungchia in southwestern Kweichow province. Most of these minorities are living in special national autonomous districts as indicated below:[12]

Table 3

National Autonomous Districts

DISTRICTS	NATIONAL MINORITIES
Yunnan	
Te-hung	Thai and Chingpo
Hsi-shuang-pa-na	Thai
Hung-ho	Hani and Yi
Nu-chiang	Lisu
Ti-ch'ing	Tibetan
Ta-Li	Pai
Wen-shan	Chuang and Miao
Ch'u-hsiung	Yi
Kweichow	
Southeastern Kweichow	Miao and Tung
Southern Kweichow	Puyi and Miao
Szechwan	
Kan-tzu	Tibetan
A-pa	Tibetan
Liang-shan	Yi
Sinkiang Vigur Autonomous Region	
I-Li	Kazak
K'e-tzu-Le-su	Khalka
Ch'ang-Chi	Hui
Pa-yin-kuo-leng	Mongol
Po-erh-ta-la	Mongol
Tsinghai	
Hai-pei	Tibetan
Hai-nan	Tibetan
Huang-nan	Tibetan
Yü-shu	Tibetan
Kuo-lo	Tibetan
Hai-hsi	Mongol, Tibetan and Kazah
Kansu	
Liu-hsia	Hui
Southern Kansu	Tibetan
Hunan	
Western Hunan	Tuchia and Miao
Kwangtung	
Hainan	Li and Miao
Kirin	
Yen-pien	Korean

How much the Chinese population (including minorities) has increased since the 1957 official estimate is anybody's guess. United Nations sources have accepted Peking's 1957 reported total population and in 1966 estimated that China had reached a population of 710 million at a growth rate of 1.4 percent annually since the 1953 census. The U.S. Bureau of the Census, on the other hand, accepts the reported growth rate of more than 2 percent and projects the present population at more than 840 million. The U.S. Department of State also accepts the more than 2 percent growth rate but arrives at somewhat smaller population totals, showing 750 million in 1966 and a current population of 800 million. Where the Census Bureau estimate incorporates a belief that population growth was set back by some

Table 4

Population Increases by Administrative Areas

| | | | AVERAGE ANNUAL GROWTH RATE | |
| | 1953 POPULATION | 1957 POPULATION | 11-YEAR BASIS | 14-YEAR BASIS |
AREA	MILLION	MILLION	PERCENT	PERCENT
Peking	2,768	7,000	6.8	8.8
Tientsin	2,694	4,000	2.9	3.4
Shanghai	6,204	10,000	3.5	4.4
Hopei	41,146	43,000	0.3	0.4
Shansi	14,314	18,000	1.7	2.1
Inner Mongolia	6,100	13,000	5.6	7.1
Liaoning	18,545	28,000	2.9	3.8
Kirin	11,290	17,000	3.0	3.9
Heilungkiang	11,897	16,210	2.2	2.8
Shensi	15,881	21,000	2.0	2.6
Kansu	12,928	13,000	0.03	60.04
Ninghsia	n/a	1,970	n/a	n/a
Tsinghai	1,677	2,000	1.3	1.6
Sinkiang	4,874	6,150	1.7	2.1
Shantang	48,876	57,000	1.1	1.4
Kiangsu	41,252	47,000	1.0	1.2
Anhwei	30,344	35,000	1.0	1.3
Chekiang	22,866	31,000	2.2	2.8
Fukien	13,143	15,980	1.4	1.8
Honan	44,215	50,000	0.9	1.1
Hupeh	27,790	32,000	1.0	1.3
Hunan	33,227	38,000	1.0	1.2
Kiangsi	16,773	22,000	2.0	2.5
Kwangtung	34,770	40,000	1.0	1.3
Kwangsi	19,561	24,000	1.5	1.9
Szechwan	65,685	70,000	0.5	0.6
Kweichow	15,037	18,420	1.4	1.8
Yunnan	17,473	23,000	2.0	2.5
Tibet	1,274	1,390	0.6	0.7
TOTAL	582,604	705,120	1.4	1.8

20 million during the Chinese famine of the early 1960s, the Department of State estimates assume a more serious setback of some 50 million.[13]

Because there has been no official data since 1957, estimates made by Chinese Nationalists offer a third figure, which indicates that the annual population growth since 1953 has been from 1.4 percent to 1.8 percent, decreasing to 1.3 percent after 1957. Table 4 on page 15 indicates population increases by administrative areas (1953–67).[14]

Suggested Readings

AIRD, JOHN S. "Estimating China's Population." *Annals of the American Academy of Political and Social Science* 369 (January 1967) : 61–72.

BUCHANAN, KEITH. *The Transformation of the Chinese Earth.* London: C. T. Bell and Sons, 1966.

CHANG, SEN-DOU. "The Million City of Mainland China." *Pacific Viewpoint* 9, no. 2 (September 1968) : 128–53.

CRESSEY, GEORGE B. *Asia's Lands and Peoples.* New York: McGraw-Hill, 1963, chapters 4–10.

GINSBURG, NORTON, ed. *The Pattern of Asia.* Englewood Cliffs, N.J.: Prentice-Hall, 1958.

HERRMAN, ALBERT. *An Historical Atlas of China.* Chicago: Aldine Publishing Co., 1966.

HO, PING-TI. *Studies on the Population of China, 1368–1953.* Cambridge, Mass.: Harvard University Press, 1959.

HSIEH, CHIAO-MIN. *China: Ageless Land and Countless People.* Princeton: D. Van Nostrand, 1967.

LATTIMORE, OWEN. *Inner-Asian Frontiers of China.* New York: American Geographic Society, 1951.

MURPHEY, RHOADS. "Man and Nature in China." *Modern Asian Studies* 1, no. 4 (October 1967) : 313–33.

RICHARDSON, S. D. *Forestry in Communist China.* Baltimore: Johns Hopkins Press, 1966.

SHABAD, THEODORE. *China's Changing Map.* New York: Praeger Publishers, 1956.

TREGEAR, T. R. *A Geography of China.* Chicago: Aldine Publishing Co., 1965.

TUAN, YI-FU. *The World's Landscapes: China.* Chicago: Aldine Publishing Co., 1969.

U.S.S.R. ACADEMY OF SCIENCES. *The Physical Geography of China.* 2 vols. New York: Praeger Publishers, 1969.

WATSON, FRANCIS. *The Frontiers of China: A Historical Guide.* New York: Praeger Publishers, 1966.

WIENS, HAROLD J. *Han Expansion in South China.* New Haven: Shoe String Press, 1967.

CHAPTER TWO

CHINA IN TRANSITION

The years between 1839, when China was opened to the West, and 1949, when it became a Communist society, might be viewed as the vital link between the waning of the old order, ancient political system, social institutions, and cultural values, and the beginning of a new era, the period of the People's Republic of China. To understand this dramatic background, one must examine the foreign influences after the Opium War and the internal environment during the past 100 years to see which factors were responsible for the eventual demise of the traditional order.

When China first began to have extensive contact with Western nations in the beginning of the sixteenth century, she regarded them as barbarians, as in the ancient days when there was a sharp distinction between the *Hua Hsia* (the Chinese) and the *Yi-Ti* (the barbarians). With the exception of Russia, foreign traders were not allowed to enter Peking, and they were restricted to the port of Canton where business was conducted through special agents, the Co-hongs, without treaty arrangements.

When King George III sent Lord Macartney to Peking in 1793 in an attempt to improve trade relations, he requested that a diplomat be accredited to the Manchu court and that trade conditions be improved. To these requests, Emperor Ch'ien-lung replied:

> As to your entreaty to send one of your nationals to be accredited to my Celestial Court and to be in control of your country's trade with China, this request is contrary to all usage of my dynasty and cannot possibly be entertained. . . . Our dynasty's majestic virtue has penetrated into every country under Heaven, and Kings of all nations have offered their costly tribute by land and sea. As your Ambassador can see for himself, we possess all things. I set no value on objects strange or ingenious, and have no use for your country's manufactures. . . .[1]

In 1816 the British sent another mission under Lord Amherst. He was not treated as hospitably as Macartney had been, and when he complained, he was ordered to leave the country. Unrealistically, Peking refused to open its door to the West, except on her own terms.

THE OPIUM WAR

However, in the search for commodities which the Chinese would buy, the Western traders finally discovered a very profitable product—opium. In fact, the immediate profits of the opium trade were so high that practically all Western traders took part in it, including the Americans.

In 1839, the Chinese emperor appointed a special commissioner, Lin Tse-hsu, to enforce the prohibition of the opium trade at Canton. Commissioner Lin forced the foreign traders to surrender all their opium and then burned the opium in Canton. The Americans submitted to the Chinese demands, while the British decided on the use of force to obtain satisfaction and reparation from the Chinese.

The Opium War lasted from November 1839 to August 1842 with complete victory for the British. A treaty was signed in Nanking in 1842 which provided for the opening of five Chinese ports, Canton, Amoy, Foochow, Ningpo, and Shanghai to British traders. It imposed upon China an indemnity of 21 million taels, and it provided that the island of Hong Kong, which controls the sea entrance to Canton, be ceded to England. Furthermore, in the supplementary Treaty of Bogus concluded with China in 1843, the British introduced the infamous "most-favored-nation" clause, guaranteeing the British any further concessions which China might subsequently grant to other nations. Thereafter, all foreign treaties with China contained this clause.

The Treaty of Wanghia, signed in July 1844, allowed American citizens a special legal protection to compensate for the lack of a naval base, such as the one the British had secured in Hong Kong. This new advantage is known as the principle of extraterritoriality, and it allowed resident aliens and corporations to be exempt from Chinese law and authority in both civil and criminal cases. Another treaty with the French was signed in October 1844. These treaties set a pattern for China's relations with the West that lasted for 100 years, as illustrated in the following table:[2]

Table 5

Major Treaties Ratified by the Manchu Empire with Foreign Powers (1689–1901)

TREATY, AGREEMENT, OR CONVENTION	DATE	PARTIES
Nerchinsk (on Amur)	27 August 1689	Russia
Peking (trade)	Winter 1720–1	Russia
Kiachta (border and trade)	August 1727	Russia
Nanking (Opium War)	29 August 1842	England
Bogus (trade)	8 October 1843	England
Wanghia (trade)	3 July 1844	U.S.A.
Whampoa (trade)	24 October 1844	France
Canton (trade)	March 1847	Sweden
Aigun (border and trade)	16 May 1858	Russia
Tientsin (trade)	13 June 1858	Russia
Tientsin (peace)	18 June 1858	U.S.A.
Tientsin (trade)	26 June 1858	England
Tientsin (privileges)	27 June 1858	France
Shanghai (Customs)	8 November 1858	England
Peking (privileges)	24 October 1860	England
Peking (tariff)	25 October 1860	France
Peking (border)	14 November 1860	Russia
Tientsin (trade)	2 September 1861	Prussia
Peking (trade)	20 February 1862	Russia
Peking and Tientsin (trade)	13 July 1863	Denmark
Tientsin (trade)	6 October 1863	Holland
Tientsin (trade)	10 October 1864	Spain
Tientsin (trade)	2 November 1865	Belgium
Peking (privileges)	31 May 1868	England
Washington (privileges)	28 July 1868	U.S.A.
Peking (trade)	15 April 1869	Russia
Tientsin (trade)	2 September 1869	Austria
Tientsin (trade)	Autumn 1871	Japan
Tientsin (trade)	26 June 1874	Peru
Tientsin (privileges)	7 August 1875	Peru
Chefoo (privileges)	13 September 1876	England
Peking (Cuba affairs)	17 November 1877	Spain
Peking (Cuba affairs)	6 December 1878	Spain
Peking (privileges)	31 March 1880	Germany
Peking (immigration)	17 November 1880	U.S.A.
St. Petersburg (border and trade)	12 February 1881	Russia
Tientsin (Korea)	Spring 1885	Japan
Tientsin (Tonkin)	9 June 1885	France
London (opium)	18 July 1885	England

Table 5 (Continued)

TREATY, AGREEMENT, OR CONVENTION	DATE	PARTIES
Peking (trade)	25 April 1886	France
Hongkong (opium)	11 September 1886	England
Peking (opium)	26 June 1887	France
Peking (Macao)	1 December 1887	Portugal
Calcutta (Sikkim)	17 March 1890	England
Peking (Chungking)	31 March 1890	England
Washington (immigration)	17 March 1894	U.S.A.
Shimonoseki (peace and cessions)	17 April 1895	Japan
Peking (privileges)	20 June 1895	France
Peking (Liao Tung)	8 November 1895	Japan
London (sphere of influence)	15 January 1896	England and France (China not included)
Peking (trade)	21 July 1896	Japan
Peking (privileges)	19 October 1896	Japan
Peking (Cassini)	September 1896	Russia
Peking (penalties)	4 February 1897	England
Peking (Kiaochou and other privileges)	6 March 1898	Germany
Peking (Port Arthur)	27 March 1898	Russia
Peking (Kwangchou Wan)	April 1898	France
St. Petersburg (Chinese railway interests)	28 April 1898	England and Russia (China not included)
Peking (Kowloong)	9 June 1898	England
Peking (Wei-hai Wei)	1 July 1898	England
Peking (trade)	7 July 1898	Congo
Boxer Protocol (peace, cessions, punishments, indemnity, foreign troops, and additional privileges)	7 September 1901	11 countries: Austria-Hungary Belgium France Germany Great Britain Italy Japan The Netherlands Russia Spain and U.S.A.

Foreign Spheres of Influence

During the two decades following these treaties, China had to surrender more and more of its sovereignty to foreign powers. Foreigners administered China's maritime customs and postal service until 1929, for example. They also had the right to establish factories, open mines, navigate in coastal and inland waters, and build railways for the expansion of their commerce. In addition, foreign troops were permitted to station in the concessions and foreign warships patrolled Chinese coasts and rivers.

As China's weakness grew, so did foreign aggression. This was revealed in the loss of some of China's outlying possessions. By 1860, Russia had penetrated into Manchuria, Mongolia, and Chinese Turkestan. France, victorious in a small-scale war (1884–85), acquired a protectorate over Annam; Great Britain coerced China again to yield sovereignty over Upper Burma in 1886; and the Portuguese, who had occupied Macao for 300 years, obtained its formal cession in 1887. Japan, only recently emerged from its centuries-long isolation, enforced a claim to suzerainty over the Ryukyu Islands (1881) by defeating the Chinese in Korea (1894–95). In addition, Japan also acquired the islands of Formosa.

Japan's defeat of China in 1895 stripped her of any remaining prestige and precipitated a scramble for new concessions. The closing decades of the nineteenth century found foreign powers engaged in a battle of concessions, through which they leased territory from the Chinese government. In the year 1898, the leading powers had acquired leaseholds on the coast of China, ranging from 25 to 99 years.

In the continuing scramble for China, foreign powers negotiated the partition of China into spheres of influence, with Russia in Manchuria, Germany in Shantung, and Great Britain in the Yangtze Valley. They wrested assurance from China that she would not allow any other power to extend its influence to any territory in their respective spheres of influence. The powers understood the leased territories and spheres of influence as the first steps toward annexation. The complete disintegration of China, which seemed to be imminent, was checked by the bitter rivalries among the powers themselves. Thus in the course of a few decades after the Opium War, these concessions not only discredited the "Celestial Dynasty" once and for all, but also made China economically dependent on the great powers, a fatal blow to the welfare of the state and the livelihood of the people.[3]

Breakdown of Agrarian Economy

The course of Chinese history has been marked by the changes in the relationship of the peasants to agriculture. Three-fourths of the people are peasants, and four-fifths of the national revenue is derived from agricultural production. Agriculture dominates the national economy. The age-long superiority of the *root* (agriculture) over the *branch* (commerce), the principle of the fair distribution of wealth, the ideal of the *well-field* system, and the various measures for limiting the ownership of land adopted by the various dynasties, were all intended to rehabilitate the traditional agrarian economy. With the exception of outlying areas, they hoped to maintain agricultural land in due proportion to the population, all over the country.

The development of an agrarian economy in China started at the Yellow River basin, then gradually focused in the Yangtze valley, and finally moved to the coast in the southeast. What is significant is the fact that although economic development changed from the river basin to the sea coast, there had been no great tendency toward over localization. At that time, water was the main problem for the farmers. When water failed, crops failed, and famine quickly spread. Famine, flood, irrigation, and water control had shaped the policies of the empires.

This type of agrarian economy was by no means unprofitable or devastating. In fact, the Chinese economy had been a balanced one up to 1800, and the efficient use of water was most notable. The water transport network throughout Central and South China was remarkably serviceable and well-developed, and the methods of application of abundant manpower to the process of the economy had been well-utilized. But for the new factors from abroad, China would have been self-contained and remained economically intact.

The Impact of Opium Trade

The economic situation was greatly worsened when the Manchu government failed to suppress the trade in opium. During the late eighteenth century, about 1,000 chests (a chest equals some 133 pounds) of opium were being imported from India to China per year. From 1800 to 1810, the average trade was about 4,500 chests a year. By 1838, the annual growth was increased to 40,000 chests. The following figures give some indication of the increase in the opium trade:[4]

Table 6

Opium Trade 1800–38

YEARS	ANNUAL AVERAGE IN CHESTS	EST. VALUE (IN DOLLARS)
1800–1810	4,500	4,500,000
1811–20	10,000	10,000,000
1821–30	16,000	16,000,000
1831–35	18,712	18,712,000
1835	26,000	26,000,000
1838	40,000	40,000,000

The tragedy of the opium trade was a dual one. It became a social problem for China because somewhere between two and ten million Chinese had become opium addicts. It also caused a great outflow of silver since a chest of opium sold for somewhere between $1,000 and $2,000 Mexican dollars.

After the opening of China, foreigners had seized local points along the sea coast and made them trade ports for the penetration of the interior. By 1899, there were 32 treaty ports in China, and that number increased to 48 in 1913. Under the Inland Navigation Regulation of 1898, foreigners could travel and do business freely along the sea coast of 5,000 nautical miles and through the inland rivers as long

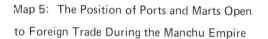

Map 5: The Position of Ports and Marts Open
to Foreign Trade During the Manchu Empire

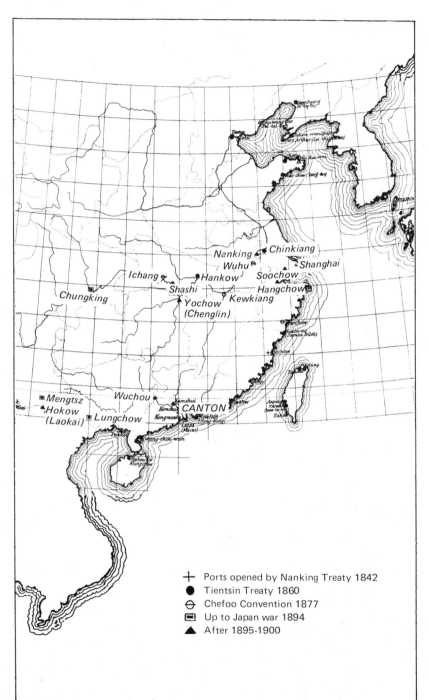

Chinkiang
Nanking
Wuhu
Shanghai
Ichang
Hankow
Soochow
Shashi
Hangchow
Chungking
Kewkiang
Yochow
(Chenglin)

Mengtsz
Wuchou
Hokow
CANTON
(Laokai)
Lungchow

Kowloon
(Hong-Kong)
Lappa
(Macao)

+ Ports opened by Nanking Treaty 1842
● Tientsin Treaty 1860
⊖ Chefoo Convention 1877
▣ Up to Japan war 1894
▲ After 1895-1900

23

as 10,000 nautical miles. After 1895, some 7,671 miles of railroads were built, mostly with foreign capital, cutting the major portion of the mainland from north to south as well as east to west. From then on, foreign commerce not only greatly increased, but also quickly penetrated to the rural areas of China, as illustrated in Map 5.[5]

Foreign trade grew as foreign governments extended political control. Consequently, the traditional political-social structure disintegrated and new groups emerged. Urban development spread from the city to the village and changed ways of life and patterns of values. Rural communities were affected to a degree that was deep and far-reaching.

But urbanization brought no significant increase in industrialization. Industry was centered in trade cities. China derived no benefit of the kind that could in any way help the development of her industrial or agricultural production. Moreover, the foreign goods, under the protection of unequal treaties, were dumped on the Chinese market, and native products could not successfully compete with them. Machine-made cotton goods were proving cheaper and better than those hand-made by peasants. The existing handicraft industries, once an important source of supplementary income for farmers, began to disappear; and yet, at the same time, the few newly formed Chinese industries failed to prosper because of foreign competition.

Consequently, the constant population increase, the ever increasing excess of imports over exports, and the imbalance between the high market value of manufactured goods and low market value of agricultural products, all joined together to cause the bankruptcy of China's agrarian economy.

DECADENCE OF THE IMPERIAL RULE

As China entered the nineteenth century, the symptoms of dynastic decay were evident in the Manchu government's failure to handle its external and internal problems. The reasons for this are not hard to find. Under the K'ang-hsi emperor (1654–1722) and his grandson Ch'ien-lung (1736–95), the Middle Kingdom, which enjoyed almost 150 years of internal peace and prosperity, might be compared to Great Britain (of the same period). However, by the middle of the Tao-kuang period (1821–50), Britain had undergone the industrial revolution, pacified the Chartist Movement, passed the Great Reform Bill of 1832, and witnessed tremendous economic, political, and intellectual progress, while the Manchu empire still followed the traditional system of government and clung slavishly to the family tradition, such as the K'ang-hsi's *Sacred Edict*:[6]

> Be filial to parents and affectionate to brothers;
> Be loyal to clans and friendly to neighbors;
> Pay attention to agriculture and sericulture;

Practice thrift and be frugal;
Devote one's self to one's own pursuit.

The unshaken faith in the past as a guide to the present prevented the Chinese rulers from perceiving the desirability of any change and comprehending the danger of having unwelcome change forced upon their country.

In the nineteenth century, China had found herself in an entirely new kind of decline, but the Manchu rulers remained stubbornly unaware. When coercion and war broke upon the empire from the onslaught of the West, they turned to the past for time-tested solutions and held wishful illusions that the Europeans ultimately would submit to China's civilizing influence as had her historical invaders. However, these illusions were dispelled by the events of the second half of the nineteenth century, for this time, the new invaders brought weapons, machines, and ideas which could not be fitted into the imperial system without tearing at the roots of its basic traditions.

Decadence in Bureaucracy

The nineteenth century was also the period of decadence in the imperial system of government. Political life was monopolized less by the bureaucracy and centered more in the personality of the emperor. The early Manchu emperors exercised not only the usual prerogatives of the Chinese sovereign, but also had the power of appointment and removal for all official posts. The Manchu emperors were making sure that social degradation reinforced political subjection by degrading their officials from the proud status of functionaries of state to the status of slaves (nu-tsai). This was the term Manchu officials used in referring to themselves when addressing the emperor.

As a result, the emperors were not inclined to listen to the suggestions of their officials about good government or against the abuses of personal power, despite the extensive setup of a bureaucratic government, as shown in Chart I.[7]

Inertia of the Leadership

Contributing to the inertia of the Manchu leaders were their vested interests in maintaining the power structure and ensuring their personal gain. During the T'ung-chih reign (1862–75), for example, the emperor was a young boy, under a regency dominated by his mother, the Empress Dowager (1835–1908). She became entrenched in power and governed with the aid of palace eunuchs and trusted personal friends. The Empress Dowager had no grasp whatsoever of China's problem of modernization. Her government suffered from the evils of nepotism and cliquish favoritism, squeeze, and lack of risk taking initiative.

*Chart I: Organization of the Manchu Government
during its Last 50 Years*

The Grand Secretariat

The Council of State

The Censorate

The Six Departments

1. Department of Civil Service
2. Department of Rites
3. Department of Revenue
4. Department of Military Affairs
5. Department of Justice
6. Department of Public Works

The Academy of Letters

The Colonial Office

Office of Transmission

Grand Court of Revision

The Four Minor Courts

The Imperial Board of Astronomy

The Imperial Household

Metropolitan Administration

Viceroy

Governor

Finance Commissioner

Judicial Commissioner

Educational Commissioner

Circuit Intendant

Prefect

Sub-Prefect

Conton Official

District Magistrate

Local Administration

The Emperor

The situation of the Empress's Court was, of course, inherited from a long past. For instance, the imperial government's fiscal system was based on the antiquated tax-farming setup, which meant that local officials were expected to make certain tax quotas available to the Imperial Court while maintaining themselves and their administrations on the remainder of what they collected. There was no budgeting, no accounting, and no central planning.

Even the time-honored systems of civil service and literacy examinations were completely disintegrated and became ineffective. Memorizing the Confucian classics was the cornerstone of all education. The content and direction of education were under the rigid control of the Department of Civil Service of the Metropolitan Administration.

Disinterest and apathy in the metropolitan administration was also reflected in the activities and attitudes of local authorities. During the Manchu dynasty, there were some 1,500 *chou* or *hsien* governments distributed among some 18–22 provinces under the personal supervision of the viceroys and governors. Provincial administrative functions were divided among several commissioners who were independently appointed by the metropolitan administration and responsible to the emperor. At the very bottom were the district magistrates who were called *chi-hsien*, or more popularly the father and mother officials of a district. Each of the magistrates was likely to take charge of an area of some 300 square miles with a population of a quarter of a million people. They were aided by varied retinues of personal and semiofficial assistants, who, at times, were their personal servants.

The local governments had always occupied a semiautonomous status in relation to the metropolitan authorities. Although legally they were all responsible to the emperor, they were free from interference as long as they furnished their quota in taxes, supported the vague general policies of the metropolitan administration, or avoided outrage to the general scheme of Confucian morality.

After the Tao-kuang period, there was a general decline of Imperial power in the provincial and local regions. Often independent groups emerged and some were organized into secret societies which became the vehicles for all sorts of illegal activities—as well as open rebellion.

Reform and Rebellion

The decadent Manchu government escalated the rise and progress of internal revolts and rebellion, while at the same time they were undermined by these happenings. In two decades before the Opium War, revolts had already occurred with alarming frequency in Honan (1822), Taiwan (1826), Hunan (1833), Shansi (1835), and many other parts of the country.

After the Opium War, there were six serious rebellions: one in the south by the Taipings (1850–64); one in the north by the Niens (1853–68); and four by the Moslems in the northwest (1855–72), southwest (1862–73), and central Asia (1862–76 and 1866–78).[8]

More often than not these rebellions gained momentum through affiliation with one or another of the secret societies, such as the White Lotus Sect in the north and the Hung Society in the south, which were animated by nationalism and religious ideology. These internal uprisings succeeded one another with shocking military violence and political disturbance, resulting in tremendous loss of lives and serious property damages throughout the empire.

The most formidable of all uprisings in China was the movement known as the Taiping rebellion, which was an almost fatal challenge to the Manchu dynasty. It began in 1850 out of local conflicts in south China, but rapidly grew into a popular movement which affected 17 out of then 18 provinces of China and resulted in a tremendous loss of life; estimated between 20 and 40 million people.

The Taiping rebellion was in many ways a standard Chinese antidynastic movement, born of agrarian distress and justified by the *mandate of Heaven*. Such movements generally combined political and economic purposes: a new dynasty was to replace the old and the have-nots were to become the haves. However, the religious tenets and political ideology gave the Taiping movement a distinctive character.

The leader of the revolt, Hung Hsiu-ch'uan (1814–64), frustrated in seeking office and influenced by the tracts of Protestant missionaries, held a conviction that he had a divine mission to perform. In 1848 he inaugurated the *Shang Ti Hui* or the *Worshippers of Shang Ti* (a Protestant term for God). This later became a political and religious movement which sought to overthrow the Manchu dynasty and establish a new *Heavenly Kingdom (Taiping Tien Kuo)*.[9]

From the outset, the movement acquired tremendous momentum by preaching its utopian and socialist ideologies (independent of European socialism) such as land redistribution, communal property, brotherhood of man, and equality of sexes. The rebel movement made rapid progress and by 1853 had occupied Nanking and much of central and south China. For a time, it appeared that the Taipings would successfully overthrow the Manchu dynasty and establish their Heavenly Kingdom.

In a certain sense the Taiping rebellion was a social and economic revolt; an uprising of impoverished peasants against oppressive landlords and corrupt officials. In their reform program, there was a mixture of Christian ideas and ideology of ancient China. Serious efforts were made at public ownership of money and property, the reduction of taxes on the peasantry, prohibition of bribery and opium, and the demand for a new calendar and colloquial literature, etc.

The Taipings, in fact, had all the ingredients for a successful revolution at hand, such as an inspiring ideology, an audacious leader, an oppressed people, and a real program for reform. However, they were unable to make the best of their opportunity. They lacked qualified personnel and were unable to devise an effective administrative system over all the regions they conquered. In addition, the failure of the Taipings had been accelerated by their inability to establish relations with the Western powers. After the new treaties between the Manchu court and the Western powers in 1858 and 1860, the imperial government received Western support and was able to crush the revolution.

The Reform Movement

During the Taiping rebellion, men like Tseng Kuo-fan (1811–72) and Li Hung-chang (1823–1901) launched a movement to enrich the nation and strengthen the army. Tseng and Li commanded the famous Hunan and Anhwei armies that suppressed the Taiping rebellion and various other uprisings. They had restored order for the Manchu government. They had also encouraged the manufacture of arms, the building of ships, the construction of railways, and the improvements in telegraphic communication as part of their goal to establish an industrial base in China.[10]

In reorganizing political and economic modernization for China, they also instituted foreign language schools, and sent Chinese students to study abroad. In addition, Li Hung-chang established a modern foreign office, the *Tsungli Yamen*, and he later played an indispensable role in foreign diplomacy for the Manchu dynasty.

Furthermore, Li Hung-chang introduced a new operational principle for the government based upon "government supervision and merchant operation." Under this new principle, for example, profit-oriented enterprises were managed by merchants while government maintained its control of policy as boards of directors. Li's projects included the China Merchants' Steamship Line, a modern coal mine in the Kaiping area, and a Chinese textile mill to compete with foreign imports, among others. The slow progress of "take-off" initiated by Li in the 1870s and 1880s could have proved successful in modernizing the Manchu dynasty, if it had not been obstructed by additional foreign encroachment and aggression.

Russia began to invade the Manchu empire's territories in Central Asia; and France attacked China's tributary states in the South, such as Annam (Vietnam) and other parts of Indochina. The outbreak of domestic rebellion in Korea in 1894, provided the occasion for Japanese intervention, which led to the disastrous Sino-Japanese War (1894–95).

In Simonoseki, China signed a treaty with Japan in which the independence of Korea was recognized; Taiwan, the Pescadores Islands, and the Liaotung Peninsula were to be ceded to Japan; an indemnity of 200,000,000 taels of silver was to be paid to Japan; and four more ports were to be opened to foreign trade. The mad scramble for concessions to the Great European powers began with this treaty.

Hundred Days Reform

China's defeat by Japan in the war of 1894/95 was destined to have profound effects on the Chinese mind. A progressive reformer, K'ang Yu-wei (1858–1927), led a group of 1,200 young scholars who were candidates for the metropolitan examination. He submitted an important memorial to the emperor, in which he called for a repudiation of the treaty, transfer of the capital to the safer interior of the country, and the total reform of the government. This demand had no effect, but in 1898, K'ang submitted another critical memorial to the emperor, in which he set forth a whole new program for the government.[11]

In the summer of 1898, the emperor began to issue a series of reform edicts, based on the program spelled out by K'ang, and he instituted what was later known as the Hundred Days' Reform, which lasted from June 11 to September 16. K'ang wanted a constitutional monarchy similar to that of the Meiji era in Japan. K'ang also proposed the abolition of the traditional examination and a complete renovation of the educational system in which Western sciences and practical arts would be studied together with the Chinese classics. He further proposed to use Buddhist temples for modern schools and wanted to establish a bureau of translation of Western works.

K'ang's general economic plans were to encourage commerce and industry through the construction of railways and factories in various parts of China. In addition, steps were to be taken to develop mining and to promote agricultural improvements. A modern budget system was to be introduced, and there were many other measures which were aimed at social and institutional reforms. To pave the way for his reform program, K'ang tried to reorganize the government machinery and eliminate the old officialdom.

K'ang's reforms aroused a storm of opposition from those who, by conviction or interest, were wedded to the old order. The situation was complicated by the rivalries of two factions at the Imperial Court, one of them disposed to countenance reforms, and the other taking the conservative viewpoint. The conservatives looked to the Empress Dowager for support and leadership. When the empress saw that the young emperor was actually launching reforms, she went to work with lightning speed. The empress resumed her regency and made the emperor a prisoner; many reformers were arrested and executed. She finally annulled all the reform edicts.

After the failure of the Reform Movement, K'ang Yu-wei went abroad and continued to write and raise funds in behalf of the movement. However, he no longer played any important part in Chinese politics and his place was soon taken over by Sun Yat-sen (1866–1925), who turned the Reform Movement into a national revolution.

SUN YAT-SEN AND COMMUNISM

In contrast to K'ang Yu-wei, Sun Yat-sen was not only a republican revolutionary, but also a man of magnetic political personality. He came of a poor peasant family in Canton and received his education in Western schools. He was not bound to conventional Chinese scholarship but became an ardent believer in Western culture and science.

In 1879, at the age of 12, Sun joined his brother in Honolulu, where he studied Western democracy. He was so influenced by these studies that they later played an important part in the formation of his own political philosophy. From 1884 to 1886, he studied medicine in Hong Kong, and after graduation from Hong Kong University Medical School he took his practice to Macao. However, even at this early stage of his life, his real interest was the revolutionary movement.[12]

After the calamities of the Sino-Japanese War, Sun founded the China Regeneration Society (*Hsing-chung Hui*) in Honolulu in 1894 for the sole purpose of overthrowing the Manchu dynasty. He returned to Canton the following year to participate in an abortive uprising. He then went to London where he was kidnapped by the Chinese legation, only to be saved by his college professor, Sir James Cantlie.

Sun then went to Japan to reorganize his society into a new organization, the League of Common Alliance (*T'ung-meng Hui*), so that he could express his political philosophy through a better organized political movement, which included:

1. The expulsion of the Manchus and the restoration of China to the Chinese. This was later formulated as the "Principle of People's Rule" (*Min-tsu*, translated as nationalism).
2. The establishment of a republic—later formulated as the "Principle of People's Authority" (*Min-ch'uan*, translated as democracy).
3. Equal distribution and nationalization of land—later formulated as the "Principle of People's Livelihood" (*Min-sheng*, translated as socialism.)[13]

This program included the main points which served as the basic text of the Nationalist Movement, and was later known as the Three People's Principles. Although there were again many reverses, persecutions, and rebuffs, the revolutionary work led by Sun Yat-sen finally broke out in October 1911 and culminated in the overthrow of the Manchu dynasty.

The success of Sun's revolution did not, however, free China from the economic difficulties, ideological conflicts, political chaos, and foreign intervention of the old empire. Governmental power was, in fact, soon passed into the hands of political opportunists and militarists and China was torn by civil wars among the warlords for 13 years.

During these years of political chaos, Sun Yat-sen continued his revolutionary work in China. He reorganized his League of Common Alliance into the Kuomintang (the Nationalist Party), as a democratic political party with open membership. His purpose was to implant his own political program—the Three People's Principles—in the minds and lives of the Chinese people.

Since he was largely ignored by the Western powers which were backing one Chinese warlord against another, Sun accepted offers of assistance and guidance from the newly formed Soviet government. In 1923, he invited a host of Soviet advisers to China to reorganize the Kuomintang and to train Chinese cadres. By 1924, a new Kuomintang was patterned after the Soviet model, including a military school at Whampoa to train future Chinese military officers. Chiang Kai-shek was named its first president and Chou En-lai, a founder-member of the Chinese Communist Party, was its chief political officer.[14]

Birth of the Chinese Communist Party

The founding of the Chinese Communist Party (CCP) can be traced to the formation of a society for the study of Marxism founded by Ch'en Tu-hsiu and Li Ta-chao in 1918.[15] Various other Marxist study groups were formed after the May 4 Movement, including the Enlightenment Society in Tientsin led by Chou En-lai and Teng Ying-chao, and the Benefit Book Club in Hupei, organized by Yun Tai-ying. These study groups were not purely Marxist, however. In fact, many groups were directed by two agents of the Third International—Gregory Voitinsky and a Chinese who resided abroad, Yang Ming-chai. With their assistance, Communist groups were brought into existence in Shanghai in May, in Peking and Changsha (Hunan) in September, and in Canton at the end of 1920. Before long, Chinan, Hangchow, Wuhan, Tokyo, and Paris had Chinese Communist groups. In addition, Ch'en Tu-hsiu initiated the socialist youth corps in August, and Ch'en's example was followed by Mao Tse-tung in Changsha.

These groups were small in number. The Shanghai group had only seven members, but later four left it; the Peking group had eight anarchists in addition to Li Ta-chao and Chang Kuo-t'ao; the Canton group, organized by Ch'en Tu-hsiu during his visit, included T'an P'ing-shan, Ch'en Kung-po, and several anarchists, and later all the anarchists withdrew. Finally, Ch'en Tu-hsiu began a reorganization campaign with the establishment of a 55 member socialist youth corps at Peking University. This Peking group ran workers' evening classes and published *Labor's Voice*. The Shanghai group also ran evening classes and published a worker's tabloid, *Labor World*, and the Canton group followed the same pattern by setting up workers' schools and publishing *Labor's Echo*.

First Party Congress

Certainly Moscow was keeping a watchful eye on developments in China. In order to transfer the Chinese Communist movement from the intellectuals to the workers, the Comintern dispatched an important agent, G. Maring (also known as Henricus Sneevliet) to attend the formal organization meeting of the Chinese Communist Party. For the purpose of subterfuge, the delegates to the First Congress of the CCP gathered at the Po-ai Girls' School in the French Concession of Shanghai on 1 July 1921. Later, to avoid police harassment, the Congress was moved to the South Lake of Chiah-sing. The 12 delegates—Chang Kuo-t'ao, Ch'en Kung-po, Ch'en Tan-chiu, Chou Fo-hai, Ho Shu-heng, Li Han-chun, Li Ta, Liu Jen-ching, Mao Tse-tung, Teng En-ming, Tung Pi-wu, and Wang Ching-mei—representing only 57 members—opened a new chapter in Chinese history and grew to become the largest Communist party in the world with effective control over 700 million people.

Much of the records for the First Congress have been lost. It is known, however, that the delegates adopted a party constitution and elected a central committee, which consisted of Ch'en Tu-hsiu as party secretary (he was in Canton during the Congress meeting in Shanghai); Chang Kuo-t'ao as head of the organization department; Li Ta as head of the propaganda department; and three alternate members, Chou Fo-hai, Li Han-chun and Liu Jen-ching. Mao Tse-tung was sent back to his native province, Hunan, as the secretary of the Hunan branch of the CCP. His tasks included the reeducation of the members of the former socialist youth corps to prepare them for induction into the Chinese Communist Party.

The labor movement began in earnest after the First Congress, and strikes were held in many parts of China. It is true, of course, that the success of the Communists was due to the fact that industrial labor in China was long overdue for organization. In fact, China at this time had no organized labor and working conditions were most deplorable. No effective remedy had ever been introduced on the workers' behalf.

Second Party Congress

The Second Congress, which was held in June and July of 1922 in Hangchow (the official Communist record says Shanghai), adopted a party constitution and several important documents including the First Manifesto and the Manifesto of the Second National Congress. In the First Manifesto, the Party had urged the calling of a conference "to be participated in by the revolutionary elements of the Kuomintang (KMT) and revolutionary socialists, to discuss the question of creating a united front for struggle against the warlords of the feudal type and against all relics of feudalism."[16] In the July manifesto, it made clear that support for the Kuomintang was temporary and did not imply surrender to the capitalists. In addition, the Second Party Congress made a formal decision to join the Comintern and set up a political bureau within the Party. Ch'en Tu-hsiu was reelected secretary-general and chairman of the political bureau.

In August 1922, Maring, the Comintern representative, proposed to a special plenum of the CCP Central Committee that a Communist bloc be formed inside, instead of alongside, the KMT, so as to make the KMT "the central force of the national revolution," as instructed by the Comintern. The Party leaders, including Ch'en Tu-hsiu, opposed this plan on the ground that it would cost the Party its class independence. Maring countered this objection by declaring that the KMT was, in fact, a multiclass party. This view, as advanced by Maring, was "clearly in conflict with the Marxist concept of parties as organs of single, individual class interest."[17] As a result, Maring invoked the Party discipline of the Comintern to force the adoption of the plan by the Chinese Communists.

Alliance with Sun Yat-sen

To the Comintern, Sun's revolutionary movement seemed to have the greatest potential for mass appeal, and offered an instrument for armed struggle against the warlords, then in control of the rest of China. By allying themselves with this movement under the leadership of Sun, the Chinese Communists would be able to utilize the prestige of the Kuomintang and operate openly in KMT-controlled areas, thereby broadening their contacts with the masses and strengthening their own power. At the same time, by influencing the policies adopted by the KMT, they would lay the foundation for a socialist revolution, once they had gained the hegemony they sought.

To carry out the plan as initiated by Maring, the Soviet representative, Adolf Joffe, came to China and built up relations with Sun. On 26 January 1923, they issued a joint statement, which was actually a strictly limited arrangement. It stated that "Dr. Sun is of the opinion that, because of the non-existence of conditions favorable to their successful application in China, it is not possible to carry out either Communism or even the Soviet system in China"; that "M. Joffe agrees with this view; he is further of the opinion that China's most important and pressing problems are the completion of national unification and the attainment of full national independence." Sun now sought and accepted Comintern aid, and Joffe assured Sun that the Russian people were willing to lend that aid.

However, the Sun-Joffe Manifesto only marked the opening of the negotiations which were to end a year later with the conclusion of the KMT-CCP alliance at the First KMT Congress in January 1924. During the summer of 1923, these negotiations were continued between Joffe and Liao Chung-kai, a vigorous leader of the KMT left wing. On the basis of these negotiations, Sun agreed to adopt the Soviet system of party organization and government. He also agreed to allow Communists to join the KMT as individuals and to participate in the cause of the national revolution simply because their anti-imperialist aims coincided with those of the KMT. This policy, which came to be known in KMT circles as *yung-kung* (let the Communists join as individuals), did not however, imply cooperation between the KMT and the CCP as equals (known as *lien-kung*).

In the fall of 1923, a Soviet mission headed by Michael Borodin came to Canton with military supplies and began to reorganize the KMT and its armies to follow the Soviet pattern. Meanwhile, Chiang Kai-shek was sent to Moscow to study the Red Army. It was upon his return that Chiang was named by Sun Yat-sen as president of the Whampoa Military Academy for the training of Nationalist officers. From the time of this appointment, Chiang played a decisive role in the KMT and in the Nationalist government.

Third Party Congress

In June 1923, the CCP held its Third Congress in Canton, attended by 30 members, 27 of whom were delegates representing 432 members. After heated debates on the question of a united front with the KMT as proposed by the Comintern agent, the Congress passed a resolution that Party members might join the KMT as individuals, but that the Party's political and organizational independence should be preserved. The Communist strategy was to build up Party strength within the KMT and ultimately capture the KMT machinery, thereby seizing total power in China. (At this congress, Mao Tse-tung was elected to the Party's Central Committee.)

In 1924, the Chinese Communists received instructions from the Party to join the KMT as individuals. Accordingly, many important Communists, such as Mao Tse-tung, Li Ta-chao, Chang Kuo-t'ao, and Ch'ü Ch'iu-pai, joined the KMT, and worked either as commissars in the army or as cadres in central and local Party headquarters. Under the protection of the KMT, the Chinese Communists embarked on a period of rapid expansion in size and influence within the KMT. In January 1925, the Fourth Congress of the CCP, held in Shanghai, reported 950 members, but within a year after this congress, membership had soared to over 10,000.

It was at this time that Sun reorganized the KMT and set up the Whampoa Military Academy for the training of an officer corps. Sun also recast his Three Principles of the People, and in a new version of his book with this title he showed a friendly attitude toward Soviet Russia. For the first time, he announced the oft-quoted formula that "essentially there is no difference between the Principle of People's Livelihood and Communism."[18]

The Fourth Party Congress

The Chinese Communists held the Fourth National Congress in Shanghai in January 1925. The Congress discussed, among other items, matters relating to the proposed National Convention and KMT-CCP cooperation.

It issued a manifesto, revised the Party Constitution, and adopted resolutions on the national revolutionary movement. Asserting that the Kuomintang had split into three factions, the resolution reaffirmed the CCP's support of the KMT's leftists. At this point the Chinese Communists began to create incidents, organize a federation of trade unions, and widen Communist influence among the masses to thus provide a basis for the future hegemony of the proletariat. On 30 May 1925, a nationwide anti-imperialist patriotic movement consisting of demonstrations, strikes, and boycotts broke out in Shanghai.

More significant, in view of the later KMT-CCP rupture, was the Communist attempt to install themselves in key positions within the KMT organization. At the First Congress of the reorganized KMT in 1924, seven Communists who had only recently joined the KMT on an individual basis were elected to its Central Executive Committee. Li Ta-ch'ao and T'an P'ing-shan were named regular members, while five others, including Ch'ü Ch'iu-pai, Chang Kuo-t'ao, and Mao Tse-tung were made alternate members.

Communist influence was further extended at the Second Congress of the KMT, held at Canton early in January 1926. At this congress, one-fourth of the places on the executive committee fell to the Communists. Of the 36 regular members of the Central Executive Committe, seven were now Communists, as were seven of the 24 alternate members—Mao Tse-tung remaining one of the seven. It is understandable that the rise of Communist influence within the KMT stirred apprehension and opposition elsewhere in the Party, and particularly among its senior members.

Sun steadfastly discouraged anti-Communist feeling within the KMT and suppressed any open expression of it. In his own mind, he felt that he needed Soviet aid and support for the national revolution. He believed, though naively, that it was the KMT and not the CCP the Russians wanted to support. He wrote early in 1924: "If Russia wants to cooperate with China, it must cooperate with our Party and not with Ch'en Tu-hsiu. If Ch'en disobeys our Party, he will be ousted."[19]

After the death of Sun on 12 March 1925, there followed a time of tension between the right and left wings of the KMT over the question of collaboration with the CCP. However, the three strong men in Canton after Sun's departure to Peking—Borodin, Chiang Kai-shek, and Wang Ching-wei—were all determined, for various reasons, to prevent any immediate break in the KMT-CCP alliance at this time.

While this alliance was still in force, the National Revolutionary Army under the supreme command of Chiang Kai-shek set out on 9 July 1926, on the famous Northern Expedition from Canton to central China. The purpose of this important military campaign, long planned by Sun Yat-sen before his death, was to destroy the northern warlords and unify China. It was also aimed at rising above local conflicts at Canton and expanding the revenue area of the Nationalist government. Under the supreme command of Chiang Kai-shek there were six main armies, mostly reorganized warlord forces. Preceded by its newly trained propagandists, the expedition forces advanced rapidly against opposition. They showed respect for the people and were welcomed by them. They overtook some 34 warlord armies by the time they reached the Yangtze River valley.

By the spring of 1927, the KMT and the CCP had each achieved the primary objective of their alliance; a position, attained with the help of the other, from which it could claim the conquest of power in China. With the support of the Communists, the KMT had built up a party apparatus and a party army to defeat the warlords. Under the protection of the KMT, the CCP had expanded its membership and extended its sway over the masses. Thus each had won a lever with which to strive against the other.

Suggested Readings

BECKMANN, GEORGE M. *The Modernization of China and Japan.* New York: Harper & Row, 1962.

CHAI, CHU, and CHAI, WINBERG. *The Changing Society of China,* rev. ed. New York: Mentor Books, 1969.

CLUBB, O. EDMUND. *Twentieth Century China.* New York: Columbia University Press, 1964.

DE BARRY, WILLIAM T., ed. *Sources of Chinese Tradition.* New York: Columbia University Press, 1960.

FAIRBANK, JOHN KING. *The U.S. and China,* 3d ed. Cambridge, Mass.: Harvard University Press, 1971.

FAIRBANK, JOHN KING; REISCHAUER, EDWIN O.; and CRAIG, ALBERT M. *East Asia: The Modern Transformation.* Boston: Houghton Mifflin, 1965.

FEUERWERKER, ALBERT, ed. *Modern China.* Englewood Cliffs, N.J.: Prentice-Hall, 1964.

HARRISON, JAMES P. *The Communists and Chinese Peasants Rebellion.* New York: Atheneum, 1969.

HO, PING-TI, and TSOU, TANG, ed. *China in Crisis.* Vol. 1. Chicago: University of Chicago Press, 1968.

HSU, IMMAMUEL C. Y. *The Rise of Modern China.* New York: Oxford University Press, 1970.

HSÜEH, CHUN-TU, ed. *Revolutionary Leaders of Modern China.* New York: Oxford University Press, 1971.

LENG, SHAO-CHUAN, and PALMER, NORMAN D. *Sun Yat-sen and Communism.* New York: Praeger Publishers, 1960.

LEVENSON, JOSEPH R. *Confucian China and Its Modern Fate.* 3 vols. Berkeley: University of California Press, 1958, 1964–65.

LI CHIEN-NUNG. *The Political History of China, 1840–1928.* Princeton: D. Van Nostrand Co., 1956.

NORTH, ROBERT C. *Moscow and Chinese Communism,* 2d ed. Stanford: Stanford University Press, 1963.

TENG SSU-YU, and FAIRBANK, JOHN K. *China's Response to the West: A Documentary Survey 1839–1923.* Cambridge, Mass.: Harvard University Press, 1954.

TSOU, TANG. *America's Failure in China.* Chicago: University of Chicago Press, 1963.

TUNG, CHI-MING. *A Short History of China.* Peking: Foreign Language Press, 1965.

CHAPTER THREE

THE CHINESE COMMUNIST PARTY ANd MAOISM

"The birth of the Chinese Communist Party ushered in a new epoch in the development of Chinese history," declared a 1971 Chinese editorial commemorating the fiftieth anniversary of the Communist Party in China. And a position paper issued at the celebration stated:

At the time of the founding of the Chinese Communist Party there were only a dozen members organized in a few communist groups. But they represented a new force, and new forces are always invincible by nature. . . .

A review of the fighting course traversed by our Party over the past 50 years confirms this truth. When our Party departs from Chairman Mao's leadership and goes against Mao Tse-tung's thought and Chairman Mao line, it suffers setbacks and defeats; when our party closely follows Chairman Mao . . . it advances and triumphs.

While Mao Tse-tung's friends praised him as representing the new force of light and progress, his foes condemned him as seeking an "idiosyncratic and extreme vision of immortality."[1] However, no one can deny the tremendous impact of the Chinese Communist Party and its chairman, Mao Tse-tung—his political ideology, unfaltering confidence, and charismatic personality—upon Chinese society and world politics.

The Chinese Communist Party under Mao has offered hope to millions of living Chinese who have endured decades of war, hunger, sickness, and foreign intervention. It has provided a new set of national goals, institutions, and priorities. Again, the Chinese Communist Party under Mao has furnished the Chinese people with a new set of basic moral values which stress a spirit of personal self-sacrifice, and it has overturned the traditional gentry class with a value system of the superiority of the leisure class over the manual laborer. Finally, the Chinese Communist Party under Mao has restored Chinese national pride and self-reliance as a model for political, social, and economic development.

However, the road which led Mao and his Party to unchallenged predominance was a long and tortuous one. As Mao himself wrote:

> There have been several occasions in the history of our Party when great conceit manifested itself and we suffered in consequence.... Comrades throughout the Party should take warning from these instances of pride and error. And they should not repeat the error of becoming conceited at the moment of success.[2]

THE GROWTH OF THE CHINESE COMMUNIST PARTY

We have already seen the birth of the Chinese Communist Party and its initial growth in the formative years from 1920 to 1925. This was largely because of Sun Yat-sen's policy of cooperation with the Soviet Union. The Chinese Communist Party (CCP) members were able to infiltrate into the Kuomintang (KMT), while maintaining their separate organization. Meanwhile, the KMT itself was helplessly divided into two major factions: the leftist KMT and the rightist KMT.

The KMT Left, now more fearful of Chiang Kai-shek's military power, moved the National government from Canton to Wuhan where it was supported by the Communists. And the Communists devoted their energies to the peasant and labor movements. Communist-led labor unions in Shanghai and Hankow carried out major strikes. In Shanghai, they even tried to prevent Chiang Kai-shek's army from occupying the city; in Hunan the peasant movement carried out a bloody agrarian revolt in which hundreds of landlords and rich peasants lost their lives.

To meet this challenge to his own position, Chiang had to make a decision: Should he continue to support the KMT Left and cooperate with the Communists and Soviet advisers? Or should he turn to the

KMT Right, which was allied with the capitalists, to oust all the Communists and end the two-party alliance? At the siege of Shanghai in 1927, during the northern expedition campaign waged against the northern warlords, Chiang and his closest colleagues, now established in headquarters at Nanchang in Kiangsi, decided on the second alternative. Shanghai came into Chiang's hands with the aid of the capitalists without a fight on 22 March 1927. Moreover, Shanghai financiers and industrialists placed capital at his disposal, so that he could finance his troops and administration independently of the KMT Left. Assured of financial resources, Chiang made a clean break with the Communists and set up a new regime in Nanking on 5 April 1927.

Although the KMT Left and the Communists had moved the Canton government to Wuhan, they controlled only two provinces, lacked internal unity, and depended on armies of dubious loyalty. Moreover, the Comintern had no real intention of upholding the KMT Left under the leadership of Wang Ching-wei, who had returned from abroad. In contrast, Chiang's Nanking government now controlled rich eastern coastal provinces and had large, loyal, unified armies. Assured of support from the KMT Right and Western powers, on the morning of 12 April 1927, Chiang began a bloody purge of the Communists which lasted four days. This purge has since been denounced by the Communists as the April 12 Massacre.

Fifth Party Congress

To counteract Chiang's estrangement from the Communists, the Chinese Communist Party held its Fifth Congress in Hankow in late April and early May 1927, where it was reported that the membership had increased to 57,968. The question discussed was how to settle accounts with the Kuomintang and thereby reorientate the revolutionary movement. Ch'en Tu-hsiu came in for vigorous criticism and attack, though he was reelected as secretary-general of the Party. Mao Tse-tung attended the Congress but was deprived of the right to vote by Ch'en's group. His report on the Hunan peasant movement was suppressed. In accordance with the Comintern's directive, the Communists, while maintaining the alliance with the KMT Left, were to work out a program of their own for taking over the leadership from the bourgeois elements within the Wuhan KMT. Meanwhile, Stalin, who had gained control of the Soviet government, issued a set of instructions, among which were the following:

1. Combat peasant excesses by means of the peasant unions rather than by KMT troops and form a new huge army of peasants and workers under the CCP's control.
2. Call for the purge of "reliable" KMT generals and reshuffle the KMT Central Executive Committee.

3. Reorganize and strengthen the KMT's Wuhan government headed by Wang Ching-wei.

In order to achieve this collaboration, M. N. Roy, the Indian Comintern delegate then in Wuhan, showed these instructions directly to Wang on 1 June 1927. In this manner, Wang learned of the conspiracy by which the CCP was to take over the leading role in the KMT. He therefore took steps leading to the suppression of the Communist-led mass movement and to the expulsion of the Communists from the Wuhan KMT (June/July 1927). After these suppression campaigns, the CCP was smashed, and the united front was destroyed. Thus the period from 1924 to 1927, called the First Revolutionary Civil War, ended in the rupture between the two parties.

Something more may be said about the unrealistic and misleading Comintern directives. After the death of Lenin in 1924, the CCP became subject to the influence of Stalin and the internecine Kremlin intra-Party struggle. It was required to obey Comintern directives issued to help Stalin and Bukharin, who at that time were on the same side. Their policy was one of cooperation with the KMT, which represented the bourgeoisie. But Trotsky, joined by Zinoviev, warned that the CCP would be the victim of this misleading policy. After the Wuhan disaster, the CCP should have left the KMT. In fact, the CCP had been cast out of the KMT. However, in the intra-Party struggle, Stalin needed the alleged KMT-CCP alliance as a shield to hide the facts that belied his infallibility. It is therefore understandable that the Comintern ordered the CCP to remain in the KMT in name, in order to "reorganize the KMT and make it a genuine mass organization."[3]

First Major Crisis

On 7 August 1927, the CCP held an emergency meeting to meet the new situation which marked its transition from that of a legal party to an outlawed party. This is now known as the August 7 Conference; it was attended by 22 delegates. Ch'en Tu-hsiu was condemned for his rightist opportunism, which was said to be responsible for the total failure of the Party. Ch'ü Ch'iu-pai, a Russian-trained Communist, replaced him as Party secretary-general. Meanwhile, the old Comintern delegation had been recalled and replaced by a new group under the leadership of Besso Lominadze. This was to show that the Comintern would tighten its control over the CCP. In fact, the Congress was convened by telegraphic order of the Comintern and was under the guidance of the Comintern delegates.

The CCP at this juncture had been expelled from the Wuhan KMT and outlawed by the Nanking KMT. Hence rebellion was the only means for Communist survival. It is no wonder that the August 7 Conference adopted a new policy of armed uprisings. On 1 August

1927, Communist led troops staged an uprising in Nanchang. But by August 8, the city was recaptured by the KMT Army and the rebel troops were dispersed. A series of peasant uprisings followed the decision of the August 7 Conference. The most significant of these revolts was the so-called August Harvest Insurrection, led by Mao Tse-tung on September 8, but this peasant revolt also ended in a bitter defeat. In these abortive uprisings, many Communists lost their lives and many cities suffered looting. The Chinese Communist Party became badly demoralized and disorganized.

The Sixth Party Congress

In November 1927, the Central Committee of the CCP called an enlarged meeting of the provisional political bureau set up at the August 7 Conference. This meeting, presided over by Ch'ü Ch'iu-pai and dominated by Moscow-trained Communists, adopted a new policy of emphasizing the leadership in the cities. This policy, which later was denounced as left Putschism, caused heavy losses to the Party. The CCP could not hold its conference in China, and accordingly, the leaders went to Moscow, where the Sixth Congress was held from July to September 1928. Under the auspices of Bukharin, the Congress, after reviewing the events of the Chinese Revolution since the Fifth Congress of April/May 1927, passed four important resolutions on the political question, propaganda work, the land question, and peasants' movements. These four resolutions are hailed by Communist historians as comprising a theoretically sound policy which overcame Ch'en Tu-hsiu's "right opportunist mistakes," as well as Chü Ch'iu-pai's "left Putschist errors."[4]

The Congress adopted the Ten Policies (also known as the Ten Great Demands of the Chinese Revolution) and a new Party constitution of 15 chapters and 53 articles.[5] It was significant that the Congress failed "to make a proper estimate of the importance of the revolutionary bases in the countryside, of the protracted nature of the democratic revolution, and of the characteristics of the national bourgeoisie in China."[6] As a result, the Congress still emphasized leadership in the cities and elected Hsiang Chung-fa, a former boatman, as secretary-general, replacing Ch'ü Ch'iu-pai.[7] Because of the intellectual incompetence of the new secretary-general, actual power fell to Li Li-san, another Moscow-trained Communist, who dominated the Central Committee and followed Moscow directives to carry on the city uprisings that led to the collapse of the CCP.[8]

It is worth noting that Mao's feat in carrying out the peasant movement in Hunan did not win him any key position in the Party leadership. On the contrary, as Mao proceeded to organize the Autumn Harvest Insurrection in Hunan, he was reprimanded several times by the Central Committee for deviations, and once dismissed from his position as an-alternate member of the provisional Politburo of the

CCP.[9] While the Communist leaders continued to direct the policy of urban uprisings as prescribed by Moscow, Mao, after the failure of the peasant uprising in Hunan, led the remnants of his forces to the Ching-kang-san area on the Kiangsi-Hunan border. Later joined by Chu Teh, he established the first peasant revolutionary base for the development of a disciplined, trained, and equipped Red army, and soviet-type government.

The Rise of Mao Tse-tung

The road that led Mao to unchallenged predominance in the CCP was a difficult one.[10] Mao's role in the CCP prior to 1927, is not clearly known. On the basis of his report on the peasant movement in Hunan, we may assume that Mao remained inwardly opposed to the policy of urban proletarian revolution pursued by the Communist leadership. The essence of his line was a rural strategy based on the peasantry. By making the peasantry the main force of the revolution, Mao diverged from the dogma of the Marxist-Leninist school. It was only after the total failure of the armed uprisings in cities that Mao separated the CCP from its urban base and established the theory that a Communist Party might function on a base of peasant and army support. This shift in the theory and framework of the CCP operations made it possible for the CCP to emphasize a program of agrarian reform. Everywhere it went, Mao's group organized the landless peasants, and set up village soviets (councils). After 1928, Mao's influence increased, the Red Army gained strength, and the area governed by soviets grew in size.

After 1929, a string of Chinese soviets spread eastward through Kiangsi to Fukien. At first these soviets were essentially local in character. It was not until 1931, when the Japanese invasion of Manchuria on 18 September 1931 diverted the attention of the Nanking government, that Mao succeeded in organizing a nationwide soviet in the Kiangsi-Hunan border region. On 7 November 1931, the First National Congress of the Soviets was convened in Juichin, the capital of Mao's Kiangsi soviet. A Chinese Soviet Republic, embracing all the soviet areas under Communist control, was formally established.[11] Over 600 delegates attended this congress and adopted a draft constitution, a land law, a labor law, and resolutions on economic policies and other matters. They elected a 64 member Central Executive Committee (CEC), including Mao, Chu Teh, Liu Shao-chi, Chou En-lai and Ch'en Shao-yü, who still remained the secretary-general of the CCP. On November 27, the CEC of the Republic in turn elected Mao Tse-tung chairman and Hsiang Ying and Chang Kuo-t'ao vice-chairmen.

The Long March

The battle lines were thus drawn between the KMT under Chiang Kai-shek and the CCP under Mao Tse-tung. In November 1930, the KMT forces began the first of the six extermination campaigns, designed to destroy the Chinese soviets, the Red Army, and the Chinese Communists. However, these campaigns, extending over a period of four years, failed to dislodge the Communist held bases. Finally, the Nationalists changed their tactics and began to circle the Communist bases with fortresses. They then applied a blockade of supplies and forced the Communists to retreat.

The Communist forces under the command of Mao Tse-tung, Chu Teh, Lin Piao and P'eng Teh-huai made a breakthrough in October 1934, and set out on the Long March (1934–35) to the border-lands of northwest China. This march of more than 6,000 miles through the whole of west China, was traversed in one year's time. The soldiers marched on foot and covered the territory of 12 different provinces, passed over 18 high mountain ranges, and went through the forbidding areas of the Chinese-Tibetan borderland. Needless to say, the march greatly weakened the Communists. Over 90,000 men had departed from the soviet area of southern Kiangsi at the beginning of the Long March, but only 20,000 men, including new recruits, reached the final destination in northwest Kiangsi.

However, the Long March marked the rise of Mao Tse-tung as the leader of the Chinese Communist Party. Mao had been chairman of the Soviet Republic in Kiangsi but now he became the undisputed leader of the whole Party. Mao obtained formal control over the CCP in January 1935, when an enlarged session of the Central Politburo was held at Tsungyi, Kweichow, to remove the Moscow-directed group from central Party leadership. In October 1935, the Central Red Army arrived in northern Shensi, where it established its new headquarters. After the seizure of the city of Yenan in December 1936, the Communists transferred their headquarters to that city and made it their capital early in 1937.

The United Front Policy

During the earlier years, Mao Tse-tung's basic strategy was one of a united front with the national bourgeoisie. Speaking in December 1935, Mao ascribed the severe setbacks suffered by the CCP between 1927 and 1934 to "the advocates of closed-door tactics."[12] By 1935, Mao became convinced that the strategy of forming a united anti-Japanese front would afford the Chinese Communists the possibilities of winning the wide support of the people. Mao's strategy paralleled that of the Comintern, which, at its Seventh Congress in 1935, proposed the formation of an anti-Fascist popular front in order to support the isolated U.S.S.R.

However, it would be wrong to assume that the strategy of the united front was entirely "channeled to the CCP from a Comintern source." On the contrary, it "grew as a response to national conditions."[13] As early as 1932, following the Japanese invasion of Manchuria in 1931, the CCP announced its willingness to conclude an agreement with all anti-Japanese groups, but no agreement with the KMT was intended at this time. Technically, this was still a united front from below, or a united front formed for the overthrow of the KMT regime. In July 1934, a similar proposal was made without eliciting any response from the KMT. As late as August 1936, the CCP presented a formal proposal of a united anti-Japanese front to the KMT. This proposal remained unanswered. In carrying out his anti-Communist campaign, Chiang Kai-shek refused to listen to arguments for a united front. His program was to placate the Japanese as long as they did not take Peking, and to wipe out the Communists and their weak northwestern base.

However, as the threat of Japanese invasion became more serious toward the end of 1936, anti-Japanese sentiment enveloped the whole country, punctuated by popular demands for resistance. Meanwhile, the National Salvation Association was organized to promote a resistance movement against Japanese aggression.[14] The association made demands which were meant to embarrass Chiang and strengthen Communist efforts for a united anti-Japanese front. Chiang's stubborn refusal to yield to demands for war against Japan led to his strange kidnapping in Sian, in December 1936.

This act was the work of Chang Hsüeh-liang, former warlord of Manchuria, whose troops were garrisoned at Sian, capital and strategic key city of south central Shensi. In 1936 he was one of Chiang's deputies and commander-in-chief of the Bandit (Communist) Suppression Campaign in the northwest. His Manchurian troops, cut off from their homeland, were especially susceptible to the Communist demand for the united front against Japan and they became increasingly bitter about Chiang's anti-Communist campaign. In December 1936, when Chiang flew to Sian to urge Chang and his troops to move against the Communists, they mutinied, kidnapped Chiang, and held him prisoner. At first it appeared certain that Chiang's arrest would end in his execution.

At this point Moscow interceded and sent agents to participate with Chou En-lai in negotiations which eventually led to Chiang's release, effected on the condition that the anti-Communist campaign was to be terminated, and a new truce worked out between the KMT and the CCP. This marked a decisive turning point in the history of the CCP.[15]

United Anti-Japanese Front

At the time of Chiang's release at Sian, the war to resist Japanese aggression was decided upon and it broke out in July 1937. The United Anti-Japanese Front, consisting of the KMT, the CCP, and other parties, was soon formed as a symbol of national unity. In September

1937, the Central Committee of the CCP issued a manifesto—"The United Front for the National Emergency." In it the Communists agreed to accept the Three People's Principles of the KMT as "the paramount need of China today," and to abandon their policy of forcible confiscation of land. They also promised to abolish the soviet government and to incorporate the Red Army into the National Revolutionary Army under Chiang's supreme command. While negotiations went on concerning incorporation of the Communist forces, the Red Army under the command of Chu Teh and P'eng Teh-huai was officially recognized as the Eighth Army, consisting of three divisions and assigned to the Second War Zone in northern Shensi. By the end of 1937, the New Fourth Army, made up of the old Red Army units under the command of Yeh T'ing and Hsiang Ying, was constituted and assigned to the Third War Zone in the area south of the Yangtze.

This united front agreement was more a tactical truce than a peaceful settlement, and was agreeable to each side for different reasons. In the course of its first year, certain measures were taken on each side which appeared to meet the terms of the agreement. From the end of 1937 until the fall of 1938, there seemed to exist a common war strategy under which Communist forces coordinated their moves and attacks with those of the KMT troops. KMT-CCP relations began to deteriorate in 1939–40 as the Japanese pressure on China lessened and the war became an endurance contest. It also became apparent that the Communists had no intention of submitting to real direction and control by the KMT government; instead, they insisted after 1937 on retaining control of their own territorial bases and maintaining their own armed forces. On the other hand, the KMT became increasingly fearful that under the guise of anti-Japanese activity the CCP would arouse a mass revolutionary movement, which for the KMT was almost as unhappy a prospect as Japanese victory.[16]

The Civil War

The first major clash between the KMT and CCP forces broke out in January 1941, on the lower Yangtze River, where the New Fourth Army had successfully established its guerilla bases. In the ensuing clash the commander of the Red Army, Yeh T'ing, was captured and his deputy, Hsiang Ying, was killed in action. This clash marked the end of the new KMT-CCP alliance. From then on, hostilities and clashes continued intermittently.

These clashes certainly weakened China's war efforts against the Japanese. It is true that from the end of 1941 until the early part of 1944, the KMT massed its forces to blockade the Red base in the northwest, with Sian as the key fortress. And yet it is also true that the CCP devoted its main effort to develop its military strength and expand its controlled areas. These years, therefore, were marked by the steady collapse of the KMT-CCP united front.

When the United States, Great Britain, and other Western powers entered the Pacific War at the end of 1941, they were interested that China should unite against Japan. The United States, in particular, was disposed to build up a united and powerful China to become a balance wheel in postwar Far Eastern politics. Toward this end, American envoys were sent to China, to try to bring about reconciliation between the KMT and the CCP.[17] However, the KMT-CCP cleavage was too far advanced for their efforts to succeed.[18] When the Japanese surrendered in August 1945, China was hopelessly divided. The glory of victory was overshadowed by the KMT-CCP struggle for control of the Japanese-occupied areas.

The Growth of Communist Power

During the war years, the Chinese Communists under the leadership of Mao Tse-tung not only gained territory and organizational strength, but also built up a very powerful Red Army and a highly disciplined Party. Before the war, the Chinese Communists had been considered outlaws and bandits, but during the war their status was legalized; they were regarded as patriots. Many young men left Szechwan and Yunnan to join them. Now they were no longer contained as they had been in Kiangsi; on the contrary, they had free access to large areas in north China. From there they could send their military forces into Manchuria and establish contact with Soviet Russia.

The Long March had left the CCP with only 20,000 men, but eight years later, by the end of 1943, the Communists claimed to have a People's Liberation Army of 470,000 men, including the Eighth Route Army, the New Fourth Army, and other anti-Japanese people's troops, with a militia force of two million men.[19] They also claimed to control 90 million people in the nineteen liberated areas, which extended across the north China plain from Shensi to Shantung; thus cutting off central China from overland access to Peking and Manchuria.

Moreover, the Party grew from 40,000 members in 1937 to about 1,200,000 in 1945. This great expansion of Party membership made the Chinese party the world's second largest Communist party at the end of the war. The increase in the number of Party members added to those in the liberated areas, made it all the more essential that the Party should be welded together into a well-disciplined and well-indoctrinated body. For the purpose of indoctrination, in 1941, the Communist leaders inaugurated a study campaign consisting of group discussion, criticism, and self-criticism. From 1942 to 1944, they carried on a thoroughgoing *cheng-feng* or Party Rectification Movement in which rightist and leftist deviationists within the Party were purged or brought into line.[20]

When the Seventh Party Congress convened at Yenan on 23 April 1945, Mao had established himself as the undisputed leader of a greatly strengthened Communist Party. He was reelected Party chairman, and a Politburo of his loyal comrades was also designated. The Party constitution, adopted by the Congress, provided the basis of a disciplined Party organization. Before the war was over, in sum, the balance of military and political power had shifted to the side of the CCP.

Table 7

Growth of Communist Party 1921–1969[21]

YEAR	MEMBERSHIP
First Party Congress, 1921	57
Second Party Congress, 1922	123
Third Party Congress, 1923	432
Fourth Party Congress, 1925	1,000
Fifth Party Congress, 1927	57,900
Sixth Party Congress, 1928	40,000
Seventh Party Congress, 1945	1,210,000
Eighth Party Congress, 1956	10,734,000
Ninth Party Congress, 1969 (est.)	20,000,000

THE MEANING OF MAOISM

The term Maoism is a "handy coinage of Western, or more precisely, of Harvard scholars," which has now gained wide circulation.[22] The Chinese simply describe it as the thought of Mao Tse-tung.

Mao Tse-tung, who reads no foreign languages himself, had to rely on second-hand accounts of Marxism and a very limited number of translations of Marxists works. According to Edgar Snow, Mao cited only the *Communist Manifesto*, Kantsky's *Class Struggle*, and *A History of Socialism* by Kirkuppas, as those works which made an important impression upon him in the earlier stages of his intellectual development.[23]

Moreover, a recent study made by a Western scholar revealed that in the four volumes of *Selected Works of Mao Tse-tung*, only 4 percent of all references and quotations are from Marx and Engels, as compared to 18 percent from Lenin and 24 percent from Stalin.[24] Mao only refers specifically to Engels' *Anti-Dühring* and *Ludwig Feuerbach*, Marx's *Theses on Feuerbach*, Lenin's *Materialism and Empiriocriticism*, and two sections from Lenin's *Philosophical Notebooks*.[25]

While this indicates that Mao Tse-tung's academic background in Marxism-Leninism is relatively weak, he nevertheless has made some important contributions to the theory of dialectical materialism, as illustrated by his two published works: *On Practice* (1957) and *On Contradiction* (allegedly written in 1937 and published in 1952).[26]

In *On Practice*, Mao perpetuated dialectical materialism and the neo-Confucian school of idealism. In this work he stressed that the process of knowledge has three stages: perception, conception, and verification. Mao also emphasized the relevancy of ideology to action; that is, the unity of theory and practice. On the basis of this analysis, Mao is said to have discovered the criterion of scientific truth, which can be applied to the criticism of opposing policies as well as to the maintenance of leadership infallibility.

An illustration of this theory can be found in a 1971 study by the Writing Group of the Communist Party:

> Chairman Mao not only affirmed in clear terms the Marxist viewpoint of practice but scientifically summarized the practical contents as something applied in the practice of production, in the practice of revolutionary class struggle and revolutionary national struggle, and in the practice of scientific experiment.[27]

The other essay, *On Contradiction*, was a companion piece to *On Practice*. Again taking the Marxist-Leninist doctrine as a base, Mao Tse-tung insisted that because contradictions are inherent in human relations, they therefore govern politics. In this work, Mao stressed the universality of contradiction, such as in war, offense and defense, advance and retreat, etc.; but also noted that their particularity was determined by the needs of time and place.

Since the essay's publication, the theory of contradictions has played a prominent part in the official ideology of the Chinese Communists. This essay became supremely important in Chinese Communist ideology after Mao's speech "On the Correct Handling of Contradictions Among the People," published in 1957. In it he differentiated two types of contradictions: "the first, called antagonistic contradictions, which exist between hostile classes and hostile social systems." There are contradictions, he explained, "between the enemy and ourselves," and because they are essentially violent, these contradictions can be resolved only by force—though not necessarily by war. The second type is called "non-antagonistic contradictions," which exist within the socialist society. Because they are essentially nonviolent, these contradictions can be resolved through the process of "uniting, criticizing, and education."[28]

The Chinese assert that Maoism with its repeated moral exhortations has filled the gap in the writings of Marx and Engels, which were widely regarded as without any ethical criteria. According to Sidney Hook, Marx and Engels were determined to get away from abstract moralizing about right and justice, and wanted to establish an ethic

firmly based in the real, class-divided world.[29] Maoism, on the other
hand, remains to some extent within the Chinese tradition which has
always regarded moral instruction as its first duty.

Maoism and Psychism

The Chinese also believe that Maoism is the "microscoped tele-
scope" of their revolutionary cause; the instrument for analyzing the
problems of the present. In other words, Maoism has served as a means
to achieve a goal. Or as Robert J. Lifton called it, a *way* (*tao*), a call to a
particular mode of being on behalf of a transcendent purpose. In this
respect, Lifton also used the term psychism to denote Maoism.[30]

However, Lifton's analysis of Maoism is fundamentally critical.
For example, he views ideological mobilization as an aberration which
can only be counterproductive to the goals of economic and political
development, without recognizing the subjective attitudes for the developmental process. Contrariwise, Joseph J. Spengler, an economist,
assigned a central role to ideology when he suggested that the state of
a people's politico-economic development depends largely upon what
is in the minds of its members, particularly the elite.[31] Or in other
words, "the thought of Mao Tse-tung has placed primary emphasis on
the reform of the mind and the spirit."[32]

Goal Orientation

Much of Mao's writings are centered on his goal for China to
develop a new national, scientific, and mass culture. This may be
traced to the early revolutionary days in the 1920s. When Mao first
wrote his important "Hunan Report" (1927), he complained that
"China has always had a landlord's culture, but never a peasant's culture."[33] He subsequently raised the question of cultural revolution
(*wen-hua ke-ming*) in his next most original thesis, "On New Democracy" in 1940.[34]

Mao wrote,

> On the cultural or ideological front, the two periods preceding
> and following the May 4 Movement form two distinct historical
> periods. Before the May 4 Movement, the struggle on China's
> cultural front was one between the new culture of the bourgeoisie
> and the old culture of the feudal class.... But since the May 4
> Movement, things have been different. A brand-new culture force
> came into being in China, that is, the Communist culture and
> ideology guided by the Chinese Communists, or the Communist
> world outlook and theory of social revolution....

And Mao continued:

> The new democratic culture is the anti-imperialist and anti-feudal
> culture of the broad masses.... This culture can be led only by

the culture and ideology of the proletariat, by the ideology of communism ... a national, scientific and mass culture ... combine the politics, the economy and the culture of the New Democracy, and you have the new-democratic republic, the Republic of China both in name and in reality, the new China we want to create.[35]

Maoism and Mass Line

The strategy used by Mao Tse-tung to achieve his goal of a national, scientific, and mass culture was through mass line. The mass line, as defined by John W. Lewis, "is the basic working method by which Communist cadres seek to initiate and promote a unified relationship between themselves and the Chinese population and thus to bring about the support and active participation of the people."[36] This method includes the two techniques of "from the masses, to the masses," and "the linking of the general with the specific."[37]

The mass line placed particular emphasis on the points of direct contact between the people and Party cadres. This was illustrated in the technique of group study (hsüeh-hsi), which required participation by the entire population—the official study group under the leadership of a propagandist. The propagandist was not only responsible for the preparation of posters and wall newspapers, but he had to give street-corner shows and lead the shouting of slogans at mass meetings. In addition, he constantly created an agitation among the people in his study group. In this plan, everyone in the study group was expected to express an opinion, and a mere parroting of the official line was not considered sufficient. Finally, using a correct standard, the ideas of each member were criticized by others of the group.

It has been estimated that by December 1950, there were already more than 1,920,000 trained propagandists in the country. The distribution throughout different regions was:

North China	606,000
Northeast	300,000
East	650,000
Central South	236,000
Southwest	85,000
Northwest	30,000

The practices of group study lasted some 20 years, until the outbreak of the Korean War in 1951. The process then turned from the milder form of group study to a more coercive method of reformative study (kai-tsao hsuen-hsi). New programs to eradicate deviant ideologies were introduced, such as the "three-anti" campaigns (against corruption, waste, and bureaucratism) and the "five-anti" campaigns (against crimes of bribery, tax evasion, fraud, theft of state assets, and leakage of state economic secrets).

These campaigns usually began with a series of articles and editorials in newspapers or on radio broadcasts. Mass accusation meetings were held together with smaller reformative study groups in which the aim was redemption through criticism. Each group would not only discuss the facts as presented by the Party, but they would also consider what kind of thought could have produced such actions. The group would then proceed to look for traces of the same in themselves. In fact, these sessions are remarkably similar to sensitivity training used by Western modern psychiatry for group therapy.

Despite these intensified campaigns, Mao became seriously disturbed by the negative response of the intellectuals. The decision then made by the Communist Party was for a tactical retreat allowing more freedom of independent thinking. This new policy was dramatically announced by the chairman himself in his famous "Let a Hundred Flowers Blossom, Let a Hundred Schools (of thought) Contend" speech on 2 May 1956 at the Supreme State Conference. But the reactions of the intellectuals were apathetic and nonresponsive. Again, on 27 February 1957, Mao reaffirmed this policy in another address entitled, "On the Correct Handling of Contradiction Among the People." This reaffirmation of free and independent thinking generated a storm of criticism upon the Party by the intellectuals, and they charged the Party with incompetence in leading China in science, education, and the arts. They declared that Party bureaucratism was worse than capitalism. Many even questioned the infallibity of Mao's thought as an ideology. As a result, Mao adopted new strategies including many great purges and finally, to insure the successful implementation of his program and ideology he effected total mass mobilization against his opponents.

THE GREAT PURGES 1949–68

Mao Tse-tung was successful in implementing his program and ideology upon the Party members. In spite of this however, there were currents of disputes, both doctrinal and tactical, on how China should be governed as a Communist nation. These disputes split the Party leadership right to the core of its hierarchy.

The Purge of Kao Kang and Jao Shu-shih

The first important dispute among Chinese leaders was revealed in 1955 when the National Conference of the Chinese Communist Party adopted a resolution, "On the Anti-Party Bloc of Kao Kang and Joa Shu-shih," which was a reaffirmation of the 1954 Central Committee's decision to expel Kao Kang and Jao Shu-shih from the Party membership.[38] According to the Party resolution,

Kao Kang carried on conspiratorial activities aimed at seizing leadership in the Party and the State. In Northeast China particularly, he created and spread many rumors slandering the Central Committee of the Party but lauding himself. His aim was to sow discord and dissension among the comrades of the Central Committee of the Party; he thus carried on activities to split the Party and, in the course of these activities, formed his own anti-Party faction . . . Jao Shu-shih was Kao Kang's chief ally in his conspiratorial activities against the Party. . . .[39]

This was surprising since both Kao and Jao were Tse-tung's comrades-in-arms since the Long March days. One could say that without the help of Kao and Jao, perhaps Mao would never have gained his present position and power in China.

Background of Kao and Jao

Kao Kang was born in 1891 in Hengshan, Shensi, an area of great importance to Mao during the Sino-Japanese War. Kao became a Communist under the influence of the Russian advisers employed by Warlord Feng Yu-hsiang in north Shensi.[40] In 1927, he and Liu Chih-tan, another earlier Communist, established a soviet area in the Northwest, persisted in guerrilla operations in the Shensi-Kansu-Ninghsia border area, and established many revolutionary base areas. These areas became the fountainhead for Mao Tse-tung after the completion of his Long March in 1935, when Mao retreated to Paoan, Shensi. The Red capital, Yenan, was also located here in this province.

During the ensuing years, Kao achieved tremendous success as the protegé of Mao. He held such important positions as chairman of the advisory council of the Shensi-Kansu-Ninghsia border area (1939); secretary of the Chinese Communist Party Northwest Subbureau (1944); and finally, he was elected to membership in the powerful Central Committee in 1945. When the Sino-Japanese War ended, he went to Manchuria together with Lin Piao and Peng Chen. In May 1949, Kao was named political commissar of the entire Northeast Military Region. When the People's Republic was established in Peking on 1 October 1949 he was named a vice-chairman of the People's Central Government and chairman of the Northeast People's Government. In fact, he became the undisputed ruler of Manchuria.

Jao Shu-shih also had a distinguished career within the Chinese Communist movement. He was born in 1905 in Nanchang, Kiangsi. He joined the Chinese Communist Party when he was a student at Shanghai University in the 1920s. During the Chiang Kai-shek coup against the Communists in 1927, with Soviet assistance he escaped to the U.S., and then went to eastern Europe before returning to Kiangsi to serve in the Red Army. In 1943, he became the political commissar of the New Fourth Army and secretary of the Chinese Communist Party East China Bureau.

After the Chinese Communist victory on the mainland, Jao was named secretary of the Shanghai Municipal Committee in May 1949, and chairman of the East China Military and Administrative Committee in December 1949. His brilliant career ended with his arrest in February 1954.

Issues over Economic Development

The open rifts between Kao Kang and Jao Shu-shih and other members of the Central Committee began in 1950. These disputes questioned whether to follow Soviet models of economic development, which featured concentration on heavy industry and relative autonomy for professional management.

Kao Kang, for example, introduced (with the approval of Soviet advisers in China) a single-director system for individual accountability at all levels of organization. The purpose of this line of organization was to provide for a course of gradual reduction of the Party Committee's authority in industrial management. Kao Kang wrote: "The secretaries of the Communist Party committees (or branches) in enterprises . . . cannot supplant the factory director; they cannot supplant the system of factory-director responsibility."[41]

On the other hand, Liu Shao-chi, Teng Hsiao-Ping, and Chou En-lai suggested a collective leadership of the Party Committee as an alternative for the industrial management by a single-director. Their argument against single-directorship as presented by Li Hsueh-feng, director of the Industrial Department of the Central Committe, was

> an erroneous overemphasis on the person responsible for plant administration as the person fully empowered to lead. The functions of the Party organizations in the plant were reduced to assurance of production target fulfillment and control. . . . As a result, negating the Party's leadership over management, and putting the Party in subordinate position. . . .[42]

When Kao and Jao feared their proposal would be defeated by the Party Central Committee, they attempted to secure the support of a number of high ranking army officers. Kao argued that the Party had to be reorganized because the Party was created by the Army, not by the professionals of the so-called "party of white areas."[43] Since Liu Shao-chi, Teng Hsiao-ping, and Chou En-lai were members who had spent much of their time in the white areas, they should have taken a secondary role in the reorganization of the Party.

Meanwhile, Liu, Teng, and Chou had already anticipated this move and had enlisted the strong support of Peng Chen, mayor of Peking, to expel Kao and Jao at the 1954 Party Central Committee meeting. Kao commited suicide and Jao was allegedly put in prison.[44] The Kao-Jao purge thus created a balance of power within the CCP hierarchy. Liu Shao-chi was named chairman of the National People's Congress in 1954 and chief-of-state in 1959; Teng Hsiao-ping was made secretary-general of the Party; and Chou En-lai remains as the powerful premier of the State Council.

The Purge of P'eng Teh-huai and Huang Ke-cheng

Disputes in Communist China seldom involve the military, for Mao Tse-tung has always kept the military under his own control. However in 1959, tumultuous political events occurred with the announcement of the replacement of two key men in the military establishment of China: Marshal P'eng Teh-huai, the minister of defense and the noted revolutionary war hero, and General Huang Ke-cheng, chief of staff of the army and P'eng's senior vice-minister. They were replaced by Lin Piao and Lo Jui-ch'ing.

Both P'eng and Huang were denounced as right-wing opportunists at the eighth plenum of the Central Committee meeting, held at Lushan in August 1959. However, the full resolution adopted by the Party to purge Peng and Huang was not revealed until 1967 during the Great Proletarian Cultural Revolution when the attack upon P'eng and Teh-huai was renewed. According to the official accusation, P'eng's and Teh-huai's and Huang Ke-cheng's crime was "a continuation and development of the case of anti-Party alliance of Kao Kang and Jao Shu-shih."[45] The resolution then continued:

> P'eng Teh-huai joined the Party and the revolutionary army led by the Party with the idea of "investing in a share." He only wants to lead others, to lead the collective, but does not want to be led by others, to be led by the collective. He does not look upon the achievements in the revolutionary work for which he is responsible as achievements in the struggle conducted by the Party and the people, but instead takes all the credit himself.[46]

P'eng had been a model Communist. He had lost both his parents early in life, had scarcely any formal schooling, had run away from home to escape from the tyranny of his stepmother, and had worked in mines and at various other forms of hard physical labor. Later, he joined Chinese warlord Lu Ti-p'ing's army and participated in the Communist uprising in Peking in the early 1920s. Finally, he reorganized his forces into the Chinese Workers' and Peasants' Red Fifth Army and helped Mao Tse-tung during the Long March. He was Mao's righthand man during the early period of the Communist revolutionary activities in China and after the Sino-Japanese War, P'eng became the deputy commander-in-chief of the People's Liberation Army in 1945. He commanded the Chinese People's Volunteers in the Korean War and was awarded the title of "Hero" by North Korea. After 1945 he was concurrently appointed a vice-premier of the State Council and minister of national defense.

Issues Involved

The political undoing of P'eng and Teh-huai can be traced to a letter of opinion which P'eng sent to Mao Tse-tung on 14 July 1959.[47] He charged that capital construction under the Great Leap Forward had been hasty and excessive, creating imbalances in the economy. He then discussed the shortcomings and errors of the formations of rural communes. In addition, P'eng also resisted the Party's control of the army and questioned the validity of Mao's theories of people's wars as well as China's nuclear strategy. P'eng, in fact, had for sometime championed the cause of a professional armed forces including the following principles: (1) to put "the army before the Party"; (2) to counterpose "regularization and modernization" against "proletarian revolutionization of the army"; (3) to substitute "the system of one-man leadership" for the "collective leadership of Party Committee" in the army; and finally, (4) to "place military technique" in the first place in army building.[48]

P'eng received substantial support from other senior military figures, including the heads of the General Logistics Department, General Training Department, General Political Department, and a half-dozen lesser military leaders who were subsequently purged.

In fact, after P'eng's and Huang's removal, the Party decreed that all members of the People's Liberation Army must work in the villages and communes and intensively study the thought of Mao Tse-tung. Meanwhile, on 20 June 1959, the Soviet Union cancelled its previous agreements to assist China in the development of advanced weapons.

After the purge of P'eng Teh-huai and Huang Ke-cheng in 1959, Mao Tse-tung's own position was considerably weakened and in fact, he was obliged to give up his chairmanship of the Republic to Liu Shao-chi at the important Lushan meeting in August 1959. Liu Shao-chi, with the support of Teng Hsiao-ping, Party secretary-general and Peng Chen, mayor of Peking, gradually effectively organized a new anti-Mao force within the Party.

The Great Purges of Peng Chen and Liu Shao-chi

When the news of the purge of Peng Chen reached the West, shock and disbelief were the first reactions of many China-watchers. Chinese Communist purges were nothing new, as witnessed in the cases of Kao Kang and Jao Shu-shih, and P'eng Teh-huai and Huang Ke-cheng. But the purge of Peng Chen, a most powerful and reasonably secure member of the inner sanctum of the ruling clique in China—this was almost unbelievable.

Peng Chen, a devoted Communist from his youth—as were the

others purged before him—was also an important Party theoretician. He was president of the Party's Central Party School from 1938 to 1942; he worked closely with both Mao and Lin Piao during the war years. In 1948, he was a deputy director of the Organizational Department of the Party Central Committee. Then, in 1951, he was appointed mayor of Peking, the capital of Communist China, and later he served as vice-chairman of the Chinese People's Congress. He was internationally known because he was one of the few Chinese Communist Party members entrusted with the responsibility of interpreting Maoism to other Communists. For example, he had often represented China at numerous international congresses and also participated in the important but unsuccessful negotiations with the Soviet Communist Party on resolving Sino-Soviet ideological differences.

It must have been difficult for Mao to dismiss Peng Chen, especially because Peng Chen belonged to the most powerful hierarchy in China which included Liu Shao-chi, China's chief-of-state; Teng Hsiao-ping, the Party's all-powerful secretary-general; Lo Jui-ch'ing, the army's chief-of-staff and one-time head of the secret police; Liu-Ning-i, China's labor boss; and Lu Ting-yi and Chou Yang, propaganda chiefs. In dismissing Peng Chen, Mao took the risk of casting doubts on others of the Party's power-elite.

But, Mao's purge of Peng Chen can be read only as another dramatic chapter of Imperial Chinese drama. The Maoists had to manufacture incriminating evidence of Peng Chen's so-called deviation from the Maoist line. This was necessary because of the people's respect for Peng, his many years of distinguished service in the Party, and his reputation as a Party theoretician. Maoists deviously plotted to uncover hidden faults and radically alter Peng's public image.

The Maoists found a convenient tool to accomplish their plot in the form of a popular play written by Wu Han, a scholar specializing in Ming history and a close friend of Peng Chen. Wu Han, a faithful backer of the CCP during the civil war period, was once a professor of history at Tsinghua University. In 1961, he wrote a play, "The Dismissal of Hai Jui," which dealt with a benevolent Chinese official in the sixteenth century who "always fought with all his might against corrupt officials and, therefore, lost favor with the Emperor."[49] Wu Han portrayed Hai Jui as a good and clean official, full of honesty, forthrightness, moral integrity, and courage to resist unjust pressures from his superiors. What made the incident noteworthy was the accusation that Wu Han was actually writing an allegory based on the dismissal of P'eng Teh-huai.

Maoists, seizing this opportunity, planned a complicated strategy.[50] From November 1965 to April 1966 many articles appeared in the newspapers, bitterly denouncing Wu Han.[51] Peng Chen—a friend of Wu Han—without realizing that the attack on the play was a political trap, came to Wu's rescue as the Maoists expected. Peng asked two prominent Chinese journalists, Teng T'o, editor-in-chief of the *People's Daily* and Liao Mo-sha, head of the United Front Department of the Party, to defend the play. They immediately responded and wrote many favorable articles in defense of Wu Han.

With the positions of these men publicly exposed, the Maoists opened fire. First, the *Liberation Army Daily*, a Maoist newspaper representing the armed forces, published fierce attacks on these men as did the official Party paper, the *People's Daily*. The Maoist paper asserted that "this anti-Party small clique is not an incidental and isolated phenomenon" and urged a nationwide movement so that the group could be dealt with "thoroughly and mercilessly."[52] With Mao's encouragement, a nationwide campaign was launched, attacking these men. Finally, the carefully planned attack was centered upon Peng Chen and several other party persons in authority, until Peng was forced from office.

As Peng Chen was being purged, the entire power structure of the Chinese Communists consequently was altered: Lu Ting-yi, Chou Yang, Liu Ning-i, Lo Jui-ch'ing, Teng Hsiao-ping; one by one, and finally Liu Shao-chi himself.

Liu Shao-chi, five years younger than Mao, was born in the same province as Mao. Unlike most Chinese Communist leaders who are specialists in one area, military, culture, labor, or foreign affairs, Liu Shao-chi has played every position on the field. He started as a professional trouble shooter among the labor unions of the coastal cities like Shanghai and Canton in the early twenties, and later switched to Party organization. In fact, he wrote the present Party constitution. For many years, his writings such as "How to be a Good Communist" (1939) and "On the Intra-Party Struggle" (1941) have become the Bible of aspirants and old Bolsheviks alike. However, Liu differs from Mao in that he has shown great admiration for the Soviet Union, which he expressed openly in his book, *On Nationalism and Internationalism* published in 1948.[53]

After the Lushan meeting in 1959, Liu's plan was to capture the leading Party cadres, or China's organizational men. For example, in 1962, he organized a Central Work Expansion Conference in Peking which included 7,000 leading cadres from all parts of China. In fact, Liu was so confident during the conference that he openly criticized Mao and his policies.[54] Then, he began to exercise greater control of governmental affairs. He took personal command of China's foreign affairs, limiting the role played by Premier Chou En-lai and his foreign minister, Chen Yi, to suit his plan to replace Chou En-lai with Peng Chen. Liu also personally travelled to many foreign states, including visits to the Soviet Union, several East European countries, Burma, Cambodia, North Korea, and North Vietnam. From 21 May to 5 June

1965 he was in Indonesia conferring with Sukarno for the proposed Peking-Djakarta axis, which was supposed to be his creation.[55] These roles should have been taken by Premier Chou En-lai.

However, Mao is an old revolutionist. He could not give up his power without a counterplan to recover it. During the 1959 Lushan meeting, he insisted that his man, Lin Piao, be appointed as the new defense minister as his price for relinquishing the chairmanship of the Republic. Lin was then only 52 years of age and considered to be the youngest and most brilliant vice-chairman of the Chinese Communist Party Central Committee. Lin Piao also had an outstanding record in the liberation army. In 1932, at the age of 25, he commanded the First Front Red Army, which acted as the vanguard in the Long March in 1934. During the Sino-Japanese War, he headed both the Chinese Worker-Peasant Red Army University and the Anti-Japanese Military and Political University, from which many of the leading military cadres of Communist China were trained. Lin Piao was wounded several times. However, in 1945, he led the Red Army into Manchuria and commanded the powerful Fourth Field Army. It was while under his command that the Chinese Communists conquered half of the Chinese mainland from Manchuria to the Hainan Islands (opposite North Vietnam). In October 1950 he was the commander-in-chief of the Chinese Volunteers in Korea until he was again wounded and replaced by P'eng Teh-huai. After his full recovery in 1958, he was appointed by Mao as vice-chairman of the Chinese Communist Party Central Committee.

When he succeeded P'eng as defense minister in 1959, Lin Piao immediately started to reorganize the Chinese Liberation Army, utilizing the strategy of "propagating Mao's thinking."[56] He abolished the ranking system in the army so as to gain support and confidence of the lower cadres and soldiers. He introduced a new system of political departments, not only in the army, but also in industry, communications, trade, financial units, and educational and scientific research organizations. This was done in 1964, and all in the name of the study of Mao's thought and to combat revisionism. Finally, to compete with the Party organizations headed by Liu Shao-chi and Teng Hsiao-ping, he made regional army commanders of the newly appointed Party secretaries in charge of the Central Committee's six regional bureaus. In addition, he enlisted Mao's wife, Chiang Ching, a former actress, to help him advance the cause of promoting Maoism among the Chinese masses.

Meanwhile, Liu Shao-chi began to consolidate his forces in Peking intending to impeach Mao.[57] Mao had already left the capital sometime in November 1965 and gone to Shanghai. There, he plotted the complicated strategy against Wu Han. As we have already seen, apparently without realizing the seriousness of the attack on Wu Han by the pro-Mao forces in Shanghai as a plot against the power-holders in Peking, Peng Chen, Teng Hsiao-ping, and Liu Shao-chi continued their support of Wu Han and their plan to remove Mao from office. In fact, Liu Shao-chi was so confident of his power status within the Party, that he left Peking with his wife, on 26 March 1966 for a state visit to Pakistan and Afghanistan. His absence afforded his opponents the perfect opportunity to complete their power play.[58]

On 18 April 1966, the *Liberation Army Daily* sounded the trumpet call of the Great Proletarian Cultural Revolution with a strong editorial on "Hold High the Great Red Banner of Mao Tse-tung's Thought and Actively Participate in the Great Socialist Cultural Revolution," and declared war against the literary world of Mao's opponents. Although Liu Shao-chi returned to China immediately thereafter, there was no publicized reception for him in Peking, and his political career was coming to an end.

Again the central issue, as in the case of earlier purges, seemed to revolve around the debate of accepting only Mao Tse-tung's model or following the Soviet or other roads, for the reconstruction of Chinese society.

Issues Involved

For example, during the foreign policy debate in Peking in 1965–66, because of the urgent military crisis in Indo-China, the Peng Chen–Liu Shao-chi groups urged a limited and conditional rapprochement with the Soviet Union. In fact, the Peng-Liu faction was supported by Lo Jui-ch'ing, then China's general chief-of-staff, who demanded more militant action in Vietnam under the guise of limited reconciliation with Moscow. This possibility was already implicit in the Soviet's suggestion that China lease airfields in the south to Soviet planes and personnel to provide air cover for Hanoi. It is important to note that in 1965–66 the Mao-Lin group consistently advocated an approach that was "far more cautious and restrained" toward the U.S. than the policy favored by their opponents.[59]

Moreover, as the chairman of the Republic in 1959, Liu Shao-chi began a series of liberalization programs including the reintroduction of personal incentives and private farm plots. Between 1959 and 1962, Liu's liberation program was notable for its greater emphasis on cost-consciousness and profitability than on output goals in state enterprises. Liu Shao-chi's domestic policy also was in direct opposition to Mao Tse-tung's ideology and directives.

The great purges were indeed titanic power struggles for the final determination of, not only the immediate, but also the ultimate, goals of the Communist revolution in China. While the purpose of the purges was mainly to maintain the purity of the Chinese Communist Party's ideology, the violence and instability, on the other hand, were inherent characteristics of any major revolutionary movement, as C. K. Yang explained: ". . . Goal instability and its concomitant violent conflicts will continue to characterize the process of a major revolution until institutional stabilization is achieved for a new pattern of social order."[60]

Suggested Reading

BRANDT, CONRAD, et al. *A Documenary History of Chinese Communism.* Cambridge, Mass.: Harvard University Press, 1952.

CHAI, WINBERG, ed. *Essential Works of Chinese Communism,* 2d ed. New York: Bantam Books, 1971.

CH'EN, JEROME. *Mao and the Chinese Revolution.* New York: Oxford University Press, 1967.

————. *Mao's Papers.* New York: Oxford University Press, 1970.

COHEN, ARTHUR. *The Communism of Mao Tse-tung.* Chicago: University of Chicago Press, 1964.

HSIAO, TSO-LIANG. *Power Relations within the Chinese Communist Movement, 1930–1934.* Seattle: University of Washington Press, 1961.

JOHNSON, CHALMER A. *Peasant Nationalism and Communist Power.* Palo Alto: Stanford University Press, 1962.

KLEIN, DONALD W., and CLARK, ANNE B., eds. *Biographic Dictionary of Chinese Communism, 1921–1965.* 2 vols. Cambridge, Mass.: Harvard University Press, 1971.

LOWE, DONALD M. *The Function of "China" in Marx, Lenin and Mao.* Berkeley: University of California Press, 1966.

MAO TSE-TUNG. *Selected Works of Mao Tse-tung.* 4 vols. Peking: Foreign Language Press, 1965.

SCHRAM, STUART. *The Political Thought of Mao Tse-tung,* rev. and enl. New York: Praeger Publishers, 1969.

SCHURMANN, FRANZ. *Ideology and Organization in Communist China,* new ed., enl. Berkeley: University of California Press, 1968.

SCHWARTZ, BENJAMIN I. *Chinese Communism and the Rise of Mao,* new ed. New York: Harper Torchbook, 1967.

————. *Communism and China: Ideology in Flux.* Cambridge, Mass.: Harvard University Press, 1968.

SHEWMAKER, KENNETH E. *Americans and Chinese Communists 1927–1945.* Ithaca: Cornell University Press, 1971.

SNOW, EDGAR. *Red Star Over China,* enl. ed. New York: Grove Press, 1968.

TREADGOLD, DONALD W., ed. *Soviet and Chinese Communism: Similarities and Differences.* Seattle: University of Washington Press, 1967.

chapter four

The Great Mass Mobilization

In China, it is nothing new to use mass mobilization for the purpose of involving the broadest possible participation of the people in state affairs. Mao Tse-tung first developed this strategy during the Kiangsi Soviet period (1931–34), and later incorporated it into his important policy guide of mass line.[1]

The great mass mobilization which has shaken mainland China began as a socialist education campaign in 1962, changed its face to the Great Proletarian Cultural Revolution in late 1965, and finally metamorphosed as the Red Guard Movement in mid-1966. These three new phases of mass mobilization represent the three additional stages of development toward a goal set by Mao.

In its first form, mass mobilization served both as an educational campaign for the peasants and a rectification campaign against cadres and intellectuals; the second stage intensified the cultural-ideological campaign for a nationwide suppression of ideological dissidence and promotion of the thought of Mao Tse-tung. Finally, the third phase, a high-level purge, was directed against "those within the party who are in authority and are taking the capitalist road."[2] The significance of this great mass mobilization at its final stages was a titanic struggle, whose main force was directed squarely at the party apparatus. To this extent, it was not merely a purge, or power struggle, but also a means to revitalize Party institutions. Its principal importance on the culture-ideology front was its intensive indoctrination and involvement in the study and application of Mao's thought. The goal was to overcome obstacles to political and economic development and provide the will or incentive for modernization, as noted by the late French Sinologist, Etienne Balazs:[3]

> Bringing politics into the daily life of the whole population has radically altered their former habits. Innumerable demonstrations, reunions, marches, committees, meetings, and public trials; theatrical performances, dances, public rejoicings; notices, pamphlets, journals—by every possible means official slogans are constantly drilled into every brain. In this way, what was formerly a sluggish, lethargic, undifferentiated mass of people has been shaken up, enlivened, turned topsy turvy, thus releasing an elemenal force that will have incalculable consequences.

THE SOCIALIST EDUCATION CAMPAIGN

The first phase of the new mass mobilization was the aftermath of the disastrous results of the Three Red Flags policy: the general line for building socialism, the Great Leap Forward, and the People's Communes during 1958–60. The conditions in China worsened as a result of the abrupt withdrawal of Soviet experts (mid-1960), and the natural calamities of the three bad years (1959–61).

These economic disruptions led to a revision of key economic policies in Communist China which were known as "Readjustment, Consolidation, Filling-out and Raising Standards."[4] The methodological guidelines for the new economies were "gradualness, a modicum of intersectoral balance, an appreciation of the overwhelming rural realities of China's society, and a new understanding of quality as an important dimension of economic growth."[5]

This change stressed agricultural production as the foundation of China's economic development, a reversal of the 1953–57 Soviet type, intensive, heavy, industrially oriented planning exemplified by the 1958–60 Great Leap Forward. According to an American economist, this new policy included the following features:[6]

1. The defacto dissolution of the People's Commune as a production and accounting unit.
2. Emphasis on maximizing the area of high and stable yields in respect to staple crops.
3. Mechanization and tool improvement.

4. Stress on the application of chemical fertilizers, natural manure, pesticides and insecticides.
5. Pushing ahead with water and soil conservancy on a local basis.
6. Tightening-up of central control over the countryside.

The socialist education campaign was implemented to insure the success of the new economic program.

The signal for this socialist education campaign came in September 1962 when Mao Tse-tung at the tenth plenum of the Central Committee "called upon the whole party and the entire Chinese people never to forget classes and class struggle;" that is, "the struggle to foster what is proletarian and liquidate what is bourgeois on the cultural front."[7] The main purposes were: (1) to purify ideology and rectify revisionist tendencies, and (2) to reestablish socialist, collective controls over economy, especially in the rural areas.

According to a study made by Richard Baum and Frederick C. Teiwes, the socialist education campaign, in fact, passed through five discernible stages prior to merging with the Great Proletarian Cultural Revolution.[8] The first stage lasted from September 1962 through the summer of 1963, with emphasis on the general investigations of rural conditions in China. In the second stage, from 1963 to 1964, it turned the campaign into a nationwide movement, including the organization of the peasant associations. The third stage, which was marked by severe attacks on basic level cadres and intellectuals for their errors and deviations, lasted from 1964 to January 1965; and the fourth stage followed immediately with a search for new theoretical guidelines for the movement. Finally, the fifth stage of the campaign began in late summer and fall of 1965 with new emphasis upon the rectification of Party officials at county (*hsien*) levels. They were subjected to intensive criticism and self-criticisim, in order to overcome the errors of bureaucratism, conservatism, and commandism.

During the social education campaign, several interesting mass movements were organized.[9] For example, the "Four Withs" were instituted, whereby policy cadres were sent to the countryside and by eating and living with, and working and communicating with the poor and lower-middle peasants, they were able to investigate abuses of socialist morality. Another part of the campaign was called the "Four Clearance" movement which was to correct cadre corruption in respect to financial affairs, work points, accounts, and storage of produce. Still another was called the "Three Fixes and One Substitution," which involved the assignment of rural—as well as industrial and trade—cadres to fixed labor bases to which they had to report at fixed hours and work for a fixed length of time each day. The substitution was the requirement of learning the jobs of regular workers so as to be ready to replace the regular workers whenever necessary. Peasant associations were also reactivated for the express purpose of helping the central organs supervise and report on the local rural cadres. Finally, in the spring of 1964, a movement of "Comparing, Learning, Overtaking, and Helping" (originally applied only in industry) was extended to the agricultural front.

In addition to its economic implications, the socialist education campaign also involved the intensive study of Mao Tse-tung's thought as well as a general uplift of the educational standards of the peasantry. There were, for example, some 19,000 sales stations established for Mao's works during the campaign and more than 12 million copies of Mao's works were published for the peasants during the initial stage of the campaign.

Moreover, many mass educational schools were expanded in the rural areas. Regular schools were to be assured for children and youngsters. However, schools to train young men and women in rural areas on a half-work and half-study basis, and schools for adult education were also organized and expanded. The purpose was to wipe out illiteracy in China.

In addition to schools, the Communists also utilized other media, such as newspapers, operas, dramas, novels, motion pictures, and radio broadcasts to carry out their campaign. It was in the field of radio broadcasting that success was most apparent.

In 1962 there were more than 5,400 radio (wired) broadcasting stations in villages, and more than 6,700,000 loudspeakers.[10] Every village, agricultural cooperative, and even some peasant homes now have radio receiving equipment and are able to listen to radio broadcasts from Peking. Most local radio stations broadcast during three periods: the first period begins early in the morning and ends after about two hours; the second period commences around noon and runs for another hour; the third period begins about 6 P.M. and continues until about 10 P.M. Included are announcements, educational programs, newscasts (both domestic and international), weather reports, and agricultural and entertainment programs. The entertainment programs include a variety of shows ranging from Peking Opera to poetry readings. Strangely enough, it is Peking Opera and other literary writings that have caused the greatest controversy in contemporary Chinese politics.

Rectification Campaigns Against Intellectuals

Whatever the success of this socialist education movement in rural areas, it is clear, in retrospect, that in the intellectual community this movement encountered stiff and stubborn resistance. For example, Mao Tse-tung himself complained in December 1963 that in the various fields of literature and art "very little had been achieved so far in socialist transformation," and termed "absurd" the fact that "many Communists showed enthusiasm in advancing feudal and capitalist art, but no zeal in promoting socialist art."[11]

There was some truth to this charge by Mao. During the period of 1961/62, there was definitely renewed interest in traditional Chinese literature, China's old popular novels, and particularly China's history. In line with this awakened interest in ancient literature, there were large reprints of old, popular works. For example, it was alleged that 7,500 tons of paper were used to reprint ancient Chinese classics in 1962 while only 70 tons were devoted to Mao's works. In fact, in 1961–62 there was a sort of cultural renaissance for Communist China; and many leading intellectuals, both inside and outside of the Party, used this opportunity to criticize Mao Tse-tung and his policies.

In June 1964, Mao charged that literary intellectuals within the powerful All-China Federation of Literary and Art Circles had "failed in the main to carry out the policies of the Party; had in recent years, even slid to the verge of revisionism; and would, if unchecked, be bound at some future date to become groups like the Hungarian Petofi Club."[12] As a result, in 1964 the Party launched a thoroughgoing rectification campaign in literature and art, screening the literary and artistic output of the intellectual cadres, in the preceding few years. Ironically, the man who was selected by Mao to take charge of this task was Peng Chen, the mayor of Peking, who himself was later purged in 1966.

This rectification campaign, which had started in September 1964 and extended to mid-1965, pushed the socialist education movement into a new stage. Many eminent philosophers, historians, novelists, and playwrights were all deeply involved. The first real casualty was Yang Hsien-chen, director of the Higher Party School. He was attacked for his theory of "combining two into one" as opposed to the "Revolutionary dialectic of 'dividing one into two'."[13] Yang's theory of combining two into one, in fact, according to his opponents, "harmonizes contradictions, emasculates struggle, and eliminates development and change."[14] He had also overstressed class peace and class cooperation while preferring the Soviet interpretation to the Maoist version of Marxism-Leninism. Consequently, Yang was removed from his position and dropped out of the CCP's Central Committee.

Another important literary theorist under criticism was Shao Ch'uan-lin, formerly vice-chairman of the Chinese Writers' Union. In *Wen-yi Pao* (*Literary Daily*), published on 20 September 1964, Shao advocated the theory of "deepening realism" and honored "people in the middle," that is, people who vacillate between the old way of life and the new one the Party had imposed on them.[15] Shao maintained that depicting the people in the middle, riddled with inner contradictions, summarizing "the spiritual burdens of individual peasants through centuries," and presenting the "painful stages of peasants in the transition from an individual to a collective economy" was the only realist writing in Communist China, or in his own words, the only way to "deepen realism."[16]

His critics saw his writings as an attempt to criticize the Party's treatment of peasantry during the Great Leap Forward and his theory of deepening realism as an echo of bourgeois critical realism. In fact, his theory and his writings reminded his opponents too much of Russia's Pasternak and *Doctor Zhivago*. Naturally, Shao was purged out of existence.

Another intellectual who came under attack in September 1964, was the well-known professor of Marxist philosophy at Peking University, Feng Ting. He was denounced for his views expounded in his works, *The Communist View of Life (Kung-ch'an chu-i jen sheng-kuan)*, 1956, *The Commonplace Truth (P'ing-fan chen-li)*, 1955, and *The Historical Mission of the Working Class (Kung-jen chieh-chi ti li-shih jen-wu)*, 1953. These works had been reprinted since their first publication and had received a wide circulation of over 1.5 million copies. Feng held the view that social history is the history of the pursuit of happiness by all men, and at the same time he regarded the need for food and shelter as one of the main motivations of human actions.[17] However, his critics charged that his view of life overstressed the forces of instinct and obliterated the influence of social practice. Moreover, he was accused of making the political mistake of calling the class struggle a "waster of human labor and energy," and of advocating "peaceful co-existence" and the "realization of socialism by peaceful means." Finally, Feng Ting was charged with supporting "the modern revisionist absurdity of opposing ideological orthodoxy."[18]

Prominent playwrights were involved in the controversy and such an important man as T'ien Han was included in the dispute. T'ien was secretary of the Union of Chinese Stage Artists. Since the early thirties he had used the stage as a vehicle for commentary on the political and social scene (on behalf of Chinese Communism). One of his controversial works was the drama, *Hsieh Yao-huan*. The play centered around Hsieh Yao-huan, a court lady of the T'ang empress, Wu. By lauding the empress' liberal rules against the exploitation of the peasantry by corrupt, local bureaucrats in the play, T'ien Han was charged with using the historical analogy to criticize the Party treatment of the peasantry during the Great Leap Forward.

However, there is nothing new about using historical analogy to criticize the contemporary scene, providing that it is not at variance with Party directives. Mao Tse-tung on 17 September 1961, for example, after watching the opera *The Monkey King Thrice Fights the Skeleton Spirit*, wrote a reply to a poem written by his companion Kuo Mo-jo. He used the monkey as a symbol of Marxism-Leninism, the skeleton spirit was portrayed as modern revisionism, the character

Hsuan-tsang represented Mr. Khrushchev, and the Pig represented Moscow's satellites.[19] Kuo's poem was as follows:[20]

> Confused are men and slaves: so are right and wrong.
> Kindness is bestowed upon foes and meanness upon friends.
> The Golden Hoop Spell is heard ten thousand times
> As the Skeleton Spirit thrice escapes.
> Hsuan-tsang's flesh should have been cut with a thousand knives.
> But to pull out a hair does no harm to the Monkey King.
> Education in time deserves praise
> For making the Pig more intelligent than men.

Mao replied as follows:

> Since the thunderstorm has broken out over this earth
> A spirit has emerged from a heap of skeletons
> The Monk, though stupid, is capable of correction,
> But the evil spirit will bring disasters.
> The Monkey King raises his mighty staff
> To disperse the spectral dust that fills the world.
> Let us hail him today,
> For the noxious fog is returning once again.

Many important intellectuals were either purged or banished to the countryside. Another old timer, the dean of Chinese culture affairs, Mao Tun (pen name Shen Yen-ping) who was minister of culture until his dismissal in September 1965, could not escape this fate.[21] Mao Tun's downfall was related to his novel, written in 1931, *Lin Chia P'u-tzu* (*Lin's Shop*). It was made into a movie and adapted by Hsia Yen, his vice-minister of culture, who was also dismissed in 1965. This motion picture sympathetically treated the story of a small town shopkeeper who became bankrupt because of the boycott of Japanese goods and the manipulation of the Shanghai businessmen during the Sino-Japanese war years. From the opponents' point of view, since he was a capitalist, the bankruptcy of the small town shopkeeper could not be regarded as tragic.

Other prominent authors purged included Chao Shu-li, one of China's most popular writers, for his story *Facing the Test* (*Tuan-lien tuan-lien*); Ou-yang Shan, chairman of the Kwangtung Writers' Union, for his fiction *In the Soft Seat Sleeping-Car* (*Tsai juan-hsi wo-ch'e li*). It seems, therefore, that the rectification campaign against the intellectuals had divided the Chinese Communist Party. Not all of the members, especially the intellectuals, were committed to the Maoist interpretation of Marxism-Leninism, nor were they readily accepting Maoism as the guiding ideology for China of tomorrow. Consequently, the second phase of mass mobilization as envisioned by Mao (the Great Proletarian Cultural Revolution) became inevitable.

THE GREAT PROLETARIAN CULTURAL REVOLUTION

On 9 January 1963, in Chinese fashion, Mao Tse-tung replied to
a poem written by his closest friend, Kuo Mo-jo and wrote a poem to
the melody of *Man Chiang Hung* in the traditional *tzu* form:[22]

> On this tiny globe
> A few flies dash themselves against the wall,
> Humming without cease,
> Sometimes shrilling,
> Sometimes moaning.
> Ants on the locust tree assume a great nation swagger
> And mayflies lightly plot to topple the giant tree.
> The west wind scatters leaves over Changan,
> And the arrows are flying, twanging.
>
> So many deeds cry out to be done,
> And always urgently;
> The world rolls on,
> Time presses.
> Ten thousand years are too long,
> Seize the day, seize the hour!
>
> The Four Seas are rising, clouds and waters raging,
> The Five Continents are rocking, wind and thunder roaring.
> Away with all pests!
> Our force is irresistible.

The humming, shrilling, and moaning flies who "dash themselves
against the wall" symbolize those who oppose Mao. The "ants" may
represent Communist Party of Soviet Union leaders, and "the may-
flies" could be the government of the United States.

At that time, no one except perhaps a few intimate friends could
have guessed the meaning of this literary work. Then, on 31 November
1966, with the Great Proletarian Cultural Revolution in full swing,
the three major newspapers, the *People's Daily*, *Liberation Army Daily*,
and *Kung-ming Daily* all reprinted the poem on their front pages. The
world now knows that a revolution of great magnitude had occurred
in China under the personal direction of the poet, Mao Tse-tung.

Although the Great Proletarian Cultural Revolution can be
viewed as a logical extension of the rectification campaign against the
intellectuals in 1964, it differs from all the previous movements in that
it did not enjoy the support of the majority of the Central Committee
of the Chinese Communits Party.[23] As the events unfolded, the Cultural Revolution turned against the entire Party apparatus. In fact,
of a total 172 full and alternate members of the powerful Central
Committee, some 106 were either purged or fell into disgrace.[24]

The Beginning of the Cultural Revolution

In the summer of 1966 a volcanic mass movement swept over the mainland of China. Article after article appeared in the Chinese newspapers attacking anti-Party, anti-Socialist elements. Many of China's leaders, one after another, had fallen from power. Peng Chen disappeared from the public scene and the Peking Municipal Party Committee was reorganized on June 4. Mao demoted Liu Shao-chi from the second to the eighth position in the Party, while Lin Piao, backed by the army, became the second in command. In the universities, left-wing students began to form bands which publicly attacked leading university officials. From cities to the countryside, the tremors were felt.

Despite the involvement of plots and counterplots in the initial stage of the mass revolt, one must not assume that a power-struggle was the single cause of it. In fact, a power-struggle was merely the byproduct of the Cultural Revolution and a continuation of the earlier ideological campaigns.

According to James Chieh Hsiung, the use of *cultural* in the Maoist phrase "Cultural Revolution" is significant: It recalls the traditional Chinese belief in the didactic function of all forms of culture, and in cultural regeneration as the key to social or national regeneration.[25] After all, Mao raised the question of cultural revolution as early as 1940. Therefore, in truth, the Cultural Revolution was a spirited attempt to rectify the thinking of the entire nation through an all-out assault on revisionism and capitalism for the final achievement of Mao's goals: a national, scientific and mass culture and a new stage of social development for China.

Thus, in the largest sense, cultural revolution denotes a philosophy of selfless struggle as well as reforms in arts and letters. This can be seen from the decision made by the eleventh plenum of th CCP's Central Committee concerning the Great Proletarian Cultural Revolution on 8 August, 1966.[26]

> The great proletarian cultural revolution now unfolding is a great revolution that touches people to their very souls and constitutes a new stage in the development of the socialist revolution in our country, a stage which is both broader and deeper. . . .
>
> Although the bourgeoisie has been overthrown, it is still trying to use the old ideas, culture, customs and habits of the exploiting classes to corrupt the masses, capture their minds and endeavor to stage a come-back. The proletariat must do the exact opposite: It must meet head-on every challenge of the bourgeoisie in the ideological field and use the new ideas, culture, customs and habits of the proletariat to change the mental outlook of the whole of society. At present, our objective is to struggle against and overthrow those persons in authority who are taking the capitalist road, to criticize and repudiate the reactionary bourgeois academic "authorities" and the ideology of the bourgeoisie and all other

exploiting class and to transform education, literature and art
and all other parts of the superstructure not in correspondence
with the consolidation and development of the socialist system.[27]

In conjunction with this decision, a 16-point program was adopted
at the August meeting, including the following:[28]

1. Put daring above everything else and boldly arouse the masses.
2. Let the masses educate themselves in the movements.
3. Firmly apply the class line of the party.
4. Correctly handle contradictions among the people.
5. Establish cultural revolutionary groups, Committees and Congresses.
6. Initiate educational reform.
7. Mao Tse-tung's thought is the guide to action in the Great Proletarian Cultural Revolution.

Development of the Cultural Revolution

The first phase of the Cultural Revolution which lasted until the
autumn of 1966, might be regarded as the warming-up period in which
forces were mobilized and gradually steered in the desired direction.
The second phase saw the beginning of a clarification of the issues and
the spreading out of the struggle from Peking to the countryside. The
third phase began about the end of January 1967, and lasted until
September 1968. It was a period of chaos and violence from time to
time in one area or another, as illustrated in Table 8 on page 72 detailing the chronology of events from 1967–68.

One of the most dramatic changes during the Cultural Revolution was the change of the decision-making process in the central leadership.

Mao changed the control apparatus of the CCP into a *troika*
system consisting of the Military Affairs Committee of the Central
Committee, the newly established Central Cultural Revolution Group,
and the State Council.[29] Policy making power was taken away from the
CCP's Central Committee and placed in the hands of the Military
Affairs Committee after reorganization of that committee in 1966
(although policy pronouncements are still issued in the name of the
disintegrated Central Committee). The implementation of decisions
made by the Military Affairs Committee was given to the Central Cultural Revolutionary Group and the State Council, bypassing the party's
functional department (see Chart 2).[30]

The Central Military Affairs Committee

Mao Tse-tung has always assumed personal leadership of the
Central Military Affairs Committee, which originally included Lin
Piao, Ho Lung, and Nieh Jung-chen as vice-chairmen, Lo Jui-ch'ing as
secretary-general, and Hsiao Hua as deputy secretary-general. Lin Piao

Table 8

Great Proletarian Cultural Revolution
Monthly Chronology of Events (1967–68)

1967

January	January Revolution erupts in Shanghai
	Red Guards exhorted to seize power throughout China
	China's *first* revolution committee inaugurated in Heilungkiang Province
February	"February Adverse Current" with countermoves by Party power-holders
	Chou En-lai issues orders to protect State Council
March	Army instructed to support agriculture
April	Liu Shao-chi officially denounced as "China's Khrushchev"
	Red Guards exhorted to love and cherish veteran cadres
May	Rectification campaign launched within the army
June	China explodes first hydrogen bomb
July	Wu Han incidents—Chou En-lai intervenes
August	Foreign Ministry temporarily seized by Red Guards
September	Mao Tse-tung tours China issuing latest instructions urging rebel factions to reconcile differences
October	Drive to establish revolutionary committees accelerated
November	Teng Hsiao-ping officially denounced
December	*People's Daily* editorials stress unity

1968

January	Campaign to support the army
February	Army instructed to support the left but not any particular faction
March	Leftists regain initiative—army chief of staff purged (Yang Cheng-wu)
April	Factionalism of the proletariat lauded in *People's Daily*
May	Leftists step up attacks on power holders
June	Violence on upswing throughout China
July	Mao Tse-tung criticizes Red Guards for lack of discipline
August	Chou En-lai announces completion of revolutionary committees throughout China
	Army ordered to restore order

represented the military establishment of the old People's Liberation Army's (PLA) Fourth Field Army group (one of the four most important PLA groups organized during the Civil War period), while Ho Lung represented the First Field Army group.

In February 1967, Mao tightened his control in the committee by dropping Ho Lung and Lo Jui-ching. They were replaced by Chen Yi, a close associate of Chou En-lai and leader of the old Third Field Army group, and Liu Po-cheng and Hsu Hsiang-chien, who represented the PLA's Second Field Army group. Hsiao Hua was temporarily appointed to the position of secretary-general, and Yang Cheng-wu to that of deputy secretary-general. However, in 1968 Hsiao Hua and Yang Cheng-wu both were dropped from the committee and replaced

Reorganization of the

Chinese Communist Party

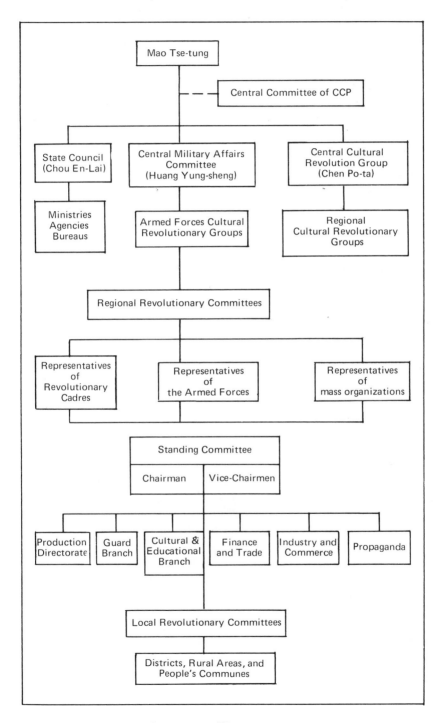

by Huang Yung-sheng, commander of the Canton military region and
acting chief of General Staff; Hsieh Fu-chih, a deputy premier of the
State Council and minister of Public Security; and Su Yu, vice-minister
of National Defense.

Chou En-lai also attends the meetings of the Military Affairs
Committee as an ex-officio member. This, in fact, makes the committee
roughly comparable to the National Security Council of the U.S. government.[31]

The Central Cultural Revolution Group

The Central Cultural Revolution Group was first established as
a 17-member team on 22 November 1966.[32] The first published list of
group members included Chen Po-ta as chairman, Chiang Ching (Mao's
wife) as first deputy chairman, and Wang Jen-chung, Liu Chin-chien,
and Chang Chun-chiao as deputy chairmen. Members consisted of
Chang Ping-hua, Wang Li, Kuan Feng, Chi Pen-yu, Mu Hsin, Yao
Wen-yuan, Hsieh Chang-hou, Liu Wei-chen, Cheng Chi-chiao, and
Yang Chin-lin. Tao Chu and Kang Sheng served as principal advisers.
This group has been drastically revised, and by 1968 there were only
five active members: Chen Po-ta, Chiang Ching, Chang Chun-chiao,
Yao Wen-yuan, and Kang Sheng. Lin Piao's wife, Yeh Chun, also serves
as an adviser to Chiang Ching.

Chen Po-ta, chairman of the group, is a leading Party theoretician
and has been closely associated with Mao since their early days in
Yenan. In addition to serving as Mao's personal political secretary, he
was deputy director of the Propaganda Department of the CCP Central
Committee in 1949 and a vice-president of the Peking Institute of
Marxism-Leninism. He was a member of the entourage when Mao went
to Moscow to negotiate the Sino-Soviet Friendship Treaty (December
1949–February 1950), and in 1955–56 he was Mao's chief spokesman
during the drive to accelerate agricultural collectivization. He was made
an alternate member of the Politburo in 1956. Chen became chief
editor of Hung Chi (Red Flag) with its founding in 1958.[33]

By including Mao's wife, Chiang Ching, in the central Cultural
Revolution group, it was ensured that Mao's personal interests would
be met. Chiang Ching has taken an active part in the educational
campaign within the military establishment under the guidance of
Lin Piao.

Chang Chun-chiao was formerly the powerful secretary of the
CCP's East China Bureau: and Yao Wen-yuan, chief editor of Chieh-
fang Jih-pao, wrote articles in 1965–66 that sounded the trumpet call
of the Great Proletarian Cultural Revolution.[34] Kang Sheng heads
China's secret police.

The State Council

Originally the executive body of the government, the State Council was reorganized into three separate groups during the Cultural Revolution.[35] The first group consisted of 29 important military, industrial, and communication ministries and agencies: National Defense, Public Security, Finance, Allocation of Materials, Commerce, Metallurgical Industry, Chemical Industry, Coal Industry, Petroleum Industry, Railways, Communications, Post and Telecommunications, Agriculture, State Farms and Land Reclamation, Water Conservation, Electric Power, Geology, Building Construction, Textile Industry, eight machine-building ministries, two light industry minstries, and the Physical Culture and Sport Commission. These bodies are under the direct supervision of the Military Affairs Committee.

The Central Cultural Revolution Group has primary responsibility over the State Council's second group, which includes the ministries of Culture, Higher Education and Education, and other agencies such as the New China News Agency, the Broadcasting Administrative Bureau, Foreign Languages Publishing House, and Circulation Administrative Bureau.

Premier Chou En-lai takes personal responsibility for such administrative departments as the Ministry of Foreign Affairs, the State Economic Commission, the Ministry of Internal Affairs, etc., which are included in the third group. In addition, Chou also coordinates the activities of all premiers (Lin Piao, Chen Yi, Ki Fu-chun, Li Hsien-nien, Nieh Jung-chen, and Hsieh Fu-chih). In fact, Chou has replaced Liu Shao-chi as chief-of-state (government) of China.

Changes in Local Organizations

On the local level (province, county, and commune), the changes made by Mao have been slow and at times difficult and bloody. Since the constitution of the Republic was adopted in 1954, China has been divided administratively into 21 provinces, 5 autonomous regions, and 2 municipalities directly under the central government. Below these divisions are more than 2,000 counties and cities, which in turn are subdivided into people's communes (towns and villages). Under the current new program envisioned by Mao, all these local areas are to be taken over first by the preparatory group or military committee, and eventually by the newly organized revolutionary committee.

The difficulties can be seen in the activities of 1967. In the first quarter of the year, the Cultural Revolution group began to move against the regional and local power holders; however, by the third quarter during July and August, there was considerable opposition including army backing of one group against another. The Maoists succeeded in setting up new revolutionary committees in only one quarter of China's provincial level administrative districts at the end of the year.

To cope with this difficult situation, the central troika system initiated a number of strategies. First of all, representatives of various contending factional groups in China's provinces were ordered to Peking to hammer out agreements under the supervision of the central leadership. At times, negotiating sessions lasted a month or more before agreements were reached.

Meanwhile, with the help of youthful Red Guards and the army, local cadres accused of being "anti-Party, anti-Socialist Rightists" were to be arrested or dismissed. Other cadres who had made "serious mistakes but have not become anti-Party, anti-Socialist Rightists" were retained by "giving them a chance to make up for their mistakes."[36]

Finally, on 7 September 1968, Premier Chou En-lai, at a mass rally in Peking, announced that as a result of the "tremendous victory" in the 20-month long struggle "to seize power from the capitalist roaders," China was now "all Red."[37]

THE RED GUARD MOVEMENT

In 1957, Premier Chou En-lai warned his Party: "If we don't change our bureaucratic ways, there will be a youth rebellion a decade hence."[38] His prophetic words were to be recalled a decade later and on 19 August 1966, newspapers in China described an event which had occurred the day before:[39]

> At five o'clock in the morning when the sun had just risen above the eastern horizon and had begun shedding its brilliant rays, Chairman Mao arrived at Tienanmen Square which was covered by a vast sea of people and a forest of red flags. There he met the revolutionary people, who even earlier had converged on the square from all sides....
>
> Tens of thousands of Red Guards, wearing red arm bands and brimming over with high spirit and vigor, caught the eye of all present. The Red Guards are members of the revolutionary mass organizations set up in the Great Proletarian Cultural Revolution by the Capital's college and middle school students. Members pledge that they will remain red vanguards defending Chairman Mao, the Chinese Communist Party and their motherland all their lives. Representatives of the Red Guards filled the rostrum on Tienanmen Gate and the reviewing stands on both sides of the gate....
>
> During the rally, a Red Guard from the Girls' Middle School attached to Peking Normal University mounted the rostrum and put a red arm band of the Red Guards on Chairman Mao. The Chairman cordially shook hands with her. "Red Guards" on and off the rostrum were beside themselves with joy. Some of them jumped a foot in the air and exclaimed with great excitement:

"Chairman Mao is our supreme commander and we are his soldiers." Some said: "Chairman Mao joins our 'Red Guards.' This is the greatest support and inspiration to us. With Chairman Mao's backing, we have nothing to fear."

One thousand and five hundred student representatives mounted the rostrum to attend the rally together with Party and Government leaders. Chairman Mao and Comrades Lin Piao, Chou En-lai and Chiang Ch'ing received them in groups, talked with them and had pictures taken together with them. When Chairman Mao received them, the students excitedly crowded around him and shouted repeatedly "Long Live Chairman Mao."...

The crowd leapt with joy. A great many hands, holding *Quotations from Chairman Mao Tse-tung* covered with red plastic jackets, stretched toward Tienanmen Gate. A million warm hearts flew out to Chairman Mao and a million pairs of eyes sparkling with revolutionary fervor were turned on him....

Thus, the Red Guards whose activities would reverberate in worldwide headlines, had come to the fore.

Young Red Guard Sung Yau-wu puts an armband on Chairman Mao
People's Daily (July 17, 1971) Announcement of President Nixon's Visit

The Red Guard in Action

At the beginning, Red Guards were cladestine organizations of disenchanted young students, frowned on by the Party apparatus which controls the Communist Youth League (CYL), the official organization for young people in China.[40] Although the Party Central Committee had directed the handful of power holding CYL officers to allow greater leadership opportunities for their fellow students, members of the hierarchy continued to enjoy additional advantages in the league. There existed a gap between the proletarian youth and the better-prepared sons and daughters of revolutionary social classes or Party bureaucrats. The proletarian youths took seriously the Communist promises of a glorious future for the working class; but they soon discovered that the system really was not destined for them, but for the better-prepared children of the middle class bureaucrats.

The Maoists could not use the existing machinery, the Communist Youth League, for mobilization of the students, since the league was well protected and controlled by the anti-Maoists' ruling Party hierarchy. Thus, Maoists leaders circumvented the official machinery and called upon the nation's youth to act spontaneously. Careful planning and months of preparation had been necessary before hundreds of thousands of Red Guards would erupt into action all over China.

The master strategy was first to strike down the school officials, since in the past, they had discriminated against those students of worker and peasant origin. During the period immediately before the Great Proletarian Cultural Revolution of mid-1966, the emphasis in education was clearly on expertness.[41] Often, the students of worker and peasant origin simply could not compete with students of middle class backgrounds. The Maoists chose Lu Ping, president of Peking University, as their logical target, because Lu Ping had not only discriminated against students of worker-peasant origin, but he was also an anti-Maoist and close associate of Mayor Peng Chen of Peking and Chairman of the Republic Liu Shao-chi.[42]

At first, the pro-Mao students quietly organized their own groups within Peking University, and began to agitate trouble.[43] For example, students in the Chinese literature faculty of the university refused to use the notes prepared by the instructors and compiled their own notes based on Mao's philosophy. When their plots were uncovered, Lu Ping requested help from the Peking Municipal Committee which had jurisdiction over the university. The municipal Party then sent a work-team to the university to investigate student disturbances.[44] Upon the team's arrival at the campus, they packed Lu Ping off to the city, ostensibly to have him write his self-criticism, but really to shield him from attack by students. Then the work-team told the students that if they wished to reform the university they must first get work-team sanction. Students defied these instructions and hauled Lu Ping away to a struggle meeting in 18 June 1966. A struggle meeting is the Chinese technique for resolving acute contradictions in politics or ideology. The usual practice is for the person involved to appear before a meeting of every concerned worker of the organization and make a detailed statement of his position. This statement is subjected to criticism by anyone who wishes to do so. During the June 18 struggle meeting at Peking University, President Lu Ping was condemned and forced to make a self-criticism.

The work-team counterattacked with the organization of their own struggle meeting using professional work-team students against supporters of the June 18 struggle meeting. They also locked all the gates of the university. One report has it that Mao Tse-tung's wife, Chiang Ching, was refused admittance to the university in the early stage of the struggle.[46]

Meanwhile, many pro-Mao students organizations began to function at various middle schools and universities in Peking and other areas. They used different names; for example, the students in the Middle School of Peking University called themselves the Red Flag Fighting Groups while another group at Tsinghua University Middle School named themselves the Fighting School of the Red Guards. Finally the one they adopted was *Hung wei-ping* or Red Guard, a name taken from a peasant organization which sprang up in the early days of the Chinese Communist revolution in Hunan province in 1928 under Mao.[47] In the initial stage of development, the Red Guards in Peking met with strong opposition, especially from those work-teams representing the Party hierarchy. For example, in one Peking middle school, the Red Guards had increased its membership from 14 (on 2 June 1966) to 300 (early in July), only to shrink to 140 under pressure from the visiting work-team.[48]

In fact, by the end of July, the situation became so critical that Mao Tse-tung had to intervene openly. He sent Chen Po-ta, his personal secretary, Kang Sheng, chief of the secret police, and Chiang Ching, his wife, to the University of Peking on July 22. In three days, they organized pro-Mao forces and gave encouragement to Maoist students and teachers. On August 4, they met again at the university and organized a new Cultural Revolution Committee to take over the administration of the university. As we know, on August 8, Mao induced the Central Committee to adopt the resolution on the Great Proletarian Cultural Revolution. A mass rally was planned in Peking on August 18, and Mao gave instructions to make transportation available for the students. With the eventual success of the August mass rally, the Red Guard Movement mushroomed all over China.

The Expansion of the Red Guards

Within three months of the official debut of the Red Guards at the Peking rally, some 20 million young people had emerged as the Red Guards, and were organized into units corresponding to their educational institutions.

No fixed pattern regarding organizational structures for the Red Guards was given, but membership was limited to the children of the so-called five *pure classes* workers: poor and middle class peasants, soldiers, revolutionary cadres, and martyrs. Students of bourgeois origin were admitted only if they could prove that they had renounced their class background. Each and every Red Guard was required to wear a red insignia identification which bore three Chinese characters, *hung wei-ping*, which were personally written by Mao Tse-tung.

There was no set curriculum, however, all Red Guards were required to read daily the works of Mao, and follow certain routine rituals, such as rising early in the morning and reading wall posters throughout the city, returning to their campus for discussion. Of course, manual work was required, specific tasks were designated, and the singing of revolutionary songs was encouraged. They were all offered free rail transportation and food so that they could travel to Peking and be reviewed personally by Mao. In fact, from August 1966 to mid-November, an estimated ten million Red Guards had come to Peking.

The Red Guards were told by Mao first to revolt against the "four olds" old thought, old culture, old custom, and old habits; to exchange revolutionary experiences; and finally to become revolutionary successors. In order to achieve these goals, they were to emulate and become *Chuang-chiang*, an intricate term originating in popular Chinese literature in the seventeenth century.[49] This term was also used in the seventeenth century by the rebel leader Li Tzu-cheng, who hastened the downfall of the Ming dynasty (1368–1644).[50] Within this historical context, Chuang-chiang suggests "rebellious spirit with a strong touch of bravado, somewhat an outlaw, a desperado." This perhaps explains why Chinese Public Security Minister Hsieh Fu-chieh credited the Red Guards with the following war results:

1. Attack against the enemy: a. Arrests including land owners, rich farmers, counterrevolutionary elements, evil elements, and rightist elements, totalled 16,623 persons. b. Members arrested in the act of counterrevolutionary moves totalled 17,888 cases. c. Political cases other than the above totalled 3,368.
2. Confiscated arms and ammunition: 85 guns, 22 machine guns, 13,700 rifles, 13,800 old model rifles, 1,368,000 bullets, 26,700 shells, 210,000 *chin* of ammunition, 389,000 detonation caps, 230,000 bayonets, 6,000 *chin* of poison, and 13,600 copies of Chiang Kai-shek's portrait and Kuomintang flags.

3. Confiscated properties: 1,198,000 *liang* of gold; 306,00 *liang* of silver; 9,789,000 pieces of silver coins; 3,558,000 *yuan* worth of U.S. dollars; 3,739,000 *yuan* worth of pounds and other curriencies; and 482,000 million *yuan* worth of cash and securities.[51]

According to Western sources, details of some of the incidents in the provinces included:[52]

1. Anhwei: The first secretary of the provincial Communist Party was reported to have been kidnapped on November 11 by Red Guards, who tortured him for several days. Fighting between workers and Red Guards followed on November 16–17 with many people injured.
2. Fukien: Red Guards were reported on September 27 to have stormed and sacked the Communist Party offices in Foochow.
3. Hopeh: In Tientsin the Red Guards were reported to have assaulted over 40 people and beaten two to death on August 26. The first secretary of the city's Communist Party died after being forced by Red Guards to stand under a hot sun for seven hours.
4. Kansu: Fighting between Red Guards and workers took place at the end of August and the beginning of September in Lanchow and Kingtai, where over 140 people were injured.
5. Kiangsu: Red Guards forcibly occupied the Communist party headquarters in Shanghai on September 4. On December 8, seven people were reported to have been killed in a two-day battle between Red Guards and employees of a local newspaper.
6. Kwangsi: Fighting was reported on September 15 to have taken place at Kweilin, where 100,000 people resisted a demand by Red Guards for the deposition of the mayor.
7. Kwangtung: Street fighting broke out in Canton on September 9 when 600 factory workers attacked Red Guards who had imprisoned the director of the factory for three days; many people were injured, and troops had to be called in to restore order.
8. Kweichow: About 30,000 workers led by Communist Party officials were reported to have clashed with Red Guards at Kweiyang at the end of August.
9. Shensi: The secretary of the provincial Communist Party was reported on September 21 to have been paraded through Siao by Red Guards, who denounced him as a "black bandit."
10. Szechwan: After 411 people had been killed and 200 injured in fighting at Chungking on December 4, Red Guards demanded "a period of red terror" in the district.

Obviously, a mass movement on such a scale which attacks the Party hierarchy and society in general is bound to generate opposition. In addition to street fighting, rival groups were organized within the Red Guard movement. For example, not one but three headquarters of Peking's Red Guards were organized on 26 October 1966.[53] They included the Capital University and College Red Guards Headquarters, the General Headquarters of Capital University and College Red Guards, and Capital University and College Red Guards Revolutionary Rebel Command. The three were serving as three separate head-quarters and were acting independently. They each published their own newspapers and issued separate instructions.[54] The third head-quarters eventually gained recognition as the Red Guards' main command with the help of the public security forces and the Liberation Army. Although this organization is supposedly national in character, its control of membership outside of Peking is weak and ineffective.

Factions within the Red Guards continued elsewhere. A Soviet report mentioned some ten separate factions within the Red Guard Movement including:[55]

1. The rebellious group
2. The stubborn group
3. The restoration group
4. The suspicious group
5. The opportunists group
6. The compromisers group
8. The timid group
9. The commercial group
10. The fence-sitting group

In addition there were reports of terrorism and fighting among the various factions of the Red Guards. Finally, to restore order, Premier Chou-En-lai issued new directives and travel restrictions.[56] To temper the young people, emphasis was then placed on "walking in emulation of the Long March." Marchers became a common sight in China; always carrying red flags, with packs on their backs, sometimes with musical instruments, and singing revolutionary songs—and always reading quotations from Chairman Mao Tse-tung.

At last, Mao ordered the People's Liberation Army to formally take control of all the future activities of the Red Guards. This is evident in Mao's March 7 Directive (1967):

> Comrades Lin Piao, En-lai, and the Comrades of the Cultural Revolution Group:
> This document could be distributed to the whole country to be acted upon accordingly. The army should give military and political training in the universities, middle schools and the higher classes of primary schools, stage by stage, group by group. It should help in re-opening school classes, strengthening organization, setting up the leading bodies on the principle of the "three-in-one" combination and carrying out the tasks of "Struggle-criticism-transformation." It should first make experiments at selected points and acquire experience and then popularize it step by step. And the students should be persuaded to implement the teaching of Marx that only by emancipating all mankind can the proletariat achieve its own final emancipation, and in military and political training. . . . Apart from the aged and the sick, these people should be allowed to take part so as to facilitate

their remolding. Provided all this is done conscientiously, it is not difficult to solve the problems.

By September 1967, with the setting up of new revolutionary committees in China's cities and provinces, the activities of the Red Guards began to be submerged into the background of Chinese politics.

The Significance of the Red Guard Movement

Three times in modern history, students have shaped and changed events in Chinese society. The first student movement may be traced to the Hundred Day Reforms by K'ang Yu-wei in 1898, when K'ang together with over 1,200 young candidates for the metropolitan examination, submitted memorials to the emperor demanding reforms of the Manchu government. The Hundred Day Reforms failed, but the movement had opened the door on questioning the validity of the entire Confucian tradition, and had liberated the Chinese mentality from traditionalism.

The second great student movement was the May 4 Movement in 1919 when some 5,000 university students in Peking, concerned about China's status among the nations, unequal treaties, and political unity within China, assembled at Tienanmen Square* and endorsed a manifesto which concluded: "China's territory may be conquered, but it cannot be given away. The Chinese people may be massacred, but they will not surrender. Our country is about to be annihilated. Up, brethren!"[57]

Then in 1966, the Red Guard Movement came to the fore. The main significance of this movement lies in the fact that despite its magnitude, passion, and intensity, the participants accomplished their mission of purging the power holders throughout the entire country without involving the country in a self-destructing civil war. When compared with other mass revolts in Chinese history, such as the Taiping Rebellion of 1850–64 which resulted in a loss of life estimated to have been between 20 and 40 million people, the recent violence and bloodshed seems indeed minimal.

There are, in addition, several unique features of the movement. First, there is the writing of wall posters—or as the Chinese call them, big character posters (ta-tzu-pao)—which are a new means to arouse the interest of the masses. In one sense, they resemble the letters to the editor columns in Western presses, with the exception that they ignore the laws of libel. In another sense, perhaps rather remote, they are like Martin Luther's 95 theses posted on the door of the church at Wittenberg in 1517. The posters are used as a channel for generating the demands of the masses to the policy makers of the state; and at the

*Same square as the Red Guards' August rally.

same time, this media is used as a means of communication to transmit political ideologies or orders to the masses themselves. Mao himself reportedly had one put up on 5 August 1966 entitled, "Bombard the Headquarters."[58]

One interesting factor associated with the big character posters is the political language used in them. Symbols and slogans have been created to propagandize the correct Party line. Often with rhyme and certain syncopated rhythm, these slogans have mass appeal which fix the propaganda message into the mind of the audience, especially when shouted and chanted in unison at Red Guards' rallies. A sample of the often repeated slogans printed on posters and shouted over loudspeakers includes the following:[59]

> *ch'in-mi chan-yu (close comrade-in-arms)*, epithet for a most trusted supporter or follower
>
> *Mao Tse-tung ssu-hsiang wei-ta hung-ch'i* (the great red flag of Mao Tse-tung's thought) avowed guiding light of the cultural Revolution
>
> *niu-kuei she-shen* (bull-ghosts and snake-gods) the anti-Mao elements to be fought and hated
>
> *p'o-chiu li-hsin* (destroy the old and foster the new), a slogan menacing even the Communist established order
>
> *pu-shih tung-feng ya-tao hsi-feng, chiu-shih hsi-feng va-tao tung-feng* (either the east wind prevails over the west wind, or the west wind prevails over the east wind), either the East dominates over the West, or vice versa.

There are many phrases which may seem to be associated with tremendous violence, but these terms are strictly metaphorical and are no more violent than the terms understood in the West's sports contests such as "kill the umpire" or "tromp the Tigers," etc.

Another unique feature in the Red Guard Movement was the intensity, religious fervor, and total involvement in the study of the works of Mao Tse-tung. For example, 86 million sets of *Selected Works of Mao Tse-tung* were published in 1967; 350 million copies of the *Quotations from Chairman Mao Tse-tung* and 48 million copies of the *Selected Readings from the Works of Mao Tse-tung* were also distributed during the same year.[60] Mao's writing, in this sense, has become the bible of Chinese Communism today, and there is no question that the Maoists in China intend to indoctrinate the Chinese youth as successors, and thus perpetuate the revolutionary cause.

Among Mao's works, three essays are particularly treasured by the Red Guards. They are: (1) "In Memory of Norman Bethune" (1939); (2) "Serve the People" (1944); and (3) "The Foolish Old Man Who Removed the Mountains (1945). Norman Bethune was a Canadian physician who was sent as a field surgeon to Yenan by the Canadian Communist Party in 1938, and died in China of blood poisoning on

12 November 1939. Mao praised him for being "without any selfish motive." In Mao's eulogy, he wrote:

> Comrade Bethune's spirit, his utter devotion to others without any thought to self, was shown in his great sense of responsibility in his work and his great warmheartedness towards all comrades and the people. Every Communist must learn from him. We must all learn the spirit of absolute selflessness from him. With this spirit everyone can be very useful to the people. A man's ability may be great or small, but if he has this spirit, he is already noble-minded and pure, a man of moral integrity and above vulgar interests, a man who is of value to the people.[61]

The second essay, "Serve the People" was originally a eulogy delivered at a memorial service for Chang En-teh, a soldier and body-guard of Party officers. Mao praised Chang En-teh and thus gave encouragement to all who work for the cause of Chinese Communism. In this essay, Mao wrote:

> All men must die, but death can vary in its significance. The ancient Chinese writer Szuma Chien said, "Though death befalls all men alike, it may be heavier than Mount Tai." . . Comrade Chang Szu-teh died for the people . . . From now on, when anyone in our ranks who has done some useful work dies, be he soldier or cook, we should have a funeral ceremony and a memorial meeting in his honor. This should become the rule. And it should be introduced among the people as well. When someone dies in a village, let a memorial meeting be held. In this way we express our mourning for the dead and unite all the people.[62]

The final essay, "The Foolish Old Man Who Removed the Mountains," was first embodied in a speech delivered by Mao at the Seventh National Congress of the Chinese Communist Party on 11 June 1945. In his address, Mao recounted an ancient Chinese fable of a stubborn old man who decided he could remove two great peaks obstructing the road. With great determination, every day the old man led his sons in the effort to dig up the mountains. When a "wise old man" saw them and laughed at their seemingly impossible task, the old man replied: "When I die, my sons will carry on; when they die, there will be my grandsons, and then their sons, and grandsons. . . ." Finally God was moved by this and sent down two angels, who carried the mountains away on their backs.

To this fable, Mao added:

> Today, two big mountains lie like a dead weight on the Chinese people. One is imperialism, the other is feudalism. The Chinese Communist Party has long made up its mind to dig them up. We must persevere and work unceasingly, and we, too, will touch God's heart. Our God is none other than the masses of the Chinese

people. If they stand up and dig together with us, why can't these
two mountains be cleared away?[63]

These are some of the examples of the indoctrination in which
the youth of China are currently being immersed: mountainous tasks
that can be surmounted, selflessness, the discipline of criticism, constant
improvement, and close links with the masses to build a modern society.
The Maoists definitely believe that only by stressing group need
over individual need can they hope to realize the twin interrelated
goals of motivating the individual to work hard and increase the
society's gross output.[64] However, in the last analysis, mass poverty will
be a fact of life for many years, regardless of the political system.
Although the resulting internal conflicts need not be carried out with
the degree of extreme violence that characterized the Red Guard movement, Mao's hope—to give the youth of China a taste and sense of the
commitments forged in his great mass mobilization—may well have
succeeded.

Suggested Readings

ASAHI EVENING NEWS. *The "Diary" of the Cultural Revolution.* Tokyo: Asahi
Shimbun Publishing Co., 1967.
ASIAN RESEARCH CENTER. *The Great Cultural Revolution.* Tokyo: Charles E.
Tuttle Co., 1968.
BARNETT, A. DOAK. *China After Mao.* Princeton: Princeton University Press,
1967.
BAUM, RICHARD, with BENNETT, LOUIS B., eds. *China in Ferment.* Englewood
Cliffs, N.J.: Prentice-Hall, 1971.
_____, and TEIWES, FREDERICK C. *Ssu-ch'ing: the Socialist Education Move-
ment of 1962–1966.* Berkeley: University of California Center for Chi-
nese Studies, 1968.
CHUANG H. C. *The Great Proletarian Cultural Revolution: A Terminological
Study.* Berkeley: University of California Center for Chinese Studies,
1967.
FAN, K. H., ed. *The Chinese Cultural Revolution: Selected Documents.* New
York: Grove Press, 1968.
GRANQVIST, HANS. *The Red Guard.* London: Pall Mall Press, 1967.
GRAY, JACK, and GAVENDISH, PATRICK. *Chinese Communism in Crisis: Maoism
and the Cultural Revolution.* London: Pall Mall Press, 1968.
HUNTER, NEALE. *Shanghai Journal, an Eyewitness Account of the Cultural
Revolution.* New York: Praeger, 1969.
LIFTON, ROBERT J. *Revolutionary Immortality: Mao Tse-tung and the Chinese
Cultural Revolution.* New York: Random House Vintage Books, 1968.
MEHNERT, KLAUS. *Peking and the New Left: At Home and Abroad.* Berkeley:
University of California Center of Chinese Studies, 1969.
NEE, VICTOR. *The Cultural Revolution at Peking University.* New York:
Monthly Review Press, 1969.
ROBINSON, THOMAS; BAUM, RICHARD; DORRILL, WILLIAM F.; GURTOVE, MELVIN; and
HARDING, HARRY, JR. *The Cultural Revolution in China.* Berkeley: Uni-
versity of California Press, 1971.
TOWNSEND, JAMES R. *The Revolutionization of Chinese Youth.* Berkeley: Uni-
versity of California Center for Chinese Studies, 1967.

PART TWO

Policy and Process

CHAPTER five

THE EMERGING NEW POLITICS

The emerging new politics in China is very much a part of the modernization process directed toward the establishment of a modern society. There are many roads to modernization. In Great Britain, for example, the process was gradual: social, economic, and political alternatives were not concurrent. In the Soviet Union, by contrast, modernization was much more compressed: industrialization and forced collectivization of agriculture occurred simultaneously. The modernization of Japan did not take place under the auspices of a revolutionary party, but under the benevolent guidance of an aristocratic bureaucracy.

In China, the modernization process cannot be understood from the static modes of thought deriving from Western structural functionalists or Weberian thought. As we have seen in the preceeding chapter, China's modernization follows a pattern of mass mobilization evolving from Mao Tse-tung's thought that "the forces of society control the state and not the reverse."[1] Time and again in Mao's writing, he returns to education, persuasion, and ideological work as a means of achieving his goal of a national scientific and mass culture for the new China.

This strong emphasis upon ideology, as David Apter has noted, can "at crucial moments during the cycle of perception give individuals a sense of identity and solidarity with their fellows—all in a political context."[2]

Chinese ideology has in fact three basic dimensions: (1) the epistemological aspect of ideology; (2) the theoretical aspect of ideology; and (3) the practical aspect of ideology. Because ideologies do not spring from a sudden revelation but have first passed through a latent period, the emerging new politics in China serves as the indispensable link between practical and theoretical considerations of Maoism and China's developing ideology.

THE RISE OF CHOU EN-LAI

One cannot speak of the new politics of China today without referring to the important role that Premier Chou En-lai has played in shaping China's policies. Kai-yu Hsu, in his excellent biography of Chou En-lai, wrote:

> Chou En-lai's stature in the Party has grown not by knocking others down, nor by staying away from controversy, but by taking the orthodox party line and sticking to it until the tide was really turning. Then he plunged into the deadlocked controversy to cast his deciding vote.[3]

Personal Background

Chou En-lai was born in Shaohsing, Chekiang in 1898. Upon graduation from Nankai Middle School in Tientsin in 1912, he went to Japan, enrolled in Waseda University for one year, and then returned to Tientsin and studied at Nankai University. He was imprisoned for six months for taking part in the anti-Japanese students' demonstrations during the May 4 Movement in 1919.[4]

After release from jail, Chou left for France under a work-study program. There he organized the Socialist Youth League in Paris and in 1922, became one of the founders of the European branch of the Chinese Communist Party. He traveled to Belgium and Germany before returning to China to assume the new post of secretary of the Chinese Communist Party in Canton in 1924.

For a short period during the Communist-Nationalist alliance, he was Chiang Kai-shek's chief political officer of the Whampoa Military Academy in 1925. He was twice engaged in leading China's labor movement and helped organize three successive workers' armed uprisings in Shanghai just prior to the arrival of Chiang Kai-shek's Northern Expedition Forces in 1927. After the failure of the Nanchang uprising, he escaped to Hong Kong and then went to Moscow to attend the Party's Sixth National Congress, where he was named director of the Organizational Department of the Party. He returned to China and from then on, Chou became a multi-faceted and indispensable member of the Party's ruling circles.

After World War II, Chou accompanied Mao Tse-tung to Chungking for negotiations with Chiang Kai-shek; he was Mao's personal representative during General George Marshall's mission in China. After the establishment of the People's Republic, he was named premier of the State Council, a position he continues to hold until the present day.

Chou's Role in the Cultural Revolution

Chou En-lai has faithfully followed the strategies and policies of the Cultural Revolution, and as events unfolded he became one of the principal policy makers of the Chinese polity. At the start of the Cultural Revolution, Chou was the first Chinese leader to make public policy pronouncements. For example, on 30 April 1966, at a mass rally to welcome an Albanian delegation, he said: "The Cultural Revolution is a key to the continued development of the socialist revolution in the present stage in China."[5] And again on 17 June 1966, he spoke before the Rumanian Communist Party Central Committee in Bucharest: "The spearhead of the Cultural Revolution is directed chiefly against a small handful of anti-Communist villians who have donned the cloak of communism."[6]

As the Cultural Revolution evolved into various stages, Chou became the spokesman for Chairman Mao at many mass rallies throughout China, as well as Mao's problem solver, trouble shooter, and negotiator. Chou also established a harmonious working relationship with the army leadership during the period of military ascendency. For example, in late July 1967, there was a case of actual military insubordination in the capital of Hupeh province, Wuhan. Two Central Committee members sent by Mao Tse-tung were kidnapped by the Wuhan Military District commander, Ch'en Tsai-tao. Chou personally flew to Wuhan and dramatically negotiated the release of the Central Committee members and presided over the trial of the Wuhan military commander.[7]

Moreover, when the Red Guards emerged with unrestrained impetus during the Cultural Revolution, it was Chou who rebuked them and told them to cease their excesses, although at times his unpopular action made him the target of Red Guards' attacks. Chou En-lai persistently limited the excessive Red Guard activities so that the social and economic fabric of the country was not seriously threatened.

Whenever the goal of assisting revolutionary takeover of factories, enterprises, and ministries may cause damages to the industrial plant and/or intellectual-managerial capital in China, Chou En-lai is always careful to restore the equilibrium once the revolutionary fervor has subsided. In these instances, his technique is to accept short-term damage if it will ensure long-range survival of these resources.

Chou's Political Style

According to a study made by Thomas W. Robinson, Chou En-lai's political style differs considerably from that of Mao Tse-tung or Lin Piao.[8] First of all, Chou wishes to preserve what has been gained although it may not be totally satisfactory. Mao, on the other hand, does not hesitate to overthrow everything if it is not in accord with the correct ideology. In other words, Chou is a gradualist, Mao is not.

Secondly, Chou En-lai is a conformist and often swims with the tide. Mao Tse-tung, it is often said, wants to cause and reverse the tide if necessary. Chou is not always the first to sense a change in the political tide, but at a proper point in time, he will move forcibly to remain with the moving tide.

Thirdly, Chou En-lai relies heavily upon his seemingly endless personal energy and contact, while Mao relies upon his charisma, his very remoteness from the masses. In other words, Chou likes to attend to the details of state affairs while Mao has not had the time nor patience to deal with them. As a result, Chou is a better administrator and negotiator than Mao.

An interesting observation was made by James Reston during his recorded interview with the premier:

> While Premier Chou talked, an elaborate dinner was served.... Though the dinner had run through almost two hours and many courses, Mr. Chou never let the conversation loiter. His mind seemed to jump from one topic to another, and as it was getting on toward midnight, he suddenly began talking about America again....[9]

In fact, Chou En-lai has ofen relied upon his own personality and energy to get himself out of tight spots. He protected and defended many of his key subordinates on countless occasions during the Cultural Revolution, which resulted in the maintenance and continuity of China's civil bureaucracy, the State Council.

If we compare Chou with Lin Piao, we may conclude that Lin is very much like the chairman, while Chou is not. There is a great difference in attitudes toward planning of policy. Lin Piao often plans to the extreme, and he would rather overcome problems by direct action. Lin also likes to simplify problems. Chou En-lai, on the other hand, seems to adopt a posture of muddling through; to make problems complex so that no simple solutions should be used. In addition,

Chou prefers bureaucratic solutions to political problems, while Lin is not comfortable with them.

A leader of the Young China Party, who had become acquainted with Chou over the years and had visited him during the Yenan period, said:

> He is at least very clever, and he has polish. He does not pretend to know much and—this is his virtue—he listens and learns, and he is always asking questions about everything he wishes to know. There is no one else among the Communist leaders who can listen, or when they rarely do, can understand what you are saying. . . . Chou En-lai is the only man the Communist Party has now and, survival or collapse, the Peking regime depends upon him.[10]

THE BEGINNING OF THE NEW POLITICS

The birth of the new politics may be traced to the joint editorial in China's three leading official newspapers on New Year's Day of 1968:[11]

1. To develop creative study and application of Mao Tse-tung's thought.
2. To promote and consolidate the revolutionary great alliance and revolutionary "three-in-one" combination (revolutionary masses—revolutionary cadres—armymen).
3. To rectify the Party organization and strengthen the Party building.
4. To implement still further Chairman Mao's great call to "support the army and cherish the people"; and greatly strengthen the unity between armymen and civilians.
5. To grasp revolution and promote production and other work, and promote preparations against war.

Another policy statement, published in Shanghai's influential *Wen Hui Pao* with a call to fight against "ten crimes of factionalism," gave further evidence to the emergence of the new political style on the Chinese scene.[12] Some of these crimes included: failure of various rebel organizations to obey the highest directives; lack of regard for the best interest of the Party, the country, and the broad masses; undue concern for status, titles, and rank of individual cadres; and distortion of excerpts from Chairman Mao's quotations.

Then, during the same month in 1968, the powerful *Liberation Army Daily* published another important statement demanding the army "support the left, but not any particular faction."[13] This slogan, in fact, was a call issued by authority of the military "to restore order no matter whose toes have to be trod on in the process"[14] Finally, when the newly established revolutionary committees were largely identified with conservative and moderate regional or provincial army commanders, we knew a new politics had emerged.[15]

Table 9

Chronology of the Establishment of the Revolutionary Committees (1967–1968)

DATE OF ESTABLISHMENT	ADMINISTRATIVE AREA	COMMITTEE CHAIRMAN
January 31, 1967	Heilungkiang	Pan Fu-sheng (party secretary)
February 5, 1967	Shanghai	Chang Chun-chiao (party secretary)
February 13, 1967	Kweichow	Li Tsai-han (military commissar)
February 23, 1967	Shantung	Wang Hsiao-yu (military commissar)
March 18, 1967	Shansi	Liu Ke-ping (military commissar)
April 24, 1967	Peking	Hsieh Fu-chih (security officer)
August 12, 1967	Tsinghai	Liu Hsien-chuan (military commander)
November 1, 1967	Inner Mongolia	Teng Hai-ching (military commander)
December 6, 1967	Tientsin	Hsieh Hsueh-kung (party secretary)
January 5, 1968	Kiangsi	Cheng Shih-ching (military commander)
January 24, 1968	Kansu	Hsien Heng-han (military commissar)
January 27, 1968	Honan	Liu Chien-hsun (military commissar)
February 3, 1968	Hopei	Li Hsueh-feng (party secretary)
February 5, 1968	Hupei	Tseng Ssu-yu (military commander)
February 21, 1968	Kwantung	Huang Yung-sheng (military commander)
March 6, 1968	Kirin	Wang Wei-hsiang (military commissar)
March 23, 1968	Kiangsu	Hsu Shih-yu (military commander)
March 24, 1968	Chekiang	Nan Ping (military commissar)
April 8, 1968	Hunan	Li Yuan (military commander)
April 10, 1968	Ninghsia Hui	Kang Chien-ming (military commissar)
April 18, 1968	Anhwei	Li Teh-sheng (military commander)
May 1, 1968	Shensi	Li Jui-shan (party secretary)
May 10, 1968	Liaoning	Chen Hsi-lien (military commander)
May 31, 1968	Szechuan	Chang Kuo-hua (military commander)
August 13, 1968	Yunnan	Tan Fu-jen (military commander)
August 19, 1968	Fukien	Han Hsien-chu (military commander)
August 26, 1968	Kwangsi	Wei Kuo-ching (party secretary)
September 5, 1968	Tibet	Tseng Yung-ya (military commander)
September 5, 1968	Sinkiang	Lung Shu-chin (military commander)

New Political Style

The development of a new political style has the approval of Chairman Mao Tse-tung, especially because of the leftist-instigated disorders in the Chinese countryside and the proven resilience of the army. The central authority in Peking now decided to revise priorities and emphasize preservation of the army as a viable institution, restoration of a minimum of public order, and revival of China's stagnated economic production.

By 1969, political stability was achieved to the extent that delegates to the post–Cultural Revolution Ninth Party Congress were already chosen by a new method: "full democratic consultation" by Party organizations at various levels and "extensively seeking the opinion" of the broad masses.[16]

On 1 April 1969, the official Ninth Party Congress convened in Peking and was attended by 1,512 delegates. It may be of interest to note that in the half-century history of the Chinese Communist Party, only nine congresses had been held: six of these were convened during the first seven years; and only three congresses have been held since the Sixth Congress in 1928.

The Ninth Party Congress held the second longest Party caucus in history (24 days), elected 279 full and alternate members to the new Central Committee, adopted a new constitution, and accepted a policy report by Lin Piao to be used as the official guide to the 1970s. (*See* Appendix 9.)

There are many significant facts with respect to the Ninth Party Congress. For one thing, out of the total 177 full members on the new Central Committee, 122 (or 72 percent) were elected for the first time to this policy making committee. There are only 53 members from the previous Eighth Committee (53 of whom were reelected to full member status and five as alternate members).

There are also an unprecedented number of common workers and peasants on the Central Committee (about 73 of them); and most of them are from China's provinces. All the new leaders of provincial revolutionary committees are elected to the ruling organ, which increases the representation of regional groups (only a limited number of provincial Party secretaries were represented in the old Eighth Central Committee). In addition, total army representation on the Central Committee has risen from 27 percent in 1956 to 41 percent in 1969.[17]

While occasionally there are still references in the Chinese press to such terms as anarchism, factionalism, and similar political labels, the old bitterness represented by factional quarrels seemingly has disappeared. Practical and constructive programs have been introduced and promoted. For instance, some 80,000 soldiers were mobilized into some 7,000 medical teams in an effort to boost the effects of "barefoot doctors" (medical auxiliaries).

Meanwhile, the first of a series of new drafts of a revised constitution for the People's Republic was approved by the second plenary session of the Ninth Central Committee held from August 23 to 6 September 1970. The first draft constitution was quickly under review and discussion by various study groups throughout the country. (*See* Appendix 2.)

In 1970, evidence was also provided that the militant foreign policy and practices of the Cultural Revolution period had ceased.[18] Beginning with the New Year's Day editorial, official statements began to emphasize China's willingness to improve diplomatic relations with all countries. Accordingly, Chinese ambassadors had returned to nearly three-quarters of their overseas posts in one-year's time; and China began to repair relations with long-standing enemies such as Yugoslavia, Burma, the U.S.S.R. and even the U.S.

The overall picture of the closing months of 1970 was one of "general administrative stability, clear policy directives from the top and firm military control at local levels."[19]

By 1971, it became clear that with her moves toward reconciliation in international relations, her continuing drive against Cultural Revolution extremes and a call to "learn from past mistakes to avoid future ones," China had now entered a period of new politics.[20] (See Appendix 4.)

THE MEANING OF THE NEW POLITICS

New politics means a synthesis of idealism and realism; a more practical application of Mao Tse-tung's theory of combining knowledge and experience. The purpose is to generate a new revolutionary pragmatism in order to develop a national, scientific and mass culture in Chinese society.[21]

This is illustrated in Lin Piao's important policy statement at the Ninth Party Congress in April 1969, in which he enumerated a number of important operational guides, among them:

1. Learn from past mistakes to avoid future ones.
2. Cure the sickness to save the patients.
3. Grasp revolution, promote production.
4. Go all out, aiming high and achieving greater, faster, better, and more economical results in building socialism.
5. Be prepared in case of war, be prepared in case of natural disasters; and do everything for the people.
6. Take agriculture as the foundation and industry as the leading factor.
7. Strive for peaceful coexistence with countries having different social systems. (See Appendix 3.)

Specifically, in the area of governmental work, new politics means the assurance of organizational responsiveness, including simplification of the structures of governmental organs, reduction of administrative personnel, and broader participation in the decision making process at all levels. There is also an attempt to strike a balance between organizational responsiveness and direction. For example, in the proposed new constitution of the Republic, Party and state merge in a nucleus of leadership which may prevent further conflicts and contradictions of policies as witnessed in the earlier periods of Communist rule in China.

In fact, new politics under the new proposed constitution follows closely the strategy and ideology which Mao used over many years in his drive for reforms in China—mass line and mass mobilization. This perhaps explains why Article 2 of the new constitution includes "Mao Tse-tung's thought as the guiding compass of all the work of the people of the whole nation"; and Article 13 states that "blooming and contending on a big scale, big character posters, and great debates are forms of socialist revolution created by the masses of people. . . ." (*See* Appendix 2.) Of course, mass line and mass mobilization will continue without excessive violence of the "past mistakes."

The military is a component of China's modernizing agents, as provided for in Article 15 of the constitution which stipulates, "the Chinese People's Liberation Army is perpetually and simultaneously a combat unit, a work unit and a production unit. . . ." This new role of the army is very much in line with modern social science theories that contend that armies in the developing nations can not only provide a sense of citizenship and appreciation of political action, but also provide a relatively high degree of psychological security. In addition, the acculturation process in the army tends to be more thorough and of a broader scope than the urbanization process as it has taken place in most Asian, African, and Latin American societies which have generally tended to produce a highly restless insecure population.

In domestic intergroup relations, Article 4 of the proposed constitution would be of greatest importance to the future stability and growth of the Chinese minorities. This article states,

> the People's Republic of China is a unitary multi-national nation-state, with national autonomous regions as inseparable parts of the People's Republic of China. All the nationalities are equal, and are opposed to great nationalism as well as parochial nationalism.

This could resolve many of the difficult minority frictions that now exist in the three zones of tension—the inner Asian sector, the Far Eastern sector (from the uplands of Trans-Baykalia to the Pacific coast southwest of Vladivostok), and the Mongolia sector—homelands of many ethnic groups. It is also conceivable that Taiwan could eventually return as an autonomous region with its own social, political, and economic institutions.

In the area of the political process, new politics means three-in-one combinations or three way alliances of armymen, cadres, and masses, with each group assuming a different role while uniting under the "guiding compass of the thought of Mao Tse-tung."[22] The army, for example, is responsible for maintaining order and political socialization; the cadres are responsible for administrative expertise; and the masses must maintain revolutionary enthusiasm and support. At the same time, the three-in-one combination is also expected to provide a system of checks and balances while broadening participation in decision making.

Economically, China's new politics will be a sensible program of gradual, proportional, economic development. This economic policy is based upon the developmental ideology of Maoism which stresses agricultural priority, small industry, geographical balance, and egalitarian distribution. In other words, one short-term goal is to give agriculture a vastly increased share of resources with a view to generating a significant increase in farm production in order to achieve self-reliance in China's economic development. The final goal involves the redistribution of investment capital and social services to reduce the disparities between urban and rural areas, and between coastal and interior provinces.

The new politics in the educational field are more open, egalitarian, integrative, and experimental programs that will achieve the goal of a new mass culture. Peasants and workers who have been traditionally neglected in the educational politics will now play important policy roles in China's arts, literature, and scientific expression. There will be continued programs to reeducate China's bourgeois intellectuals and to revise university and secondary school curricula and admission standards in order to meet the demands and expectations of millions of Chinese youth in the decades ahead.

According to a report published in the *Far Eastern Economic Review*, new educational policies such as those linking the universities with factories have already produced important dividends in raising technical standards.[23] China's elite intellectuals are required to assist in raising popular levels of technical competence by leavening the work force with qualified personnel. For the future, opening the doors of advanced education institutions to ordinary workers and peasants should result in the breaking down of cultural barriers to industrial modernization. Meanwhile, universities will benefit by the selection of new undergraduates with solid production experience.

Finally, in the field of foreign relations, new politics in China denotes conciliation and pragmatism with more emphasis on people-to-people relationships and cultural diplomacy. However, China will continue to support revolutionary movements to strike down the last vestiges of imperialism and colonialism in industrially advanced countries.

In the last analysis, it must be remembered that new politics denotes a new style of action for the Chinese, based upon moderation, not arrogance. The policy paper commemorating the fiftieth anniversary of the founding of the Chinese Communist Party states:

... efforts must be made to guard against arrogance. This is of particular importance to a Party which has won great victories, a Party which is in power and leads the people of all nationalities of the country in carrying out the socialist revolution and construction.

And then quoting Chairman Mao, the paper declares, "modesty helps one to go forward, whereas conceit makes one lag behind. This is a truth we must always bear in mind." (*See* Appendix 4.)

Suggested Readings

Bulletin of the Atomic Scientists. "China After the Cultural Revolution." February 1969.

COMMITTEE OF CONCERNED ASIAN SCHOLARS. *China: Inside the People's Republic.* New York: Bantam Books, 1972.

DORRIL, W. F. *Power, Policy and Ideology in the Making of China's Cultural Revolution.* Santa Monica: Rand Corp., 1968.

Far Eastern Economic Review 1972 Yearbook. Hong Kong: December 1971.

GEOFFROY-DECHAUME, FRANCOIS. *China Looks at the World: A New Way to see China as a Civilization in Change.* New York: Pantheon Books, 1967.

GRAY, JACK. *Modern China's Search for a Political Form.* New York: Oxford University Press, 1969.

HSIUNG, JAMES CHIEH. *Ideology and Practice: The Evolution of Chinese Communism.* New York: Praeger Publishers, 1970.

HSU, KAI-YU. *Chou En-lai.* Garden City: Doubleday and Co., 1968.

KAROL, K. S. *China, the Other Communism.* 2d ed. New York: Hill and Wang, 1968.

KITAGAWA, JOSEPH M., ed. *Understanding Modern China.* Chicago: Quadrangle Books, 1969.

KUO, PING-CHIA. *China.* New York: Oxford University Press, 1971.

New York Times, Report From Red China. New York: Quadrangle Books, 1971.

ROBINSON, THOMAS W. *Chou En-lai's Role in China's Cultural Revolution.* Santa Monica: Rand Corp., 1970.

TRAGER, FRANK N. and HENDERSON, WILLIAM, eds. *Communist China, 1949–1969.* New York: New York University Press, 1970.

TSOU, TANG, ed. *China in Crisis.* Vol. 1, book 2. Chicago: University of Chicago Press, 1968.

CHAPTER SIX

THE NEW POLITICAL PROCESS

Let us begin our study of the new political process in
China by clarifying some important factors which are
fundamental concepts in the developmental process.
First of all, the Chinese Communists speak not of a
nation-state, but of a people (*jenmin*). In the view of
Franz Schurmann, such a concept denies the idea of
an essential national unity. Schurmann maintains that
the *people* concept excludes the exploiting class which
still exists in China. In other words, China, theoretically speaking, is not yet fully an integral national
unity.[1] This concept varies considerably from that of
the Soviet Union, which speaks of the *sovietskii narod*;
the essential unity of all elements that make up the
Soviet Union.

Second, the Chinese place tremendous impor-
tance on Mao Tse-tung's theory of contradiction which
acknowledges the existence of contradictions in the
Chinese society in spite of the Communist revolution.
This theory differs again with the accepted ideology of
Soviet communism. Stalin denied the existence of hu-

man contradiction in Soviet society, while Mao's theory stresses the antagonistic contradictions within China and nonantagonistic contradictions within the Chinese people. Thus for the Chinese, the state exists as an essentially oppressive instrument, although it is used in the interests of the dictatorship of the proletariat.

Third, Chinese ideology calls for politicizing almost all spheres of social life, which means putting Mao Tse-tung's thought first and foremost. This politicizing process originated in guerilla days in the 1930s and is now being used as a short-term expedient to reconstruct new patterns of social relationships. Putting Mao Tse-tung's thought first does not mean blind obedience; in fact, his constant stress on activism or positive political participation seems to represent an attempt to move away from the passive and dependent quality of traditionally dealing with authority. Mao himself has said that greater organizational strength could come from a policy of self-reliance, or "regeneration through one's own efforts" (tzu-li-keng-sheng).[2]

Fourth, the Chinese place tremendous faith in the infinite ability of man. One of the major aspects of Chinese political thought relates to the centrality of man. Thus, the three articles written by Mao Tse-tung in the Yenan days—"In Memory of Norman Bethune," "Serve the People," and "the Foolish Old Man who Removed the Mountains"— which stress the importance of personal sacrifice and human efforts, have been designated as required readings in China today.

Finally, the Chinese concept of *the people* implies a continuing revolution in society, as demonstrated in recent Chinese history. This concept not only differs from Soviet theory and practice, it in fact implies a negation of the importance of institutional organization and structure in the Chinese political process. Perhaps this explains why, during the Cultural Revolution, the chairman of the Party violated many, if not all, of its most important norms and prescribed procedures, and ignored its regular structural arrangements. Thus, he insured that personal legitimacy may be used to override structural legitimacy.

Such are the theories and practices of the Chinese. While, on one hand, they will strengthen the position of the charismatic leader and his thought, they will at times delay the process of routinization and make institutionalization in the political sphere more difficult. Conseqently, political stability achieved at any particular time will be more precarious.[3]

DECISION MAKING

The Chinese Communist Party directed the revolution and war which led to the seizure of state power in 1949. After that, the Party created state bureaucratic structures; and the Party and the state merged. However, in China prior to the Cultural Revolution, as in all communist countries in the world, there remained a distinction between Party and state.

Chinese communist literature makes it clear that the state (*kuo-chia*) refers to the formal organization which is bureaucracy, army, and law, which dominates the society. The Party on the other hand, is the expression of the interest of the people which, as Franz Schurmann defined, "actualizes the control of society over the state."[4] However the Party does not command, for formal command must flow from some instrument of the state. In other words, the Party may initiate policy, but technically it cannot issue orders; orders must come from an organ of the state.

The Communist Party

The formal decision making process of the Chinese Communist Party is essentially like that of the Soviet Communist Party. It is hierarchially organized, and pictorially the whole decision making process resembled a pyramid. The Party is structured along geographic lines, with the essential chain of command running from the Party committee to committees at the commune, county, provincial, and national levels. At the top of the leadership apparatus stands the Party Central Committee, elected by the National Party Congress. It is empowered to elect the membership of the central Party organs, including the Politiburo, the Standing Committee of the Politiburo, and the Secretariat, as well as the chairman, vice-chairman, and secretary-general of the Central Committee.

The secretary-general supervises administrative work through a general office and distributes the work on a functional basis to departments such as Communication Work, Finance and Trade Work, International Liaison, Organization, Propaganda, Rural Work, Social Affairs, and United Front Work. He also coordinates the activities of other committees such as Military Affairs—central state organs which are under the direct control of the Central Committee.

Below the central level, Party organization parallels the administrative divisions of the country. The next-to-lowest level of Party organization is parallel to the subprovincial units of administration: counties and cities. The basic-level Party units constitute the lowest echelon of Party organization, although not its smallest units. The biggest basic-level units of Party organization are the communes. Here again, as in the central organization, the Party committee technically is distinct from the communes' administrative committees.[5]

However, after the Cultural Revolution, local and provincial state and Party leadership merged, i.e., leadership positions now are held by the same Party members. They therefore function in a dual capacity: as Party leaders and administrative cadres.

The People's Government

The decision making process of the People's government in China is not like that of the Soviet Union. However, because of extreme secrecy about the operations of the Chinese government, it is often difficult to say how structure relates to function. In fact, what a governmental agency actually does may not be what it is formally empowered to do.

The governmental structure, according to the 1954 constitution, maintains that the National People's Congress is "the highest organ of the state authority" (Article 21), and the State Council is the "executive organ of the highest state authority" (Article 47). Similarly, " People's Congresses and People's Councils are established in provinces, municipalities, counties, etc." (Article 54).[6] A good illustration can be found in the chart on page 104.

There are in fact several important characteristics identified with the decision making process in the People's government.[8] First, the Chinese governmental designs combine structural conservatism with functional flexibility; second, as an organization, the Communist Party plays a far more important role in government than in the Soviet Union; third, the regional government has a unique importance in China's decision making process.

The general functional principles on the allocation of authority to governmental agencies are those of "vertical rule and dual rule."[9] Vertical rule means that an agency has full policy and operational control over all units of organization within its jurisdiction. Commands flow directly down; information comes directly up. Examples of vertical rule are the ministries and other branch-type agencies such as the People's Bank.

Dual rule means multiple rather than single channels of command and information. A lower level agency receives commands from two or more higher agencies. At times, an agency can be partly under the jurisdiction of another organ on the same level. In short, dual rule may be seen as a combination of vertical and horizontal control, which means, one channel of command and information going up, and another going sideways. An example would be the State Economic Commission or the State Planning Commission. Here dual rule is exercised both at central and regional levels, although both commissions named above are primarily responsible to regional governments.

The Judicial System

The Chinese have made use of two different models to formulate a judicial system. The first model is based upon the establishment of a formal, detailed, and usually written set of rules, plus formal organizational structures: people's courts and the procuratorate.

The people's courts have also adopted the so-called three-level

Chart 3:

Supreme State Organs

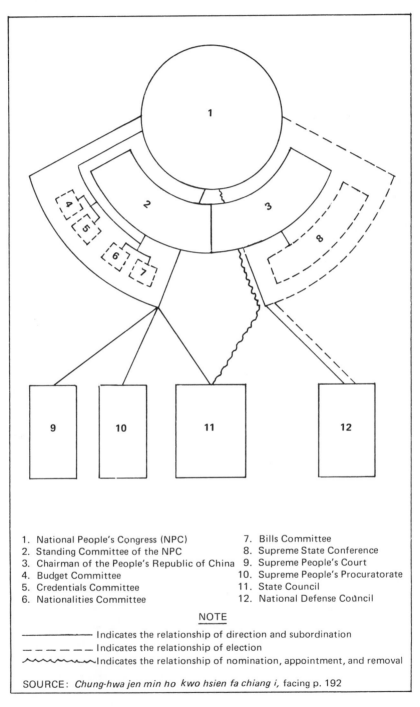

1. National People's Congress (NPC)
2. Standing Committee of the NPC
3. Chairman of the People's Republic of China
4. Budget Committee
5. Credentials Committee
6. Nationalities Committee
7. Bills Committee
8. Supreme State Conference
9. Supreme People's Court
10. Supreme People's Procuratorate
11. State Council
12. National Defense Council

NOTE

———————— Indicates the relationship of direction and subordination
— — — — — — Indicates the relationship of election
〰〰〰〰〰〰Indicates the relationship of nomination, appointment, and removal

SOURCE: *Chung-hwa jen min ho kwo hsien fa chiang i,* facing p. 192

and two-trial system; as a result, a single appeal ordinarily may be allowed from the judgment of a lower-level court. The district people's courts are the basic courts of first trial, and the provincial people's courts are the basic courts of the second trial. Generally, the provincial people's court trial is the final one, but in more important cases the provincial people's courts may conduct the first trial, with the appeal to the supreme people's court for a second trial. The procuratorate system parallels that of the courts, and is empowered to supervise decisions and prosecute criminals. The charts on pages 106 and 109 illustrate the judicial system.[10]

The second model of the Chinese judicial system is a reflection of a combination of traditional and foreign influences. Under this second model, proper modes of behavior are not taught through written rules, but rather through a lengthy and continuing educational process. At the beginning, the second model was intended to complement the first, well-organized system.

However, after 1957, a change of attitude toward law and legal work occurred in China; and many writers began to argue against having legal codes—or even a formal set of laws. As a result, the Party played a much more active role in adjudicating cases within the framework of the second model. As in purely criminal cases, the task was taken over by the public security forces, since the public security system originates from its national headquarters under the direct influence of the Ministry of National Defense.

New Decision Making Process

Prior to the Cultural Revolution, the existence of two parallel political systems (Party and state) had contributed to the excessiveness of competing power groups and compartments. Mao Tse-tung's own frustration with the system was probably compounded by the constitutional provision that as Party chairman he shared power with state chairman, Liu Shao-chi.

The undesirable effects may be seen from the policy paper adopted at the Ninth Party Congress: "A duplicate administrative structure divorced from the masses . . . are destructive to the socialist economic base, advantageous to capitalism, and disadvantageous to socialism." Quoting Chairman Mao, Lin Piao suggested that a formula was being sought that would enable the newly organized revolutionary committees to "exercise unified leadership, eliminate duplication in the administrative structure, follow the policy of better troops and simpler administration. (*See* Appendix 3.)

Several new methods evolved from the Party congress: more flexibility of the central leadership with the merger of Party and state into a unified political system; less rigidity in provincial and local organizational structures; a new decision making process which must

Chart 4:

People's Courts

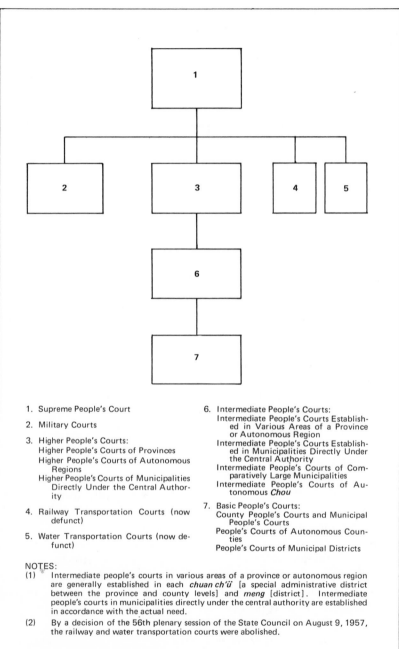

1. Supreme People's Court

2. Military Courts

3. Higher People's Courts:
   Higher People's Courts of Provinces
   Higher People's Courts of Autonomous
   Regions
   Higher People's Courts of Municipalities
   Directly Under the Central Author-
   ity

4. Railway Transportation Courts (now
   defunct)

5. Water Transportation Courts (now defunct)

6. Intermediate People's Courts:
   Intermediate People's Courts Established in Various Areas of a Province
   or Autonomous Region
   Intermediate People's Courts Established in Municipalities Directly Under
   the Central Authority
   Intermediate People's Courts of Comparatively Large Municipalities
   Intermediate People's Courts of Autonomous *Chou*

7. Basic People's Courts:
   County People's Courts and Municipal
   People's Courts
   People's Courts of Autonomous Coun-
   ties
   People's Courts of Municipal Districts

NOTES:
(1) Intermediate people's courts in various areas of a province or autonomous region
     are generally established in each *chuan ch'ü* [a special administrative district
     between the province and county levels] and *meng* [district]. Intermediate
     people's courts in municipalities directly under the central authority are established
     in accordance with the actual need.

(2) By a decision of the 56th plenary session of the State Council on August 9, 1957,
     the railway and water transportation courts were abolished.

SOURCE: *Chung-hwa jen min ho kwo hsien fa chiang i,* facing p. 252

Chart 5:

People's Procuratorates

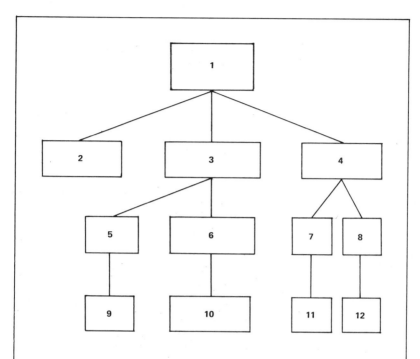

1. Supreme People's Procurate
2. Military People's Procuratorates
3. People's Procuratorates of Provinces, Autonomous Regions, and Municipalities Directly Under the Central Authority
4. Railway and Water Transportation Procuratorates (now defunct)
5. People's Procuratorates of Municipalities
6. Branches of People's Procuratorates of Provinces, Autonomous Regions, and Municipalities Under the Central Authority

People's Procuratorates of Autonomous *Chou*

7. Railway Transportation Procuratorates (now defunct)
8. Water Transportation Procuratorates (now defunct)
9. People's Procuratorates of Municipal Districts
10. People's Procuratorates of Counties, of Autonomous Counties, for Municipal Districts
11. Branches of the Railway Transportation Procuratorates (now defunct)
12. Branches of the Water Transportation Procuratorates (now defunct)

NOTES:
(1) Branches of people's procuratorates of provinces and autonomous regions are generally established in each *chuan ch'ü* [a special administrative district between the province and county levels] and *meng* [district]. The number of the branches of people's procuratorates of municipalities directly under the central authority is determined by the actual need.

(2) Autonomous regions and autonomous *chou* also have people's procuratorates of municipalities.

(3) In the provinces, autonomous regions, and autonomous *chou* where there are people's procuratorates of municipalities, no people's procuratorates for municipal districts are established if there are no municipal districts.

(4) Railway and water transportation procuratorates were abolished "to be in tune with the abolition of the railway and water transportation courts" in accordance with a decision of the 56th plenary session of the State Council on August 9, 1957.

SOURCE: *Chung-hwa jen min ho kwo hsien fa chiang i,* facing p. 258

involve "repeated consultations" from "below and from above"; and finally, implementation of the three-in-one combination of armymen, cadres, and masses in preventing any one particular faction from acquiring an excessive share of political power in the new political system.[11]

In 1970–71, for example, among cadres, there was a tremendous amount of traffic from one area of China to another. They attended consultation sessions which required a complex and protracted process of negotiation and bargaining between various groups within a given level and between different levels of the new power structure. This seems to confirm that the new decision making procss is now being fully applied.[12]

In the final analysis, the extension of the three-in-one combination, the decentralization of power to intermediate and local levels, and the encouragement of local initiative and mass participation in the new governmental policy and programs, at least in its present form, constitute an implicit recognition of group interest and group conflict as an integral part of China's new political system and process.[13]

THE MILITARY POLITICS

The military's role in civil administration, an outgrowth of the Cultural Revolution, is now legitimized. As the only nationwide organization capable of restoring order and imposing administrative control, the army has tended to dominate the new revolutionary structure of power, especially at provincial and local levels. However, the Chinese military politics is a complex one, because of its unique history, background, and role in Chinese political life.

The Chinese People's Liberation Army dates back to the Nanchang uprising on 1 August 1927, when dissident communist leadership revolted against Chiang Kai-shek's government in Nanking. Although the rebellion failed, its leaders and most of its combat units survived to form the nucleus of the forces that finally established the People's Liberation Army. In fact, August 1 is now officially memorialized as Army Day in the People's Republic.

Evolving Army Systems

Most of the key positions within the military establishment in China are allocated and dominated by members of the original five field armies. Thus, in today's military politics of China, a PLA officer might accept the fall or purge of his Party's oldest leaders if the small officer elite with whom he has spent most of his career retains its political existence as an informal vehicle for his own political-military survival. In order to understand this unique military system, one must take a brief look at the evolution of the five field armies from the days of the Nanchang uprising.[14]

When the early revolts failed, the Communist forces spent the next few years moving into several provinces, adopting guerilla tactics, organizing Chinese Soviet Republics, and developing a military system which included:[15]

1. The Red First Front Army under Chu Teh and Mao Tse-tung organized the central (Kiangsi) Soviet. This army had two important groups: the Red First Army Corps under Lin Piao and the Red Third Army Corp under P'eng Teh-huai.
2. The Red Second Front Army under Ho Lung organized the Hsiang-O-Hsi Soviet.
3. The Red Fourth Front Army under Chang Kuo-t'ao and Hsu Hsiang-chien organized the O-Yu-Wan Soviet.
4. The Red Northern Kiangsu Army under Kao Kang and Liu Chi-ta.

After Chiang Kai-shek's extermination campaign against them, and Mao Tse-tung's subsequent Long March of more than 6,000 miles, the Communists went to north Shensi, a barren and remote highland where they renewed their strength and rebuilt the army into four new groups:

1. The Red First Front Army became the 115th Division of the Eighth Route Army under Lin Piao.
2. The Red Second Front Army became the 120th Division of the Eighth Route Army under Ho Lung.
3. The Red Fourth Front Army, after purging Chang Kuo-t'ao, reorganized as the 129th Division of the Eighth Route Army under Liu Po-cheng and Hsu Hsiang-chien.
4. The Red Northern Kiangsu Army was dissolved and units were absorbed by a new Fourth Army Corp under Chen Yi.

In spite of these reorganizations, the Red Army did not participate in any positional warfare other than guerilla raids during World War II. After the Soviet troops occupied Manchuria at the end of the war, for the first time, the U.S.S.R. supplied Chinese Communists with vast stocks of captured Japanese weapons. With more and better arms, and assurance of popular peasant support in rural areas, Mao Tse-tung then called for total mobilization and formation of a new revolutionary army, to be known as the People's Liberation Army which could seize power from the Kuomintang.

This People's Liberation Army was organized into five important groups:[16]

1. Those operating in the interior of China, under the command of P'eng Teh-huai, were called the Northwest Liberation Army. They were formerly the 120th Division of the Eighth Route Army.
2. Those in central China, under Liu Po-cheng, became the Central Plains Liberation Army. They were formerly the 129th Division of the Eighth Route Army.

3. Those in Shantung, under Chen Yi, were organized into the East China Liberation Army. They were the former Fourth Corps.
4. The units in Manchuria, under Lin Piao, were designated as the Northeast Liberation Army. They were formerly part of the 115th Division.
5. The forces in the area north of Peking, under Nieh Jung-chen, became the North China Reserve Liberation Army. They were also part of the former 115th Division of the Eighth Route Army.

As the civil war continued, these armies came to be known respectively as the First, Second, Third, Fourth and Fifth Field Armies of the People's Liberation Army. When the People's Republic was proclaimed in Peking, each of the five armies was responsible for controlling one of the five military districts in China. Later in 1955, these five districts were further divided into 13 military districts:[17]

1. First Field Army: Northwest China Region: Sinkiang, Lanchou, and Chengtu military districts.
2. Second Field Army: Central China Military Region: Wuhan, Tibet, and Kunming military districts.
3. Third Field Army: East China Military Region: Nanking and Foochou military districts.
4. Fourth Field Army: Manchuria Military Region: Shenyang and Canton military districts.
5. Fifth Field Army: North China Military Region: Tsinan, Inner Mongolia, and Peking military districts.

Military Structure and Manpower

During the earlier years of the Republic, Chinese military units were organized and standardized on the Soviet model. Territorial command was divided into administrative regions through which the Party Central Committee exercised its political authority under unified area command responsible to the Military Affairs Committee. But much of the reorganization and modernization program was delayed because of the Korean War.

Not until the adoption of the new constitution in 1954, was the army changed from a Party organ to an agency of the government. The Ministry of National Defense was formed under the control of the State Council. The ministry was divided into various general staff departments which served as army headquarters and general staff for the entire unified establishment.

After the establishment of the 13 military districts for ground operation, nine air regions were established for air defense and three naval districts were to control fleet operations in the Yellow, East China, and South China seas. The following chart indicates the organization of the People's Liberation Army:

Chart 6: Organization of the

People's Liberation Army

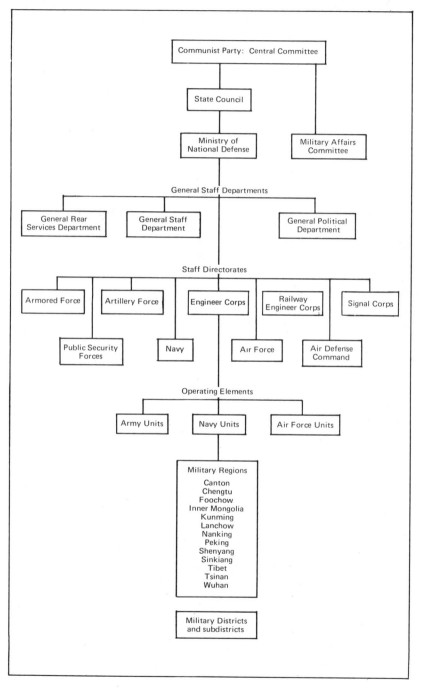

Military manpower is drawn selectively from every segment of society under a national annual conscription program. All males 18 years of age, plus a smaller number of females are subject to draft, provided they pass a rigorous political, educational, and physical examination. Preference is given to poor, lower-middle peasant and fishermen families from the rural areas, and to worker-laborer families in the cities.

For the army, 35 percent of the draftees must be middle school graduates, but for 65 percent of the draftees an elementary school education is sufficient. For the navy, the precentage is higher (40 percent to 60 percent), and it is much higher for the air force (65 percent and 35 percent respectively).

There are no commissioned officers in the PLA as the system of ranks and grades was abolished in 1965. The function of leadership remains, however, and is discharged by men who are simply referred to by job titles. Since leadership positions are maintained, there are three channels through which the status of leader may be achieved.

First, young men who show leadership ability and an unusually high degree of political orientation are recommended for leadership positions by special committees within the company. The nominee is then trained at one of several service academies for three years; and upon completion of training, he is assigned to a combat unit as a common soldier for six months before assuming a command post.

Second, leaders are chosen directly from graduates of universities and colleges if they have participated in the reserve officer training program. Again, they must serve for six months in the ranks before being given leadership status. Finally, leaders are selected or promoted directly from the ranks after unusual achievement by the individual soldier or leader.

The typical Chinese soldier is a fine physical specimen (Chinese standards). Years of hard, unrelieved labor have made him strong and durable. He is used to hardship and is capable of withstanding extremes of cold, damp, or dryness. He undergoes sustained periods of physical exertion and can make forced marches over incredible distances in a single day. His physical fitness is generally greater than that in most Western trained armies as exemplified by the decisive victories over the Indian Army in the 1959 and 1962 border wars.

The army has a total personnel strength of something under 2.5 million men. Military practice seems to follow task force, rather than rigid, formal principles of organization. The ground forces, according to U.S. estimates, are "adequately equipped with a range of infantry weapons . . . all produced in China."[19] In addition, the militia, a vast organization of armed civilians between 18 and 50 years of age, forms the basic reserve for the regular armed forces. The number of units has never been disclosed, but is estimated at 20 million.

The air force is the third largest in the world with a personnel strength of about 150,000 men. The complement of planes totals 3,000 with a rather limited number of TU–16 Badger jet medium-range bombers (1,600 miles). No reliable data on the organization and mission of the air force is available to the public. Its territorial organization consists of nine air defense regions operating at least 20 military airbases, which are generally well-equipped with ground control devices.

The navy is the smallest and least capable unit of all the Chinese armed forces. It has a strength of less than 150,000 men (including naval air force and marines) with no effective capability to support an amphibious operation; they have very few Soviet-type G-class, diesel-power, missile-launching submarines.

As far as China's nuclear development is concerned, U.S. Secretary of Defense Melvin Laird noted that from 16 October 1964 to the end of September 1969, the Chinese had detonated ten nuclear devices. Laird further stated on 20 February 1970, that China had been working on an MRBM system for a number of years and had actually delivered a nuclear device by missile in the October 1966 test. With the launching of an earth satellite on 24 April 1970, China demonstrated "a capability of delivering a payload at ICBM range."[20]

The Pacesetter

As early as 1938, Mao Tse-tung told his people: "Every Communist must grasp the truth, political power grows out of the barrel of a gun."[21] By 1945, he further explained:

> This army is powerful because all its members have a conscious discipline; they have come together and they fight not for the private interests of a few individuals or a narrow clique, but for the interests of the broad masses and of the whole nation. The sole purpose of this army is to stand firm with the Chinese people and to serve them whole-heartedly.[22]

Although the PLA has always played an important role in Chinese revolution, it did not become involved in the internal political struggle until after the Ministry of National Defense was reorganized by Lin Piao in 1959. Thereafter, there was the so-called "three-eight" working-style campaign in 1960. The three-eight working style is derived from Mao's three famous phrases (firm, correct, political orientation; a plain, hard-working style; and flexibility in strategy and tactics), and eight additional Chinese characters, which in English mean "unity, alertness, earnestness and liveliness."

In the spring of 1961, it burgeoned into a nationwide campaign to build what was known as "Four Good Company." All units in the company level were urged to become good in four aspects of their work and rated accordingly:[23] good in political and ideological work; good in three-eight working style; good in military training; and good in management of army livelihood.

The last one is most interesting, because in the past ten years, the PLA men have had to devote considerable time (varied from company to company) to raising some part of their own food supply. This took place in several provinces after the expansion of the production and construction corps.

During the end of the Cultural Revolution, Mao Tse-tung demanded that teachers as well as students learn from the army cadres. According to Mao, the reason for this was that,

> they can learn from the liberation Army, they can learn politics, military affairs, the "four first," the "three-eight" working style and "the three main rules" of discipline and the "eight points for attention," and strengthen their sense of organization and discipline.[24]

The four firsts are simply first place to man, first place to political work, first place to ideological work, and first place to living (creative) ideas. The three main rules of discipline are old rules of obeying orders during the Yenan revolutionary days; and the eight points for attention are (1) speak politely, (2) pay fairly for what you buy, (3) return everything you borrow, (4) pay for anything you damage, (5) do not hit or swear at people, (6) do not damage crops, (7) do not rape or take advantage of women, and (8) do not ill-treat captives; again rules of the army during the early revolutionary days.[25]

It seems that the Maoists in China believe that the armed forces are more than just a fighting machine. In fact as well as in theory, they are a special school of pace setters where soldier-workers study politics and culture, practice military science, and still have time to grow crops, run factories, construct public works, and establish close contact with the people. To this long list of difficult tasks, is now added the additional responsibility of running the government, both in national affairs and provincial and local revolutionary committees.

Military in Politics

On the national level, the Ninth Party Congress convened in April 1969, and 123 military men were elected to the 279 full and alternate members of the powerful Central Committee. (*See* Appendix 9.)

Of the 29 Party committees established for provincial politics, 94 or 60 percent of a total of 158 new regional leaders are military men; and of the 29 revolutionary committees, 20 are chaired by men from the army. Moreover, among the 189 special administrative districts below the provinces, 160 are headed by military cadres; and out of 2,359 counties, 2,000 have again been captured by the military.

In addition, important administrators on the national level have been selected from the ranks of the military. There are four heads (ministers) of ministries in the State Council: Sha Feng, Agriculture and Forestry; Pai Hsiang-kuo, Foreign Trade; Yang Chieh, Communication; and Li Shui-ching, First Machinery Minister. Li Yoa-wen, another armyman, also serves as vice-minister of Foreign Affairs.[26] Other important policy makers within the central government in Peking include:[27]

> Foreign Affairs: Li Yao-wen and Ma Wen-po
> Interior: Shih Yi-chih
> Nationality Affairs Commission: Wan Hai-feng
> Metallurgical Industry: Chen Shao-kun and Chu Hu-ming
> Second Machinery Industry: Yuang Hsieh-kai
> Third Machinery Industry: Chou Hung-po
> Fourth Machinery Industry: Pen Lin
> Fifth Machinery Industry: Chang Ming-yuan
> Sixth Machinery Industry: Huang Chung-hsueh
> Seventh Machinery Industry: Tsao Kuang-lin
> Water Conservancy and Hydroelectric Power: Chang Wen-pei
> Finance: Tuan Cheng-cheng
> Food: Fan Sheng-huan
> Commerce: Fan Tzu-yu
> Bureau of Supply: Liu Jen
> Bureau of Geology: Wan Lo-tien
> Bureau of Labor: Yen Chun
> Construction Engineering: Chang Kuo-chuang
> Construction Materials Industry: Li Ta-tung and Chen Jen-hung
> Health: Hsin Cheng-ching

Furthermore, some 16 important industrial and transportation works are now chaired by military men:

> Wuhan Iron Works: Kang Hsing-ho
> Tayuan Iron Works: Yuan Tao
> Capital Iron Works: Kuo Ying-chun
> Penghsi Iron Works: Li Tzu-cheng
> Fushin Mining Company: Chang Chien-kuei
> Fushun Drilling and Dredging Equipment Manufacturing
>   Company: Kao Shih-ping
> Changchun First Automobile Plant: Yu Hai-ying
> Shanghai Kiangnan Shipyard: Chang Chen-chun
> Dairen Red Flag Shipyard: Chang Chih-tung
> Nanchang Harbor Administration: Pan Chin-yang
> Nanking Harbor Administration: Yao Piao
> Peking Railway Administration: Hsiao Feng
> Canton Railway Administration: Liu Chan-yung
> Peking Knitwear Factory: Sun Yi
> Tsinan Third State Cotton Textile Mill: Hsu Nan

While the military has become a permanent feature of Chinese politics, it is not, however, the controlling element of Chinese society, and its impact is still to be measured.

THE ROLE OF CADRES

According to A. Doak Barnett, the term cadre (*kan-pu*) has a variety of meanings.[28] In its restricted use, cadre is someone who holds a formal leadership position in the bureaucratic hierarchies in China. In this sense, the term implies authority. For example, a Party secretary is a party cadre. However, over the years, it has been increasingly applied to a larger number of people in China, both Party and nonparty members. Some have authority and others are in low-level functionary posts. A file clerk in China's travel service agency may still be called a cadre.

In spite of a great many different types of cadres in China, one important distinction is made between the state cadres (*kuo-chia kan-pu*) and local cadres (*ti-fang kan-pu*). The former describes persons in the bureaucratic hierarchies of Party and government who receive their salaries from the state; the latter are those at the commune levels and below who receive their incomes from local institutions.

Generally, a state cadre is an administrative cadre in government or Party office who is paid on the basis of a standard ranking system which includes 24 salary classifications in urban areas and 26 in rural areas. This does not apply either to military cadres or commercial cadres who have their own separate ranking system.

Importance of Cadres

The important role played by cadres in Chinese polity is first measured by size. In 1949, there were 720,000 cadres in China; and by September 1952 they had increased to 2,750,000, exclusive of cadres in military, mass, or local organizations. By 1958, the number of state cadres had increased to 7,920,000, about 1.2 percent of China's total population, or roughly one cadre for every 80 people. This is a favorable picture when compared with the ratio of one cadre for 700 people with which the regime began in 1949.

Another aspect of importance is measured by the role they play. In agriculture, for example, more than a million new cadres were used to implement the land reform programs in the early fifties. By 1963, there were 20 million cadres at the brigade and production team levels alone. To these, of course, should be added the cadres of various state agencies operating in the countryside, and cadres and activists of social or political organizations, including visiting work-teams engaged in specific political tasks.

In order to measure the significant role of the cadres, it is necessary to study the training process. For example, of the 2,750,000 state cadres in mid-1952, 66,000 had graduated from regular universities; 100,000 had been trained at people's revolutionary universities; and over 1,100,000 had been trained in on-job, rotating training courses.

In a study made by Ezra A. Vogel, many schools and rotating training centers were organized by the Party and government organs at all levels, from the central authority in Peking to the regional, provincial, municipal, and county levels.[29] In some special areas of finance, public security, and the military, schools gave special courses in technical subject matter. In addition, these cadre training centers also served as screening centers for meaningful judgment and evaluation of the trainees.

Finally, the importance of the cadres can be seen from their personal backgrounds. Most of the earlier cadres were drawn largely from the following five groups:[30]

1. Long March cadres: those who had joined the Communist movement by 1934 either as members of the Party, or the Red Army, and took part in the epic Long March with Chairman Mao.
2. War of Resistance cadres: those who joined the Communist movement following the completion of the Long March but before the victory over Japan.
3. Liberation cadres: those who did not take part in the Sino-Japanese war but joined the cause before the Civil War ended.
4. Uprising personnel (chi-i jen-yuan): those who defected to the Communist side during the Civil War.
5. Retained personnel: those who had served under the Kuomintang but were allowed to remain and serve because of their individual specialization and ability which were urgently needed.

New Role of the Cadres

The cadres are the primary link between the government and the governed in China, whether they be state, local, or military. However, there are two opposing philosophies with respect to the cadres' proper role within the leadership of the Chinese Communist Party.

One school of thought, supported by the former chief-of-state, Liu Shao-chi, and deposed Party secretary-general, Teng Hsiao-ping, stressed professionalism for the cadres, with emphasis on technical competence and efficiency. They were supported by the great majority of Chinese intellectuals and Party cadres at central and provincial levels.

Another philosophy was upheld by Chairman Mao, who placed emphasis upon ideological awareness and motivation rather than professional ability. This difference of attitudes and philosophies resulted in heated controversies of the "Red versus the Expert" which raged throughout the Chinese countryside.

In this connection, the 1964 decision to set up special political departments of the Central Committee was significant because it served as the first step to bolster the political power of Chairman Mao. These new departments represented the application of a system of political control already initiated in the PLA by Lin Piao in the 1960s. Under the instructions of political departments, professional cadres are required to take part in productive labor in the factories as well as in the countryside.

The true test of the applicability of the Maoist school of thought came during the Hsia Fang movement in 1957, when cadres were required to participate downward in manual labor throughout the countryside.[31] Liu Shao-chi, Teng Hsiao-Ping, and a host of high state cadres vigorously opposed this new directive. They expressed the fear of progressive alienation of professional cadres, especially at a time when there was a serious shortage of competent specialists in every field in Chinese society. As we have noted, these opposition leaders were purged from their authority in the Party; and the Hsia-Fang movement became a regular feature of the cadres' activities.

The Maoists consider separation of professional cadres from manual labor as detrimental to Mao Tse-tung's thought, and a hindrance to China's economic and political development.[32] The Maoists further argue that a separation of these two groups fosters a set of elite values that are antithetical to production and capital accumulation. It also wastes human resources and burdens the state with unnecessary administrative expense; it gives rise to a bureaucratic style of work which is divorced from the immediate problems of production; and it lowers the morale of producers.[33]

In the final analysis, what the Maoists hope to achieve are new *kinds* of cadres—but not a new class. It is hoped that by engaging in productive labor in the countryside, they will be able to learn the nature of the soil, to draw on the accumulated wisdom of the peasants, and to develop more productive methods of cultivation. Hopefully, the new kinds of cadres—specialists in industry and science—will make timely discoveries and help to solve immediate problems while laboring as ordinary workers in production. Finally, these new cadres in the front lines of administration and participating in the three-in-one combination in the decision making process, will give impetus to the activism of a traditionally rather timid peasantry and may bring about a transformation of Chinese society into what Mao called "democratic, scientific and mass culture."[34]

Suggested Readings

Area Handbook for Communist China. (Washington, D.C.) DA PAM No. 550–60, 1967.

BARNETT, A. DOAK. *Cadres Bureaucracy and Political Power in Communist China*. New York: Columbia University Press, 1967.

————, ed. *Chinese Politics in Action*. Seattle: University of Washington Press, 1969.

COHEN, JEROME ALAN, ed. *Contemporary Chinese Law.* Cambridge, Mass.: Harvard University Press, 1971.

GITTINGS, JOHN. *The Role of the Chinese Army.* New York: Oxford University Press, 1967.

GRIFFITH, SAMUEL B., II. *The Chinese People's Liberation Army.* New York: McGraw-Hill, 1967.

HARDING, HARRY. *Maoist Theories of Policy-making and Organization: Lessons form the Cultural Revolution.* Santa Monica: Rand Corp., 1969.

LEWIS, JOHN WILSON, ed. *Party Leadership and Revolutionary Power in China.* New York: Cambridge University Press, 1970.

LINBECK, JOHN M. H., ed. *China: Management of a Revolutionary Society.* Seattle: University of Washington Press, 1971.

PRYBYLA, JAN S. *The Political Economy of Communist China.* Scranton: International Textbook, 1970.

SCHURMANN, FRANZ *Ideology and Organization in Communist China,* new ed., enl. Berkeley: University of California Press, 1968.

SOLOMON, RICHARD H. *Mao's Revolution and the Chinese Political Culture.* Berkeley: University of California, 1971.

TOWNSEND, JAMES R. *Political Participation in Communist China.* Berkeley: University of California Press, 1968.

VOGEL, EZRA F. *Canton Under Communism: Programs and Politics in a Provincial Capital, 1949–1968.* Cambridge, Mass.: Harvard University Press, 1969.

CHAPTER SEVEN

THE NEW ECONOMIC PROCESS

For the Chinese, the process of economic modernization is especially intense, reflecting far greater ambitions for rapid change than many other developing
nations. Modernization in China began, in fact, after
the mid-nineteenth century. Initially, the state played
an important role in the construction of modern factories and the transportation system. Private modern
industries, mostly under foreign sponsorship, emerged
with the success of the Kuomintang revolution in 1911.
By 1936, foreign capital constituted 73.8 percent of
China's total industrial capital.[1]

   The Sino-Japanese War (1937–45) destroyed whatever hopes existed for China's economic development.
To support its ever-increasing war expenditures, the
Kuomintang government increasingly resorted to issu-
ing bank notes. From June 1937 to June 1939, for
example, the volume of note issues increased from $1.4
billion (Chinese national currency) to $2.6 billion—
representing 97 percent expansion. The wholesale price
index in China's wartime capital, Chungking, rose from

101 in June 1937 to 216, two years later. The national economy became chaotic.

The end of the Sino-Japanese War in 1945 failed to normalize China's national economy however, despite massive U.S. economic assistance. From 1945 to 1947, the wholesale price index rose twelvefold, and from 1947 to 1949, it increased another 45 times. The economic situation worsened when the Kuomintang government introduced its August 1948 currency reform which originally was intended to stop inflation. The public was ordered to convert all foreign currencies, and silver and gold savings in private possession into the Chinese *gold-yuan* bank-note issued by the government. Not only was the currency reform a failure, but instead the wholesale price index increased an unprecedented 5,482.9 times (based upon the 1937 index).[2] This hyperinflation of the postwar years shattered the confidence of the Chinese people and paved the way for the final victory of the Chinese Communists.[3]

ECONOMIC POLICIES AND PLANNING

Following Mao Tse-tung's theory of revolution by stages, the Chinese at first moved rather cautiously in the field of economic policy. Between 1949 and 1952, the principal goal was simply to rehabilitate the economy and restore some semblance of order to an economy badly battered by inflation. Although it had succeeded in eliminating the landlord class, the government in Peking was carefully proclaiming its adherence to a coexistence policy for private sectors in the urban areas, as outlined in the Common Program, adopted by the Chinese People's Political Consultative Conference in September 1949.

Meanwhile a comprehensive plan of balances specifying interindustry and intersectoral relationships was established. According to a study made by Yuan-li Wu, the plan was supported by a set of sectoral and partial plans with the following objectives:[4]

1. A plan for industrial production including one for heavy industry and one for light industry.
2. A plan for agriculture including both the volume of consumption in the agricultural sector itself and the amount marketable in the nonagricultural sectors.
3. A transport plan whose objectives were to safeguard the adequate flow and distribution of industrial and farm products.
4. A plan for capital construction or investment in fixed assets.
5. A labor plan whose goal was to increase labor productivity.
6. A technological plan to insure that all sectors of the national economy have the latest scientific and technological information at their command.
7. A cost plan to specify the standard costs for each individual segment of the economy; to fix the targets of cost reduction; and

to provide guidance to the correct relationship between increase in labor productivity and increase in wages.

8. A plan for the allocation and supply of materials.

9. A plan for the flow of commodities to insure that the industrial and farm products demanded by the urban and rural workers will be available to them in planned quantities.

10. A plan for the social and cultural welfare of the people under the guidance of Maoism.

There were additional plans to deal with exports and imports; financial plans to deal with the national budget and the accumulation and allocation of capital funds and short-term credit; and a regional plan concerning regional specialization and the administration of enterprises under local control.[5]

To implement these national economic plans, several governmental agencies including information-gathering agencies, various planning organs, and executive departments were reorganized under a new constitution adopted in 1954. The complete organization of the economic administration of China can be seen from the chart on the following page.[6]

Economic Policies

The new constitution set forth a blueprint for transforming the economy by "gradually replacing capitalist ownership with ownership of the whole people."[7] Pressure toward nationalization was brought to bear on the private sector through state control of economic activities; cooperatives were established; and capital of enterprises that were said to be hostile to the state was confiscated.

Mass pressure movements also were undertaken to induce private firms to become joint state-private enterprises. By 1956 all industry, finance, domestic trade, transportation, and communications had been absorbed by the state; and almost all farms became cooperatives.

By 1958, a more radical approach to economic development was introduced, such as the three Red Flags—the general line for building socialism, the great leap forward, and the people's communes—which became a part of the total mass mobilization.[8] The goal of this new policy was to break away from dependence on the Soviet model and develop China's own economic style.[9]

Although the move was led by Chairman Mao himself, it met considerable resistance from the leading authorities within the Party and economic planning groups. By August 1959, Mao's policies were under severe attack at the important Lushan Plenum.[10] Meanwhile, Mao's great leap forward movement was compounded with three bad harvest years and the withdrawal of Soviet technicians and aid in 1960. By the end of 1960, China clearly was facing a major economic crisis and Mao Tse-tung was temporarily forced to step aside when Liu Shao-chi began a rightist policy towards people's communes, industry,

Chart 7: Central Economic Administration

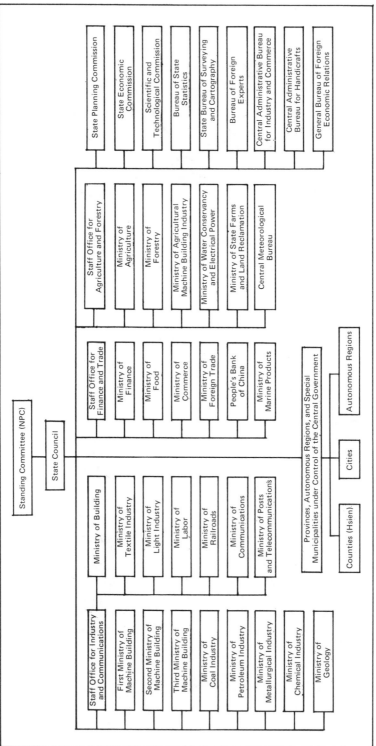

Standing Committee (NPC)

State Council

Staff Office for Industry and Communications
- Ministry of Building
- First Ministry of Machine Building
- Ministry of Textile Industry
- Second Ministry of Machine Building
- Ministry of Light Industry
- Third Ministry of Machine Building
- Ministry of Labor
- Ministry of Coal Industry
- Ministry of Railroads
- Ministry of Petroleum Industry
- Ministry of Communications
- Ministry of Metallurgical Industry
- Ministry of Posts and Telecommunications
- Ministry of Chemical Industry
- Ministry of Geology

Staff Office for Finance and Trade
- Ministry of Finance
- Ministry of Food
- Ministry of Commerce
- Ministry of Foreign Trade
- People's Bank of China
- Ministry of Marine Products

Staff Office for Agriculture and Forestry
- Ministry of Agriculture
- Ministry of Forestry
- Ministry of Agricultural Machine Building Industry
- Ministry of Water Conservancy and Electrical Power
- Ministry of State Farms and Land Reclamation
- Central Meteorological Bureau

- State Planning Commission
- State Economic Commission
- Scientific and Technological Commission
- Bureau of State Statistics
- State Bureau of Surveying and Cartography
- Bureau of Foreign Experts
- Central Administrative Bureau for Industry and Commerce
- Central Administrative Bureau for Handicrafts
- General Bureau of Foreign Economic Relations

Provinces, Autonomous Regions, and Special Municipalities under Control of the Central Government
- Counties (Hsien)
- Cities
- Autonomous Regions

NOTE: Since 1969, it has been replaced by the Central Committee of the Communist Party.

123

and commerce. Although during the Cultural Revolution many charges were made against Liu Shao-chi, including policy differences (with Mao) during the earlier years of economic redevelopment in China, the serious differences in fact had not developed until after the failures of the great leap forward in 1958.[11]

Before the great leap forward, the Chinese economy went through two distinct phases—the initial regime of the Common Program and the subsequent first Five-Year Plan (1953–57) which was based upon a pre-Liberman Soviet model: central planning, bureaucratic control, emphasis on modern technology, and expanding state sector. However, this kind of program, in the eyes of the Maoists, manifests "a lack of faith in the wisdom of the masses and gives preference to direct both the government and economy by administrative decree rather than through spontaneous grassroots initiative. It also places sole reliance on material incentive and oblivion to the need for continuing revolution."[12]

The Maoists' viewpoint envisages modernization by mass movement, which in the economic process can be transformed into a wave-like motion—a series of great forward leaps succeeded by periods of consolidation and adjustment. The consolidation periods are not supposed to be phases of absolute decline, as was the case with the Chinese economy in 1961/62 under the direction of Liu Shao-chi.

The Maoists suffered certain temporary economic setbacks during the Cultural Revolution when many of the authorities in power were purged, including specialists in the industrial sector. In the long run, however, we may discover that even in their failures, they did much to prepare the Chinese people for further economic development. This is because the "thought of Mao Tse-tung has functioned to transform the perceptions of the Chinese and to infuse them with a spirit of commitment sufficient to break the barriers of inertia and stagnation identified with tradition."[13]

As the curtain rose on China's fourth Five-Year Plan on National Day 1970, Premier Chou En-lai said that "the successful fulfillment of China's national economic plan for 1970 would lay the foundation for the Fourth Five-Year Plan"; and that agriculture had been identified as the key development of the plan with rural industrialization to provide the inputs for agricultural expansion.[14] The intent is for a wide range of rural reforms to generate a significant increase in farm production, and spur overall economic development.

AGRICULTURAL REFORMS

Agricultural policy was probably the greatest single factor responsible for the Communist Party's rise to power in China. With 85 percent of her population living in the rural areas, China depends upon agriculture to directly provide the livelihood for at least four-fifths of her people. Agriculture products also provide the major portion of China's foreign exchange and the bulk of raw material for light industry. The well-being of the people and the strength and stability of the government depend upon the success or failure of agricultural policies.

The primary agrarian society of pre-Communist China was confronted with three critical problems—the growing agrarian population, the scarcity of agricultural capital, and inadequate food production. The Chinese Communist's policy goal therefore involves land reform, including reclamation of land and increase in the cultivated acreage; water conservation and increase in irrigation; and intensification of existing agriculture techniques.

After a preparatory stage which gave priorities to the reduction of land rent and interest, and the redistribution of land, the Party Central Committee issued its first call for the lowest form of collectivism—the establishment of mutual-aid teams—on 15 December 1951.[15] The simple mutual-aid teams involved a seasonal or temporary arrangement for limited sharing of manpower, draft animals, and agricultural tools, and provided for some improvements in agricultural techniques.

However, the mutual-aid teams failed to stem the tendency of class differentiation: member households with greater economic resources could still utilize a part of the labor of other member households to obtain greater returns. As a result, a higher form of collectivism—the agricultural producers' cooperative—was pushed vigorously from the beginning of 1954 until 1958.

In contrast to the mutual-aid arrangements, the early form of producers' cooperative combined land resources with the resources of farm implements, draft animals, and labor. The land was considered to be the peasants' investment in the cooperative. However, this too revealed a series of internal and external contradictions: the contradiction of the collective economy and individual subsidiary occupations; the contradiction of the better-off cooperatives and the poor cooperatives; and the contradictions between the collective economy and the state economy.

The Maoists attributed these contradictions to the ownership of private property, and the sense of individualism rooted in the traditional Chinese family system. Therefore, a system of people's communes was introduced in September 1957. By 1958 a call was issued by the Party for the establishment of communes throughout the country. However, during the first three years of existence (1958–61), it underwent a series of changes. The following chart illustrates the evolution of the people's communes into four stages:[16]

Chart 8: Changes in the People's Rural Commune System

Development:			
First Stage – – –➤ Second Stage – – –➤ Third Stage – – – –➤ Fourth Stage			
Time:			
1958 – 59	1959 – 60	1960 – 65	1968 –
Function:			
Commune as the functional organ	Production brigade as the functional organ	Production team as the functional organ	Production brigade as the functional organ
Organization:			
Three levels:	Three levels:	Four levels:	Two levels:
1. Commune management committee	1. Commune management committee	1. Commune management committee	1. Commune revolutionary committee
2. Administrative division	2. Production brigade	2. Large production brigade	2. Production brigade
3. Production brigade	3. Production team	3. Production brigade	
		4. Working groups	

NOTE: Some interruptions and changes not accounted for from the third stage to the fourth stage.

Learn From Tachai

One of the most interesting developments with respect to China's communes was the 1970/71 *Learn from Tachai* campaign. Peasants in countless village meetings pondered ways to better acquire the Tachai spirit, while provincial leaders convened conferences and study groups to analyze Tachai's remuneration methods and work-style. Even the People's Liberation Army has been called upon to learn from Tachai.[17]

In fact, the new remuneration system developed by the peasants in Tachai is very much in keeping with Maoist concepts of egalitarian principles. Tachai, unlike other Chinese communes, did not follow a complex and cumbersome method of contracting work under quota and of recording individual work points for piece labor. Tachai experimented with at least six remuneration schemes before settling upon the present one.

For example, at first, the villagers in Tachai attempted to do farm work according to the rotation system, which resulted at times in a gross misallocation of labor, with the physically weak members occupied at the most arduous tasks. Then, the Tachai brigade developed a pace-setter system, wherein all members computed their own remuneration by comparing their endeavors with those of the brigade's most highly-skilled and productive model workers. Again they developed a standard work system, wherein a job's classification was judged in relation to the season's principal task. For instance, during the season for land clearing, carrying stones was the standard job and points were assigned on a sliding scale in terms of exertion required.

The standard work system was in turn abandoned. Finally a new system of from each according to his ability was developed, with each brigade member rewarded principally for laboring to the best of his ability. For instance, physically strong peasants reportedly needed little encouragement to take on the heaviest jobs, while the infirm could select easier chores without substantial loss of income. Tachai reports that individual abilities now are allocated properly, allegedly without cadre controls.

According to Tachai pronouncements, the new remuneration system has strengthened the sense of mutual responsibility among the people. Among other things, the peasants reportedly agreed to distribute grain, green vegetables, and fruits according to need. Aged brigade members receive nearly the same work points thy received when younger, provided they take part in collective labor to the best of their ability.[18] Tachai's cadres, eschewing special privileges, now stipulate that their own portions of the year-end imbursements should never exceed the brigade's median.[19]

New Emphasis on Agriculture

Since the Ninth Party Congress in 1969, there has been new emphasis that agriculture needs to be supported by industry. Provincial press reports imply that many small, local plants that have been in existence for some time have switched from production of nonessential items to the manufacture of products for use directly in farming. Similarly, some reports not only reflect this narrow form of priority, but indicate what seems to be a national policy: cutting back funds for capital construction in certain areas while concentrating in others.[20] One of the policy papers developed included the following directives:[21]

1. To modernize the habits and attitudes of the peasants.
2. Modernization must be carried out collectively with local, not state funds.
3. Follow Chairman Mao's "eight-character charter" for agriculture (a rather general philosophy for scientific farming).
4. Follow Chairman Mao's call to send youth to the rural areas. (Graduates of middle schools and universities who have departed for the countryside are said to total several million.)
5. Transformation of consumer units in the villages—which means

dispersal of skilled workers and others, even from small towns and villages—to farm units in order to achieve self-sufficiency within each unit.

Finally, China has expanded farm land acreage, increased construction of large as well as small water conservation projects, made wider use of high-yielding, short straw varieties of rice seed, and adopted a new advanced technique of transplanting. It has been claimed that the Chinese have built more than a million small reservoirs and ponds, dug 9 million wells, and developed new canals and storage basins which increased the irrigated area by 120 million acres. The taming of the Haiho River, for example, has brought control over water supplies covering an area of 85,000 square kilometers in northern China; and some 350,000 men worked on this project. Elsewhere, the weather has been overcome by primitive schemes. A Fukien production brigade fought drought by leading water to the fields through a network of only 500 bamboo tubes.[22] There is little doubt that significant progress has been made in tackling many of the age-old problems of agriculture in China today.

INDUSTRIAL DEVELOPMENT

The Chinese Communists inherited a damaged and poorly functioning industrial base. Therefore, initial emphasis (1949–52) was placed upon rebuilding and restoring production to pre-war levels, a goal which was reached and sometimes exceeded by the end of 1952. Then in 1952, the Chinese clearly formulated twin goals of socialization (including agricultural collectivization) and industrialization as their major policy of economic development.

According to a study by Kang Chao, the specific policies adopted by China during the various periods in its industrial development are threefold.[23] There is a need to develop a comprehensive and independent industrial system. The insistence on this policy is motivated by a number of reasons, not the least of which are political and military considerations. The major problems encountered by the planners have been how to maintain an equilibrium among the various branches of industry, and between industry and agriculture. In addition, this policy has also generated a major conflict of interests between the Chinese and Soviet leaders in recent years.

It is deemed necessary to relocate and reestablish industrial centers in the inland cities, close to their sources of raw materials, their fuel supply, and their consumption centers. The reasons for these are twofold: First, most factories were originally constructed in or around the treaty ports by Chinese firms with foreign connections. (*See* Map 5.) They were too far away from domestic sources of raw materials. Second,

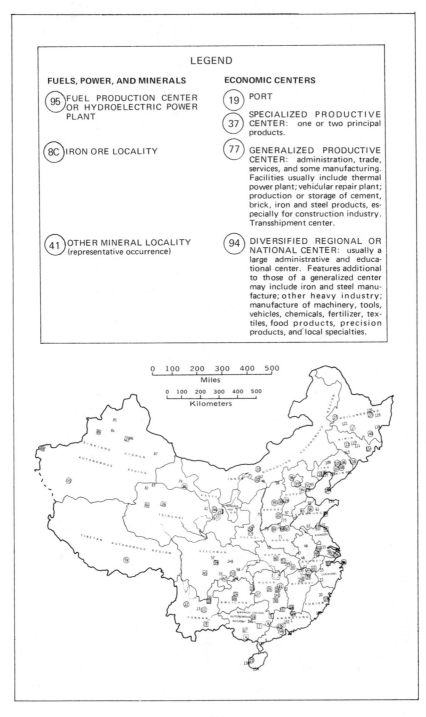

LEGEND

FUELS, POWER, AND MINERALS

(95) FUEL PRODUCTION CENTER OR HYDROELECTRIC POWER PLANT

(8C) IRON ORE LOCALITY

(41) OTHER MINERAL LOCALITY (representative occurrence)

ECONOMIC CENTERS

(19) PORT

(37) SPECIALIZED PRODUCTIVE CENTER: one or two principal products.

(77) GENERALIZED PRODUCTIVE CENTER: administration, trade, services, and some manufacturing. Facilities usually include thermal power plant; vehicular repair plant; production or storage of cement, brick, iron and steel products, especially for construction industry. Transshipment center.

(94) DIVERSIFIED REGIONAL OR NATIONAL CENTER: usually a large administrative and educational center. Features additional to those of a generalized center may include iron and steel manufacture; other heavy industry; manufacture of machinery, tools, vehicles, chemicals, fertilizer, textiles, food products, precision products, and local specialties.

COMMUNIST CHINA: 155 PRINCIPAL ECONOMIC CENTERS AND REPRESENTATIVE PRODUCTION LOCALITIES LISTED BY PROVINCE

ANHWEI
44 Ma-an-shan — Iron mine, iron and steel plant
45 Fo-tzu-ling — Kaolin
46 — Hydroelectric power plant
47 Mei-shan — Hydroelectric power plant
48 Haui-nan — Coal
134 Wu-hu — Port; paper

CHEKIANG
32 Huang-t'an-K'ou — Hydroelectric power plant
33 Hsin-an-chiang — Hydroelectric power plant
34 Chou-shan — Fishing grounds
35 Hang-chou — Textiles, foodstuffs

FUKIEN
19 Foochow (Fu-chou) — Port; chemicals
20 Ku-t'ien — Hydroelectric power plant
136 Amoy (Hsia-men) — Port; fishing

HEILUNGKIANG
115 Chia-mu-ssu — Paper
117 Harbin (Ha-erh-pin) — River port; machinery, electrical equipment
118 Chi-hsi — Coal
119 Shuang-ya-shan — Coal
120 Hao-Kang — Coal
121 An-ta — Ta-ch'ing oil field, oil refinery
123 Ch'i-ch'i-ha-erh and Fu-la-erh-chi — Steel, tools, railroad equipment
140 Mu-tan-chiang — Tires

HONAN
67 K'ai-feng — Agricultural machinery
68 Cheng-chou — Textiles; railroad junction
69 Lo-Yang — Heavy machinery, cement
70 San-men-hsia — Dam (completed); hydroelectric power plant (under construction)
71 P'ing-ting-shan — Coal
72 Chiao-tso — Coal
73 Hao-pi — Coal

HOPEH & PEKING
93 Peking (Pei-ching) — Diverse industries
94 Tientsin (T'ien-ching) — Port; diverse industries
95 K'ai-luan — Coal (K'ai-p'ing — Luan-hsien area)
96 Lung-yen — Iron mines
97 Feng-feng — Coal (Han-tan area)
124 Shih-chia-chuang — Textiles
130 T'ang-ku — Port
151 T'ang-shan — Cement, steel

HUNAN
26 Hsi-k'uang-shan — Antimony mine and smelter
27 Hung-chiang — Timber
28 Shan-shan-ch'ung — Manganese
30 Shui-k'ou-shan — Lead and zinc mines
31 Ch'ang-sha, Hsiang-t'an, Chu-chou — Tricities: heavy industry, chemicals
141 Heng-yang — Machinery, mineral products

HUPEH
40 Chung-hsiang — Phosphate
49 "Wu-han": Wu-chou, Han-k'ou, Han-yang — Tricities: port; iron and steel, heavy machinery, food processing
50 Huang-shih — Ta-yeh iron mine, iron and steel, copper, cement
51 Ying-ch'eng — Gypsum
52 Tan-chiang-k'ou — Hydroelectric power plant (under construction)

INNER MONGOLIAN AUTONOMOUS REGION (IMAR)
102 Pao-t'ou — Iron and steel complex
103 Pai-yun-o-po — Iron mine
142 Shih-kuai-kou — Coal

KANSU
77 Lan-chou — Oil refinery; petro-chemicals, aluminum
78 Liu-chia-hsia and Yen-kuo — Hydroelectric power plants (under construction)
79 Yü-men — Oil field and refinery
80 Ch'i-lien-shan area — Iron ore deposits

143 Pai-yin-ch'ang — Copper
144 Yung-teng — Cement

KIANGSI
21 Ching-te-chen — Porcelain
22 P'ing-hsiang — Coal (serves Huang-shih, 50)
23 Ta-yü — Representative tungsten mine
24 Lung-nan — Representative tungsten mine
25 Nan-ch'ang — Aircraft assembly
29 Lo-p'ing — Manganese, lead, and zinc mines
135 Chiu-chiang — Port

KIANGSU
36 Shanghai, with Min-hang, P'u-t'ung — Port; many primary and secondary industries; facilities include oil refinery; shipbuilding, iron and steel, textiles, chemicals, pharmaceuticals, electrical equipment
37 Soochow (Su-chou) — Textiles
38 Wuhsi — Textiles
39 Nanking (Nan-ching) — Chemicals, cement; oil refinery
41 "Huai-pei," — Salt fields
42 Süchow (Hsü-chou) — Coal; railroad junction
43 Hsin-hai-lien — Phosphate
132 Lien-yün-kang (or -chiang) — Port
133 Chen-chiang — Port

KIRIN
111 Feng-man (Sungari Reservoir) — Hydroelectric power plant
112 Ch'and-ch'un — Trucks, railroad equipment, tools, pharmaceuticals
113 Liao-yüan — Coal
114 T'ien-pao-shan — Lead and zinc mine
116 T'ung-hua — Iron mines, coal
122 Kirin (Chi-lin) — Chemicals, cement

KWANGSI CHUANG AUTONOMOUS REGION
4 Ch'in-hsien area — Manganese mines
6 Ho-hsien (Hsi-wan) — Tin mines
7 Kuei-p'ing — Manganese mines
8 Wu-chou — River port; timber, pitch, rosin
17 Nan-ning — Light industry
18 Liu-chou — Cement
146 Ho-shan — Coal

KWANGTUNG
1 Hsin-feng-chiang — Hydroelectric power plant
2 Canton (Kuang-chou) — Port; shipbuilding, chemicals, fertilizer, sugar, paper
3 Mao-ming — Shale oil, oil refinery
5 Shao-kuan area — Tungsten, antimony, bismuth, tin deposits and mines
125 Shih-lu — Iron mines
137 Chan-chiang — Port
138 Tung-fang [Hainan] — Port
139 Yü-lin [Hainan] — Port
152 Liang-k'ou — Hydroelectric power plant
153 Fo-shan — Silk
154 Chiang-men — Sugar, paper

KWEICHOW
14 K'ai-yang — Phosphate
15 T'ung-jen area — Mercury (many small deposits)
16 Kuei-yang — Cement, aluminum, tools

LIAONING
90 Chin-hsi — Oil refinery, cement
91 Sup'ung (N.Korea) — Hydroelectric power plant
104 "Lü-ta": Ta-lien (Dairen) and Lü-shun — Port; steel, shipbuilding and auxiliary industries, locomotives, chemicals, cement
105 Shen-yang (Mukden) — Railroad hub; diverse primary and secondary industries; iron and steel, heavy machinery, tools, electrical equipment, aircraft, copper refining

106 Fu-shun — Coal, shale oil, oil refinery, aluminum, cement
107 An-shan — Iron and steel complex
108 Pen-ch'i — Coal, cement, iron and steel complex
109 Fou-hsin — Coal
110 Yang-chia-chang-tzu — Lead, zinc, molybdenum mines
128 Ying-k'ou — Port; magnesite
129 Hu-lu-tso — Port

SHANSI
98 Ta-t'ung area — Coal, cement
99 T'ai-yüan and Yü-tzu — Iron and steel, chemicals, machinery
100 Yang-ch'üan — Iron mines, coal
101 Lu-an (Ch'ang-chih area) — Iron mines, coal

SHANTUNG
61 Wei-fang — Coal
62 Po-shan — Coal, aluminum
63 Tsao-chuang (I-hsien) — Coal
64 Tsingtao (Ch'ing-tao) — Port; textiles, tires, locomotives
65 Tsinan (Chi-nan) — Agricultural machinery, tools
66 Tzu po — Iron mines (T'ieh-shan)
92 Sheng-li — Oil field
131 Chefoo (Yen-t'ai) — Port

SHENSI
74 Sian (Hsi-an) and Hsien-yang — Textiles, electrical equipment
75 Yen-sh'ang — Oil field
76 T'ung-ch'uan — Coal
150 Yao-hsien — Cement

SINKIANG UIGHUR AUTONOMOUS REGION
84 Tu-shan-tzu — Oil field, oil refinery
85 K'o-la-ma-i (Karamai) — Oil field
86 Liu-tao-wan — Coal
87 Ha-mi — Coal
88 Wu-ch'ia — Lead and zinc mines
89 Ni-lo-k'o (Nilki) — Zinc deposits
127 Urumchi (Wu-lu-mu-ch'i) — Cement, agricultural machinery, small iron mines
155 Khotan (Ho-t'ien) — Textiles

SZECHWAN
53 Chungking (Ch'ung-ch'ing) — Heavy industry, coal, iron and steel, cement

54 Ch'eng-tu — Precision and electronics industries; copper
55 Tzu-kung — Natural gas, brines, chemicals
57 Tzu-p'ing-p'u — Dam
58 Shih-tzu-t'an — Hydroelectric power plants
145 Shih-mien — Asbeston
147 Lu-chou — Fertilizer
148 Nan-ch'ung — Oil field and refinery
149 Nan-t'ung Basin — Coal at Wan-sheng-ch'ang

TIBETAN AUTONOMOUS REGION
59 Lhasa (La-sa) — Textiles, small hydroelectric power plant

TSINGHAI
60 I-k'o-ch'ai-ta-mu — L. Boron salts
81 Ta-t'ung — Coal
82 Mang-yai — Oil field
83 Leng-hu — Oil refinery
126 Ch'a-erh-han Basin — Potassium salts

YUNNAN
9 Ko-chiu — Tin mine and smelter; lead
10 Tung-ch'uan (Hui-tse) — Copper mines
11 K'un-ming — Iron and steel; copper, cement, chemicals
12 Hsia-kuan — Cement
13 I-p'ing-land — Coal
56 I-li River — Hydroelectric power plants under construction

The 68 economic centers and the 87 production localities were selected to illustrate provincial contrasts as well as to identify major production centers. Economic centers, in general, are so designated because they provide services and principal production facilities that help support region and province, as well as nation. A more discriminating study is intended for orientation. The Spatial Economy of Communist China (Hoover Institution, Palo Alto, 1968) by Wu Yuan-li, in it assesses the industrial and economic significance of 117 cities in relation to location and transportation. Additional descriptive information on those cities and their hinterlands will be found in various regional geographies and special monographs by Soviet and Chinese authors. These have been translated in the JPRS series.

from a military viewpoint, the Chinese navy is particularly weak and the coastal area is strategically vulnerable. In time of war, the concentration of industry in that area might jeopardize the whole economy. Because of these considerations, a more balanced development was established in China, as illustrated in map 5.

A new system of industrial administration and management is also needed. However, this is one area where policies have varied over a period of time. In the early years (1949–53), the central government had no real control over state enterprises, except for those located in the north China region. Each regional government had its own industrial ministries to exercise the administrative power vested in it. However, the importance of centralized control of industry has gradually increased since 1954. Then, in 1958, during the great leap period, local governments were again empowered to supervise the enterprises belonging to the industrial ministries in Peking. By 1960, the Chinese authorities had restored the system of central responsibility only to see it changed again during the Cultural Revolution. The post-Cultural Revolution seems to have established a new balance of power between central and local governments, including the principle of mass participation at the enterprise level.

To carry out these policies, several Five-Year Plans were established and promulgated. The first plan (1953–57) called for almost doubling the value of gross industrial output, increasing gross agricultural output by close to one-quarter, and increasing by about one-half the gross commodity output of agriculture and industry combined. Strong priority was given to expanding the output of basic industrial commodities and increasing the production of capital goods to broaden the industrial base and increase national self-sufficiency. There was also a stepup in the machine-building and armaments industries.

Under the Treaty of Friendship, Alliance, and Mutual Assistance, announced on 14 February 1950, the Soviet government promised China a credit of $300 million (U.S. currency) over five years, subject to repayment within ten years from the end of 1954 with interest at one percent.[24] In mid-1957 the Chinese Communists stated that they had received loans and credits of all kinds from the Soviet Union totaling about $2.24 billion (U.S. currency), of which about $1.31 billion had been received during the first Five-Year Plan. Much of the loan included charges for Russian military equipment and services, and for Soviet shares in the joint stock companies which were turned over to exclusive Chinese ownership during 1954 and 1955.[25]

Specific Soviet aid for the first Five-Year Plan covered 156 major industrial enterprises, including seven iron and steel plants, 24 electric power stations, and 63 machinery plants. By the end of 1957, the number of projects was expanded to 166. In 1958 and 1959 an additional 125 projects, scheduled for completion in 1964, were added, which became the very core of the Chinese industrialization program. The Soviet Union also provided China with technical assistance—some 11,000 Russian specialists worked in China. China also received 10,000 sets of specifications from the U.S.S.R., ranging from machine design to blueprints for large construction projects.[26]

According to the final account for the first Five-Year Plan period, about 10,000 industrial projects, above and below norm, were under construction. Of these, 921 were above-norm units, exceeding the planned number by 227. The actual investment in industry made in this period was 25,030 *yuan*, slightly less than the planned amount. Thus, according to a study by Kang Chao, the actual average investment per project was smaller than that contemplated in the original plan (2.5 million *yuan* as compared with 8.9 million *yuan*).[27]

Soviet assistance programs began to decline when China entered into a second Five-Year Plan (1958–62), as announced at the Party Congress in September 1956. As with the first plan, industrial construction was to be carried out with heavy industry at the center. However, the economic situation in China was not as favorable as expected. As investment in heavy industry increased, particularly in 1956, shortages began to appear in raw materials, consumer goods, and skilled labor. Strict rationing of essential consumer goods failed to ease the situation. Criticism began to be heard.

In order to reverse this situation and mobilize all resources for a maximum degree of industrialization in a minimum amount of time, with a minimum use of scarce sources and labor, Chairman Mao called for the anti-rightist campaign and subsequent great leap forward program in 1958. The campaign was to last three years throughout the countryside to ensure popular enthusiasm and support.

In the implementation of the new drive, production targets for all major products were raised; to a greater extent, management and planning were transferred to local authorities; and plants mushroomed throughout the country. In addition, small backyard pig-iron furnaces were set up in every area where raw materials were available.

As we have already noted, a combination of adverse circumstances caused a serious recession in China. Finally, the withdrawal of all Soviet technicians and advisors—taking with them blueprints for the construction and operation of plants and machines—resulted in a period of readjustment at the end of 1960 and in early 1961. From 1960 to 1966 no official statistical information was published on industrial production, investment, or output of individual sectors. The third Five-Year Plan was launched in 1963, only to be postponed until 1966.[28]

The third Five-Year Plan was intended as a plan of recovery from recession. The emphasis included increased construction of new plants and improvement of old ones, including the redesign of machine tools for greater efficiency in production. In addition they increased the pro-

Table 10: Economic Indicators — 1970 Compared to 1969

Region / Indicator	Change	Period
National		
Coal	24%	Jan.-Aug.
Crude oil	34%	Jan.-Aug.
Tax revenues	budget surplus	Jan.-Aug.
Sales by retail organizations	16%	Jan.-June
Purchases by retail organizations	19%	Jan.-June
Wheat & rice crops	"an all-time high"	
Farm machinery (value)	22%	Jan.-June
Farm equipment, manufacturing, and repair plants	80% of all countries	
Anhwei		
Industrial output (value)	34%	Jan.-Sept.
Coal	19%	Jan.-Aug.
Industrial products purchased by commercial departments (value)	15%	Jan.-Sept.
Industrial products sold by local markets (value)	20%	Jan.-Sept.
Wheat crop	20%	
Chekiang		
Coal	20%	Jan.-Aug.
Freight	18%	Jan.-Aug.
Sales	31%	Jan.-Aug.
Chinghai		
Industrial output (value)	increased	Jan.-Aug.
Financial revenue	increased	Jan.-Aug.
Inner Mongolia		
Industrial output (value)	21%	Jan.-June
Spring wheat crop	35%	
Autumn grain crop	20%	
Wheat procurement	200%	Jan.-Aug.
Kansu		
Industrial output (value)	25%	Jan.-Aug.
Coal	37%	Jan.-June
Crude oil (Yumen)	17%	Jan.-Aug.
Kiangsi		
Capital construction	81%	Jan.-Aug.
Engineering production (value)	100%	Jan.-Aug.
Early rice crop	30%	
Pigs (no.)	30%	
Kiangsu		
Pigs raised (no.)	8%	Jan.-June
Fruits harvest	50%	
Kirin		
Industrial output (value)	15%	Jan.-Aug.
Steel	100%	Jan.-Aug.
Coal	21%	Jan.-Aug.
Grain & cotton crops	21%	
Kwangsi		
Grain procurement	21%	Jan.-Sept.
Kwangtung		
Industrial output (value)	19%	Jan.-Sept.
Steel	100%	Jan.-Aug.
Coal	64%	Jan.-Aug.
Pig iron	150%	Jan.-Aug.
Capital construction	70% of the year's planned projects completed by end June	Jan.-June
Shantung		
Industrial output (value)	29%	Jan.-Aug.
Retail organizations: sales	5%	Jan.-Aug.
Retail organizations: purchases	12%	Jan.-Aug.
Retail organizations: stocks	22%	Jan.-Aug.
Cotton crop	10%-20%	
Synthetic ammonia	24%	Jan.-Sept.
Chemical fertilizers	20%	Jan.-Sept.
Sinkiang		
Industrial output (value)	40%	Jan.-Aug.
Cotton crop	30%	
Livestock (no.)	5%	
Szechwan		
Grain crop	10%	
Yunnan		
Steel	39%	Jan.-Aug.
Pig iron	87%	Jan.-Aug.
Coal	21%	Jan.-Aug.
Coke	63%	Jan.-Aug.
Freight	25%	Jan.-Aug.
Industrial output (value)	"marked increase"	
Grain	20%	Jan.-Aug.
Canton		
Industrial output (value)	29%	Jan.-June

134

Chemical, fertilizer employed	50%	Jan.-Aug.

Fukien

Coal	85%	Jan.-Aug.
Hainan		
Industrial output (value)	28%	Jan.-Aug.
Freight	30%	Jan.-Aug.

Heilungkiang

Crude oil (Taching)	"record increase"	Jan.-Aug.
Peasant sideline income	30%	Jan.-June
Spring wheat crop	10%-20% of total area	
Farm mechanization:	40% of total area	
Scientific farming:	60% of total area	

Honan

Diesel engines	134%	Jan.-Aug.
Agricultural pumps	170%	Jan.-Aug.
Tractor-drawn farm implements	175%	Jan.-Aug.

Hunan

Industrial output (value)	42%	Jan.-Aug.
Electricity	40%	Jan.-Aug.
Coal	57%	Jan.-Aug.
Electronic factories (no.)	400%	Jan.-Aug.
Revenue collection:	90% of year's task completed by end Aug.	

Hupeh

Industrial output (value)	20%	Jan.-Aug.
Steel	15%	Jan.-Aug.
Iron	18%	Jan.-Aug.
Tractors	200%	Jan.-Aug.
Motor vehicles	500%	Jan.-Aug.
Early rice crop	60%	Jan.-Aug.
Summer grain crop	20%	Jan.-Sept.

State transport: freight moved	24%	Jan.-Aug.
Early rice crop	10%	
Pigs (no.)	10%	Jan.-Sept.
Marine products	10%	

Liaoning

Industrial output (value)	16%	Jan.-June
"Major electronic products"	100%	
Silicon steel (Anshan)	22%	Jan.-Aug.
Steel tubes (Anshan)	20%	Jan.-Aug.
Coal	28%	Jan.-June
Retail organizations: sales	5%	Jan.-Sept.
Retail organizations: purchases	40%	Jan.-Sept.

Ninghsia

Industrial output (value)	"all-time high"	Jan.-Oct.
Coal	39%	Jan.-Aug.

Shansi

Total industrial output	25%	Jan.-July
Electronic enterprises	100%	Jan.-Oct.
Electronic products	100%	Jan.-Oct.
Chemical fertilizers	110%	Jan.-Aug.
Fuel supplies	30%	Jan.-Aug.
Consumer sales	30%	Jan.-Aug.
Electricity generated	40%	Jan.-Sept.
Steel ingots	148%	Jan.-Sept.
Pig iron	157%	Jan.-Sept.
Rolled Steel	130%	Jan.-Sept.
Tractors	650%	Jan.-Sept.
Diesel Engines	900%	Jan.-Sept.
Agricultural machinery (value)	180%	Jan.-Sept.

Steel	110%	Jan.-June
Rolled steel	23%	Jan.-June
Pig iron	150%	Jan.-June
Machine tools	44%	Jan.-June
Vehicles	250%	Jan.-June

Sian

Industrial output (value)	54%	Jan.-July

Tientsin

Industrial output (value)	14%	Jan.-June

Wuhan

Industrial output (value)	31% (compared with any previous year)	Jan.-Aug.
Commercial department's sales	10%	Jan.-Aug.

Shanghai

Industrial & agricultural output	"surpassed any previous peak"	

Peking

Industrial output (value)	33%	Jan.-Sept.

*Based on provincial radio broadcasts and the New China News Agency.

vision for fertilizer to raise agricultural productivity. However, during this period, progress was slow because of the Cultural Revolution which had had a profound effect upon China's economic elite and upon the economic administration.[29]

China entered a new phase of industrial development in January 1971, with the start of the fourth Five-Year Plan. The basic guideline called for agriculture as the base, simultaneous development of both large and small industries, and the creation of self-sufficient industrial and farming communities across the nation. Industry must now provide the inputs for agricultural expansion: chemical fertilizers, electric power, agricultural tools and machinery, irrigation and drainage facilities, etc.[30]

Since China's resources are larger, the means of mobilization are more readily available, and the vast numbers of peasantry are the chief resource for the new economic take-off. With the economic structure more balanced than in the past, China ought to be able to become a major industrial nation before the end of the century.[31] (See Table 10, pages 134–35.)

Suggested Readings

CHAO, KANG. *Agricultural Production in Communist China, 1949–1965.* Madison: University of Wisconsin Press, 1971.
CHEN, C. S., ed. *Rural People's Communes in Lien-chiang.* Palo Alto: Hoover Institution, 1969.
CHEN, NAI-RUENN. *Chinese Economic Statistics.* Chicago: Aldine Publishing Co., 1967.
_____, and GALENSON, WALTER. *The Chinese Economy Under Communism.* Chicago: Aldine Publishing Co., 1969.
DAWSON, OWEN L. *Communist China's Agriculture: Its Development and Future Potential.* New York: Praeger Publishers, 1970.
ECKSTEIN, ALEXANDER; GALENSON, WALTER, and LIU, T-CHUNG, eds. *Economic Trends in Communist China.* Chicago: Aldine Publishing Co., 1968.
HUGHES, T. J., and LUARD, D. E. *The Economic Development of Communist China, 1949–1960.* New York: Oxford University Press, 1961.
PERKINS, DWIGHT H. *Agricultural Development in China, 1368–1968.* Chicago: Aldine Publishing Co., 1969.
RICHMAN, BARRY M. *Industrial Society in Communist China.* New York: Random House, 1969.
U. S. Congress, Joint Economic Committee. *An Economic Profile of Mainland China.* 2 vols. Washington, D.C.: U.S. Government Printing Office, 1967.
WU, YUAN-LI. *The Economy of Communist China: An Introduction.* New York: Praeger Publishers, 1965.
_____. *The Spatial Economy of Communist China.* Palo Alto: Hoover Institution, 1967.

chapter eight

The New Cultural Process

Maoism has served as a means to a goal: to develop a new national, scientific, and mass culture for the Chinese people. The strategy used by Maoists has been that of mass line or mass mobilization. From the founding of the People's Republic in 1949, they have persistently called upon the Chinese intellectuals—cadres, teachers, scientists, engineers, doctors, writers, and artists—to serve the Chinese peasantry, and have insisted that together they should be mobilized in a collective effort to serve the goal of the revolution.

However, there are a number of insurmountable problems which have been obstacles to China's cultural reforms. First of all, the Chinese population is largely rural, probably to the extent of over 85 percent. In addition, the population is relatively young. In 1953, for example, 36 percent of the population was below 15 years of age; 53 to 56 percent was below 25; and 86 percent was below 50. (In the U.S. the population below 15 years of age is estimated at 21 percent). The problem of providing education for such a large young population is extremely difficult and expensive. In one estimate, it has been calculated that it takes three working peasants to support one full-time student at school in China.[1]

Then there is always the problem of the serious dialect differences among the Chinese people; some of these are mutually unintelligible. In fact, there are really two major language problems: the development of a standard spoken form and the reform of the writing system.

While the Chinese government has had considerable success with the simplification of the Chinese written language, the progress has been limited in scope. But China has not been able to eliminate the dialect differences. At present, some 387 million people speak Mandarin dialects, which are themselves divided into northern, northwestern, southwestern, and river dialects; 46 million Chinese speak Wu dialects with several variations; 26 million speak Hunanese dialects; 20 million communicate in Hakka dialects; 13 million speak Chianghsi dialects; 27 million use the Cantonese dialects; and some 22 million speak in Fukienese dialects.[2]

Finally, there are always the problems of cultural heritage and tradition. Although, in principle, equal access to a Confucian education was open to all in imperial China, in practice, the cultural system of old China served only the interests of the gentry class. This tradition was further reinforced after the overwhelming military, economic, political, and cultural intrusion of Western powers, which produced a new Chinese elitist class, with a highly disdainful attitude toward the manual labor of the peasantry. This was so despite the fact that the peasants have been the backbone of the Chinese nation for more than 2,000 years.

PROLETARIAN EDUCATIONAL POLICIES

The Communist education policy was born out of the realities of the Yenan days. Because of the shortage of trained manpower during the revolutionary period, those with some education and training performed several different tasks. It was then that the Maoist idea of the all-around man emerged: the intellectual soldier-peasant.

Early Policies

During 1949 to 1951, the new Chinese government in Peking held a series of national conferences on different aspects of education in order to implement the earlier recommendation of the Common Program of September 1949. This included the reorganization of educational institutions and the liquidation of private schools.

Another directive was soon passed by the administrative council of the government on 10 August 1951, to provide guidelines for the types of schools, the length of the curriculum, students' age limits, and other educational philosophy. The new directive further provided equal opportunity of education for all, systems of schools and universities under unified control, opportunities for revolutionary political training and continuing education, and flexible methods and procedures.[3]

To implement this policy, an average of 7 percent of the national budget was allocated for educational reforms from 1951 to 1956. The allocation increased to 10 percent by 1957. A regular school system under national control was established from the kindergarten to university level; and a parttime system with accelerated programs was also established to be maintained under local auspices.

Official statistics for 1958, for instance, claimed that 81 million persons were enrolled in spare-time classes: 40 million in literacy classes, 26 million in spare-time primary school, 15 million in spare-time middle schools, and 150,000 in spare-time higher education. The regular school enrollment is illustrated in the following table:[4]

Table 11

Enrollments in Schools and Universities (in thousands of students)

	ELEMENTARY SCHOOLS	MIDDLE SCHOOLS	UNIVERSITIES
1949–50	24,391	1,267	111
1951–52	43,154	1,964	156
1953–54	51,504	3,628	217
1955–56	53,100	4,437	290
1957–58	63,000	5,160	447
1959–60	90,000	n.a.*	810
1960–61	n.a.*	n.a.*	855

*n.a.—not available

The Soviet Union was the only source of foreign influence upon the Chinese educational reforms in the formative years. From 1950 to 1958, several hundred Russian teachers taught in the Chinese school systems; and some 2,700 Chinese teachers received training in Soviet schools and colleges. In addition, enormous amounts of Soviet educational material and literature, either in Russian or in translation, were exported to China. From 1952 to 1956, the Chinese themselves translated 1,400 Russian textbooks and 2,746 literary works: a total of 295 million books were printed and distributed throughout China. However, after the Sino-Soviet split, China began to import or exchange books with other foreign countries: some 110,000 different titles from 160 countries in 1961.[5]

Educational System

By 1954, China had established a unified educational system divided into three catagories: primary education, middle schools, and universities.

Primary education was divided into preschool kindergartens and junior schools, which were usually separated into a lower school and an upper school. Kindergartens normally cater to the age range of three to seven. While kindergartens are serving the goal of the state with early indoctrination, they also serve economic needs, by releasing women (mothers) from child care and allowing them to engage in productive labor. In most regions in China the development of preschool education is tied in with child welfare programs.

The Ministry of Education in Peking decided the primary educational curriculum: physical education, language arts, and general knowledge. Physical education is supposed to include health habits, free play, gymnastics, and dance. Language arts are verbal skills: conversation and story telling. One of the problems facing children in rural areas is the distance between home and school. Children in the lower primary school may walk a distance of three and four kilometers, and the walk to an upper primary school may be even longer.

Secondary schools, usually called middle schools, build on the primary curriculum by adding courses in literature, science, more advanced mathematics, and foreign languages (including a choice of English and Russian). Formal political study is also begun at this level. Prior to the Cultural Revolution, admissions to middle schools were based upon examination, and final examinations determined the award of diplomas (graduation).

The highest educational system is made up of the colleges, universities, and post-graduate institutes. By 1963, the number of Chinese higher educational institutions grew to a total of 400, including 23 universities, 20 polytechnical universities, 100 engineering institutes, 90 agricultural colleges, 120 medical schools, and a number of colleges for teacher training, economics, politics, physical education, fine arts, and foreign languages. Admission to an institution of higher education is limited in number, and acceptance standards are highly selective. A few selected graduates may be allowed to do post-graduate work at research institutes.

The regular school system is supplemented by an extensively organized part-time and spare-time education subsystem. The difference between part-time and spare-time education is that the former involves more or less equal amounts of time spent at work and study, while spare-time education involves study in addition to full-time work. The following chart illustrates the educational system in China prior to the Cultural Revolution:[6]

Chart 9: China's Educational System Prior to the Cultural Revolution

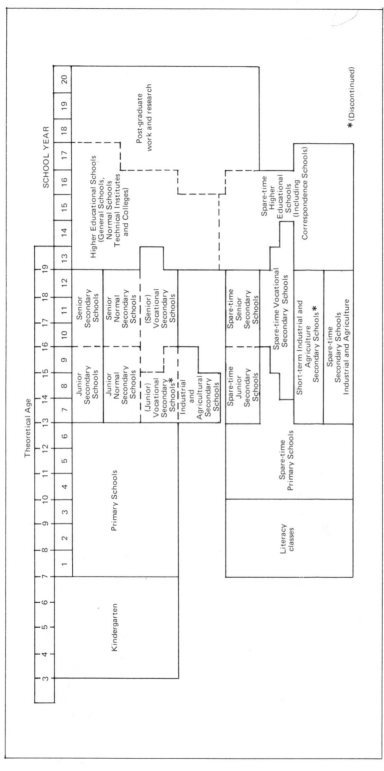

New Proletarian Education

The Chinese educational process from 1950 to 1965 should have been considered a tremendous success, especially when compared to the pre-Communist period: in 1949 there were only about 75,000 college level intellectuals. However, the system was not responding fully to the expectations of the great majority of China's youth. In addition it tended to discriminate against children of peasant origin in rural areas.[7]

As a direct result of the Cultural Revolution, reform policies have been formulated in order to handle the "ten different relations" of the new proletarian education:[8]

1. The relation between politics and vocational study.
2. The relation between leadership and masses and between unity and struggle.
3. The relation between destruction and construction.
4. The relation between study, the main task of the students, and learning other things such as industrial production, agricultural production, and military affairs.
5. The relation between theory and practice, between book knowledge and practical knowledge gained in the three great revolutionary movements of class struggle, production struggle, and scientific experimentation.
6. The relation between using, remolding, and training the three-in-one combination teaching staff.
7. The relation between popularization and raising standards.
8. The relation between running school through diligence and frugality and state aid.
9. The relation between classroom and society, between the activities carried out inside the school and outside.
10. The relation between the revolution on the educational front and the revolution in other fields.

The thrust of new reform policies is intended to thoroughly structure the educational system in order to reach Maoists goals and resolve existing problems. Specifically, the most important changes are the reduction in the number of years required to fulfill preuniversity requirements; emphasis on the acquisition of diverse practical skills through manual work; and the garrisoning of worker-military propaganda teams in the schools.

In urban areas, for example, the primary school curriculum, formerly set at six years, has now been reduced to five. Secondary studies, covering both junior and senior middle school, have been reduced to four years. And in rural areas, the new system of primary and middle school education provides for a seven-year combined term to be run by production brigades, followed by a two year senior middle school run by the communes.[9]

At the university level courses of study have been reduced from six years to three years, as evidenced in the reforms at the prestigious Tsinghua University in Peking. However, a student must have had at least two years' prior experience as a worker, peasant, or soldier before qualifying for admission.[10] According to a 1971 report, the incoming student body that year consisted of 45 percent workers, 40 percent peasants, and 15 percent military men.[11]

In the final analysis, there will be new structures, new curricula, and new procedures which will enable the system to become a vehicle to mold the participants to a socialist consciousness of unselfishness through an integration of intellectuals, common workers, and peasants. After a four-week visit to China in 1971, a Chinese-American, Nobel-laureate physicist, Chen-ning Yang, said:

> Since everyone is required to do (manual work), it is no longer regarded as a form of punishment. The scientists take it in stride. Some of them get so interested in the farms that they even go back on Sundays to check on the crops. . . . I went to a country I find very exciting. There is a need of many material things. But what I found to be very moving is a spirit. I wondered, looking back at this country (the U.S.), if there was not too much of the material here and not enough spirit.[12]

LITERATURE AND ARTISTIC EXPRESSION

No one denies that literature is closely affiliated with both philosophy and ideology. Philosophy is the soul of literature; literature is the expression of philosophy. In the West, literature and philosophy constitute two separate branches of culture, even though they are closely associated. On the other hand, Chinese literature is intimately allied with philosophy. Traditional Chinese literature originated from the *Five Classics* and various schools of philosophy in the classical time. However modern Chinese Communist literature is derived from the theoretical foundation of Marxism-Leninism, and more recently, the thought of Mao Tse-tung.

Development of New Literature

In the formative years of Chinese Communist literature and arts, Chinese policies had been affected by Russian experiments and experiences in the attempt to fashion socialist realism. This has been defined as "truthful, historical, concrete representation of reality in its revolutionary development . . . it linked with the task of ideological transformation and education of workers in the spirit of socialism."[13]

This early impact of Marxism-Leninism helped to create the type of intellectual and emotional environment necessary for the development of a unified literary line in the Chinese Communist Party. This was clearly demonstrated in Mao Tse-tung's speech on "Talks at the Yenan Forum on Art and Literature" in May 1942.[14]

In this policy speech, Mao initiated sharp criticism against various petit bourgeois ideas and tendencies that existed in art and literature. By reasserting the Marxist-Leninist view that art and literature must subserve the political ends of revolution, Mao exhorted Chinese artists and writers to measure themselves against five yardsticks: standpoint, attitude, audience, work, and study. The five yardsticks would constitute control over ideological content in order to ensure the appearance of new revolutionary literature. He further urged the primacy of popularization, but stressed that "no hard and fast line can be drawn between popularization and the raising of standards." While he acknowledged the distinction between artistic standards and political standards, he insisted that the former should be subordinate to the latter.

After the founding of the new Republic, a national cultural conference was convened in 1949, and the All-China Federation of Literary and Art Circles was formed. They adopted the principles enunciated by Mao Tse-tung at the Yenan Forum, and made the federation the new oracle for all workers in literature and the arts.

In conjunction with Maoists' mobilization drives, many rectification campaigns were launched in order to purify ideology within the literary and art circles. A great number of workers in art and literary fields were sent to rural areas, mines, factories, or into the armies to temper themselves through physical labor.

One of the most important campaigns was the 1954 nationwide criticism of Hu Shih (1891–1962), a Chinese philosopher and writer, founder of the simplified *pai-hua* or spoken-language style of writing in China. In 1955, Hu Feng, a veteran Communist and authority on literary theories, and Ting Ling, the outstanding woman writer of Communist China were purged. Meanwhile, a number of older writers were promoted: the late Lu Hsün, idolized as "engineer of the human soul"; Kuo Mo-jo, named president of the Chinese Academy of Arts and Sciences; Mao Tun became editor of the official *Chinese Literature*, a monthly journal; and many others, including Pa Chin and Lao She, were given high positions in the government.

By 1960, another important congress (the third) of the All-China Federation of Literary and Art Circles met in Peking. During this conference the new principle concerning the "unity of revolutionary realism and revolutionary romanticism" was introduced. This amended the original policy initiated by Mao Tse-tung at the Yenan Forum and became the guiding compass of Chinese art and literature.

Development of Fine Arts

The development of fine arts in China follows the same ideological principles as literature. By far the greatest part of art creation has been in illustrative arts: posters, cartoons, woodcuts, and picture story-books. Their enormous production serves a vast number of illiterate or barely literate masses.

Picture storybooks, for example, are always present at various mass mobilization programs. Discussion of themes such as health and sanitation, care of livestock, new farming methods, love of fatherland, and more recently, planned-parenthood are available in an easily under-stood format. Workers and peasants are particularly responsive to this material.

Other forms of fine arts such as drama, films, and music, are viewed as forces that can arouse the people's proletarian consciousness and inspire their devotion to socialism. The Chinese have been putting forth their utmost efforts to develop their motion picture industry. For instance, in 1949 there were only three film studios located in Chang-chun, Peking, and Shanghai; a decade later, some 14,500 cinema studios were established throughout China. The Chinese people have been encouraged to patronize theaters of all kinds: cinemas, dramas, shadow plays, puppet shows, storytelling, ballad singing, folk dancing, acro-batics, as well as Peking Opera (a distinctive, traditional, Chinese art form). At times, theaters are used to educate the people in such practi-cal and, for Westerners, simple matters as improved sanitation, health, and agricultural practices.

In order to popularize music and use it as an education and propaganda tool, group singing has been highly developed. In addition to spontaneous group singing in the streets or places of work, many professional choirs and instrumental groups have been organized. Sing-ing contests and music festivals are regularly organized to stimulate the composition and performance of all forms of music. Nieh Erh and Hsien Hsing-hai are generally recognized as the fathers of socialist music in China. Nieh Erh composed the "March of the Volunteer," which for a time served as the Communist national anthem. Hsien composed symphonies, orchestral suites, cantatas, and operas; the best of his work is the *Yellow River Cantata*.

Under the Party tutelage, the dance has also been elevated to an independent art form. Folk dancing provides opportunity for group participation and mass attendance. For example, the "harvest song" dance (*yang-ko*), a traditional fertility dance from northwest China, has now been popularized and identified with liberation, unification, peace, and national spirit. Regional and ethnic dance troupes have con-tinuously been encouraged. The ballet also enjoys considerable popu-larity in its own right.

Revolution in Creative Expression

The Cultural Revolution began with Maoist attacks against a popular play written by Wu Han, *The Dismissal of Hai Jui*. In point

of fact, the Maoists saw a great number of revisionalist arts and literature emerge under the leadership of Liu Shao-chi and many historical
and pernicious plays were retained. Specifically, the Maoists were
angered when Peng Chen, mayor of Peking and influential member of
the Central Committee, opposed the reformation of the Peking Opera,
as proposed by Chiang Ching, wife of Mao Tse-tung.

Chiang Ching, once worked as an actress in the film studio in
Shanghai under the pseudonym of Lan Ping. She joined Mao's revolutionary Lu Hsun Art Institute in Yenan and married Mao Tse-tung during the early revolutionary years. She remained at home, bearing Mao's
two daughters, until 1950, when she was appointed to the central steer-
ing committee for the Chinese film industry under the Ministry of
Culture.

Chiang accepted the position with enthusiasm and frequently
commented and spoke on each film that was made in those years. By
1962, Chiang Ching had completed an extensive review of more than
1,000 Peking Operas. She saw some performed by the Number One
Peking Opera Company and concluded that these operas needed to be
reformed. According to Chiang Ching, too many confusions were
created by the repertoire and themes about ghosts, gods, emperors,
generals, and concubines. She saw them as poisonous weeds, incom-
patible with China's revolutionary goals. She began to talk with young
actors and actresses throughout China and urged them to reform operas
to comply with contemporary themes.[15]

A new forum on the work in literature and art in the armed forces
was held from January 2 to 20, 1966. Lin Piao, who became China's
defense minister, appointed Chiang to oversee all artistic work in the
army. The conference adopted a ten-point policy:[16]

1. Develop class struggle on the cultural front.
2. Reform Peking Operas on contemporary themes.
3. & 4. Use the Liberation Army to play an important role in the
   socialist cultural revolution.
5. Stress destruction as well as construction in the cultural revolution.
6. Urge writers and artists to practice "democratic centralism."
7. Encourage revolutionary and militant mass criticism of literature
   and art.
8. Struggle against foreign revisionism, including Chukhrai and
   Shulokhov [methods]. (Later in 1969, Stanislavsky's system was
   added to the list.)
9. Combine revolutionary realism with revolutionary romanticism.
10. Reeducate and reorganize writers and artists in the spirit of
    socialist revolution.

Furthermore, together with these ten guidelines, Chiang Ching
made an important policy statement at the conference. One year later,

the *People's Daily* proclaimed that this was the prelude to the "Cultural Revolution. (*See* Appendix 5.)

With this new responsibility, Chiang began to reform the Peking Opera. The formal *ch'u* songs were replaced by revolutionary music, and traditional Chinese music was supplemented by Western instruments, including piano. The innovation was called an example of how people armed with the thought of Mao Tse-tung could "not only destroy the old world, but also construct one totally new" (a practice of guideline 5).[17]

Another important innovation in China's arts involves the popular musical work, *Shores of the Sha Village* (*Sha-chia-pin*) which "harmoniously incorporates the original characteristic melodies, instrumentation, and percussion rhythms of Chinese opera with symphony, choruses, and other form of music expression" borrowed from the West.[18] The work also combines the use of natural voice and falsetto.

These kinds of new artistic expression indicate that a relatively eclectic and utilitarian approach has been undertaken. In order to construct a new Chinese society, Maoists have successfully translated a theory of cultural value into practice.[19]

CULTURAL HEROES, "NEW WOMEN," AND SOCIAL VALUES

In traditional China, the moral philosophy of the ruling Confucian scholars held that man was inherently good and socially harmful behavior occurred only when men lacked guidance. That guidance was provided by the virtuous examples of one's superior.

On the other hand, Mao Tse-tung regards man as a product of his social class, with his ideas and habits strongly determined by his origin. However, at the same time, Mao has an almost infinite belief in man's ability to rise above these limitations. Therefore, time and again, Mao returns to education, persuasion, ideological work, and the emulation of heroes as a means of eradicating various errors. Often, the local cadre is held up as the virtuous model to be imitated.

Emulation of Heroes

The *Liberation Army Daily* published an editorial on 23 November 1967:

> The great Mao Tse-tung era we are now in is also the era of the coming of heroes. A succession of outstanding men rising up from the masses and a profusion of good men and good deeds mark the era.... To model oneself after heroes and learn from great people has always been the mainstay of the Party and Chairman Mao's teachings.[20]

The emulation of heroes is not new, but dates back to ancient dynasties. It was the Confucian tradition to educate people by telling them stories about great historical personalities, describing their special qualities of character and filial piety: devotion and loyalty to parents. In fact, filial piety was the most important virtue stressed, and its emphasis was the backbone of the social order.

Heroes in Chinese Communist society are very carefully selected before promotion to the society, and then they most often reflect the new mood and political style of the revolutionary period. For instance, during the Yenan period, Stakhanov-type model workers were promoted as heroes in order to spur on the production drive. Alexei Stakhanov was a Russian miner of Donbas, who was cited as an example to all for supposedly having dug 14 times the amount of coal normally required.

Chinese descriptions of heroes during the Yenan period almost always began with details of the model worker's production records as well as his production methods. The model's personality and private life were not described, and there was no ideological dressing to the facts and figures.

The promotion of Stakhanou-type models continued through the 1950s and 1960s. Stories always centered on conquering a particular problem in the model's occupation, or in the conquest of nature. These earlier heroes included: Tung T'sun-jui—Liberation War hero; Huang Chi-kuang—Korean War hero; Lo Sheng-Chiao—Korean War hero; Wang Hsiao-ho—Civil War martyr; Liu Hu-lan—15 year-old girl cadre and Civil War martyr; and Ting Yu-Chun—girl cadre and Civil War martyr.

These heroes and heroines were all examples of excellence in energy, drive, endurance, resourcefulness, and devotion to their work. Pain is an essential test for the hero; it is also essential as a preparation for the ultimate test—death. In fact, heroes' deaths are somehow an occasion for pride and satisfaction. They feel that their lives are not given in vain, since they have set an example of how a man or woman should behave when he has to pass through the final ordeal of human existence.

Lei Feng–Wang Chieh Type Heroes

During the Cultural Revolution, many new heroes emerged as paragons to be emulated by all new revolutionary cadres. They are all based upon the prototypes of Lei Feng and Wang Chieh of the People's Liberation Army, and their stories are related in the form of diaries. This new form of presentation can be more didactic and soul-searching than the third person narrative style. According to a critical study by Mary Sheridan, Lei Feng's diary has a fairly "loose style, and is romantic in an adolescent vein."[21]

In Lei Feng's diary, there are 61 entries, 24 of which mention the Party frequently. Mao is not quoted, but the reference is made to his works or instructions. In 1965, the August First Film Studio made a feature film based on Lei Feng's life, and referred to him as "Chairman Mao's good fighter."[22]

Here are some entries from Lei Feng's diary:

> November 8, 1960
> Today is my red-letter day. I joined the great Chinese Communist Party and thus realized my noblest wish.
> My heart keeps beating, Oh! Our great Party, our great leader Chairman Mao, it is you who gave me my new life. . . .

> October 3, 1961
> Man must die, but some die with a significance lighter than a swan's down, while others die with a significance weightier than Mount Tai. . . . When my country and my people are faced with danger, I will come forward and defy death. I was born for the people, and I will die for them.

> March 4, 1962
> I would be a pine on a high mountain rather than a willow by the lake side. I would temper myself in a stormy struggle rather than live a life of tranquility.

Wang Chieh's diary, on the other hand, is a more sophisticated effort than Lei Feng's. It has 116 entries, and of the 59 which refer to Mao, 25 contain direct quotes. When he quotes Mao, Wang adds didactic lessons for his own benefit:[23]

> January 11, 1965
> Last night the leadership announced that I'd been made acting deputy squad leader. . . . It was a difficult problem and I hesitated to accept the job. Then I looked up Chairman Mao's works. I found the article "on the Chungking negotiations" in which he said:
>
> > What is work? Work is struggle. There are difficulties and problems in those places for us to overcome and solve. We go there to work and struggle to overcome these difficulties. A good comrade is one who is more eager to go where the difficulties are greater. . . . Hard work is like a load placed before us, challenging us to shoulder it.
>
> As I read this passage again, I felt as if it had been written for me. I asked myself: Am I really afraid of difficulties? Should I back away from them? No! I shouldn't be afraid.

> September 14, 1964
> In his article "Serve the People," Chairman Mao says:
> > Our Communist Party and the Eighth Route and New Fourth Armies led by our Party are battalions of the Revolution. These battalions of ours are wholly dedicated to the liberation of the people and work entirely in the people's interest.

> I now understand the real significance of this passage. The words "wholly" and "entirely" mean that we should whole-heartedly serve and work for the people. . . .

The characteristics of this new type of hero can be briefly stated: all are young, all are soldiers (or sailors) of lowest rank, and all are practitioners of Maoism for social reconstruction. Their stories include the ingredients of courage, sacrifice, and dependence on Mao's thought. In a sense, their diaries, real or imaginary, are guidebooks of the new social morality or values of China today.

Because youth is the most rebellious and idealistic age of man, it must have seemed an especially suitable vehicle for the Maoists to use to move China into a new age of national, scientific, and mass culture.

Women and the Family System

Not all Chinese literature and artistic expression is centered around heroes and heroines of the Chinese Liberation Army. There have been other major themes, as illustrated in Chinese films during the past 20 years: *Liberation of Women, The Feudalistic Family,* and *Reactionary Figures.*

In a study made of 23 representative Chinese films, John H. Weakland found that women were considerably more prominent than men.[24] In 10 films, the leading role was a female one; in only four films did a male have the lead; and in five films, the male and female leads were of fairly similar prominence. Furthermore, women not only were prominent in the frequency of leading roles, but also in their dramatic and emotional intensity.

Another interesting observation deriving from the study of these films involves the oppression and liberation of women in China. The nature of the oppression suffered by the heroines is not mainly related to backwardness, poverty, and starvation. But rather, as demonstrated in Chinese films, the status of women suffers overwhelmingly from sexual oppression, which includes rape and prearranged marriage.

Those women who are represented as liberated women are portrayed mainly as teachers, doctors, or workers on construction projects, and sometimes they are involved in socially constructive student activities. They may be single or married, but they study and work like men, just as the resistance heroines fight like men.

In summary, in the personal sphere of sexual relations and the traditional family, young women are regularly depicted as weak and oppressed by men. On the other hand, when women are separated from the immediate family and sexual sphere by their new social affiliations and activities, they are not oppressed or weak, since they are in contact with *good* men. For instance, the heroine in *White Haired Girl* is quite helpless to resist rape by an evil landlord, but she displays great determination and perseverance when concerned with survival and revenge.

In fact, these themes are consistent with the Chinese policy toward women and the family as outlined in the new Marriage Law of 1 May 1950, one of the first major legal pronouncements of the People's Republic.

> The feudal marriage system which is based on arbitrary and compulsory arrangements and the superiority of men over women and ignores the children's interest, shall be abolished. The New-Democratic marriage system, which is based on the free choice of partners, on monogamy, on equal rights for both sexes, and on the protection of the lawful interests of women and children, shall be put into effect. (Article I.) [25]

The right of both marriage partners to pursue their own occupations or social activities invites them to involve themselves in relationships that go beyond the traditional concept of family. The result is that the real social unit is no longer the husband-wife but a group of 20 to 30 neighboring households.

Impact upon Society

What has been the impact of the new social practices of hero emulation and women's liberation in China? Although there is no conclusive answer at the moment, an early observation may be of interest. In 1961, in Shanghai and Canton a team of Canadian child psychiatrists conducted a study based upon Murray's Thematic Apperception Test and concluded:[26]

1. The subjects are overly preoccupied with socio-political themes in contrast to their denial of intra-psychic conflicts.
2. Hostility is not expressed directly toward the immediate environment.
3. The fear of failure is associated with high ambition.
4. There is marked blocking in the area of sexuality.
5. Attitudes of dependence and submission are expressed toward authority figures and rationalized as moral acts.
6. Parental figures are consistently perceived as affectionate and supportive, in marked contrast to the T.A.T. responses (Murray's Thematic Apperception Test) of North American adolescents.

Suggested Readings

BIRCH, CYRIL, et al. "Special Survey of Chinese Communist Literature." *China Quarterly* No. 13 (January/March 1963).
BUSH, RICHARD C., JR. *Religion in Communist China.* Nashville: Abingdon Press, 1970.

CHAI, CH'U, and CHAI, WINBERG. *A Treasury of Chinese Literature*. New York: Appleton-Century, 1964.

CHEN, THEODORE H. E. *Thought Reform of the Chinese Intellectuals*. Hong Kong: University of Hong Kong Press, 1960.

CHIN, ROBERT, and CHIN, AI-LI. *Psychological Research in Communist China, 1949–1966*. Cambridge, Mass.: M.I.T. Press, 1969.

CHUNG, HUA-MIN, and MILLER, ARTHUR C. *Madame Mao: A Profile of Chiang Ching*. Kowloon, Hong Kong: Union Research Institute, 1968.

CROIZIER, RALPH C. *China's Cultural Legacy and Communism*. New York: Praeger Publishers, 1970.

FRASER, STEWART, ed. *Chinese Communist Education: Records of the First Decade*. Nashville: Vanderbilt University Press, 1965.

GOLD, MERLE. *Literary Dissent in Communist China*. Cambridge, Mass.: Harvard University Press, 1967.

GOULD, SIDNEY H., ed. *Sciences in Communist China*. Washington, D.C.: American Association for the Advancement of Science, 1961.

HOUN, FRANKLIN W. *To Change a Nation, Propaganda and Indoctrination in Communist China*. New York: Free Press of Glencoe, 1961.

MESERVE, WALTER J., and MESERVE, RUTH I., eds. *Modern Drama from Communist China*. New York: New York University Press, 1970.

PRICE, R. F. *Education in Communist China*. New York: Praeger Publishers, 1970.

RIDLEY, CHARLES, GODWIN, PAUL, and DOOLIN, DENNIS. *The Making of a Model Citizen in Communist China*. Stanford: Hoover Institution Press, 1971.

SNOW, HELEN FOSTER. *Women in Modern China*. The Hague: Mouton & Co., 1967.

YANG, C. K. *The Chinese Family in the Chinese Communist Revolution*. Cambridge, Mass.: M.I.T. Press, 1959.

YU, FREDERICK T. C. *Mass Persuasion in Communist China*. New York: Praeger Publishers, 1964.

CHAPTER NINE

THE NEW FOREIGN POLICY

The Chinese define foreign policy as,

> a tool of diplomacy and inseparable from her domestic
> policy. It includes the relations between two or more coun-
> tries, covering all kinds of activities, political, economic and
> cultural affairs. . . . Policy not only actually determines the
> contents of the foreign relations, but also determines its
> nature and steps.[1]

However, the making of Chinese foreign policy
is beset with difficulties. As in the U.S., the formulation
and execution of foreign policy has become such a
complex process that it may be actually misleading to
refer to Chinese foreign policy as if it were a single
thing.

Charles A. McClelland refers to the U.S. foreign
policy process as a game which includes the diplomatic
game of the Department of State, military game of the
defense establishment, intelligence game, information
game, national development game, and finally the security game. Professor McClelland warned that

> because organizations quickly adopt distinctive opera-
> tional codes and institutionalize their practices, dis-

agreements and tensions develop in inter-agency relations; it becomes the conviction of each and every agency that it is second to none in its devotion to national objectives in international relations.[2]

Chinese games are more complex because institutionalization was lacking in the decision making process. This was especially so during the Cultural Revolution. While the Ministry of Foreign Affairs might have been following one set of goals, other branches including the Ministry of Defense, the Party's International Liaison Bureau, the Commission for Cultural Relations, or the Chinese People's Association for Friendship with Foreign Countries may have been pursuing their own courses of action based upon their own interpretations of the situation. In fact, the increased tension and conflict during the Cultural Revolution paralyzed the routine operation of China's foreign policy.[3]

However, the extremely unfavorable reactions abroad with respect to the Chinese conduct of foreign relations made it imperative for the leadership in Peking to reverse the trend. After the important Ninth Party Congress of April 1969, Premier Chou En-lai was given the supreme authority to supervise and coordinate all foreign policy activities under the State Council in order to correct past mistakes and increase China's responsiveness to the international environment.

OPERATIONAL GUIDES

The Ministry of Foreign Affairs is the primary executive instrument that carries out foreign policy decisions of the State Council (Premier Chou En-lai) and the Politiburo of the Party Central Committee. As far as we know, the Foreign Ministry is headed by a minister (Chi P'eng-fei) and four vice-ministers. The principal organs in the ministry include four geographic departments: West European, American, and Australian Affairs; Asian Affairs; Soviet and East European Affairs; and West Asian (Middle East) and African Affairs. In addition, there are several functional departments: International Organization; Information (intelligence and research); Protocol; Consular Affairs; Legal; Personnel; and Office of General Administration (secretariat).

The Foreign Ministry is under the direction of its acting foreign minister, Chi P'eng-fei, a personal protegé of Premier Chou En-lai. He is the only senior officer in the Foreign Ministry who has survived a dozen purges since 1950. Chi was first given the important post of vice-minister in charge of Soviet and East European affairs on 31 January 1955, at a time when China began to exert thinking and action, independent of the Soviet Union.

At the end of 1959, when China began to initiate a major diplomatic offensive in the developing nations of Asia and Africa, Chi was shifted to handle West Asian (Middle East) and African affairs in the ministry. For example, he was personally involved in the 1961–62 Geneva Conference on Laos; and paved the way for Premier Chou En-lai's two successful visits to the Middle East and Africa from 1963 to 1964. He himself has also travelled in Africa.

During the Cultural Revolution, Chi P'eng-fei was criticized by the Red Guards for being a moderate on foreign policy matters; and for a short time, he did not attend any public functions in Peking. However, he emerged at the end of the Cultural Revolution as the senior vice-minister, and finally became acting minister of foreign affairs.

Operational Guides

According to a study of official Chinese documents made by this author, the basic operational guides of China's foreign policy may be summarized as follows:[4]

1. Foreign affairs officers must assume the leadership role, based upon correct political orientation, faith and self-sacrifices, and finally courage.
2. They must practice investigation and research before making a decision or implementing a decision.
3. They must practice negotiation and compromise, and avoid one-sideness in state to state relations.

As to the last principal guide, it was presented by Chairman Mao in an inner-Party circular, which set forth five conditions:[5]

1. The Chinese Communist will negotiate when he has fallen into the "quagmire of an indecisive struggle, armed or other wise";
2. The Chinese Communist will negotiate when confronted with "so strong an enemy that a combative posture would surely invite catastrophe, yet a strategic retreat or truce might enable them to conserve strength and wait for a more favorable change in the balance of power";
3. The Chinese Communist will negotiate when "negotiation appears to be a promising way of resolving a specific conflict, whereas struggle (war) would entail a cost incommensurable with the anticipated gain";
4. Chinese Communists will negotiate when they "wish to devote their attention and resources to a more important or urgent project (or problem) at home or abroad";
5. Finally, the Chinese Communist will negotiate when he can "win the sympathy of the concerned public (public opinion) and to expose the plots, hypocrisy, and other evil acts of the opponents (propaganda victory)."[6]

In fact, this author maintains that Mao's conditions for negotiation resemble certain aspects of Morgenthau's classic fundamental rules of diplomacy: "Nationals must be willing to compromise on all issues that are not vital to them" and "the objectives of foreign policy must be defined in terms of the national interest and must be supported with adequate power."[7]

Although Mao has probably not heard of Morgenthau, he nevertheless wrote, "we on our side are prepared to make such concessions as are necessary and as do not damage the fundamental interest of the people"; and "you must definitely not rely on the negotiations, must definitely not hope that the Kuomintang (opposition) will be kindhearted, because it will never be kind-hearted. You must rely on your own strength."[8]

Therefore, the most significant operational guide of China's foreign policy, like her other policies of political, economic, and social affairs, is based upon the ideology of Maoism. However, the thought of Mao Tse-tung has been broad enough to encompass not only the current of change, both gradual and rapid, but also the current of continuity, always latent and often active.

FOREIGN POLICY THEMES

Richard Lowenthal recently wrote that,

> Communist China is today the greatest dissatisfied power in the world. . . . It (the dissatisfaction) is rooted both in China's national situation and history and in the ideological needs arising from the present internal problems and the historical experience of its Communist leadership.[9]

Historically, china has long attempted to gain considerable detachment from environing states. However, when China could not keep foreigners out altogether, she then tried to limit the extent of their interactions with the natives by establishing carefully regulated tribute missions and restricted foreign enclaves. Again, when such defensive measures failed, the Chinese reversed their roles and hoped to assimilate the invaders into Chinese culture and civilization.

Even the often quoted militant policy of "people's war" can be viewed in this light: if the enemy cannot be repulsed at the frontier, he can be drawn in further and further until, lacking any local support and harassed by elusive if inferior forces, his own weapons taken over and turned against him, he is finally exhausted and submerged by the people.

Furthermore, the intensity and persistence of the Chinese distrust of any foreign influence can be seen in her insistence that anti-imperialism is a condition for peaceful coexistence and world peace. Here imperialism denotes the policies and practices of three of the world's super powers: the U.S.A., the U.S.S.R., and Japan.

The Chinese experiences with all three major industrial powers have been sad ones. The Sino-Japanese conflicts lasted more than a decade. Until 1971, Sino-American relations were caught in a hopeless deadlock over a variety of major issues: the Korean war, the status of Taiwan, and covert and overt actions against each other. These hostile positions and actions have built walls of suspicion between Peking and Washington, and webs of conflicting interest—domestic and international—exist behind these walls.[10]

China was in close alliance with the Soviet Union in the formative years of the Republic; but that alliance also called for China to make economic concessions, despite earlier massive Soviet technical assistance programs. Some public concessions made by China to the Soviet Union included: Soviet control of China's principal railways in Manchuria, Soviet use of naval bases in Chinese Port Arthur and Dairen, and Chinese acceptance of the independence of Outer Mongolia. Moreover, the U.S.S.R. began to extend her influence in the Pacific and openly challenged the traditionally Chinese stronghold in Asia.[11]

From the Chinese viewpoints, the policies and practices of these three imperialist powers have been the greatest obstacle to the economic development of the third world, underdeveloped countries. The Chinese complained that

> during the period of industrial capitalism the advanced capitalist countries in Europe and North America, backed up by gunboat diplomacy, had already begun the large-scale export of commodities to Asia, Africa and Latin America. This led to the destruction of the handicrafts of the colonial and semi-colonial countries and the throttling of their national industries, thereby turning them into suppliers of raw materials. In the period of imperialism, by means of capital exports, the monopolies took a direct part in developing the production of primary products in the underdeveloped countries, which they need themselves, particularly raw mineral materials. At the same time, they established more factories there. As a result, the national industries suffered both from competition from imported goods and directly from local factories operated by foreign capital. The economies of the underdeveloped countries thus became more lopsided.[12]

The record of the Soviet Union, although a socialist country, is equally corrupt and reprehensible in the eyes of the Chinese:

> The specialization of production and international division of labor, brayed [bragged] about and put into operation by the Soviet revisionists have brought about a lopsided development of the economics of those Eastern European countries and turned them into workshops of the Soviet revisionists for processing raw materials and dumping grounds for their goods. Moreover, by granting "credits," Soviet revisionism has savagely plundered these countries and grabbed fabulous profits from them.[13]

Because the Chinese distrust foreign powers, they have developed a major foreign policy theme of self-reliance as a model for socialist construction in developing nations. In a position paper published in June 1965, Tseng Yun, a Chinese economist, outlined four fundamental principles with respect to the concept of self-reliance:[14]

1. Self-reliance means to rely on the strength and diligent labor of our people to carry on economic construction.
2. To build socialism self-reliance means to make full use of all available resources in our own country.
3. To build socialism self-reliance means to get the necessary funds for construction through internal accumulation.
4. [Use] self-reliance in building socialism and gain knowledge of the laws of socialist construction through our own efforts instead of copying the experience of other nations.

However, the stress on self-reliance does not necessarily mean the absence of international aid or cooperation. In the same position paper, the Chinese economist continued: "self-reliance, however, by no means excludes international economic cooperation on the basis of equality and mutual benefit." The extent of Chinese involvement in international economic cooperation certainly validates the Chinese position, as illustrated by the table on the following pages.

Because the policy of self-reliance serves as the most important theme in Peking's foreign policy, Premier Chou En-lai outlined a program of Eight Principles on Economic and Technical Assistance during his first visits to the African countries in 1953/54. They were:[16]

1. The Chinese government always based itself on the principle of equality and mutual benefit in providing aid to other countries.
2. In providing aid to other countries, the Chinese government strictly respects the sovereignty of the recipient countries, and never asks for any privileges or attaches any conditions.
3. The Chinese government provides economic aid in the form of interest-free or low-interest loans.
4. In providing aid to other countries, the purpose of the Chinese government is not to make the recipient countries dependent on China, but to help them embark on the road of self-reliance step by step.
5. The Chinese government tries its best to help the recipient countries build projects which require less investment while yielding quicker results.
6. The Chinese government provides the best quality equipment and material of its own manufacture at international market prices.
7. In any given particular technical assistance, the Chinese government will see to it that the personnel are best qualified.
8. Chinese experts will have the same standards of living as those of the recipient country.

Unfortunately, at times, China's positive self-reliance program is

Table 12: China's Economic and

Other Agreements with Foreign Nations: 1949—64

State	No. Total Agreements	No. Economic Agreements	%	State	No. Total Agreements	No. Economic Agreements	%
Afghanistan	11	1	9	Mongolia			
Albania	22	14	64	(Outer)	32	18	56
Algeria	8	2	25	Morocco	1	0	0
Austria	2*	2*	100	Nepal	18	3	17
Bulgaria	30	22	73	Nigeria	1	1	100
Burma	31	9	29	Norway	2	1	50
Burundi	1	1	100	Pakistan	9	2	22
Cambodia	25	13	52	Poland	35	21	60
Ceylon	20	13	65	Rumania	36	27	75
Central Africa	3	2	67	Singapore-			
Congo (B.)	4	1	25	Malaya	1*	1*	100
Cuba	11	3	27	Somali	4	1	25
Czechoslovakia	39	23	59	Sudan	6	4	67
Denmark	4	4	100	Sweden	2	2	100
Ethiopia	2	0	0	Switzerland	1	1	100
Finland	21	21	100	Syria	8	7	88
France	3*	3*	100	Tanganyika-			
Germany (East)	48	30	63	Zanzibar	2	0	0
Germany (West)	4*	4*	100	Tunis	2	1	50
Ghana	11	5	45	United Arab Republic (Egypt)	23	17	74
Guinea	8	3	38	United Kingdom	2	2	100
Hungary	40	27	68	United Nations	1	0	0
India	10	5	50	U. S. A.	1	0	0
Indonesia	22	7	32	U. S. S. R.	40	15	38
Iraq	6	5	83	Vietnam (North)	47	27	57
Japan	26*	11*	42	Yemen	7	1	14
Korea (North)	39	11	28	Yugoslavia	15	11	73
Laos	7	0	0				
Lebanon	1	1	100				
Mali	7	2	29				

* Non-governmental agreements.
SOURCES: The thirteen volumes of the official collection, TYC, covering the period 1949-1964.
The figures of percentage are approximate, not exact.

marred by certain psychological fears such as the militarism of the
emerging, economically prosperous Japan. This was demonstrated in
James Reston's interview with Premier Chou En-lai:[18]

> We oppose the Japanese reactionaries. . . . The budget for
> the fourth defense plan reached the amount of more than $16

Table 13:

China's Economic and Technical Assistance Program, 1969

(A) Project Completed

COUNTRY	PROJECT	REMARK
COMMUNIST BLOC — Asia		
Albania	Concrete Mixing Plant, Mao Tse-tung Hydro-Electric Station	Located on Drin River, the plant was completed on May 21.
	Dam, Mao Tse-tung Hydro-Electric Station	Located on Drin River, the work was completed on July 21.
	Mao Tse-tung Textile Combine in Berat	The combine was completed on Nov. 22.
	Thermo-Electric Station	Completed on Nov. 23.
	Petroleum Processing Plant	Completed on Nov. 23.
	Electric Bulb Factory in Vlona	Construction started on Nov. 24.
FREE WORLD — Asia		
Yemen	Medical service	A new medical team arrived in Sana in early May to replace the old one.
	Water works	Chinese technicians returned to China after two years of work a-long the Sana-Sada Highway.
Pakistan	Construction of highway leading from Latak through northern Kashmir to Lhasa Highway	Construction reported in first half of 1969.
	Construction of highway from Gilgit in Kashmir to Sinkiang	Part of the road has been open to traffic since late August.
Cambodia	A hospital and its facilities in Phnom Penh	Dedication ceremony held on Jan. 10.
	Tea seeds	Presented to Cambodian government in April.
	Overhauling of a paper mill	Completed on May 21.
Nepal	Construction of a brick factory	Completed on March 12.
	Construction of a hydro-electric station some 80 miles from Kat-mandu	Foundation stone laid on June 9.
	One million doses each of small pox vaccine and combination diph-theria-tetanus-typhoid-paratyphoid vaccine	Presented by Chinese Red Cross Society.
Afghanistan	Assistance in fish-breeding at Ka-runta Experimental Fish-Breeding Center	Ceremony marking the first catch at the center was held on Dec. 21.
	Water conservation works	Inspected by king of Afghanistan on June 23.
Ceylon	Anti-malaria medicine	Presented by Peking on Aug. 31.

	FREE WORLD — Africa	
Tanzania	Two water works in Zanzibar	One completed on June 25 and the other on June 27.
	Two water works in southern Pemba	One completed on Oct. 10 and the other on Oct. 11.
	State farm in Zanzibar	Completed on Jan. 10.
	Ruvu State Farm	Completed at end of May.
	Another large state farm	A Chinese team has completed observation and is now doing the planning work.
	Construction of a hospital	Ground was broken on July 12.
	A farm tool repair plant in Zanzibar	Chinese technicians returned to China in early October after completing their assignment.
	A state leather and shoe manufacturing plant in Zanzibar	Visited by Kuo Lu on Dec. 14.
	Prospects for Tanzania-Zambia Railway	Preparatory work completed at end of 1969.
	Medical Service	A new team left for Tanzania in May to replace the old one in the African country.
Zambia	Preparatory work for Lusaka-Mankoya Highway	Technicians arrived in Zambia in September.
	Construction of three transmitting stations	Technicians arrived in Zambia on Sept. 29.
The Congo (B)	Kinsoundi Textile Combine	Completed on Aug. 12.
	Kombe State Farm	Inspected by Congolese premier.
	Shipyard	Chinese work team arrived in Brazzaville on Aug. 5.
Guinea	Kankan Brick Factory	Chinese engineering and technical team arrived in Conakry on Oct. 20.
	Tinkisso Hydro-Electric Station	Observation team arrived in Conakry on Nov. 21.
	Medical Service	A medical team arrived in 1968.
Somali	Expansion of medical team	15 more medical personnal arrived in Somali at end of April.
	Station for experimental planting of rice and tobacco	Visited by Somali minister of planning and cooperation on Aug. 13.
Algeria	Medical service	A medical team arrived in August 1968.
	U.S. $40,000 of canned goods and blankets	Presented by Chinese Red Cross Society on Oct. 13.
	Vocational training program	Algerians received training in China.
Mauritania	3,000 tons of food	Arrived at Nouakchott on April 29.
Mozambique	24 transport airplanes	Part of the planes have arrived in southern Tanzania.
Mali	Medical service	A medical team arrived in Mali in 1968.
	TOTAL	
16	49	

Table 13:

(continued)

(B) New Projects, 1969

COUNTRY	TITLE	DATE & PLACE OF SIGNING	SIGNATORIES
COMMUNIST BLOC			
North Vietnam	Agreement and Pertinent Protocol on Chinese Communist Assistance to North Vietnam for 1970	Sept. 26 Peking	Li Hsien-nien Le Thanh Nghi
FREE WORLD — Asia			
Yemen	Minutes of Talks on Chinese Communist Grant to Yemen for Construction of a Secondary Technical School	July 14 Sana	Li Ching-chun Yemeni Minister of Public Works
Afghanistan	Minutes of Talks on Chinese Communist Assistance to Afghanistan for Fish Breeding at Karunta Experimental Fish-Breeding Center	March 8 Kabul	Peiping's Technical Team on Fish Breeding Afghan Minister of Agriculture and Irrigation
	Minutes of Talks on Experimental Tea Planting in Afghanistan with Peking's aid	Dec. Kabul	Lin Kuei-tang Abdul Aghafour
Southern Yemen	Protocol on Dispatching of Chinese Communist Medical Team to Southern Yemen	Dec. 4 Aden	Li Chiang-fen Muhammad Saif Thabet
	Minutes of Talks on Chinese Communist Assistance to Tanzania for Construction of State Athletic Field	June 6 Dar es Salaam	Chung Hsi-tung C. Y. Mgonja
	Third Protocol on Joint Shipping Line between Peking and Tanzania	July 12 Dar es Salaam	Board chairmen of the shipping companies of two sides
FREE WORLD — Africa			
Tanzania	Supplementary Agreement between Peking and the government of Tanzania and Zambia on Construction of Tanzania-Zambia Railway	Nov. 14 Lusaka	Kuo Lu E.H.K. Mudenda A.H. Jamal
	Minutes of Talks Relating to Preparatory Work for Construction of Tanzania-Zambia Railway	Nov. 14 Lusaka	Kuo Lu E.H.K. Mudenda A.H. Jamal
	Supplementary Proposal on Matters of Some Technical Principles for Tanzania-Zambia Railway	Nov. 14 Lusaka	Kuo Lu E.H.K. Mudenda A.H. Jamal
Zambia	Documents Concerning Peking-Aided Highway from Lusaka to Monkoya	Feb. 14 Lusaka	Li Chen-ho E.H.K. Mudenda
The Congo (B)	Agreement on Peking's Assistance to Congo (B) for Construction of Small-Sized Wooden Board Building Yard	Sept. 6 Brazzaville	Wang Yu-tien Alfred Raoul
Guinea	Agreement on Chinese Communists Providing Loan in Commodities to Guinea	Feb. 28 Peking	Lin-Hai-yun Nfamara Keita
	Agreement on Economic and Technical Cooperation	Oct. 9 Peking	Li Hsien-nien Lansana Diane
Somali	Agreement on Chinese Communist Assistance to Somali for Drilling of Wells and Geological Survey	March 18 Mogadiscio	Chang Chi-fang Ali Alio Mohamed
Mauritania	Contract on Chinese Communist Assistance to Mauritania for Drilling of Wells	Nov. 27 Nouakchott	Feng Yu-chiu Mauritanian Minister of Equipment
	TOTAL		
10	16		

billion . . . and two to two-and-a-half years will be sufficient (for Japan to complete that plan). . . . Japan with her present industrial capabilities is fully able to have the means of delivery (nuclear weapons), she is able to manufacture ground-to-air, ground-to-ground missiles, and sea-to-ground missiles. As for bombers, she is all the more capable of manufacturing them. . . . Japan's output of nuclear power is increasing daily. . . . You have helped her develop her economy to such a level. And she is bound to demand outward expansion. (*See* Appendix 8.)

Mao Tse-tung is known as a great strategist who turns weakness into strength,[19] and he does not personify the image of the impetuous

People's Daily (July 17, 1971) Announcement of President Nixon's Visit

新华社十六日讯　公告

周恩来总理和尼克松总统的国家安全事务助理基辛格博士，于一九七一年七月九日至十一日在北京进行了会谈。获悉尼克松总统曾表示希望访问中华人民共和国，周恩来总理代表中华人民共和国政府邀请尼克松总统于一九七二年五月以前的适当时间访问中国。尼克松总统愉快地接受了这一邀请。

中美两国领导人的会晤，是为了谋求两国关系的正常化，并就双方关心的问题交换意见。

man who is blind to the reality of his enemy's superiority. Because of this, it is expected that China will *not* initiate any major policy of military aggression either directly against Japan or any other country in Asia. China may very well adhere to a paper-tiger psychology[20] to combat "big-power hegemony and imperialist aggressions" in the years ahead.[21] Otherwise, how is one to explain the historic Nixon–Mao summit conference in 1972?[22]

CHINA AND THE UNITED NATIONS

Since China now participates in the United Nations, what will be her attitude and role with respect to the world organization? Let us remember that historically the Communist Party of China supported the formation of the United Nations. Mao Tse-tung wrote on 24 April 1945 that:

> in regard to the establishment of an institution to preserve international peace and security, the Chinese Communist Party completely approves of the proposals made at the Dumbarton Oaks Conference and the decision concerning this question made at the Crimea (Yalta) Conference. . . . The Chinese Communist Party has already sent its own representative to join the Chinese delegation at the San Francisco Conference in order to express the will of the Chinese people.[23]

Indeed, the Chinese Communist Party delegate, Tung Pi-wu had joined the 12-member delegation representing the State of China at the San Francisco opening conference. Tung Pi-wu has since been named vice-chairman of the People's Republic and, since the Cultural Revolution, has been often called upon to act as China's chief-of-state in receiving foreign visitors.

On the other hand, China indeed has a bitter relationship with the United Nations, especially because of the Korean conflicts in 1950. She has been barred from the world organization for more than 20 years. Nevertheless, she has never once repudiated the charter of the United Nations, nor announced her formal withdrawal from the world organization.[24]

It may be of interest to note that while not a member of United Nations, China approvingly cited the charter of the United Nations in a number of bilateral treaties with foreign countries: U.S.S.R. (14 February 1950); East Germany (25 December 1955); Czechoslovakia (27 March 1957); Hungary (6 May 1959); and Afghanistan (26 August 1960) to name but a few. Her public pronouncements have also supported the principles of the U.N. as exemplified by Tung Pi-wu's speech in 1955 that "our support for the purposes and principles of the charter of the United Nations is consistent."[25] Similar views were also expressed by Premier Chou En-lai on a number of occasions.

Moreover, China also supported a fundamental revision of the United Nations Charter when it was adopted by the majority of member states. When the General Assembly adopted two resolutions amending the charter so as to provide for enlarging the membership of the Security Council and the Economic and Social Council on 17 December 1963, the Soviet delegates voted against these two resolutions on the grounds of Chinese opposition to these revisions.[26] But the foreign minister of China immediately issued a statement to correct the Soviet error and voiced approval for the charter revision.[27]

However, when Indonesia withdrew from the world organization in 1965/66, Communist China, following the Indonesian example, demanded a "thorough reorganization of the United Nations" and talked about setting up a new "revolutionary United Nations."[28] It was during these months that the Chinese press denounced the U.N. as a "tool of U.S. imperial aggression," which, according to them, included the following crimes:[29] aggression against Korea, hostility to China, intervention in Indochina, hostility toward Indonesia, intervention in Cuba, aggression against the Congo (Leopoldville), hostility to the Arab countries, and intervention in Cyprus. But from 1964 to 1968, her position was reduced to a sort of "wait and see" attitude, and she ceased to demand a revolutionary United Nations.

After the Cultural Revolution, China again began to express interest in active participation in the world organization. Although she was denied representation at the twenty-fifth session of the General Assembly, Peking interpreted that vote as a major victory because she achieved a simple majority vote (51 in favor and 49 against).[30] Finally, in a tense and emotion-filled session, the General Assembly on 25 October 1971 voted overwhelmingly to admit Communist China and to expel the Chinese Nationalist government. The vote, which "brought delegates to their feet in wild applause," was 76 in favor, 35 opposed, and 17 abstentions.[31]

There is universal agreement in the United Nations that the 1971 vote to admit the People's Republic of China will further accelerate a whole series of realignments and shifts on the international scene. There will be a slow but gradual erosion of American influence over world politics, and China will emerge as a renascent great power. She is already armed with a small nuclear arsenal and is destined to share power and influence with the United States and the Soviet Union.

Therefore, the question is: Will Communist China, as one of five permanent powers of the Security Council (and with a national population of one-quarter of the human race) work for world peace and order based upon principles of international law and justice? While no one outside China can speak with certainty on Chinese attitudes and future policies, exclusive of the period of the Cultural Revolution, China's own conduct of foreign relations indicates that she is very much within the mainstream of the world system.

Table 14: United Nations Role Call Vote to

Seat the People's Republic of China, 25 October 1971

ON TWO-THIRDS REQUIREMENT	ON SEATING PEKING
Resolution declaring the expulsion of Nationalist China an "important matter" and thus requiring a two-thirds vote rather than a simple majority for passage.	Resolution to seat Communist China and expel Nationalist China.

ON TWO-THIRDS REQUIREMENT

IN FAVOR — 55

Argentina	Japan
Australia	Jordan
Bahrain	Lebanon
Barbados	Lesotho
Bolivia	Liberia
Brazil	Luxembourg
Cambodia	Madagascar
Cent. Afr. Republic	Malawi
Chad	Mauritius
China	Mexico
Colombia	New Zealand
Congo (Kirsh.)	Nicaragua
Costa Rica	Niger
Dahomey	Panama
Dominican Republic	Paraguay
El Salvador	Philippines
Fiji	Portugal
Gabon	Rwanda
Gambia	Saudi Arabia
Ghana	South Africa
Greece	Spain
Guatemala	Swaziland
Haiti	Thailand
Honduras	United States
Indonesia	Upper Volta
Israel	Uruguay
Ivory Coast	Venezuela
Jamaica	

OPPOSED — 59

Afghanistan	Kenya
Albania	Kuwait
Algeria	Libya
Bhutan	Malaysia
Britain	Mali
Bulgaria	Mauritania
Burma	Mongolia
Burundi	Nepal
Byelorussia	Nigeria
Cameroon	Norway
Canada	Pakistan
Ceylon	Peru
Chile	Poland
Congo (Brazza)	Rumania
Cuba	Sierra Leone
Czechoslovakia	Singapore
Denmark	Somalia
Ecuador	Southern Yemen
Egypt	Soviet Union
Equatorial Guinea	Sudan
Ethiopia	Sweden
Finland	Syria
France	Tanzania
Guinea	Trinidad/Tobago
Guyana	Uganda
Hungary	Ukraine
Iceland	Yemen
India	Yugoslavia
Iraq	Zambia
Ireland	

ABSTENTIONS — 15

Austria	Morocco
Belgium	Netherlands
Botswana	Qatar
Cyprus	Senegal
Iran	Togo
Italy	Tunisia
Laos	Turkey
Malta	

ABSENT — 2

Maldives	Oman

ON SEATING PEKING

IN FAVOR — 76

Afghanistan	Libya
Albania	Malaysia
Algeria	Mali
Australia	Mauritania
Belgium	Mexico
Bhutan	Mongolia
Botswana	Morocco
Bulgaria	Nepal
Burma	Netherlands
Burundi	Nigeria
Byelorussia	Norway
Cameroon	Pakistan
Canada	Congo (Brazza)
Ceylon	Peru
Chile	Poland
Cuba	Portugal
Czechoslovakia	Rumania
Denmark	Rwanda
Equador	Senegal
Egypt	Sierra Leone
Eq. Guinea	Singapore
Ethiopia	Somalia
Finland	Southern Yemen
France	Soviet Union
Ghana	Sudan
Guinea	Sweden
Guyana	Syria
Hungary	Tanzania
Iceland	Togo
India	Trinidad-Tobago
Iran	Tunisia
Iraq	Turkey
Ireland	Uganda
Israel	Ukraine
Italy	Britain
Kenya	Yemen
Kuwait	Yugoslavia
Laos	Zambia

OPPOSED — 35

Australia	Lesotho
Bolivia	Liberia
Brazil	Madagascar
Cambodia	Malawi
Cent. Afr. Republic	Malta
Congo (Kinsh.)	New Zealand
Costa Rica	Nicaragua
Dahomey	Niger
Dominican Rep.	Paraguay
El Salvador	Philippines
Gabon	Saudi Arabia
Gambia	South Africa
Guatemala	Swaziland
Haiti	United States
Honduras	Upper Volta
Ivory Coast	Uruguay
Japan	Venezuela

ABSTENTIONS — 17

Argentina	Jordan
Bahrain	Lebanon
Barbados	Luxembourg
Colombia	Mauritius
Cyprus	Panama
Fiji	Qatar
Greece	Spain
Indonesia	Thailand
Jamaica	

ABSENT — 3

China	Oman
Maldives	

China has never abandoned international law, although her legal scholars hold diversified interpretations. Some Chinese writers of international law accept only Menzhinsky's (Russian) view that a unified international law system does not exist, but instead there are two separate systems: "the bourgeois and socialist international laws."[32] There are others who believe that modern international law is comprised of three different sets of norms and institutions: the first based upon the norms and institutions of the capitalist system; the second established by the socio-economic pattern of the new socialism; and the third comprised of norms enacted commonly between all countries.[33] Recently, China has departed considerably from the Russian interpretations;[34] in fact, China has repeatedly condemned the Brezhnev Doctrine of limited sovereignty as an outright "doctrine of hegemony."[35]

In the final analysis, Chinese attitudes on war and peace are still conditioned by a multitude of variables: historical experience, domestic environment, international politics, and not least, ideology. In ideological terms, she strictly follows the Marxist-Leninist-Maoist model of dialectical materialism, refusing to acknowledge peaceful coexistence between oppressed and oppressor nations or oppressed and oppressor classes. However, in practical politics, the Chinese have never exactly defined just what are "oppressed and oppressor nations," other than to spout generalizations about revisionism and/or imperialism. Also, her own attempts at social stratification have proven to be matters of convenience: "Who is a friend and who is an enemy of the CCP?"[36]

Suggested Readings

CHAI, WINBERG. *The Foreign Relations of the People's Republic of China: Views From Inside*. New York: G. P. Putnam's Sons, 1972.

CHAO, KANG, "Sino-Soviet Exchange Rate." *China Quarterly* no. 47 (1971), pp. 546–52.

CLUBB, O. EDMUND. *China and Russia: The Great Game*. New York: Columbia University Press, 1971.

COHEN, JEROME ALAN, ed. *The Dynamics of China's Foreign Relations*. Cambridge, Mass.: Harvard University Press, 1970.

DEUTSCHER, ISSAAC. *Russia, China and the West*. New York: Oxford University Press, 1970.

HINTON, HAROLD C. *China's Turbulent Quest: An Analysis of China's Foreign Relations Since 1945*. New York: Macmillan Co., 1970.

LALL, ARTHUR. *How Communist China Negotiates*. New York: Columbia University Press, 1968.

LARKIN, BRUCE D. *China and Africa, 1949–1970*. Berkeley: University of California Press, 1971.

New York Times. 10 August 1971. (Official transcript of James Reston's conversation with Premier Chou En-lai.)

NORTH, ROBERT. *The Foreign Relations of China*. Belmont, Calif.: Dickenson Press, 1970.

OJHA, ISHWER C. *Chinese Foreign Policy in an Age of Transition*. Boston: Beacon Press, 1969.

SIMMONDS, J. D. *China's World: The Foreign Policy of a Developing State*. New York: Columbia University Press, 1971.

VAN NESS, PETER. *Revolution and Chinese Foreign Policy*. Berkeley: University of California Press, 1970.

WHITING, ALLEN. "What Nixon Must Do to Make it in Peking." *New York Review of Books*, 7 October, 1971.

CHAPTER TEN

PROSPECTS iN THE 1970S

The Cultural Revolution has addressed itself not only to the quality of the people's ideology, but to their physical and social lives as well. Therefore, China has emerged from her greatest domestic crisis, since the founding of the new Republic on 1 October 1949, as one of the world's most dynamic powers.

According to an eyewitness report:

> Chinese shops are well stocked with basic consumer goods and there is a greater variety than before the "Cultural Revolution." Food is in good supply, though meat is a little expensive. The grain ration seems quite adequate at 30 pounds or so a month for the non-manual worker. The cotton ration is tighter, but there are enough spare coupons for buying fancy clothes for the young children . . . there were no beggars . . . I only saw one child with impetigo among thousands, none with rickets or the other ghastly diseases which spell malnutrition in every other "third world" country I've visited.[1]

In the international community, as exemplified by the 25 October 1971 U.N. General Assembly decision to seat the People's Republic and expel the Nationalists, China will encounter a veritable gold mine of good will, especially from third world developing nations of Latin America, Africa, and Asia. Primarily this is because China herself is a developing nation, still rather poor and struggling. Secondly, China is a country that is pulling itself up by its own bootstraps, rather than by reliance on the largesse of the richer powers. And finally, China has become a nuclear power mainly through her own considerable efforts. In other words, the developing nations have acquired "a powerful atomic voice through China on the very top level of global policy-making."[2]

In spite of such an optimistic outlook for the new politics of China in the 1970s, there are still problems, including: the continuation of political struggles within the high-level Party politics as exemplified by the purges of Lin Piao and several high military officials associated with him prior to President Nixon's successful visit in February, 1972; important factors of overpopulation, food production, and industrialization; and the issues of boundaries and disputed territories, including the future status of Taiwan.

POPULATION AND ECOLOGICAL PROBLEMS

Whether one considers the population estimates made by the U.S. Bureau of the Census, the Department of State, or Nationalist Chinese sources, the fact remains that the problem of population in China is not a matter of absolute numbers alone, but rather a matter of balance between available income and mouths to be fed. Chinese leadership, in spite of a popular misconception, is very much aware of the problem of overpopulation.

Mao's famous speech on "Contradiction" in February 1957 had included a strongly worded statement that the Chinese people, as a whole, should begin to control their fertility.[3] The Chinese government, meanwhile, enacted new programs for transferring Chinese populations from high density areas to low density border regions, including Tibet, Sinkiang, and Inner Mongolia. This is necessary because traditionally over 95 percent of China's population lives in 40 percent of China's land territory. This area is known as China Proper, an area from Aihui in Heilungkiang in the northeast to T'eng Chung in Yunnan in the southwest—about 40 percent of the total Chinese territory.

Birth Control

After the total failure of the great leap forward and other similar economic drives, China made an intensive effort to begin a rather comprehensive, nationwide program of birth control (excluding minority groups) in 1962. The program included propaganda promoting smaller families, and educational programs of planned parenthood. In addition many medical mobile teams were created to bring doctors from cities to China's countrysides. In December 1965, some 1,000 medical mobile teams were reported. Thousands of additional medical personnel who were moved out of the cities during the Cultural Revolution have been enjoined to accelerate these activities.

Evidence from studies of Chinese medical journals have indicated that four principal methods were used to disseminate birth control information:[4]

1. Propaganda meetings: These meetings varied from larger meetings, with 1,000 participants to small meetings which were attended by as few as four or five persons.
2. Exhibitions: These were set up in places where people usually congregated.
3. Films including such titles as *What is Birth Control?*
4. Informational materials describing the advantages of abortion and sterilization, and the use of condoms, vaginal diaphragms, chemical solutions, and occasionally, the rhythm method.

These kinds of activities were further confirmed by the eye witness report of an English surgeon who spent the years from 1954 until 1969 in China:

> I attended an evening lecture on hygiene and birth control illustrated by an old style magic lantern using a pressurized paraffin lamp. The village hall was packed. . . .
>
> After dealing with such mundane subjects as night-soil disposal, fly control and food protection, the speaker, a doctor from the mobile team, described the anatomy and physiology of the male and female organs of reproduction. An animated filmstrip showed the process. . . .
>
> Then, he described various methods of contraception, discussed their advantage and disadvantage and passed around contraceptive appliances for inspection. . . .
>
> He spoke of the advantage of planned parenthood. . . . He urged the women to discuss it among themselves and with their husbands. . . . When he had finished, the barrage of questions showed that the women were deeply interested in the new possibilities opening up for them.[5]

Problems of Pollution

With an ever-increasing population, there are problems accompanying the growth of urban centers and cities. The most powerful force in promoting urban growth is the pull of rapid industrialization.

But the new urban landscapes of China have been built in haste, with huge residential blocks constructed of red brick, grouped in geometric patterns, and relieved somewhat by grassed squares where the children can play. They are plain, modern, monolithic buildings housing government offices, educational institutions, department stores, outdoor stadiums, etc. In nearly all the expanding cities there are also blocks and blocks of industrial plants, which cause problems of environmental pollution.

Beginning in 1970, Chinese newspapers began to urge a policy of multi-purpose use on the industrial front through the recycling of waste materials: gas, liquid, and slag. For example, tail gasses belching from the chimney of a Shanghai oil refinery previously fouled the air. The Chinese now maintain that these gasses have been transferred to a nearby chemical plant via a two-kilometer-long channel set up by the workers who "analyzed, separated and purified them, obtaining ethylene, propylene and butane from this noxious exhaust." Then the chemicals obtained were delivered to Shanghai's textile mills, plastic and pharmaceutical factories, and machine building plants which processed them into useful synthetic goods.[6]

There are many other examples of advances in recycling industrial waste. (*See* Appendix No. 6.) In fact, by September 1971, a national policy was proclaimed that "solving the problem of pollution was not to be regarded as simply scientific and technical tasks but as a serious political assignment."[7] Existing major industrial enterprises have been directed to take steps "without delay."

BOUNDARIES AND DISPUTED TERRITORIES

The problem of Chinese territorial disputes with her neighbors is largely an emotional one resulting from her humiliating defeats after the Opium War and the subsequent unequal treaties with foreign powers.

A Chinese handbook published in 1954, has a map included which is captioned "The Past Democratic Revolutionary Era (1840–1919)— Imperialist Encroachments of Chinese Territory." It specifies 19 individual losses of Chinese land. However, this is not a Communist propaganda document because another text, published in Nationalist China under Chiang Kai-shek in 1946, listed 22 losses with a total of 4,009,092 square kilometers of Chinese territory.[8] These lost territories include such areas as Soviet Central Asia, Kashmir, Nepal, Sikkim, Bhutan, Assam, Burma, Malaya, Andaman, Thailand, Indo-China, Hong Kong, Taiwan, and Korea.

Of course, not all of these territories are in dispute. No Chinese, now or in the past, has been taught that countries such as Korea, Indo-China, Malaya, Burma, Thailand, Nepal, or Bhutan are part of China. In addition, the Chinese Communists have signed a number of new agreements or treaties to guarantee or reaffirm the permanence of these boundaries: Burma (1960); Nepal (1961); Pakistan (1962); Afghanistan (1963); and Mongolia (1963). However, there are some very serious boundary disputes with India and the U.S.S.R. For a description of the status of current Chinese boundaries, see Map 6.

Map 7: Communist China — Boundaries

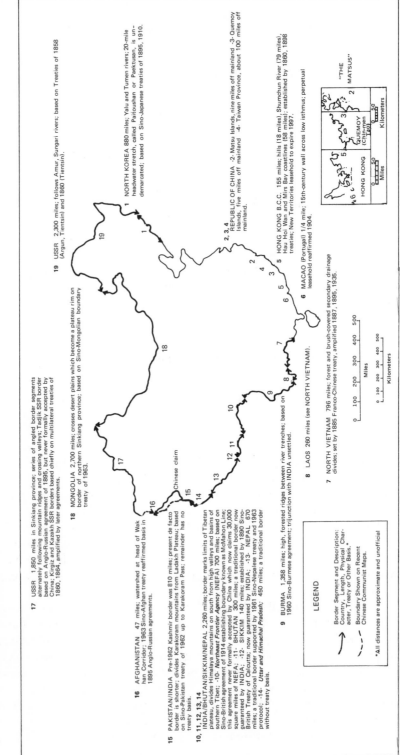

17 USSR 1,850 miles in Sinkiang province; series of angled border segments alternately following mountain ridges and crossing valleys; Tadjik SSR border based on Anglo-Russian agreement of 1895, but never formally accepted by China; Kirgiz and Kazakh SSR borders based chiefly on multilateral treaties of 1860, 1864, amplified by later agreements.

16 AFGHANISTAN 47 miles; watershed at head of Wakhan Corridor; 1963 Sino-Afghan treaty reaffirmed basis in 1895 Anglo-Russian agreements.

15 PAKISTAN/INDIA Pre-1962 Kashmir border was 810 miles; present de facto border is shorter; divides Karakoram mountains from Ladakh Plateau; based on Sino-Pakistan treaty of 1962 up to Karakoram Pass; remainder has no treaty basis.

10, 11, 12, 13, 14
INDIA/BHUTAN/SIKKIM/NEPAL 2,260 miles; border marks limits of Tibetan plateau, divides Himalaya mountains on south from high valleys and basins of southern Tibet; -10- *Northeast Frontier Agency* (NEFA) 700 miles; based on Sino-British agreement of 1914 establishing boundary known as McMahon Line; this agreement never formally accepted by China which now claims 30,000 square miles of NEFA; -11- BHUTAN 300 miles; a traditional border now guaranteed by INDIA; -12- SIKKIM 140 miles; established by 1890 Sino-British Treaty of Calcutta; now guaranteed by INDIA; -13- NEPAL 670 miles; a traditional border supported by 1961 Sino-Nepalese treaty and 1963 protocol; -14- *Uttar and Himachal Pradesh*; 450 miles; a traditional border without treaty basis.

9 BURMA 1,358 miles; high, forested ridges between river trenches; based on 1960 Sino-Burmese agreement; trijunction with INDIA unsettled.

8 LAOS 260 miles (see NORTH VIETNAM).

7 NORTH VIETNAM 796 miles; forest and brush-covered secondary drainage divides; set by 1885 Franco-Chinese treaty, amplified 1887, 1895, 1935.

6 MACAO (Portugal) 1/4 mile; 15th-century wall across low isthmus; perpetual leasehold reaffirmed 1904.

5 HONG KONG B.C.C. 155 miles; hills (18 miles); Shumchun River (79 miles); Hau Hoi Wan and Mirs Bay coastlines (58 miles); established by 1860, 1898 treaties; New Territories leasehold to expire 1997.

REPUBLIC OF CHINA -2- Matsu Islands, nine miles off mainland -3- Quemoy Islands, five miles off mainland -4- Taiwan Province, about 100 miles off mainland.

1 NORTH KOREA 880 miles; Yalu and Tumen rivers; 20-mile headwater stretch, called Paitoushan or Paektusan, is undemarcated; based on Sino-Japanese treaties of 1895, 1910.

19 USSR 2,300 miles; follows Amur, Sungari rivers; based on Treaties of 1858 (Argun, Tientsin) and 1860 (Tientsin).

18 MONGOLIA 2,700 miles; crosses desert plains which become a plateau rim on border of northern Sinkiang province; based on Sino-Mongolian boundary treaty of 1963.

LEGEND

Border Segment and Description:
Country, Length, Physical Character, Treaty or Other Basis.*

Boundary Shown on Recent Chinese Communist Maps.

*All distances are approximate and unofficial

Chinese claim

"THE MATSUS"

QUEMOY (Chin-men)

HONG KONG

Kilometers
Miles

Miles
0 100 200 300 400 500

Kilometers
0 100 200 300 400 500

Sino-Indian Disputes

Although Sino-Indian relations were friendly in the 1950s, potential conflict was present because of differences with respect to India's special interest in China's infiltration of Nepal and the Chinese friendly attitude toward Pakistan. Finally, Sino-Indian border disputes resulted in two border wars in 1959 and 1962.

Any appraisal of the Sino-Indian boundary dispute must begin with a definition claimed by both sides. The latest official position of the two countries prior to the 1962 hostilities are presented in the lengthy *Report of the Chinese and Indian Officials on the Boundary Question*.[9] It should be noted that these claims have not remained constant throughout the disputes, and that each side has deviated somewhat in its claims.

The disputed territory lies in three sections: the western sector, claimed by India to be part of the Ladakh region of the Kashmir state; the middle sector, claimed by India to be part of the Uttar Pradesh state; and the eastern sector, which consists of the entire Indian-claimed NEFA (Northeast Frontier Agency). The contested regions total approximately 50,000 square miles in area.

In her presentation, India maintained that her claim in the western sector was validated by the treaties of 1684 and 1842, that her maps have shown their present alignment for over a century, and that officials of either Ladakh, Kashmir, or India have always exercised jurisdiction in the area. The Chinese answered that the above treaties were not valid boundary agreements, but merely nonaggression pacts, and that China had exercised continuous administration throughout the area.

Furthermore, both countries in their presentation claim the entire Aksai Chin area in the western sector. India cited nine Chinese maps and four of British and German sources, dating from the sixth century through 1911, which show the Kuen Lun Mountains as the southernmost limits of Sinkiang, i.e. the boundary claimed by India. In their presentation the Chinese government listed 11 Indian maps in which the northern boundary of Ladakh was undefined or drawn along the Kara Koran Mountains, i.e. the boundary claimed by China.

India further submitted reports made by several parties which were sent to the western region to obtain salt and the accounts of one or two Kashmiri and Cadakhis traders. These traders purportedly aided in constructing trade routes and rest houses across the area. Similarly, China submitted the reports of several Indian parties expelled by Sinkiang (Chinese) soldiers while attempting to "steal salt." Finally, Indian proponents insisted that the Indian alignment adheres to a geographical principle, although the entire area is part of the Tibetan plateau which embraces all of Tibet.

Judging from the evidence that both countries presented in a report by Chinese and Indian officials on the Bombay question, based on historical jurisdiction, neither side had a strong claim to the Aksai Chin prior to 1950.[10] However, since 1950, the Chinese army passed through the area going from Sinkiang to the Ari region of Tibet. And from March 1956 to October 1957, Chinese soldiers and more than 3,000 civilians constructed the 1,200-kilometer Sinkiang-Tibet highway. India did not discover this until 1958 when a consular officer in Peking saw it depicted on a small Chinese map. India then sent patrols which confirmed the existence of this road.

With respect to the middle sector, the Indian government declared that the area as far north as Spiti was confirmed by treaties of 1684 and 1842 (the same as the western sector) and substantiated by the 1954 Tibetan-Indian Trade Agreement. While the Chinese refuse to acknowledge the 1684 and 1842 treaties as boundary treaties, the 1954 trade agreement come somewhat closer to qualifying as valid evidence, although it is still an inferred, rather than formalized, boundary treaty.

Both India and China claimed title to the eastern sector on the basis of several categories of evidence: maps, records, documents, and reports, all allegedly substantiating their respective claims to traditional and historical occupation. In addition, there is a dispute on the legality and authenticity of the Simla Conference including the status of Tibet and the McMahon Line.

The question of the validity of the Simla Conference is extremely complex and no authority has yet been able to present a clearcut case with respect to this controversy. For example, the historical status of Tibet as part of China is advanced by Tieh-Tseng Li and opposed by H. E. Richardson.[11] In fact, assessments of the Sino-Indian disputes have all been colored by the various writers' ideological orientations. This is not based solely upon personal prejudice, since if examined independently, each country does present a very convincing case.

In practical politics, China presses her claims in the eastern sector only to obtain Indian recognition of her claim to Aksai Chin in the western sector. The fact that China withdrew all her forces from all areas after clashes in 1962, except her forces in Aksai Chin, indicates that she could be induced to recognize the Indian claim in the NEFA and middle sector in exchange for acknowledged title to the western sector.

Sino-Soviet Disputes

China and the Soviet Union share a common border in three distinct sectors: 1,850 miles in the inner-Asia zone; 2,700 miles in the Mongolian sector; and 2,300 miles in the far eastern sector.[12] Many of the boundaries negotiated in the early days of the Manchu empire were never formally accepted by the modern Chinese.

After the establishment of the People's Republic in 1949, the territorial questions were not formally raised with Stalin. Mao Tse-tung however, attempted to discuss the status of Outer Mongolia with Soviet leaders in 1954; but he dropped it after receiving no response. Chou En-lai privately raised the territorial issue with Khrushchev in January 1957, but again without success. Finally, after the withdrawal of Soviet technicians from China, and immediately following the attack by Khrushchev on the Chinese Communist Party in 1960, troubles began along the Sino-Soviet borders. The Chinese charged that Soviet leaders used their "organs and personnel in Sinkiang, China, to carry out large-scale subversive activities in the Ili region and enticed and coerced several tens of thousands of Chinese citizens into going into the Soviet Union."[13]

As Sino-Soviet relations worsened because of increasing ideological, economic, and political differences, the tempo of Chinese attacks on the Russians increased with a nationalistic flavor, citing modern revisionism, phoney Communism and finally soviet socialist imperialism.[14]

After repeated failures of Sino-Soviet negotiations, more than 400 military border skirmishes occurred between the two countries in 1969. The largest clashes occurred in March 1969 in conflict over Chenpao Island (Russia's Damansky Island in the Ussuri River). According to a Chinese diplomatic note, from March 29 to 31 May 1969, 57 sorties were executed by the Soviet air force and bombers, fighters, and reconnaissance planes ranged into Chinese territory, some to a depth of over 60 kilometers.[15]

In the same month as the Chenpao Island clashes, the *New York Times* of 9 March 1969 declared that the Soviet defense ministry newspaper had published a warning that "military force would be used if necessary." In broadcasts monitored in London the Soviet Union was overheard to issue two direct threats to use nuclear missile force against China.[16]

At the same time, Soviet leaders began to propose a new Asian Security System to contain China. At the closing session of the International Conference of the Communist Parties in Moscow on 7 June 1969, Brezhnev stated that "We are of the opinion that the course of events [in China indicates] putting on the agenda the task of creating a system of collective security in Asia."[17]

Brezhnev's proposal was, in fact, foreshadowed by Averell Harriman, who was then chief U.S. delegate in the Vietnam negotiations. Six months earlier (on 26 January 1969), Harriman informed newsmen in Paris that Russia wanted to see a peaceful, neutral Southeast Asia that would check a "Chinese advance to the south."[18]

The *Times* of London, in a news item from New Delhi entitled "Soviet plan to encircle China" suggested that:

...the Russians will not encourage new military pacts in
the region, but hope to undermine China's dominating position
by sponsoring an ambitious plan for regional economic alliances.
However, the Soviet Union is prepared to step into America's role to contain China militarily by arming Asian countries
on a bilateral basis. This is the essence of the Indian government's
understanding of Russia's future policy in Asia, according to
recent clarifications received from Moscow.[19]

In response to these potential threats, China began to instigate
massive demonstrations against the U.S.S.R., and mobilized the Chinese
armed forces in preparation for war. At the same time, the Chinese
government issued a policy statement on 24 May 1969, which included
a call for "peaceful negotiations and against the resort to use force."[20]

On 20 October 1969, for the first time in several years, formal
negotiation on boundary questions reopened in Peking. Chinese dele-
gations, headed by Chiao Kuan-hua and Chai Cheng-wen, met the
Soviet delegation chaired by V. V. Kuznetsov and V. A. Matrosov. The
long negotiation continued until 1970 without reaching any agreement.
The Soviet side continued to insist upon upholding their government's
position as expressed in 1964:

...having taken shape many generations ago, the frontier
between the Soviet Union and China reflected, and continues to
reflect, the actual population of lands by the peoples of these two
states, along natural demarcation lines—mountains and rivers.
Throughout its length this frontier is clearly and precisely determined by treaties, protocols and maps.[21]

When the news of U.S. invasion of Cambodia reached Peking in
1970, the Chinese government decided to temporarily shelve the issue
of border disputes with the Soviet Union. At the same time, normal
diplomatic relations resumed between the two countries.

THE FUTURE STATUS OF TAIWAN

Although the Chinese knew of Taiwan in the seventh century,
large scale settlement by the Chinese did not begin until well into the
seventeenth century. In 1624, the Dutch established a trading station
there and imposed taxes on both the inhabitants and exported items.
Two years later, the Spaniards landed at Keelung, but they were driven
out by the Dutch in 1641.

In 1661, Cheng Cheng-kung (or Koxinga) expelled the Dutch, and
established a Ming government in exile from the Manchus, new rulers
of China. The Manchus conquered the island in 1683, and the following year the island was made a prefecture of China's Fukien province.

When Taiwan was ceded to Japan after the Sino-Japanese War

of 1894, the Chinese inhabitants objected and declared a republic, which the Japanese had to subdue by force. The Japanese turned the island into an important military and naval base. They used the island as a source of foodstuffs and raw materials, and endowed the island residents with standards of economic development and education much in advance of those on the mainland.

As a result of the Japanese surrender after World War II, Taiwan was returned to the Chinese on 25 October 1945. Two years later, a revolt against Nationalist rulers in Taiwan broke out on 28 February 1947, and was quickly and firmly suppressed. As the Communists established a new People's Republic on the mainland, the Nationalist government moved to Taipei in December 1949 and about a million former mainlanders fled to the island. After the outbreak of the Korean War, President Harry S. Truman, on 5 January 1950, ordered the U.S. Seventh Fleet to prevent any Chinese Communist attack on the island.

On 28 June 1950, Chou En-lai, acting as China's foreign minister, declared that "On behalf of the Central People's Government of the People's Republic of China, I declare that, no matter what obstructive action U.S. imperialists may take, the fact that Taiwan is part of China will remain unchanged forever."[22]

More than twenty years later, Chou En-lai, now premier of China, in an official interview with James Reston of the *New York Times* said:

> We have stated very clearly that should a state of two Chinas or one China, one Taiwan appear in the United Nations, or a similar absurd state of affairs take place in the United Nations designed to separate Taiwan from China to create a so-called independent Taiwan, we will firmly oppose it and under these circumstances we will absolutely not go into the U.N. . . . We have waited already for more than 20 years and we can wait for another year. That doesn't matter. But there must be a just solution.[23]

Although the United Nations General Assembly on 25 October 1971 voted to expel Nationalist China, it is indeed not easy to define a just solution for the future status of Taiwan. As Robert A. Scalapino wrote,

> Taiwan represents a special problem because it is the symbol of a continuing "civil war," and because both the Chinese Communists and the Nationalists have viewed it as a pawn in a game where the stakes are much higher. At its roots, the problem of Taiwan rests upon psychological and political considerations involving the modern Chinese revolution, a revolution not yet finally determined with respect to course and scope. At the same time, it also involves the fate of some twelve million (fourteen million) people, very few of whom are interested in being involved with the fate of the Chinese revolution.[24]

The fate of 14 million people in Taiwan is both a moral and political question. Among the 14 million people, there are 12 million Taiwanese whose ancestors came to Taiwan before its cession to Japan in 1895. They, in turn, can be subdivided into three groups: the aborigines (Malayo-Polynesian stock), about 2 percent of the 1970 population; the Hokkien, first immigrants from China's Amoy in southern Fukien, about 75 percent; and the Hakka group who arrived after the Hokkien, about 13 percent. The remaining 10 percent of the total population are the latecomers who arrived in Taiwan with Chiang Kai-shek after the fall of the Nationalist regime in 1949.[25] All of them are now under the rule of a one-party government, the Kuomintang, headed by 83-year old President Chiang Kai-shek, and his son, Chiang Ching-kuo, the vice-premier.

Under Kuomintang rule, the island-state is under a general state of siege, declared by the Nationalists on 19 May 1949, because of the national emergency created by the continuation of the Chinese civil war with the Communists. The Kuomintang government maintains that it is the sole legitimate government of all of China and the proclamation of the state of siege automatically carried into operation the whole body of martial law promulgated by the Kuomintang government. There is no political freedom on the island, and since 1947, American official contact has been almost exclusively with mainlanders or safe Taiwanese, who are virtually under mainlander control. For this reason, we lack even the minimal basis of knowledge with respect to the wishes of the 12 or 14 million people.[26]

In addition, polls recently taken by non-Chinese are equally unreliable. For example, one survey of student attitudes in 1970 stated that "except for the small aboriginal population, the people of Taiwan are essentially Chinese in their social and political outlooks as well as in their ancestry."[27] And a 1971 *New York Times* survey suggested that "the gulf of mistrust between Taiwanese and mainlanders is so wide that many feel it cannot be bridged within one generation."[28]

Furthermore, the politics of Taiwan has in fact been part of the U.S. political game for more than two decades. For one thing, there is the mutual security pact for the defense of Taiwan, ratified by the U.S. Senate on 9 February 1955 and signed by President Eisenhower three days later. Since 1955, U.S. military and intelligence apparatus have developed a vested interest in Chiang Kai-shek's government. According to a study made by Edward Friedman, for example,

> A CIA air arm, Air America, has been intimately related to Taiwan. Arms were run in 1956 to Khamba rebels in Tibet through Burma. Dissidents against Sukarno in 1958 were also supplied from Taiwan. In 1957, special-forces advisers moved into Taiwan. This Green Beret-CIA team has trained Chiang's troops in such things as sabotage and subversion. In 1959, they began a

decade of joint exercises called Exercise Forward Thrust, which included dropping special forces in mountainous terrain and linking up with insurgent forces already operating there.... Intelligence operatives also use Taiwan for U-2 flights over China, as well as other types of surveillance.... In July, 1969, special offensive operation of Taiwan's National Salvation Force went into China's Min River, which reportedly destroyed at least three Chinese ships.[29]

This does not mention the billions of dollars invested or spent on the island by the United States.[30]

There is one additional variable with respect to the future status of Taiwan, and it is evidenced by Japan's economic involvement on the island. From 1965 to 1970, Japan has an accumulative trade surplus with Taiwan of $1.6 billion. Total Japanese investments in Taiwan have amounted to $90 million, of which a full $80 million has flowed in during the last six years, from 1965 to 1971. The proportion of Japanese capital in Taiwan's foreign investment rose from 5.9 percent in 1965 to 26.1 percent in 1970, while the U.S. investments slid from 88.5 percent to 62.1 percent. More significantly, Japanese investments are of a kind that would bind Taiwan's economy increasingly to Japan's import-export needs.[31]

Japan's economic interest in Taiwan is further evidenced by the loans granted to the Nationalist government since 1965, which amount to $150 million.[32] The last loan agreement was signed in August 1971, and the Japanese government promised new loans of $22.4 million to be utilized over a period ending in 1976. The August agreement brought the total of Japan's loan commitments yet to be implemented in 1971 to $64.3 million.[33]

In addition to these complex issues, public opinion in the U.S. is still hostile to the mainland Chinese and many factions will definitely oppose any return of Taiwan to the Communist Chinese government.[34]

In the last analysis, the future of Taiwan is still in hands of the Chinese. At the moment, no compromise will be possible for a *modus vivendi* because of the strong oppositions of China's two aging leaders: Chiang Kai-shek and Mao Tse-tung. However, one remarkable characteristic of the Chinese mentality is its power of adaptation. With the vision of the future, the modern Chinese will never go back to the fetters of the past. After all, the stream of Maoism has been broad enough to encompass not only the current of change, both gradual and rapid, but also the current of continuity, always latent and often active.

Suggested Readings

AIRD, JOHN S. *The Size, Composition and Growth of the Population of Mainland China.* Washington, D.C.: Bureau of the Census, 1961.

Association of the Bar of the City of New York. *The International Position of Communist China.* Dobbs Ferry: Oceana Publications, 1965.

BARNETT, A. DOAK. *A New U.S. Policy Towards China*. Washington, D.C.: Brookings Institution, 1971.

BLUM, ROBERT. *The U.S. and China in World Affairs*. New York: Council on Foreign Relations, 1966.

CHAI, WINBERG. *The Foreign Relations of the People's Republic of China: Views from Inside*. New York: G. P. Putnam's Sons, 1972.

CHEN, LUNG-CHU, and LASSWELL, HAROLD. *Formosa, China and the United Nations*. New York: St. Martin's Press, 1967.

COHEN, JEROME ALAN; FRIEDMAN, EDWARD; HINTON, HAROLD C.; and WHITING, ALLEN S. *Taiwan and American Policy*. New York: Praeger Publishers, 1971.

COHEN, WARREN I. *America's Response to China*. New York: John Wiley & Sons, 1971.

DOOLIN, DENNIS J. *Territorial Claims in the Sino-Soviet Conflicts*. Palo Alto: Hoover Institution, 1965.

ECKSTEIN, ALEXANDER, ed. *China Trade Prospects and U.S. Policy*. New York: Praeger Publishers, 1971.

Far Eastern Economic Review 1972 Yearbook. Hong Kong, December 1971.

GITTINGS, JOHN. *Survey of Sino-Soviet Disputes*. New York: Oxford University Press, 1968.

GODDARD, W. G. *Formosa: A Study in Chinese History*. East Lansing: Michigan State University, 1966.

JACKSON, W. A. DOUGLAS. *The Russo-Chinese Borderlands*. 2d ed. Princeton: D. Van Nostrand Searchlight Books, 1968.

JACOBY, NEIL H. *U.S. Aid to Taiwan: A Study of Foreign Aid, Self-Help and Development*. New York: Praeger Publishers, 1966.

LAMB, ALASTAIR. *The McMahon Line*. 2 vols. London: Routledge and Kegan Paul, 1966.

————. *The China-India Border*. New York: Oxford University Press, 1964.

MAXWELL, NEVILLE. "China and India: The Un-negotiated Dispute." *China Quarterly* no. 43 (July/September 1970), pp. 47–80.

MENDEL, DOUGLAS. *The Politics of Formosan Nationalism*. Berkeley: University of California Press, 1970.

RUSSELL, MAUD. *The Sino-Soviet Ussuri River Border Clash*. New York: Far Eastern Reporter, 1969.

SALISBURY, HARRISON E. *War Between Russia and China*. New York: Bantam Books, 1970.

STEELE, A. T. *The American People and China*. New York: McGraw-Hill, 1966.

U.S., Congress. House, Committee on Foreign Affairs. *United States China Relations: A Strategy for the Future:* Hearings before the subcommittee on Asian and Pacific Affairs, 91st Cong., 2d sess., 1970.

U.S. Congress. Senate Committee on Foreign Relations. *United States Security Agreements and Commitments Abroad-Republic of China*: Hearings before the Subcommittee on United States Security Agreements and Commitments Abroad, 91st Cong. 2d sess. Part 4, November 1969 and May 1970.

ZAGONIA, DONALD S. *The Sino-Soviet Conflict, 1956–1961*. Princeton: Princeton University Press, 1962.

NOTES

Notes for Chapter One

1. Yi-Fu Tuan, *The World's Landscapes: China* (Chicago: Aldine Publishing Co., 1969), p. 197. In addition to Mr. Tuan's work, the author made extensive use of studies made by the U.S. government, including maps of China, published in *Current Scene*; and Communist China's text on China's geography, published in Peking.
2. "The Geography of Mainland China: A Concise Sketch," *Current Scene* 7, no. 17 (September 1969): 5; map is by the geographer of the U.S. Department of State.
3. Tables compiled by editors of *Current Scene* (September 1969), p. 3.
4. Shan-yu Yao, "The Chronological and Seasonal Distribution of Floods and Droughts in Chinese History, 206 B.C.–A.D. 1911," *Harvard Journal of Asiatic Studies* 7 (1942): 275.
5. Tuan, *World's Landscapes*, p. 197.
6. *Peking Review*, 15 October 1971, pp. 12–13.
7. George B. Cressey, *Asia's Land and People* (New York: McGraw-Hill Book Co., 1963), chapters 4–10.
8. Tuan, *World's Landscapes*, pp. 195–96.
9. Jesse H. Wheeler, Jr., J. Trenton Kostbade, and Richard S. Thoman, *Regional Geography of the World* (New York: Holt, Rinehart and Winston, 1969), chapter 20.
10. Jen Yu-ti, *A Concise Geography of China* (Peking: Foreign Language Press, 1964), pp. 55–59.
11. *Current Scene*, "Geography," p. 14.
12. *Peking Review*, 26 May 1959, p. 9.
13. U.S. Department of State Publications, No. 8499 (December 1969), p. 5.
14. *Issues and Studies* (November 1968), pp. 22–23.

Notes for Chapter Two

1. Sir Frederick Whyte, *China and Foreign Powers* (New York: Oxford University Press, 1927), p. 39. For a detailed study *see also* H. H. Morse, *The International Relations of the Chinese Empire*, 3 vols. (London: Longmans Green, 1918).
2. E. H. Parker, *China: Her History, Diplomacy, and Commerce* (London: John Murray, 1901), pp. 113–15.
3. *See* John King Fairbank, Edwin O. Reischauer, and Albert M. Craig, *East Asia: The Modern Transformation* (Boston: Houghton Mifflin, 1965), chapter 2.
4. Ibid., p. 131.

5. Parker, *China: Her History*, p. 161.

6. Cf. Fairbank, et al., *East Asia*, p. 276. *See also* Arthur Waley, *Opium War Through Chinese Eyes* (London: Allen and Unwin, 1958).

7. Adapted from Paul M. A. Linebarger, Djang Chu, and Ardath W. Burks, *Far Eastern Governments and Politics* (Princeton: D. Van Nostrand Co., 1956), p. 64. For a guide to material and research on the Manchu administration, *see* John King Fairbank, *Ch'ing Documents: An Introductory Syllabus*, 2 vols. Cambridge, Mass.: Harvard University Press, 1970).

8. For an evaluation of peasant uprising in Chinese history, *see* James P. Harrison, *The Communists and Chinese Peasant Rebellion* (New York: Atheneum, 1969).

9. *See* Franz Michael, with Chung-Li Chang, *The Taiping Rebellion, History and Documents*, 3 vols. (Seattle: University of Washington Press, 1967).

10. For the background on the Western effort to stimulate reform, *see* Jonathan Spence, *To Change China: Western Advisors to China 1620–1960* (Boston: Little, Brown, 1969).

11. *See* Meribeth E. Cameron, *The Reform Movement in China, 1898–1912* (Palo Alto: Stanford University Press, 1931) and Winberg Chai, *The Political Thought of K'ang Yu-Wei* (Ph.D. diss., New York University, 1968) and Jung-pang Lo, *K'ang Yu-Wei* (Tucson: University of Arizona Press, 1967).

12. *See* Leng Shao-Chuan and Norman D. Palmer, *Sun Yat-sen and Communism* (New York: Praeger Publishers, 1960) and Jack Gray, ed., *Modern China's Search for a Political Form* (New York: Oxford University Press, 1969).

13. *See* Paul Linebarger, *The Political Doctrine of Sun Yat-sen* (Princeton: D. Van Nostrand, 1956), and Milton J. T. Shieh, *The Kuomintang: Selected Historical Documents 1894–1969* (New York: St. John's University Press, 1970).

14. *See* Robert C. North, *Kuomintang and Chinese Communist Elites*, 2d ed. (Palo Alto: Stanford University Press, 1963).

15. *See* Maurice Meisner, *Li Ta-Chao and the Origins of Chinese Communism* (Cambridge, Mass.: Harvard University Press, 1967).

16. *See* Conrad Brandt, Benjamin Schwartz, and John King Fairbank, *A Documentary History of Chinese Communism* (Cambridge, Mass.: Harvard University Press, 1952).

17. Ibid., p. 52.

18. *See* Robert C. North, *Moscow and Chinese Communism*, 2d ed. (Palo Alto: Stanford University Press, 1963).

19. *See* Brandt, et al., *Documentary History*, p. 73.

Notes for Chapter Three

1. Robert J. Lifton, *Revolutionary Immortality: Mao Tse-tung and the Chinese Culture Revolution* (New York: Random House, 1968), p. 97.

2. *Peking Review* 2 July 1971, p. 19.

3. Conrad Brandt, et al., *A Documentary History of Chinese Communism* (Cambridge, Mass.: Harvard University Press, 1952), p. 122.

4. The Congress attacked Ch'en for his conciliatory policy toward the Wuhan KMT and reprimanded Ch'ü for his "ill prepared, ill directed Putschism." *See* Warren Kuo, *Analytical History of Chinese Communist Party* (Taipei: 1968), chapter 3.

5. This constitution was later revised at the Seventh Congress in April 1945.

6. *See* "From the First to the Seventh National Congress of the CCP," *People's China*, no. 18 (16 September 1956).

7. Hsiang was later executed by the Nanking government.

8. Li Li-san, who insisted on following the Comintern's directives, directed Party affairs from 1928 to 1930, when he was purged for "leftist deviationism" and recalled to Moscow. Then the Central Committee was under the control of "twenty-eight quasi-Bolsheviks," headed by Wang Mong (Ch'en Shao-yu) and included Liu Shao-chi. They continued to advocate an urban proletarian revolution and ordered general strikes and uprisings in China. *See* Tso-liang Hsiao, *Power Relations Within the Chinese Communist Movement, 1930–34* (Seattle: University of Washington Press, 1961), chapters 3 and 4.

9. At the August 7 Conference, Mao was sent to Hunan to lead the Autumn Harvest Insurrection.

10. As Mao said to Edgar Snow, he had been expelled three times from the Central Committee and received eight warnings before he rose to power. Edgar Snow, *Red Star Over China*, new ed. (New York: Grove Press, 1961), p. 169.

11. At the time of this First Congress of Soviets, the territorial bases of the CCP comprised about 300 counties, scattered through 11 of the 18 provinces of China. The total population of soviet areas, according to Communist estimates, was over 60 million. Of these areas, the most important was the Central Soviet Area, with a total population of 15 million and a territorial extent of 45 to 50 counties. For a critical analysis, *see* Benjamin I. Schwartz, *Chinese Communism and the Rise of Mao* (Cambridge, Mass.: Harvard University Press, 1951), pp. 184–85.

12. *See* report of Mao Tse-tung, "On Tactics of Fighting Japanese Imperialism," (27 December 1935), quoted in *Essential Works of Chinese Communism*, ed. Winberg Chai (New York: Bantam Books, 1969), Document 5.

13. *See* Boyd Compton, *Mao's China: Party Reform Documents, 1942–44* (Seattle: University of Washington Press, 1966), pp. xxi–xxii.

14. Its members included Shen Chun-yu (chief justice of the Supreme Court before the Cultural Revolution) and Shih Liang (minister of justice before the Cultural Revolution).

15. Details of the political negotiations carried on in Sian still remain unknown.

16. In August 1938, the KMT government, still in Hankow, outlawed the Communist mass organizations. *See* Kuo, *Analytical History*.

17. The most important of these missions were those of Henry Wallace (U.S. vice-president) in May 1944 and General Patrick Hurley, personal representative of President Roosevelt, in June 1944. *See* Tang Tsou, *America's Failure in China, 1941–50* (Chicago: University of Chicago Press, 1963), chapter 5.

18. However, on 22 August 1945, General Hurley brought Mao Tse-tung from Yenan to Chungking, thus bringing the KMT and CCP to a consultative conference which became the foundation for General George Marshall's work of mediation. *See* Tang Tsou, *America's Failure*, part 3.

19. According to the report at the Seventh National Party Congress at Yenan on 23 April 1945, the People's Liberation Army numbered

910,000 men, plus a militia of 2.25 million. *See* Samuel B. Griffith II, *The Chinese People's Liberation Army* (New York: McGraw-Hill, 1967), p. 74.

20. Boyd Compton's interpretation of *cheng-feng* has two characterisics: "purge; and intensive indoctrination and education in the principles of Mao's communism." *See* Compton, *Mao's China*, p. xxxix.

21. *Issues and Studies* 17, no. 10 (July 1971): 36–37.

22. Jerome Ch'en, *Mao and the Chinese Revolution* (New York: Oxford University Press, 1965), p. 3.

23. Edgar Snow, *Red Star*, p. 153.

24. V. Holubnychy, "Mao Tse-tung's Materialistic Dialectics," *China Quarterly*, no. 19 (July/September 1964), p. 16.

25. R. F. Price, *Education in Communist China* (New York: Praeger Publishers, 1970), p. 16.

26. Quoted in *Essential Works*, ed. Chai, Documents 6 and 7.

27. *Hongqi (Red Flag)* no. 5 (1971).

28. Mao Tse-tung, "On the Correct Handling of Contradiction Among the People" (February 1957), quoted in *Essential Works*, ed. Chai, Document 22.

29. Sidney Hook, *From Hegel to Marx* (Ann Arbor: University of Michigan Press, 1962), p. 51.

30. Lifton, *Revolutionary Immortality*, pp. 99–126.

31. Joseph J. Spengler, "Theory, Ideology, Non-Economic Values, and Politico-Economic Development," in *Tradition, Values and Socio-Economic Development*, ed. Ralph Braibanti (Durham, N.C.: Duke University Press, 1961), p. 4.

32. Dennis M. Ray, "Traditionalism and the Idea of Progress: A Case for Ideological Mobilization in Communist China." (Paper read at Western Conference of Association of Asian Studies, San Diego, October 29, 1971.)

33. Mao Tse-tung, *Selected Works of Mao Tse-tung*, vol. I, (Peking: Foreign Language Press, 1965), p. 41.

34. Ibid., 2:339–82; quoted in Chai, *Essential Works*, Document 12.

35. Ibid., pp. 371–82.

36. John Wilson Lewis, *Leadership in Communist China* (Ithaca: Cornell University Press, 1963), p. 70.

37. Mao, *Selected Works*, vol. 3, quoted in Chai, *Essential Works*, Document 15.

38. "Document of the National Conference of the Communist Party of China," in *Essential Works*, Chai, Document 23.

39. Ibid.

40. Ch'en, *Mao*, p. 165.

41. Quoted in H. Franz Schurmann, "Organizational Contrasts between Communist China and the Soviet Union," in *Unity and Contradiction*, ed. Kurt London (New York: Praeger Publishers, 1962).

42. *Jen Ming Shouts'e 1957*, p. 111.

43. *Current Background*, no. 324, p. 4.

44. Chu-yuan Cheng, "Power Struggle in Red China," *Asian Survey* 6, no. 9 (September 1966).

45. "Resolution of the Eighth Plenary Session of Eighth Central Committee of Communist Party of China Concerning the Anti-Party Clique Headed by P'eng Teh-huai," quoted in *Peking Review*, 18 August 1967.

46. Ibid, p. 9.

47. Philip Bridgham, "Factionalism in the Central Committee," in *Party Leadership and Revoluionary Power*, ed. John Wilson Lewis (New York: Oxford University Press, 1971), p. 213.
48. Ibid., p. 216; *see also* David A. Charles, "The Dismissal of Marshal P'eng Teh-huai," *China Quarterly*, no. 8 (October/December 1961).
49. Cheng, "Power Struggle."
50. Gene T. Hsiao, "The Background and Development of the Proletarian Cultural Revolution," *Asian Survey* 7, no. 6 (June 1967): 398.
51. Yao Wen-yuan wrote the first major critical analysis of Wu Han's play which was published in *Wen Wei Pao* (Shanghai). *See* A. Jackson-Thomas, K. Janaka, and A. Manheim, "How It All Started in Peking University," *Eastern Horizon* 6, no. 5 (May 1967): 22–23.
52. Cheng, "Power Struggle."
53. Winberg Chai, "China's Chief of State," *New York Times*, 3 May, 1959.
54. *Ming Pao* (August 18–20, 1967), reprinted in *Chung-chi New Asia Associated Students Weekly* (Hong Kong: 17 October 1967).
55. Cheng, "Power Struggle," p. 478.
56. Ibid., pp. 471–74.
57. *Central Daily News* (Taipei), 29 December 1966.
58. Hsiao, *Proletarian Cultural Revolution*, pp. 398–400.
59. Uri Ra'anan, "Peking's Foreign Policy Debates, 1965–1966," in *China in Crisis*, vol. 2, ed. Tang Tsou (Chicago: University of Chicago Press, 1968), pp. 23–71.
60. C. K. Yang, "Cultural Revolution and Revisionism," in *China in Crisis*, vol. 1, ed. Ping-ti Ho and Tang Tsou (Chicago: University of Chicago Press, 1968), p. 503.

Notes for Chapter Four

1. Ilpyong J. Kim, "Mass Mobilization Policies and Techniques Developed in the Period of the Chinese Soviet Republic," in *Chinese Communist Politics in Action*, ed. A. Doak Barnett (Seattle: University of Washington Press, 1969), pp. 78–98.
2. *See* "Decision of the CCP Central Committee Concerning the Great Proletarian Cultural Revolution," (8 August 1966), quoted in *Essential Works of Chinese Communism*, ed. Winberg Chai (New York: Bantam Books, 1972), Document 29.
3. Etienne Balazas, *Chinese Civilization and Bureaucracy: Variation on a Theme* (New Haven: Yale University Press, 1964), p. 169.
4. Jan S. Prybyla, "Communist China's Strategy of Economic Development: 1961–66," *Asian Survey* (October 1966), p. 589.
5. Ibid., p. 588.
6. Ibid., pp. 590–95.
7. Quoted in *The Great Socialist Cultural Revolution in China (1)* (Peking: Foreign Language Press, 1960).
8. Richard Baum and Frederick C. Teiwes, *Ssu-ch'ing: The Socialist Education Movement of 1962–66*, University of California Center for China Studies Research Monographs no. 2, (Berkeley, 1968), pp. 47–48.
9. Prybyla, "China's Strategy," pp. 593–94.
10. George P. Jan, "Radio Propaganda in Chinese Villages," *Asian Survey* (May 1967), pp. 305–15.
11. Quoted in *The Great Socialist Cultural Revolution in China (5)* (Peking: Foreign Language Press, 1966).

12. Ibid.
13. *Red Flag*, no. 16 (1964), p. 8.
14. *Kuang-ming Daily*, 25 December 1964.
15. Quoted in *The Great Socialist Cultural Revolution in China (I)*, p. 18.
16. Ibid.
17. *Kuang-ming Daily*, 25 December 1964.
18. Ibid.
19. The opera was adopted from the famous Chinese novel *Hsi Yu Chi* written by Wu Cheng-an (1500–1582). It was based on Hsuan Tsang's (602–64) pilgrimage to the kingdom of Magadha in India. Principal characters include Hsuan Tsang and his three pupils—the Monkey, Pigsy, and Sandy. For an excerpt of the novel, *see* Ch'u Chai and Winberg Chai, eds., *A Treasury of Chinese Literature* (New York: Appleton–Century, 1965), chapter 8.
20. Translated by Michael Bullock and Jerome Ch'en. *See* Jerome Ch'en, *Mao and the Chinese Revolution* (New York: Oxford University Press, 1965), p. 355.
21. For a study of Mao Tun and some of his representative writings, *see* Chai and Chai, *A Treasury*, chapter 9.
22. *Chinese Literature*, no. 5 (Peking, May 1966), p. 13.
23. Mao's wife, Chiang Ching indirectly admitted that the Maoists did not constitute a majority within the Central Committee. *See Peking Review*, 9 December, 1966, p. 9.
24. A list including several hundred prominent Party leaders was published by Chinese newspapers in November 1966. These men were called "Monsters and Demons" or "Black Gangsters." *See, The Great Cultural Revolution in China* (Hong Kong: Asia Research Center, 1967), pp. 116–93.
25. James Chieh Hsiung, *Ideology and Practice: The Evolution of Chinese Communism* (New York: Praeger Publishers, 1970), chapters 12–14.
26. According to the editor of *Current Scene*, Mao employed his enormous personal prestige and packed the Eleventh Plenum with outsiders "in order to overcome the resistance of what may have been a majority within Party leadership councils" and rammed through the revolutionary decisions on the Cultural Revolution. Quoted in Tang Tsou, "The Cultural Revolution," *Chicago Today* 4, no. 2 (Spring 1967): 25.
27. *See* note 2.
28. Ibid.
29. *Studies on Chinese Communism I* (Taipei: March 1967): 1.
30. Winberg Chai, "The Reorganization of the Chinese Communist Party, 1966–1968," *Asian Survey* (November 1968), p. 903; cf. Donald W. Klein, "The State Council and the Cultural Revolution," *China Quarterly*, no. 35 (July/September 1968).
31. Cf. Peter Grose' analysis, the *New York Times*, 25 June 1968.
32. *The Diary of the Cultural Revolution, October 1966–April 1967* (Tokyo: *Asahi Evening News*, 1967), p. 12.
33. *Red Flag (Hung Chi)* was interrupted in its publication during the 1967–68 Cultural Revolution. *See, Chinese Communist Affairs: Facts and Features* 1, no. 14 (1 May 1968): 15–16.
34. In the most famous of all his articles, "On Three-family Village," he initiated the attack on Teng To, Wu Han, and Liao Mo-sha. *See, The Great Socialist Cultural Revolution in China (I)*.
35. *Studies on Chinese Communism* 1, no. 12 (December 1967): 2.

36. Radio Foochow, 7 January 1967.
37. New China News Agency, 9 September 1968.
38. *People's Daily*, 26 April 1957.
39. New China News Agency, 18 August 1966.
40. John Israel, "The Red Guards in Historical Perspective," *China Quarterly*, no. 30 (April/June 1967), pp. 1–32.
41. C. T. Hu, "The Chinese University—Target of the Cultural Revolution," *Saturday Review*, 9 August 1967.
42. According to *Asahi* correspondent Matsuno Tanio, a small group of seven "revolutionary" Peking University students received Mao Tsetung's secret order to attack their president, Lu Ping, in September 1965. *See, Asahi Journal*, 2 October 1966.
43. For an eyewitness account, *see* A. Jackson-Thomas, et al., "How It All Started in Peking University," *Eastern Horizon* 6, no. 5 (Hong Kong: May 1967): 19–21.
44. The work-team concept had been used during the early 1964 rectification campaign by the Party to aid local organizations.
45. Jackson-Thomas "It All Started," p. 26.
46. Ibid., p. 27; another eyewitness account reported that Liu Shao-chi's wife was also a member of the Peking Municipal Committee's work-team, who had taken up residence on the campus. *See* "Eyewitness of the Cultural Revolution by a Foreign Expert," *China Quarterly*, 28 (October/December 1966), p. 3.
47. Red Guard in Chinese means "red protectors of the soldiers" (Hung wei-ping or Ch'ih wei-tui). In the earlier years, these armed peasants continued to take part in farm labor but were ready at all times to protect the Red soldiers. The organization may be traced to the Russian Revolution of 1917 when it was known as "Krasnaya Gvardia." *See* Edgard Snow, *Red Star Over China* (New York: Grove Press, 1961, p. 504; *see also, Christian Science Monitor*, 19 September 1966.
48. *Asahi Journal*, 16 October 1966.
49. A Chinese classic, *Pai-t'ou Hsien-hua* (Senile Chattering) published around 1645, described "chuang-chiang" as "some people in the capital gang together by fives or tens and swagger through the streets." *See* Hao Chai, *T'ungsu Pien (Notes on Popular Literature)* (Shanghai: Commercial Press, 1937), p. 90; quoted in *The Great Proletarian Cultural Revolution: A Terminological Study*, H. C. Chuang (Berkeley: University of California Center for Chinese Studies, August 1967), p. 12.
50. Professor Latourette wrote, "the last of the Ming to rule in Peking made desperate but vain efforts to retrieve the declining fortunes of his house.... The death blow was a rebellion led by Li Tzu-cheng, son of a village headman in Shenshi. Famine and taxation had driven Li, as they have many another Chinese, to turn brigand. He proved an able general and disciplinarian, in 1642 captured K'aifeng, made himself master of Shensi, and in 1644 proclaimed himself emperor of a new dynasty. In the latter year he marched upon Peking and took it. The Ming emperor, in despair, hung himself as the city fell." Kenneth Scott Latourette, *The Chinese: Their History and Culture*, 4th ed. rev. (New York: Macmillan, 1964), pp. 231–32.
51. *Asahi Journal*, 9 January 1967.
52. Keesing's Research Report, *The Cultural Revolution in China* (New York: Charles Scribner's Sons, 1967), pp. 21–22.
53. *The Diary*, p. 4.

54. From 1966 to 1967, the Red Guard published several thousands of "newspapers"; for a complete list *see,* the Contemporary China Research Institute release (Hong Kong), 1968–69.
55. Quoted in Stephen Pan and Raymond J. de Jaegher, *Peking's Red Guards* (New York: Twin Circle, 1968), pp. 134–35.
56. *The Diary.*
57. John King Fairbank, et al., *East Asia: The Modern Transformation* (Boston: Houghton Mifflin, 1965), p. 666.
58. *Peking Review,* 11 August 1967, p. 5.
59. *See* Chuang, *Proletarian Cultural Revolution.*
60. *Peking Review,* 3 January 1968, p. 14.
61. Mao Tse-tung, *Serve the People* (Peking: Foreign Language Press, 1966), pp. 1–4.
62. Ibid., pp. 5–7.
63. Mao Tse-tung, *The Foolish Old Man Who Removed the Mountains* (Peking: Foreign Language Press, 1966), p. 3.
64. Richard W. Wilson and Amy A. Wilson, "The Red Guards and the World Student Movement," *China Quarterly,* no. 42 (April/June 1970), p. 104.

Notes for Chapter Five

1. R. F. Price, *Education in Communist China* (New York: Praeger Publishers, 1970), p. 8.
2. David Apter, *The Politics of Modernization* (Chicago: University of Chicago Press, 1965), p. 328.
3. Kai-yu Hsu, *Chou En-lai: China's Gray Eminence* (Garden City: Doubleday and Co., 1968), p. 224.
4. For Chou's role in the May 4 Movement, *see* Chou Tse-tsung, *The May Fourth Movement* (Cambridge, Mass.: Harvard University Press, 1960), pp. 129–30.
5. *People's Daily,* 1 May 1966.
6. *People's Daily,* 18 June 1966.
7. Thomas W. Robinson, "The Wuhan Incident: Local Strife and Provincial Rebellion during the Cultural Revolution," *China Quarterly,* no. 47 (July/September, 1971), pp. 413-38.
8. Thomas W. Robinson, "Chou En-lai's Political Style: Comparison with Mao Tse-tung and Lin Piao," *Asian Survey* (December 1970), pp. 1101–16.
9. *New York Times,* 10 August 1971.
10. Quoted in Hsu, *Chou En-lai,* p. 228.
11. *Peking Review,* 3 January 1968, pp. 10–13.
12. *Wen Hui Pao* (Shanghai), 12 January 1968.
13. *Liberation Army Daily,* 28 January 1968.
14. Richard Baum, "China: Year of the Mangoes," *Asian Survey* (January 1969): 11.
15. Ibid., p. 8.
16. *Issues and Studies* 3, no. 1 (October 1971): 3.
17. Donald W. Klein and Lois B. Hager, "The Ninth Central Committee," *China Quarterly,* no. 45 (January/March 1971), p. 53.
18. *Current Scene* 9, no. 8 (7 August 1971); *see also, New York Times,* 28 June 1971.
19. *Far Eastern Economic Review 1971 Yearbook,* p. 132.

20. *Background on China,* B 71–36 (16 July 1971), p. 1.
21. Harry Harding, "China, Toward Revolutionary Pragmatism," *Asian Survey* (January 1971), pp. 51–67.
22. Philip L. Bridgham, "The Cultural Revolution and the New Political System in China" (paper delivered at the sixty-sixth annual meeting of American Political Science Association, Los Angeles, 8 September 1970). *See also* Harry Harding, *Maoist Theories of Policy-Making and Organization* (Santa Monica: Rand Corporation, 1969), pp. 1–39.
23. *Far Eastern Economic Review 1971 Yearbook,* p. 144.

Notes for Chapter Six

1.   Franz Schurmann, *Ideology and Organization in Communist China,* new ed. enl. (Berkeley: University of California Press, 1968), p. 115.
2.   *Current Scene* 9, no. 2 (7 February 1971): 2.
3.   Ping-ti Ho and Tang Tsou, eds. *China in Crisis,* vol. 1, book 1 (Chicago: University of Chicago Press, 1968), p. 347.
4.   Schurmann, *Ideology,* p. 110.
5.   John Wilson Lewis, *Leadership in Communist China* (Ithaca: Cornell University Press, 1963), chapters 4 and 5.
6.   *Constitution of the People's Republic of China,* in *Essential Works of Chinese Communism,* ed. Winberg Chai (New York: Bantam Books, 1971), Document 19.
7.   Tao-Tai Hsia, ed., *Guide to Selected Legal Sources of Mainland China* (Washington, D.C.: Library of Congress, 1967), p. 65.
8.   Schurmann, *Ideology,* pp. 173–75.
9.   Ibid., pp. 187–90.
10. Hsia, *Legal Sources,* p. 66.
11. *See* Winberg Chai, "Review of the 1970 Draft of the Revised Constitution of the People's Republic of China," *Comparative Communism* 4, nos. 1 and 2 (January/March 1971): 99–106.
12. Authoritative sources and interviews by the author.
13. Philip L. Bridgham, "The Cultural Revolution and the New Political System in China" (Paper delivered at the sixty-sixth Annual Meeting of APSA, American Political Science Association, Los Angeles, September 8–12, 1970).
14. William Whitson, "The Field Army in Chinese Communist Military Politics," *China Quarterly,* no. 37 (January/March, 1969).
15. *Chinese Communist Affairs,* no. 22 (21 August 1968): 3–9.
16. *Issues and Studies* (January 1968), pp. 7–19.
17. Whitson, "The Field Army," p. 2.
18. Cf., *Area Handbook for Communist,* (Washington, D.C.) DA Pam 550–60 (1967), p. 618.
19. U.S. Department of Army, *Communist China: A Strategic Survey,* DA Pam 20–67 (February 1966), p. 132.
20. Alice Langley Hsieh, "China's Nuclear Missile Programme: Regional or Intercontinental," *China Quarterly,* no. 47 (January/March 1971), pp. 85–99.
21. Mao Tse-tung, *Selected Works of Mao Tse-tung,* vol. 2 (Peking: Foreign Language Press, 1965), p. 224.
22. Ibid., 3:264.
23. *Peking Review,* 15 March 1968, p. 10.
24. Ibid.

25. Quoted in Winberg Chai, "The Reorganization of the Chinese Communist Party, 1966–1968," *Asian Survey* 8, no. 11 (November 1968): 908.
26. *Issues and Studies* (October 1971): 23–37.
27. Ibid.
28. A. Doak Barnett, *Cadres, Bureaucracy and Political Power in Communist China* (New York: Columbia University Press, 1967), p. 45.
29. Ezra V. Vogel, "The Regularization of Cadres," *China Quarterly*, no. 29 (January/March 1967), pp. 45–46.
30. Victor C. Funnell, "Bureaucracy and the Chinese Communist Party," *Current Scene* 9, no. 5 (7 May 1971): 1–14.
31. Rensselaer W. Lee, III, "The Hsia Fang System: Marxism and Modernization," *China Quarterly*, no. 28 (October/December 1966), p. 40; cf. T. A. Hsia, *A Terminological Study in the Hsia-Fang Movement*, University of California Center for Chinese Studies Monograph, no. 10 (Berkeley, 1968).
32. Dennis Ray, "Entrepreneurship in the Economic Thought" (Paper delivered at Berkeley Regional Seminar on Chinese Studies, November 13, 1971).
33. Lee, *Hsia Fang*, p. 52.
34. Dennis M. Ray stated that "it may be unwise to draw generalized conclusions from the temporary economic setbacks in the Great Leap Forward or the Cultural Revolution. In the long-run we may discover that even in their failures, they did much to prepare the Chinese people for industrial society. This may be especially true . . . of their leaders with a will to overcome the various obstacles to economic development." *See* Dennis M. Ray, "Traditionalism and the Idea of Progress: A Case for Ideological Mobilization in Communist China" (Paper delivered at Western Conference of Association of Asian Studies, San Diego, October 29, 1971).

Notes for Chapter Seven

1. Chu-yuan Cheng, *Communist China's Economy 1949–1926* (East Orange, N.J.: Seton Hall University Press, 1963), p. 4.
2. Cheng, *China's Economy*, p. 8.
3. *See* A. Doak Barnett, *China On the Eve of Communist Takeover* (New York: Praeger Publishers, 1965).
4. Yuan-li Wu, *The Economy of Communist China* (New York: Praeger Publishers, 1965), pp. 22–25.
5. *See* Nai-Ruenn Chen and Walter Galenson, *The Chinese Economy under Communism* (Chicago: Aldine Publishing Co., 1969).
6. Cheng, *China's Economy*, p. 86.
7. *The Constitution of the People's Republic of China* (1954), quoted in *Essential Works of Chinese Communism*, ed. Winberg Chai (Bantam Books: New York, 1972), Document 19.
8. Dwight H. Perkins, "Mao Tse-tung's Goals and China's Economic Performance," *Current Scene* 9, no. 1 (8 January 1971): 7.
9. Ibid., p. 12.
10. Quoted from *Selections from China Mainland Magazines*, Supplement, no. 21, 16.
11. Kenneth Lieberthal, "Mao Versus Liu: Policy Towards Industry and Commerce: 1946–1949." *China Quarterly*, no. 47 (July/September 1971), pp. 519–20.

12. Quoted in Yuan-li Wu, "Economics, Ideology and the Cultural Revolution," in *Understanding Modern China*, ed. Joseph M. Kitagawa (Chicago: Quadrangle Books, 1969), p. 129.
13. Dennis M. Ray, "Traditionalism and the Idea of Progress: A Case for Ideological Mobilization" (Paper delivered at Western Conference of Association of Asian Studies, San Diego, October 29, 1971).
14. "Peking's Fourth Five Year Plan," *Current Scene* 8, no. 17 (October 1970): 19–20.
15. Cheng, *China's Economy*, pp. 30–37.
16. Adapted from Cheng, *China's Economy*, pp. 52–53.
17. Jonathan Unger, "Learn from Tachai," *Current Scene* 9, no. 9 (7 September 1971): 1–11.
18. *People's Daily*, 24 November 1968.
19. New China News Agency, 28 September 1968.
20. *Current Scene* 7, no. 18 (15 September 1969): 4.
21. Ibid., p. 5.
22. *Far Eastern Economic Review* (2 October 1971): 39.
23. Kang Chao, "Policies and Performance in Industry," in *Economic Trends in Communist China*, ed. Alexander Eckstein, et al. (Chicago, Aldine Publishing Co., 1968), pp. 552–75.
24. R. G. Boyd, *Communist China Foreign Policy* (New York: Praeger Publishers, 1962), p. 66.
25. A. Doak Barnett, *Communist China and Asia* (New York: Harper and Row, 1960), p. 41.
26. *Communist China, 1949–1966* (Taipei, Institute for the Study of Chinese Communist Problems, 1970), pp. 845–55.
27. Kang Chao, *Performance in Industry*, p. 571.
28. *See* Cheng, *China's Economy*, pp. 133–49.
29. Richard D. Diao, "The Impact of the Cultural Revolution on China's Economic Elite," *China Quarterly*, 42 (April/June 1970), pp. 65–87.
30. *Current Scene* 9, no. 10 (7 October 1971).
31. W. Klatt, "A Review of China's Economy in 1970," *China Quarterly*, no. 43 (July/September 1970), p. 117.
32. *Far Eastern Economic Review, 1971 Yearbook*, pp. 138–39.

Notes for Chapter Eight

1. R. F. Price, *Education in Communist China* (New York: Praeger Publishers, 1970), p. 70.
2. Paul Kratchochvil, *The Chinese Language Today* (Hutchinson University Library, 1968).
3. *Jen-min Chiao Yu* (Peking, November 1951), quoted in *Professional Manpower and Education*, Leo A. Orleans (Washington, D.C.: U.S. Government Printing Office, 1960), p. 12.
4. Franklin W. Houn, *A Short History of Chinese Communism* (Englewood Cliffs, N.J.: Prentice–Hall, 1967), p. 210.
5. G. R. Nunn, *Publishing in Mainland China* (Cambridge, Mass.: M.I.T. Press, 1966), p. 4.
6. Orleans, *Professional Manpower*, p. 11.
7. S. Garrett McDowell, "Educational Reform in China as a Readjusting Country," *Asian Survey* (March 1971), p. 259.
8. *Red Flag*, June 1971, quoted in *Issues and Studies* (October 1971), p. 116.
9. *Current Scene* 9, no. 9 (7 September 1971): 20.

10. *Current Scene* 9, no. 9 (7 January 1971).
11. John Gittings, "Inside China—In the Wake of the Cultural Revolution," *Ramparts* (August 1971), p. 16.
12. *New York Times*, 22 September, 1971.
13. Quoted in Howard L. Boorman, "The Literary World of Mao Tse-tung," *China Quarterly*, no. 13 (January/March 1963), 17.
14. Mao Tse-tung, *Selected Works of Mao Tse-tung*, vol. 3 (Peking: Foreign Language Press, 1965), pp. 75–97.
15. *See* Chung Hua-min and Arthur C. Miller, *Madame Mao: A Profile of Chiang Ching* (Hong Kong: Union Research Institute, 1968).
16. *China Reconstruct* (August 1967), pp. 26–33.
17. *People's Daily*, 4 July 1968.
18. *People's Daily*, 9 July 1968.
19. James Hsiung, *Ideology and Practice: the Evolution of Chinese Communism* (New York: Praeger Publishers, 1970), p. 250.
20. *Liberation Army Daily*, 23 November 1967.
21. Mary Sheridan, "The Emulation of Heroes," *China Quarterly*, no. 33 (January/March 1968), pp. 47–72.
22. *China's Screen*, no. 2 (1965).
23. *The Diary of Wang Chieh* (Peking: Foreign Language Press, 1967).
24. John H. Weakland, "Chinese Film Images of Invasion and Resistance," *China Quarterly*, 47 (July/September 1971), pp. 439–70.
25. *The Marriage Law of the People's Republic of China* (Peking: Foreign Language Press, 1959), p. 1
26. Denis Lazure, "The Family and Youth in New China: Psychiatric Observation," *Canadian Medical Association Journal* 86, no. 179 (January 1962): 179–82.

Notes for Chapter Nine

1. *Hsing Ming Tsu Tsu Tien* (*A Dictionary of New Terms*) (Shanghai: Chung-ming Publishing Co., 1953), p. 77.
2. *Abstracted in the Proceedings of the Institute of World Affairs* (Los Angeles, University of Southern California, Fortieth Session, 1963), pp. 63–64.
3. Melvin Gurtov, "The Foreign Ministry and Foreign Affairs During the Cultural Revolution," *China Quarterly*, no. 40 (October/December 1969), pp. 65–102.
4. Winberg Chai, *The Foreign Relations of the People's Republic of China: View from Inside* (New York: G. P. Putnam's Sons, 1972), chapter 1.
5. Mao Tse-tung, "On Peace Negotiation with the Kuomintang" (August 1945), quoted in Chai, *Foreign Relations*, Document 5.
6. Franklin W. Houn, "The Principles and Operational Code of Communist China's International Conduct," *Journal of Asian Studies* 27, no. 1 (November 1967): 36–37.
7. Hans J. Morgenthau, *Politics Among Nations*, 4th ed., (New York: Alfred A. Knopf, 1966), pp. 542–43.
8. Chai, *Foreign Relations*.
9. Richard Lowenthal, "Communist China's Foreign Policy," in *China in Crisis*, vol. 2, ed. Tang Tsou (Chicago: University of Chicago Press, 1968), p. 1.
10. Allen Whiting, "What Nixon Must Do to Make it in Peking," *New York Review of Books* (7 October 1971), pp. 10–13.

11. Chai, *Foreign Relations*, chapter 3.
12. Kuo Wen, "Imperialist Plunder—Biggest Obstacle to the Economic Growth of Underdeveloped Countries," (June 1965), quoted in Chai, *Foreign Relations*, Document 42.
13. Quoted in Chai, *Foreign Relations*, Document 60.
14. Tseng Yun, "How China Carries Out the Policy of Self-Reliance," in *Foreign Relations*, ed. Chai, Document 41.
15. Gene T. Hsiao, "Communist China's Trade Treaties and Agreements, 1949–1964," *Vanderbilt Law Review* 21, no. 5 (October 1968): 658.
16. Quoted in Chai, *Foreign Relations*, Document 40.
17. *Issues and Studies* 6, no. 6 (March 1970): 37–41.
18. *New York Times*, 10 August 1971.
19. Arthur Cohen, *The Communism of Mao Tse-tung* (Chicago: University of Chicago Press, 1964), p. 59.
20. J. D. Simmonds, *China's World, the Foreign Policy of a Developing Nation* (New York: Columbia University Press, 1970), chapter 9.
21. *People's Daily*, 23 January 1971.
22. *New York Times*, 1972.
23. Mao Tse-tung, *Selected Works of Mao Tse-tung*, vol. 3 (Peking: Foreign Language Press, 1965), pp. 255 and 306.
24. Winberg Chai, "China and the United Nations: Problems of Representation and Alternatives," *Asian Survey* (May 1970).
25. *People's China*, no. 14 (1955), p. 6.
26. General Assembly, Official Records, 18, Special Political Committee, 423d meeting, p. 257.
27. *Peking Review*, 20 December 1963, pp. 20–21.
28. *Peking Review*, 29 January 1965, pp. 5–6.
29. *Peking Review*, 15 January 1965, "facts on file."
30. *See* Chai, *Foreign Relations*, Document 61.
31. *New York Times*, 26 October 1971.
32. *Chinese Law and Government* 11, no. 1 (Spring 1969): 39.
33. Ibid.
34. Douglas M. Johnston and Hungdah Chiu, *Agreements of the People's Republic of China* (Cambridge, Mass.: Harvard University Press, 1968); *see also* Hungdah Chiu, "Communist China's Attitude Toward the United Nations: A Legal Analysis," *American Journal of International Law* 62, no. 1 (January 1968): 33–39.
35. Quoted in Chai, *Foreign Relations*, Document 25.
36. Cohen, *Communism of Mao*, p. 82.

Notes for Chapter Ten

1. John Gittings, "Inside China: In the Wake of the Cultural Revolution," *Ramparts*, August 1971, p. 19.
2. Louis Halasz, "China's Welcome at the United Nations," *War/Peace Report* (October 1971), p. 3.
3. John S. Aird, "Population, Planning and Economic Development," *Population Bulletin* 19, no. 5 (August 1963): 114–35.
4. Leo A. Orleans, "Evidence from Chinese Medical Journals on Current Population Policy," *China Quarterly*, no. 40 (October/December, 1969), pp. 137–46.
5. Dr. Joshua S. Horn, *Away with All Pest: An English Surgeon in People's China: 1954–69* (New York: Monthly Review Press, 1969), p. 141.
6. *Peking Review*, 5 February 1971, pp. 8–10.

7. *New York Times*, 18 September 1971.
8. *See* Liu Pei-hua, ed., *A Short History of Modern China* (Peking: I Chang Bookstore, 1954); and Hou Ming-chiu, et al., *General Geography of China* (Shanghai, 1946).
9. Ministry of External Affairs, Government of India, *Report of the Chinese and Indian Officials on the Boundary Question* (New Delhi, 1961).
10. Alaistair Lamb, *The China-India Border* (New York: Oxford University Press, 1964), pp. 77–78.
11. Tieh-tseng Li, "The Legal Position of Tibet," *American Journal of International Law* (April 1956): 397; for a pro-British position, *see* H. E. Richardson, *A Short History of Tibet* (New York: Dutton and Co., 1962).
12. W. A. Douglas Jackson, *The Russo-Chinese Borderland*, 2d ed., (Princeton: D. Van Nostrand Searchlight Books, 1968).
13. "The Sino-Soviet Border Question," *China in the News* (London), no. 8 (September 1969).
14. Quoted in Chai, *Foreign Relations*, Document 23.
15. "The Sino-Soviet Border Question," *China in the News* (London), no. 8, September, 1969.
16. *New York Times*, 21 March 1969.
17. *Soviet News*, 10 June 1969, p. 132.
18. *International Herald Tribune*, 28 January 1969.
19. *Times* (London), 3 July 1969.
20. *Peking Review*, 30 May 1969, quoted in Chai, *Foreign Relations*, Document 53.
21. *Soviet News*, 17 June 1969, p. 138.
22. *Oppose U.S. Occupation of Taiwan and Two China Plot*, (Peking: Foreign Language Press, 1958), p. 6.
23. *New York Times*, 10 August 1971.
24. Robert A. Scalapino, "The Question of Two Chinas," in *China in Crisis*, vol. 2, ed. Tang Tsou (Chicago: University of Chicago Press, 1968), p. 110.
25. J. Bruce Jacob, "Recent Leadership and Political Trends in Taiwan," *China Quarterly*, no. 45 (January/March 1971), pp. 136–37.
26. Allen S. Whiting, "Morality, Taiwan and U.S. Policy," in *Taiwan and American Policy*, ed. Jerome Alan Cohen, et al. (New York: Praeger Publishers, 1971), pp. 79–105.
27. Sheldon Appleton, "Taiwanese and Mainlander on Taiwan: A Survey of Student Attitudes," *China Quarterly*, no. 44 (October/December 1970), p. 56.
28. *New York Times*, 26 September 1971.
29. Edward Friedman, "Real Interest of China and America in the Taiwan Area," in *Taiwan*, ed. Cohen, et al., pp. 46–47.
30. *See* Neil H. Jacoby, *U.S. Aid to Taiwan* (New York: Praeger Publishers, 1966).
31. *Far Eastern Economic Review* (16 October 1971), pp. 49–52.
32. Ibid.
33. *Los Angeles Times*, 29 October 1971.
34. *See* A. Doak Barnett, *A New U.S. Policy Toward China* (Washington, D.C.: Brookings Institution, 1971); *see also* U.S., Congress, House, Committee on Foreign Affairs, *U.S.-China Relations:* Hearings before the subcommittee on Asian and Pacific Affairs, 91st Cong., 2d sess., 1970.

PART THREE

Original Sources

Appendix one

The New Constitution of the Communist Party of China (April 1969)

CHAPTER ONE: GENERAL PROGRAM

The Communist Party of China is the political party of the proletariat.

The basic program of the Communist Party of China is the complete overthrow of the bourgeoisie and all other exploiting classes, the establishment of the dictatorship of the proletariat in place of the dictatorship of the bourgeoisie and the triumph of socialism over capitalism. The ultimate aim of the Party is the realization of communism.

The Communist Party of China is composed of the advanced elements of the proletariat; it is a vigorous vanguard organization leading the proletariat and the revolutionary masses in the fight against the class enemy.

The Communist Party of China takes Marxism-Leninism-Mao Tse-tung Thought as the theoretical basis guiding its thinking. Mao Tse-tung Thought is Marxism-Leninism of the era in which imperialism is heading for total collapse and socialism is advancing to worldwide victory.

For half a century now, in leading China's great struggle for accomplishing the new-democratic revolution, in leading her great struggle for socialist revolution and socialist construction and in the great struggle of the contemporary international communist movement against imperialism, modern revisionism and the reactionaries of various countries, Comrade Mao Tse-tung has integrated the universal truth of Marxism-Leninism with the concrete practice of revolution, inherited, defended and developed Marxism-Leninism and has brought it to a higher and completely new stage.

Comrade Lin Piao has consistently held high the great red banner of Mao Tse-tung Thought and has most loyally and resolutely carried out and defended Comrade Mao Tse-tung's proletarian revolutionary line. Comrade Lin Piao is Comrade Mao Tse-tung's close comrade-in-arms and successor.

The Communist Party of China with Comrade Mao Tse-tung as

its leader is a great, glorious and correct Party and is the core of leadership of the Chinese people. The Party has been tempered through long years of class struggle for the seizure and consolidation of state power by armed force, it has strengthened itself and grown in the course of the struggle against both Right and "Left" opportunist lines, and it is valiantly advancing with supreme confidence along the road of socialist revolution and socialist construction.

Socialist society covers a fairly long historical period. Throughout this historical period, there are classes, class contradictions and class struggle, there is the struggle between the socialist road and the capitalist road, there is the danger of capitalist restoration and there is the threat of subversion and aggression by imperialism and modern revisionism. These contradictions can be resolved only by depending on the Marxist theory of continued revolution and on practice under its guidance. Such is China's Great Proletarian Cultural Revolution, a great political revolution carried out under the conditions of socialism by the proletariat against the bourgeoisie and all other exploiting classes.

The whole Party must hold high the great red banner of Marxism-Leninism-Mao Tse-tung Thought and lead the hundreds of millions of the people of all the nationalities of our country in carrying on the three great revolutionary movements of class struggle, the struggle for production and scientific experiment, in strengthening and consolidating the dictatorship of the proletariat and in building socialism independently and with the initiative in our own hands, through self-reliance and hard struggle and by going all out, aiming high and achieving greater, faster, better and more economical results.

The Communist Party of China upholds proletarian internationalism; it firmly unites with the genuine Marxist-Leninist Parties and groups the world over, unites with the proletariat, the oppressed people and nations of the whole world and fights together with them to overthrow imperialism headed by the United States, modern revisionism with the Soviet revisionist renegade clique as its center and the reactionaries of all countries, and to abolish the system of exploitation of man by man on the globe, so that all mankind will be emancipated.

Members of the Communist Party of China, who dedicate their lives to the struggle for communism, must be resolute, fear no sacrifice and surmount every difficulty to win victory!

CHAPTER TWO: MEMBERSHIP

Article 1: Any Chinese worker, poor peasant, lower-middle peasant, revolutionary armyman or any other revolutionary element who has reached the age of 18 and who accepts the Constitution of the Party, joins a Party organization and works actively in it, carries out the Party's decisions, observes Party discipline and pays membership dues may become a member of the Communist Party of China.

Article 2: Applicants for Party membership must go through the procedure for admission individually. An applicant must be recommended by two Party members, fill out an application form for Party membership and be examined by a Party branch, which must seek the opinions of the broad masses inside and outside the Party. Application is subject to acceptance by the general membership meeting of the Party branch and approval by the next higher Party committee.

Article 3: Members of the Communist Party of China must:

1. Study and apply Marxism-Leninism-Mao Tse-tung Thought in a living way;
2. Work for the interests of the vast majority of the people of China and the world;
3. Be able at uniting with the great majority, including those who have wrongly opposed them but are sincerely correcting their mistakes; however, special vigilance must be maintained against careerists, conspirators and double-dealers so as to prevent such bad elements from usurping the leadership of the Party and the state at any level and guarantee that the leadership of the Party and the state always remains in the hands of Marxist revolutionaries;
4. Consult with the masses when matters arise;
5. Be bold in making criticism and self-criticism.

Article 4: When Party members violate Party discipline, the Party organizations at the levels concerned shall, within their functions and powers and on the merits of each case, take appropriate disciplinary measures—warning, serious warning, removal from posts in the Party, placing on probation within the Party, or expulsion from the Party.

The period for which a Party member is placed on probation shall not exceed two years. During this period, he has no right to vote or elect or be elected.

A Party member who becomes politically apathetic and makes no change despite education should be persuaded to withdraw from the Party.

When a Party member asks to withdraw from the Party, the Party branch concerned shall, with the approval of its general membership meeting, remove his name from the Party rolls and report the matter to the next higher Party committee for the record. When necessary, this should be made public to the masses outside the Party.

Proven renegades, enemy agents, absolutely unrepentant persons in power taking the capitalist road, degenerates and alien class elements must be cleared out of the Party and not be re-admitted.

CHAPTER THREE: ORGANIZATIONAL PRINCIPLE
OF THE PARTY

Article 5: The organizational principle of the Party is democratic centralism.

The leading bodies of the Party at all levels are elected through democratic consultation.

The whole Party must observe unified discipline: The individual is subordinate to the organization, the minority is subordinate to the majority, the lower level is subordinate to the higher level, and the entire Party is subordinate to the Central Committee.

Leading bodies of the Party at all levels shall regularly report on their work to congresses or general membership meetings, constantly listen to the opinions of the masses both inside and outside the Party and accept their supervision. Party members have the right to criticize Party organizations and leading members at all levels and make proposals to them. If a Party member holds different views with regard to the decisions or directives of the Party organizations, he is allowed to reserve his views and has the right to bypass the immediate leadership and report directly to higher levels, up to and including the Central Committee and the Chairman of the Central Committee. It is essential to create a political situation in which there are both centralism and democracy, both discipline and freedom, both unity of will and personal ease of mind and liveliness.

The organs of state power of the dictatorship of the proletariat, the People's Liberation Army, and the Communist Youth League and other revolutionary mass organizations, such as those of the workers, the poor and lower-middle peasants and the Red Guards, must all accept the leadership of the Party.

Article 6: The highest leading body of the Party is the National Party Congress and, when it is not in session, the Central Committee elected by it. The leading bodies of Party organizations in the localities, in army units and in various departments are the Party congresses or general membership meetings at their respective levels and the Party committees elected by them. Party congresses at all levels are convened by Party committees at their respective levels.

The convening of Party congresses in the localities and army units and their elected Party committee members are subject to approval by the higher Party organizations.

Article 7: Party committees at all levels shall set up their working bodies or dispatch their representative organs in accordance with the principles of unified leadership, close ties with the masses and simple and efficient structure.

CHAPTER FOUR: CENTRAL ORGANIZATIONS OF THE PARTY

Article 8: The National Party Congress shall be convened every five years. Under special circumstances, it may be convened before its due date or postponed.

Article 9: The plenary session of the Central Committee of the Party elects the Political Bureau of the Central Committee, the Standing Committee of the Political Bureau of the Central Committee and the Chairman and Vice-Chairman of the Central Committee.

The plenary session of the Central Committee of the Party is convened by the Political Bureau of the Central Committee.

When the Central Committee is not in plenary session, the Political Bureau of the Central Committee and its Standing Committee exercise the functions and powers of the Central Committee.

Under the leadership of the Chairman, the Vice-Chairman and the Standing Committee of the Political Bureau of the Central Committee, a number of necessary organs, which are compact and efficient, shall be set up to attend to the day-to-day work of the Party, the government and the army in a centralized way.

CHAPTER FIVE: PARTY ORGANIZATIONS IN THE LOCALITIES AND THE ARMY UNITS

Article 10: Local Party congresses at the county level and upwards and Party congresses in the People's Liberation Army at the regimental level and upwards shall be convened every three years. Under special circumstance, they may be convened before their due date or postponed.

Party committees at all levels in the localities and the army units elect their standing committees, secretaries and deputy secretaries.

CHAPTER SIX: PRIMARY ORGANIZATIONS OF THE PARTY

Article 11: In general, Party branches are formed in factories, mines and other enterprises, people's communes, offices, schools, shops, neighborhoods, companies of the People's Liberation Army and other primary Party committees may also be set up where there is a relatively large membership or where the revolutionary struggle requires.

Primary Party organizations shall hold elections once a year. Under special circumstances, the election may take place before its due date or be postponed.

Article 12: Primary Party organizations must hold high the great red banner of Marxism-Leninism-Mao Tse-tung Thought, give prominence to proletarian politics and develop the style of integrating theory with practice, maintaining close ties with the masses of the people and practicing criticism and self-criticism. Their main tasks are:

1. To lead the Party members and the broad revolutionary masses in studying and applying Marxism-Leninism-Mao Tse-tung Thought in a living way;
2. To give constant education to the Party members and the broad revolutionary masses concerning class struggle and the struggle between the two lines and lead them in fighting resolutely against the class enemy;
3. To propagate and carry out the policies of the Party, implement its decisions and fulfil every task assigned by the Party and the state;
4. To maintain close ties with the masses, constantly listen to their opinions and demands and wage an active ideological struggle within the Party so as to keep Party life vigorous;
5. To take in new Party members, enforce Party discipline, constantly consolidate the Party organizations and get rid of the stale and take in the fresh so as to maintain the purity of the Party ranks.

Appendix Two

The Secret Draft of the Revised Constitution of the People's Republic of China

The following draft is one of a series of secret documents adopted by the second plenary session of the Ninth Central Committee of the Chinese Communist Party held from 23 August to 6 September 1970. It has been circulated for internal distribution and discussion. The final adoption of the Constitution with considerable modification by the National People's Congress is expected including the removal of Lin Piao. This text has been translated by the author with his father, Dr. Ch'u Chai, for Comparative Communism.

CHAPTER ONE: GENERAL PRINCIPLES

Article 1: The People's Republic of China is a socialist state of proletarian dictatorship led by the working class (through the Chinese Communist Party) and based on the alliance of workers and peasants.

Article 2: Chairman Mao Tse-tung is the great leader of the people of all nationalities in the entire country, the Chief of State of the proletarian dictatorship, and the supreme commander of the whole nation and the whole armed forces. Vice-Chairman Lin Piao is Chairman Mao's close comrade-in-arms and successor, and the deputy supreme commander of the whole nation and the whole armed forces. Mao Tsetung's thought is the guiding compass of all the work of the people of the whole nation.

Article 3: All power in the People's Republic of China belongs to the people. The organs through which the people exercise power are the people's congresses at every level with the deputies of workers, peasants and soldiers as the main body. The people's congresses at every level and other state organs all practice democratic centralism. Deputies to the people's congresses are elected through democratic consensus. The original electoral units and the electorate have the power to supervise and, in accordance with the provisions of law, to recall and replace the elected deputies.

Article 4: The People's Republic of China is a unitary multinational nation-state, with national autonomous regions as inseparable parts of the People's Republic of China. All the nationalities are equal, and opposed to great nationalism and parochial nationalism. All the nationalities have the freedom to use their own spoken and written languages.

Article 5: At present, the main categories of ownership of means of production in the People's Republic of China are twofold: socialist ownership by the whole people, and socialist collective ownership by the masses of working people. The state permits nonagricultural individual laborers, under the central management of urban and township street organizations and production teams of rural people's communes, to engage in individual labor within permissive legal provisions and not exploit others. They are in the meantime to be guided step by step onto the road of socialist collectivization.

Article 6: The state sector of the economy is the leading force in the national economy. All mineral resources and waters, as well as state forests, undeveloped lands and other resources, are the property of the whole people. The state may purchase, appropriate or nationalize both urban and rural land as well as other productive resources in accordance with legal provisions.

Article 7: The rural people's commune is an organization in which government and commune are combined into one. At present, the economy of collective ownership in the rural people's communes generally operates under three levels of ownership, namely: ownership by the commune, by the production brigade, and by the production team as the basic accounting unit. Provided that the development of the collective economy of people's communes is guaranteed and occupies absolute priority, members of a people's commune may operate small pieces of land for private operation.

Article 8: Socialist public property is inviolable. The state guarantees the consolidation and development of socialist economy, and prohibits anyone from using any means to sabotage the interests of socialist economy and public property.

Article 9: The state practices the socialist principles of "no work, no food," "from each according to his ability," and "distribution according to one's labor." The state protects the citizens' right to own income from labor, savings, houses and other means of subsistence.

Article 10: Political work is the lifeline of all activity. The state acts to retain revolution, promote production and work, and to prepare for defense, as well as to promote the systematic and proportional development of socialist economy, so that on the basis of continually elevating social productivity, the material and cultural life of the people will be gradually improved, and the independence and security of the state will be consolidated.

Article 11: All working personnel of state and other organs must study and apply creatively the thought of Mao Tse-tung, place special emphasis on proletarian politics, oppose bureaucratism, align closely with the workers and peasants, as well as all laboring masses, and serve the people with whole heart and devotion. Working personnel of all organs must participate in collective labor. All state organs must practice the principle of simplified administration; their leadership organs must practice the revolutionary three-in-one combination of military men, cadres and masses, and of the old, the middle-aged and the young.

Article 12: The proletariat, which must be established in the superstructure including the various cultural fields, exercises total dictatorship over the bourgeoisie. Culture, education, literature, arts and scientific research must all serve proletarian politics, serve the workers, peasants and soldiers, and unite with productive labor.

Article 13: Blooming and contending on a big scale, big-character posters, and great debates are new forms of socialist revolution created by the masses of people. The state protects the use of such forms by the people in mass movement, to create a political situation where there is democracy and yet centralism, discipline and yet freedom, collective will and yet individual pursuit of mental gratification, so as to consolidate proletarian dictatorship.

Article 14: The state safeguards the socialist system, suppresses all treasonable and counterrevolutionary activities, and punishes all traitors and counterrevolutionaries. The state according to law deprives landlords, rich peasants, reactionary capitalists, counterrevolutionaries, and other undesirable elements of their political rights for a specific period of time; meanwhile it provides them means to earn a living, in order to enable them to reform through labor and become citizens who can earn their livelihood by their own labor.

Article 15: The Chinese People's Liberation Army and militia are the children and brothers of workers and peasants under the leadership of the Communist Party of China, and the armored power-source of the whole nation. The Chinese People's Liberation Army is perpetually and simultaneously a combat unit, a work unit, and a production unit. The duty of the armed forces of the People's Republic of China is to safeguard the socialist revolution and the achievements of socialist construction, to defend the sovereignty, territorial integrity and security of the state, and to guard against the subversion and aggression of imperialism, social-imperialism and their lackeys.

CHAPTER TWO: THE STATE STRUCTURE

Section I: The National People's Congress

Article 16: The National People's Congress is the highest organ of state power under the leadership of the Communist Party of China.

The National People's Congress is composed of deputies elected by provinces, autonomous regions, municipalities directly under the central authority, armed forces and Chinese residents abroad. A number of patriotic personalities may be invited to participate when necessary. The National People's Congress is elected for a term of five years, which may be extended under special circumstances. The National People's Congress meets once a year, but under special circumstances it may be convened sooner or postponed.

Article 17: The functions and powers of the National People's Congress are: to make and to amend the Constitution, to make laws, to appoint and remove the premier of the State Council upon the recommendation of the Central Committee of the Communist Party of China, to examine and approve the state budget and the state accounts, and to exercise such other functions and powers as the National People's Congress considers necessary.

Article 18: The Standing Committee of the National People's Congress is the permanent working organ of the National People's Congress. Its functions and powers are: to interpret the laws to the sessions of the National People's Congress, to adopt decrees, to appoint and recall plenipotentiary representatives, and to ratify and nullify treaties concluded with foreign states. The Standing Committee of the National People's Congress is composed of the chairman, the vice-chairmen, and other members, to be elected or removed by the National People's Congress.

Section II: The State Council

Article 19: The State Council is the central people's government. The State Council is accountable to the National People's Congress and its Standing Committee and submits reports to them. The State Council is composed of the premier, the vice-premiers, the ministers, the chairmen of commissions, and others.

Article 20: The functions and powers of the State Council are: to formulate administrative measures and issue decisions and orders in accordance with the Constitution, laws and decrees; to coordinate and lead the work of ministries, commissions, as well as the work of local administrative organs of state throughout the country; to formulate and put into effect the national economic plan and the provisions of the state budget; to direct the administrative affairs of the state; and to exercise such other functions and powers as are vested in it by the National People's Congress or its Standing Committee.

Section III: Local People's Congresses and Local Revolutionary Committees

Article 21: Local people's congresses at every level are local organs of state power. The term of office of people's congresses at the provincial and municipal levels in five years; that of people's congresses of special districts, cities and counties, three years; that of people's congresses of rural people's communes and townships, two years.

Article 22: Local revolutionary committees at every level are the standing organs of local people's congresses and, at the same time, local people's governments. A local revolutionary committee is composed of the chairman, the vice-chairmen and other members, to be elected or recalled by the people's congress of the corresponding level. A local revolutionary committee is accountable to the local people's congress and to the next higher state organ.

Article 23: Local people's congresses at every level and members of local revolutionary committees ensure the implementation of laws and decrees in their respective areas, stimulate the enthusiasm of local organs at every level to the utmost, provide leadership for local socialist revolution and socialist construction; examine and approve local budgets; protect revolutionary order; and safeguard the rights of citizens.

Section IV: Organs of Self-Government of National Autonomous Areas

Article 24: The organs of self-government in autonomous regions, autonomous *chou* and autonomous counties are the people's congresses and revolutionary committees. The organs of self-government of national autonomous areas may exercise, in addition to the functions and powers of local state organs as prescribed in Chapter Two, Section III of the Constitution, autonomy as provided by law. Higher state organs at every level should fully safeguard the exercise of autonomy by organs of self-government in national autonomous areas, and actively support the various minority nationalities in carrying out socialist revolution and socialist construction.

Section V: The Judicial and Procuratorate Organs

Article 25: The Supreme People's Court, local people's courts at every level and special people's courts exercise judicial authority. The people's courts at every level are accountable to the people's congresses and their standing committees and submit reports to them. The permanent organs of the people's congresses at every level appoint or remove presidents of the people's courts. The exercise of procuratorial and trial authority shall follow the mass line. Mass discussion and criticism are to be conducted in serious counterrevolutionary and criminal cases.

CHAPTER THREE: FUNDAMENTAL RIGHTS AND DUTIES OF CITIZENS

Article 26: The most fundamental rights and duties of citizens are to support Chairman Mao Tse-tung and his close comrade-in-arms

Vice-Chairman Lin Piao, to support the leadership of the Communist party of China; to support the proletarian dictatorship, to support the socialist system, and to abide by the Constitution and laws of the People's Republic of China. It is the highest responsibility of every citizen to defend the motherland and to resist aggression; and it is the glorious duty of citizens to perform military service according to law.

Article 27: All citizens who have reached the age of eighteen have the right to vote and stand for election, except those deprived by law of such rights. Citizens have the right to work and the right to education. The working people have the right to rest and leisure; and the right to material assistance in old age and in case of illness or disability. Women enjoy equal rights with men. The state protects marriage, the family, and the mother and child. The state protects the just rights and interests of Chinese residents abroad.

Article 28: Citizens enjoy freedom of speech, freedom of correspondence, freedom of press, freedom of assembly, freedom of association, freedom of procession, freedom of demonstration, and freedom to strike. Citizens enjoy the freedom of religious belief and the freedom of iconoclasm and of propagating atheism. The freedom of person and the homes of citizens are inviolable. No citizen may be arrested except by decision of a people's court or with the sanction of public security organs.

CHAPTER FOUR: NATIONAL FLAG, NATIONAL EMBLEM, CAPITAL

Article 30: The national flag of the People's Republic of China is a red flag with five stars. The national emblem is: in the center, Tien An Men under the light of five stars, framed with ears of grain and with a cogwheel. The capital of the People's Republic of China is Peking.

Appendix Three

Policy Statement to the Ninth National Congress of the
Communist Party of China, 1 April 1969

This policy paper was presented by Lin Piao on behalf of Chairman
Mao and adopted by the Party Congress as official program
guide for the Party on April 14, 1970.

Comrades!

The Ninth National Congress of the Communist Party of China
will be a congress with a far-reaching influence in the history of our
Party.

Our present congress is convened at a time when a great victory
has been won in the Great Proletarian Cultural Revolution personally
initiated and led by Chairman Mao. This great revolutionary storm
has shattered the bourgeois headquarters headed by the renegade, hidden traitor and scab Liu Shao-chi, exposed the handful of renegades,
enemy agents and absolutely unrepentant persons in power taking the
capitalist road within the Party, with Liu Shao-chi as their arch-repre-
sentative, and smashed their plot to restore capitalism; it has tremendously strengthened the dictatorship of the proletariat and our country,
tremendously strengthened our Party and thus prepared ample conditions for this congress politically, ideologically and organizationally.

ON THE PREPARATION FOR THE GREAT PROLETARIAN CULTURAL REVOLUTION

The Great Proletarian Cultural Revolution of our country is a
genuine proletarian revolution on an immense scale.

Chairman Mao has explained the necessity of the current great
revolution in concise terms:

> The current Great Proletarian Cultural Revolution is absolutely
> necessary and most timely for consolidating the dictatorship of
> the proletariat, preventing capitalist restoration and building
> socialism.

In order to comprehend this scientific thesis of Chairman Mao's fully, we should have a deep understanding of his theory of continuing the revolution under the dictatorship of the proletariat.

In 1957, shortly after the conclusion of the Party's Eighth National Congress, Chairman Mao published his great work *On the Correct Handling of Contradictions Among the People*, in which, following his *Report to the Second Plenary Session of the Seventh Central Committee of the Communist Party of China*, he comprehensively set forth the existence of contradictions, classes and class struggle under the conditions of the dictatorship of the proletariat, set forth the thesis of the existence of two different types of contradictions in socialist society, those between ourselves and the enemy and those among the people, and set forth the great theory of continuing the revolution under the dictatorship of the proletariat. Like a radiant beacon, this great work illuminates the course of China's socialist revolution and socialist construction and has laid the theoretical foundation for the current Great Proletarian Cultural Revolution.

In order to have a deeper understanding of Chairman Mao's great historic contribution, it is necessary briefly to review the historical experience of the international communist movement.

In 1852, Marx said:

> Long before me bourgeois historians had described the historical development of this class struggle and bourgeois economists the economic anatomy of the classes. What I did that was new was to prove: (1) that the *existence of classes* is only bound up with *particular historical phases in the development of production*, (2) that the class struggle necessarily leads to the *dictatorship of the proletariat*, (3) that this dictatorship itself only constitutes the transition to the *abolition of all classes* and to a *classless society*. (Marx and Engels, *Selected Correspondence*, Chinese ed., p. 63.)

Marx's theory of the dictatorship of the proletariat clearly distinguished scientific socialism from utopian socialism and sham socialism of every kind. Marx and Engels fought all their lives for this theory and for its realization.

After the death of Marx and Engels, almost all the parties of the Second International betrayed Marxism, with the exception of the Bolshevik Party led by Lenin. Lenin inherited, defended and developed Marxism in the struggle against the revisionism of the Second International. The struggle focused on the question of the dictatorship of the proletariat. In denouncing the old revisionists, Lenin time and again stated:

> Those who recognize *only* the class struggle are not yet Marxists. ... Only he is a Marxist who *extends* the recognition of the class

struggle to the recognition of the *dictatorship of the proletariat.* (Lenin, *Collected Works*, Chinese ed., Vol. 25, p. 399.)

Lenin led the proletariat of Russia in winning the victory of the Great October Socialist Revolution and founding the first socialist state. Through his great revolutionary practice in leading the dictatorship of the proletariat, Lenin perceived the danger of the restoration of capitalism and the protracted nature of class struggle:

> The transition from capitalism to Communism represents an entire historical epoch. Until this epoch has terminated, the exploiters inevitably cherish the hope of restoration, and this *hope* is converted into *attempts* at restoration. (Lenin, *Collected Works*, Chinese ed., Vol. 28, p. 235.)

Lenin stated:

> ... the bourgeoisie, whose resistance is increased *tenfold* by its overthrow (even if only in one country), and whose power lies not only in the strength of international capital, in the strength and durability of the international connections of the bourgeoisie, but also in the *force of habit*, in the strength of *small production.* For, unfortunately, small production is still very, very widespread in the world, and small production *engenders* capitalism and the bourgeoisie continuously, daily, hourly, spontaneously, and on a mass scale. (Lenin, *Collected Works*, Chinese ed., Vol. 31, p. 6.)

His conclusion was: **"For all these reasons the dictatorship of the proletariat is essential."** *(Ibid.)*

Lenin also stated that **"the new bourgeoisie"** was **"arising from among our Soviet government employees."** (Lenin, *Collected Works*, Chinese ed., Vol. 29, p. 162.)

He pointed out that the danger of restoration also came from capitalist encirclement: The imperialist countries **"will never miss an opportunity for military intervention, as they put it, i.e., to strangle Soviet power."** (Lenin, *Collected Works*, Chinese ed., Vol. 31, p. 423.)

The Soviet revisionist renegade clique has completely betrayed these brilliant teachings of Lenin's. From Khrushchev to Brezhnev and company, they are all persons in power taking the capitalist road, who have long concealed themselves in the Communist Party of the Soviet Union. As soon as they came to power, they turned the bourgeoisie's **"hope of restoration"** into *"attempts* **at restoration,"** usurped the leadership of the Party of Lenin and Stalin and, through "peaceful evolution," turned the world's first state of the dictatorship of the proletariat into a dark fascist state of the dictatorship of the bourgeoisie.

Chairman Mao has waged a tit-for-tat struggle against modern revisionism with the Soviet revisionist renegade clique as its center and has inherited, defended and developed the Marxist-Leninist theory of proletarian revolution and the dictatorship of the proletariat. Chairman Mao has comprehensively summed up the historical experience of the dictatorship of the proletariat both in the positive and negative aspects and, in order to prevent the restoration of capitalism, has put forward the theory of continuing the revolution under the dictatorship of the proletariat.

As early as March 1949, on the eve of the transition of the Chinese revolution from the new-democratic revolution to the socialist revolution, Chairman Mao explicitly pointed out in his report to the Second Plenary Session of the Seventh Central Committee of the Party: After the country-wide seizure of power by the proletariat, the principal internal contradiction is **"the contradiction between the working class and the bourgeoisie."** The heart of the struggle is still the question of state power. Chairman Mao especially reminded us:

> After the enemies with guns have been wiped out, there will still be enemies without guns; they are bound to struggle desperately against us, and we must never regard these enemies lightly. If we do not now raise and understand the problem in this way, we shall commit the gravest mistakes.

Having foreseen the protracted and complex nature of the class struggle between the proletariat and the bourgeoisie after the establishment of the dictatorship of the proletariat, Chairman Mao set the whole Party the militant task of fighting imperialism, the Kuomintang and the bourgeoisie in the political, ideological, economic, cultural and diplomatic spheres.

Our Party waged intense battles in accordance with the resolution of the Second Plenary Session of the Seventh Central Committee and the Party's general line for the transition period formulated by Chairman Mao. In 1956, the socialist transformation of the ownership of the means of production in agriculture, handicrafts and capitalist industry and commerce was in the main completed. That was the crucial moment for the question of whether the socialist revolution could continue to advance. In view of the rampancy of revisionism in the international communist movement and the new trends of class struggle in our country, Chairman Mao, in his great work *On the Correct Handling of Contradictions Among the People,* called the attention of the whole Party to the following fact:

> In China, although in the main socialist transformation has been completed with respect to the system of ownership ... there are still remnants of the overthrown landlord and comprador classes, there is still a bourgeoisie, and the remolding of the petty bourgeoisie has only just started.

Countering the fallacy put forward by Liu Shao-chi in 1956 that "in

China, the question of which wins out, socialism or capitalism, is already solved," Chairman Mao specifically pointed out:

> The question of which will win out, socialism or capitalism, is still not really settled.
> The class struggle between the proletariat and the bour-geoisie, the class struggle between the different political forces, and the class struggle in the ideological field between the prole-tariat and the bourgeoisie will continue to be long and tortuous and at times will even become very acute.

Thus, for the first time in the theory and practice of the international communist movement, it was pointed out explicitly that classes and class struggle still exist after the socialist transformation of the owner-ship of the means of production has been in the main completed, and that the proletariat must continue the revolution.

The proletarian headquarters headed by Chairman Mao led the broad masses in carrying on the great struggle in the direction he indi-cated. From the struggle against the bourgeois rightists in 1957 to the struggle to uncover P'eng Teh-huai's anti-Party clique at the Lushan Meeting in 1959, from the great debate on the general line of the Party in building socialism to the struggle between the two lines in the social-ist education movement—the focus of the struggle was the question of whether to take the socialist road or to take the capitalist road, whether to uphold the dictatorship of the proletariat or to restore the dictator-ship of the bourgeoisie.

Every single victory of Chairman Mao's proletarian revolutionary line, every victory in every major campaign launched by the Party against the bourgeoisie, was gained only after smashing the revisionist line represented by Liu Shao-chi, which either was Right or was "Left" in form but Right in essence.

Now it has been proved through investigation that as far back as the First Revolutionary Civil War period Liu Shao-chi betrayed the Party, capitulated to the enemy and became a hidden traitor and scab, that he was a crime-steeped lackey of the imperialists, modern revision-ists and Kuomintang reactionaries and that he was the arch-representa-tive of the persons in power taking the capitalist road. He had a political line by which he vainly attempted to restore capitalism in China and turn her into an imperialist and revisionist colony. In addi-tion, he had an organizational line to serve his counter-revolutionary political line. For many years, recruiting deserters and turncoats, Liu Shao-chi gathered together a gang of renegades, enemy agents, and capi-talist-roaders in power. They covered up their counter-revolutionary political records, shielded each other, colluded in doing evil, usurped important Party and government posts and controlled the leadership in many central and local units, thus forming an underground bourgeois headquarters in opposition to the proletarian headquarters headed by Chairman Mao. They collaborated with the imperialists, modern revisionists and Kuomintang reactionaries and played the kind of disruptive role that the U.S. imperialists, the Soviet revisionists and the reactionaries of various countries were not in a position to do.

In 1939, when the War of Resistance Against Japan and for National Liberation led by Chairman Mao was vigorously surging forward, Liu Shao-chi dished up his sinister book *Self-Cultivation*. The core of that book was the bertayal of the dictatorship of the proletariat. It did not touch at all upon the questions of defeating Japanese imperialism and of waging the struggle against the Kuomintang reactionaries, nor did it touch upon the fundamental Marxist-Leninist principle of seizing state power by armed force; on the contrary, it urged Communist Party members to depart from the great practice of revolution and indulge in idealistic "self-cultivation," which actually meant that Communists should "cultivate" themselves into willing slaves going down on their knees before the counter-revolutionary dictatorship of the imperialists and Kuomintang reactionaries.

After the victory of the War of Resistance Against Japan, when the U.S. imperialists were arming Chiang Kai-shek's counter-revolutionary troops in preparation for launching an all-out offensive against the liberated areas, Liu Shao-chi, catering to the needs of the U.S.-Chiang reactionaries, dished up the capitulationist line, alleging that "China has entered the new stage of peace and democracy." It was designed to oppose Chairman Mao's general line of **"go all out to mobilize the masses, expand the people's forces and, under the leadership of our Party, defeat the aggressor and build a new China,"** and to oppose Chairman Mao's policy of **"give tit for tat and fight for every inch of land,"** which was adopted to counter the offensive of the U.S.-Chiang reactionaries. Liu Shao-chi preached that "at present the main form of the struggle of the Chinese revolution has changed from armed struggle to non-armed and mass parliamentary struggle." He tried to abolish the Party's leadership over the people's armed forces and to "unify" the Eighth Route Army and the New Fourth Army, predecessors of the People's Liberation Army, into Chiang Kai-shek's "national army" and to demobilize large numbers of worker and peasant soldiers led by the Party in a vain attempt to eradicate the people's armed forces, strangle the Chinese revolution and hand over to the Kuomintang the fruits of victory which the Chinese people had won in blood.

In April 1949, on the eve of the country-wide victory of China's new-democratic revolution when the Chinese People's Liberation Army was preparing to cross the Yangtse River, Liu Shao-chi hurried to Tientsin and threw himself into the arms of the capitalists. He wildly opposed the policy of utilizing, restricting and transforming private capitalist industry, a policy decided upon by the Second Plenary Session of the Seventh Central Committee of the Party which had just concluded. He clamored that "capitalism in China today is still in its youth," that it needed an unlimited "big expansion" and that "capitalist exploitation today is no crime, it is a merit." He shamelessly praised the capitalist class, saying that "the more they exploit, the greater their merit," and feverishly advertised the revisionist theory of productive forces. He did all this in his futile attempt to lead China onto the capitalist road.

In short, at the many important historical junctures of the new-democratic revolution and the socialist revolution, Liu Shao-chi and his gang always wantonly opposed Chairman Mao's proletarian revolutionary line and engaged in counter-revolutionary conspiratorial and disruptive activities. However, since they were counter-revolutionaries, their plots were bound to come to light. When Khrushchev came to power, and especially when the Soviet revisionists ganged up with the U.S. imperialists and the reactionaries of India and other countries in whipping up a large-scale anti-China campaign, Liu Shao-chi and his gang became all the more rabid.

Chairman Mao was the first to perceive the danger of the counter-revolutionary plots of Liu Shao-chi and his gang. At the working conference of the Central Committee in January 1962, Chairman Mao pointed out the necessity of guarding against the emergence of revisionism. At the working conference of the Central Committee at Peitaiho in August 1962 and at the Tenth Plenary Session of the Eighth Central Committee of the Party in September of the same year, Chairman Mao put forward more comprehensively the basic line of our Party for the whole historical period of socialism. Chairman Mao pointed out:

> Socialist society covers a fairly long historical period. In the historical period of socialism, there are still classes, class contradictions and class struggle, there is the struggle between the socialist road and the capitalist road, and there is the danger of capitalist restoration. We must recognize the protracted and complex nature of this struggle. We must heighten our vigilance. We must conduct socialist education. We must correctly understand and handle class contradictions and class struggle, distinguish the contradictions between ourselves and the enemy from those among the people and handle them correctly. Otherwise a socialist country like ours will turn into its opposite and degenerate, and a capitalist restoration will take place. From now on we must remind ourselves of this every year, every month and every day so that we can retain a rather sober understanding of this problem and have a Marxist-Leninist line.

This Marxist-Leninist line advanced by Chairman Mao is the lifeline of our Party.

Following this, in May 1963, under the direction of Chairman Mao, the *Draft Decision of the Central Committee of the Chinese Com-*

munist Party on Certain Problems in Our Present Rural Work (i.e., the 10-Point Decision) was worked out, which laid down the line, principles and policies of the Party for the socialist education movement. Chairman Mao again warned the whole Party: If classes and class struggle were forgotten and if the dictatorship of the proletariat were forgotten,

> then it would not be long, perhaps only several years or a decade, or several decades at most, before a counter-revolutionary restoration on a national scale would inevitably occur, the Marxist-Leninist party would undoubtedly become a revisionist party or a fascist party, and the whole of China would change its color. Comrades, please think it over. What a dangerous situation this would be!

Thus Chairman Mao still more sharply showed the whole Party and the whole nation the danger of the restoration of capitalism.

All these warnings and struggles did not and could not in the least change the reactionary class nature of Liu Shao-chi and his gang. In 1964, in the great socialist education movement, Liu Shao-chi came out to repress the masses, shield the capitalist-roaders in power and openly attack the Marxist scientific method of investigating and studying social conditions initiated by Chairman Mao, branding it as "outdated." He raved that whoever refused to carry out his line was "not qualified to hold a leading post." He and his gang were working against time to restore capitalism. At the end of 1964, Chairman Mao convened a working conference of the Central Committee and, under his direction, the document *Some Current Problems Raised in the Socialist Education Movement in the Rural Areas (i.e., the 23-Point Document)* was drawn up. He denounced Liu Shao-chi's bourgeois reactionary line which was "Left" in form but Right in essence and repudiated Liu Shao-chi's absurdities, such as "the intertwining of the contradictions inside and outside the Party" and "the contradiction between the 'four cleans' and the 'four uncleans'." And for the first time Chairman Mao specifically indicated: **"The main target of the present movement is those Party persons in power taking the capitalist road."** This new conclusion drawn by Chairman Mao after summing up the historical experience of the dictatorship of the proletariat, domestic and international, set right the course of the socialist education movement and clearly showed the orientation for the approaching Great Proletarian Cultural Revolution.

Reviewing the history of this period, we can see that the current Great Proletarian Cultural Revolution with the participation of hundreds of millions of revolutionary people has by no means occurred accidentally. It is the inevitable result of the protracted and sharp struggle between the two classes, the two roads and the two lines in socialist society. The Great Proletarian Cultural Revolution is

a great political revolution carried out by the proletariat against
the bourgeoisie and all other exploiting classes; it is a continuation of the prolonged struggle waged by the Chinese Communist
Party and the masses of revolutionary people under its leadership
against the Kuomintang reactionaries, a continuation of the class
struggle between the proletariat and the bourgeoisie.

The heroic Chinese proletariat, poor and lower-middle peasants, People's Liberation Army, revolutionary cadres and revolutionary intellectuals, who were all determined to follow the great leader Chairman
Mao closely in taking the socialist road, could no longer tolerate the
restoration activities of Liu Shao-chi and his gang, and so a great class
battle was unavoidable.

As Chairman Mao pointed out in his talk in February 1967:

> In the past we waged struggles in rural areas, in factories, in the
> cultural field, and we carried out the socialist education move-
> ment. But all this failed to solve the problem because we did not
> find a form, a method, to arouse the broad masses to expose our
> dark aspect openly, in an all-round way and from below.

Now we have found this form—it is the Great Proletarian Cultural
Revolution. It is only by arousing the masses in their hundreds of
millions to air their views freely, write big-character posters and hold
great debates that the renegades, enemy agents, and capitalist-roaders
in power who have wormed their way into the Party can be exposed
and their plots to restore capitalism smashed. It is precisely with the
participation of the broad masses in the examination of Liu Shao-chi's
case that his true features as an old-line counter-revolutionary, renegade, hidden traitor and scab were brought to light. The Enlarged
Twelfth Plenary Session of the Eighth Central Committee of the Party
decided to dismiss Liu Shao-chi from all posts both inside and outside
the Party and to expel him from the Party once and for all. This was
a great victory for the hundreds of millions of the people. On the basis
of the theory of continuing the revolution under the dictatorship of
the proletariat, our great teacher Chairman Mao has personally initiated and led the Great Proletarian Cultural Revolution. This is indeed
"absolutely necessary and most timely" and it is a new and great contribution to the theory and practice of Marxist-Leninism.

ON THE COURSE OF THE GREAT PROLETARIAN
CULTURAL REVOLUTION

The Great Proletarian Cultural Revolution is a great political
revolution personally initiated and led by our great leader Chairman
Mao under the conditions of the dictatorship of the proletariat, a great
revolution in the realm of the superstructure. Our aim is to smash
revisionism, seize back that portion of power usurped by the bour-

geoisie, exercise all-round dictatorship of the proletariat in the superstructure, including all spheres of culture, and strengthen and consolidate the economic base of socialism so as to ensure that our country
continues to advance in giant strides along the road of socialism.

Back in 1962, at the Tenth Plenary Session of the Eighth Central
Committee of the Party, Chairman Mao pointed out:

> To overthrow a political power, it is always necessary first of all
> to create public opinion, to do work in the ideological sphere.
> This is true for the revolutionary class as well as for the counter-
> revolutionary class.

This statement of Chairman Mao's hit the Liu Shao-chi counter-revolutionary revisionist clique right on the head. It was solely for the purpose of creating public opinion to prepare for the overthrow of the
dictatorship of the proletariat that they spared no effort in seizing
upon the field of ideology and the superstructure, violently exercising
counter-revolutionary dictatorship over the proletariat in the various
departments they controlled and wildly spreading poisonous weeds.
To overthrow them politically, we must likewise first vanquish their
counter-revolutionary public opinion by revolutionary public opinion.

Chairman Mao has always attached major importance to the
struggle in ideology. After the liberation of our country, he initiated
on different occasions the criticism of the film *The Life of Wu Hsun*,
the Hu Feng counter-revolutionary clique, *Studies of "The Dream of
the Red Chamber,"* etc. And this time it was Chairman Mao again
who led the whole Party in launching the offensive on the bourgeois
positions occupied by Liu Shao-chi and his gang. Chairman Mao wrote
the celebrated essay *Where Do Correct Ideas Come From?* and other
documents, in which he criticized Liu Shao-chi's bourgeois idealism
and metaphysics, criticized the departments of literature and art under
Liu Shao-chi's control as being **still dominated by 'the dead,'** criticized
the Ministry of Culture by saying that **"if it refuses to change, it should
be renamed the Ministry of Emperors, Kings, Generals and Prime
Ministers, the Ministry of Scholars and Beauties or the Ministry of
Foreign Mummies"** and said that the Ministry of Health should likewise be renamed the **"Ministry of Health for Urban Overlords."** At
the call of Chairman Mao, the proletariat first launched a revolution
in the spheres of Peking Opera, the ballet and symphonic music, spheres
that had been regarded as sacred and inviolable by the landlord and
capitalist classes. It was a fight at close quarters. Despite every possible
kind of resistance and sabotage by Liu Shao-chi and his gang, the
proletariat finally scored important successes after arduous struggles.
A number of splendid model revolutionary theatrical works came into
being and the heroic images of the workers, peasants and soldiers finally
rose aloft on the stage. After that, Chairman Mao initiated the criticism
of *Hai Jui Dismissed From Office* and other poisonous weeds, focusing

the attack right on the den of the revisionist clique—that impenetrable and watertight "independent kingdom" under Liu Shao-chi's control, the old Peking Municipal Party Committee.

The *Circular* of May 16, 1966 worked out under Chairman Mao's personal guidance laid down the theory, line, principles and policies for the Great Proletarian Cultural Revolution and constituted the great program for the whole movement. The *Circular* thoroughly criticized the "February Outline" turned out by Liu Shao-chi's bourgeois head-quarters for the purpose of suppressing this great revolution. It called upon the whole Party and the whole nation to direct the spearhead of struggle against the representatives of the bourgeoisie who had sneaked into the Pary and to pay special attention to unmasking **persons like Khrushchev ... who are still nestling beside us.**" This was a great call mobilizing the people of the whole country to unfold a great political revolution. The Cultural Revolution Group Under the Central Committee, which was set up by decision of the *Circular*, has firmly carried out Chairman Mao's proletarian revolutionary line.

Under the guidance of Chairman Mao's proletarian revolutionary line, the broad revolutionary masses plunged into the fight. In Peking University a big-character poster was written in response to the call of the Central Committee. And soon big-character posters criticizing re-actionary bourgeois ideas mushroomed all over the country. Then Red Guards rose and came forward in large numbers and revolutionary young people became courageous and daring pathbreakers. Thrown into a panic, the Liu Shao-chi clique hastily hurled forth the bourgeois reactionary line, cruelly suppressing the revolutionary movement of the student youth. However, this did not win them much time in their death-bed struggle. Chairman Mao called and presided over the Eleventh Plenary Session of the Eighth Central Committee of the Party. The Plenary Session adopted the programatic document, *Decision of the Central Committee of the Chinese Communist Party Concerning the Great Proletarian Cultural Revolution (i.e., the 16-Point Decision)*. Chairman Mao put up his big-character poster *Bombard the Headquarters*, thus taking the lid off Liu Shao-chi's bourgeois headquarters. In his letter to the Red Guards, Chairman Mao said that the revolutionary actions of the Red Guards

> express your wrath against and your denunciation of the landlord class, the bourgeoisie, the imperialists, the revisionists and their running dogs, all of whom exploit and oppress the workers, peas-ants, revolutionary intellectuals and revolutionary parties and groups. They show that it is right to rebel against reactionaries. I warmly support you.

Afterwards, Chairman Mao received 13 million Red Guards and other revolutionary masses from all parts of the country on eight occasions at Tien An Men in the capital, which heightened the revolutionary fighting will of the people of the whole country. The revolutionary movements of the workers, peasants and revolutionary functionaries developed rapidly. Increasing numbers of big-character posters spread like raging prairie fire and roared like guns; the slogan "It is right to rebel against reactionaries" resounded throughout the land. And the battle of the hundreds of millions of the people to bombard Liu Shao-chi's bourgeois headquarters developed vigorously.

No reactionary class will ever step down from the stage of history of its own accord. When the revolution touched that portion of power usurped by the bourgeoisie, the class struggle became all the more acute. After Liu Shao-chi's downfall, his revisionist clique and his agents in various places changed their tactics time and again, putting forward slogans which were "Left" in form but Right in essence such as "suspecting all" and "overthrowing all," in a futile attempt to go on hitting hard at the many and protecting their own handful. Moreover, they created splits among the revolutionary masses and manipulated and hoodwinked a section of the masses so as to protect themselves. When these schemes were shattered by the proletarian revolutionaries, they launched another frenzied counter-attack, and that is the adverse current lasting from the winter of 1966 to the spring of 1967.

This adverse current was directed against the proletarian headquarters headed by Chairman Mao. Its general program boiled down to this: to overthrow the decisions adopted by the Eleventh Plenary Session of the Eighth Central Committee of the Party, reversing the verdict on the overthrown bourgeois headquarters headed by Liu Shao-chi, reversing the verdict on the bourgeois reactionary line, which had already been thoroughly repudiated and discredited by the broad masses, and repressing and retaliating on the revolutionary mass movement. However, this adverse current was seriously criticized by Chairman Mao and resisted by the broad revolutionary masses; it could not prevent the main current of the revolutionary mass movement from surging forward.

The twists and reversals in the revolutionary movement further brought home to the broad masses the importance of political power: the main reason why Liu Shao-chi and his gang could do evil was that they had usurped the power of the proletariat in many units and localities and the main reason why the revolutionary masses were repressed was that power was not in the hands of the proletariat in those places. In some units, the socialist system of ownership existed only in form, but in reality the leadership had been usurped by a handful of renegades, enemy agents, and capitalist-roaders in power, or it remained in the hands of former capitalists. Especially when the capitalist-roaders in power whipped up the evil counter-revolutionary wind of economism after failing in their scheme to suppress the revolution on the pretext of "grasping production," the broad masses came to understand still better that only by recapturing the lost power was it possible for them to defeat the capitalist-roaders in power completely. Under the leadership and with the support of Chairman Mao and the proletarian headquarters headed by him, the working class in Shanghai with its revolutionary tradition came forward courageously and, uniting with the broad revolutionary masses and revolutionary cadres, seized power from below in January 1967 from the capitalist-roaders in power in the former Municipal Party Committee and Municipal People's Council.

Chairman Mao summed up in good time the experience of the January storm of revolution in Shanghai and issued his call to the whole nation: **"Proletarian revolutionaries, unite and seize power from the handful of Party persons in power taking the capitalist road!"** Following that, Chairman Mao gave the instruction: **"The People's Liberation Army should support the broad masses of the Left."** He went on to sum up the experience of Heilungkiang Province and other provinces and municipalities and laid down the principles and policies for the establishment of the revolutionary committee which embraces representatives of the revolutionary cadres, representatives of the People's Liberation Army and representatives of the revolutionary masses, constituting a revolutionary three-in-one combination, thus pushing forward the nationwide struggle for the seizure of power.

The struggle between the proletariat and the bourgeoisie for the seizure and counter-seizure of power was a life-and-death struggle. During the one year and nine months from Shanghai's January storm of revolution in 1967 to the establishment of the revolutionary committees of Tibet and Sinkiang in September 1968, repeated trials of political strength took place between the two classes and the two lines, fierce struggles went on between proletarian and non-proletarian ideas and an extremely complicated situation emerged. As Chairman Mao has said:

> In the past, we fought north and south; it was easy to fight such wars. For the enemy was obvious. The present Great Proletarian Cultural Revolution is much more difficult than that kind of war. The problem is that those who commit ideological errors are mixed up with those whose contradiction with us is one between ourselves and the enemy, and for a time it is hard to sort them out.

Nevertheless, relying on the wise leadership of Chairman Mao, we finally overcame this difficulty. In the summer of 1967, Chairman Mao made an inspection tour north and south of the Yangtze River and issued extremely important instructions, guiding the broad revolutionary masses to distinguish gradually the contradictions between ourselves and the enemy from those among the people and to further bring about the revolutionary great alliance and the revolutionary three-in-one combination and guiding people with petty-bourgeois ideas onto the path of the proletarian revolution. Consequently, it was only the enemy who was thrown into disorder while the broad masses were steeled in the course of the struggle.

The handful of renegades, enemy agents, unreformed landlords, rich peasants, counter-revolutionaries, bad elements and rightists, active counter-revolutionaries, bourgeois careerists and double-dealers who had hidden themselves among the masses would not reveal their colors until the climate suited them. In the summer of 1967 and the spring of 1968, they again fanned up a reactionary evil wind to reverse correct verdicts both from the Right and the extreme "Left." They directed their spearhead against the proletarian headquarters headed by Chairman Mao, against the People's Liberation Army and against the new-born revolutionary committees. In the meantime, they incited the masses to struggle against each other and organized counter-revolutionary conspiratorial cliques in a vain attempt to stage a counter-seizure of power from the proletariat. However, like their chieftain Liu Shao-chi, this handful of bad people was finally exposed. This was an important victory for the Great Proletarian Cultural Revolution.

ON CARRYING OUT THE TASKS OF STRUGGLE-CRITICISM-TRANSFORMATION CONSCIENTIOUSLY

As in all other revolutions, the fundamental question in the current great revolution in the realm of the superstructure is the question of political power, a question of which class holds leadership. The establishment of revolutionary committees in all provinces, municipalities and autonomous regions throughout the country (with the exception of Tai-wan Province) marks the great, decisive victory achieved by this revolution. However, the revolution is not yet over. The proletariat must continue to advance, **"carry out the tasks of struggle-criticism-transformation conscientiously"** and carry the socialist revolution in the realm of the superstructure through to the end.

Chairman Mao says:

> Struggle-criticism-transformation in a factory, on the whole, goes through the following stages: Establishing a three-in-one revolutionary committee; carrying out mass criticism and repudiation; purifying the class ranks; consolidating the Party organization; and simplifying the administrative structure, changing irrational rules and regulations and sending office workers to the workshops.

We must act on Chairman Mao's instruction and fulfill these tasks in every single factory, every single school, every single commune and every single unit in a deep-going, meticulous, down-to-earth and appropriate way.

Confronted with a thousand and one tasks, a revolutionary committee must grasp the fundamental: it must put the living study and
application of Mao Tse-tung Thought above all work and place Mao
Tse-tung Thought in command of everything. For decades, Mao Tse-
tung Thought has been showing the orientation of the revolution to
the whole Party and the whole nation. However, as Liu Shao-chi and
his gang of counter-revolutionary revisionists blocked Chairman Mao's
instructions, the broad revolutionary masses could hardly hear Chairman Mao's voice directly. The storm of the present great revolution
has destroyed the "palaces of hell-rulers," big and small, and has made
it possible for Mao Tse-tung Thought to reach the broad revolutionary
masses directly. This is a great victory. This wide dissemination of Mao
Tse-tung Thought in a big country with a population of 700 million
is the most significant achievement of the Great Proletarian Cultural
Revolution. In this revolution, hundreds of millions of people always
carry with them *Quotations From Chairman Mao Tse-tung*, which they
study and apply conscientiously. As soon as a new instruction of Chairman Mao's is issued, they propagate it and go into action. This most
valuable practice must be maintained and persevered in. We should
carry on in a deep-going way the mass movement for the living study
and application of Mao Tse-tung Thought, continue to run well the
Mao Tse-tung Thought study classes of all types and, in the light of
Chairman Mao's *May 7 Directive* of 1966, truly turn the whole country
into a great school of Mao Tse-tung Thought.

All revolutionary comrades must be clearly aware that class struggle will by no means cease in the ideological and political spheres. The
struggle between the proletariat and the bourgeoisie by no means dies
out with our seizure of power. We must continue to hold high the
banner of revolutionary mass criticism and use Mao Tse-tung Thought
to criticize the bourgeoisie, to criticize revisionism and all kinds of
Right or extreme "Left" erroneous ideas which run counter to Chairman Mao's proletarian revolutionary line and to criticize bourgeois
individualism and the theory of "many centers," that is, the theory of
"no center." We must continue to criticize thoroughly and discredit
completely the stuff of the renegade, hidden traitor and scab Liu Shao-
chi such as the slavish comprador philosophy and the doctrine of trail-
ing behind at a snail's pace, and must firmly establish among the cadres
and the masses of the people Chairman Mao's concept of **"maintaining
independence and keeping the initiative in our own hands and relying
on our own efforts,"** so as to ensure that our cause will continue to
advance in the direction indicated by Chairman Mao.

Chairman Mao points out:

> The revolutionary committee should exercise unified leadership,
> eliminate duplication in the administrative structure, follow the

policy of "better troops and simpler administration" and organize itself into a revolutionized leading group which maintains close ties with the masses.

This is a basic principle which enables the superstructure to serve its socialist economic base still better. A duplicate administrative structure divorced from the masses, scholasticism which suppresses and binds their revolutionary initiative, and a landlord and bourgeois style of formality and ostentation—all these are destructive to the socialist economic base, advantageous to capitalism and disadvantageous to socialism. In accordance with Chairman Mao's instructions, organs of state power at all levels and other organizations must keep close ties with the masses, first of all with the basic masses—the working class and the poor and lower-middle peasants. Cadres, old and new, must constantly sweep away the dust of bureaucracy and must not catch the bad habit of "acting as bureaucrats and overlords." They must keep on practicing frugality in carrying out revolution, run all socialist undertakings industriously and thriftily, oppose extravagance and waste and guard against the bourgeois attacks with sugar-coated bullets. They must maintain the system of cadre participation in collective productive labor. They must be concerned with the well-being of the masses. They must themselves make investigation and study in accordance with Chairman Mao's teachings, dissect one or several "sparrows" and constantly sum up experiences. They must make criticism and self-criticism regularly and, in line with the five requirements for the successors to the revolution as set forth by Chairman Mao, **"fight self, criticize revisionism"** and conscientiously remold their world outlook.

The People's Liberation Army is the mighty pillar of the dictatorship of the proletariat. Chairman Mao has pointed out many times: From the Marxist point of view the main component of the state is the army. The Chinese People's Liberation Army personally founded and led by Chairman Mao is an army of the workers and peasants, an army of the proletariat. It has performed great historic feats in the struggle for overthrowing the three big mountains of imperialism, feudalism and bureaucrat-capitalism, and in the struggles for defending the motherland, for resisting U.S. aggression and aiding Korea and for smashing aggression by imperialism, revisionism and reactionaries. In the Great Proletarian Cultural Revolution, large numbers of commanders and fighters have taken part in the work of "three supports and two militaries" (i.e., support industry, support agriculture, support the broad masses of the Left, military control, political and military training) and representatives of the army have taken part in the three-in-one combination: they have tempered themselves in the class struggle, strengthened their ties with the masses, promoted the ideological revolutionization of the army, and made new contributions to the people. And this is also the best preparation against war. We must carry forward the glorious tradition of "supporting the government and cherishing the people," "supporting the army and cherishing the people," strengthen the unity between the army and the people, strengthen the building of the militia and of national defense and do a still better job in all our work. For the past three years, it is precisely because the people have supported the army and the army has protected the people that renegades, enemy agents, absolutely unrepentant persons in power taking the capitalist road and counter-revolutionaries have failed in their attempts to undermine this great people's army of ours.

Departments of culture, art, education, the press, health, etc., occupy an extremely important position in the realm of the superstructure. The line "We must whole-heartedly rely on the working class" was decided upon at the Second Plenary Session of the Seventh Central Committee. And now, at Chairman Mao's call that "The working class must exercise leadership in everything," the working class, which is the main force in the proletarian revolution, and its staunch ally the poor and lower-middle peasants have mounted the political stage of struggle-criticism-transformation in the superstructure. From July 27, 1968, mighty contingents of the working class marched to places long dominated by the persons in power taking the capitalist road and to all places where intellectuals were predominant in number. It was a great revolutionary action. Whether the proletariat is able to take firm root in the positions of culture and education and transform them with Mao Tse-tung Thought is the key question in carrying the Great Proletarian Cultural Revolution through to the end. Chairman Mao has attached profound importance to our work in this connection and personally grasped typicals, thus setting us a brilliant example. We must overcome the wrong tendency among some comrades who make light of the ideological, cultural and educational front; we must closely follow Chairman Mao and consistently do arduous and meticulous work. "On its part, the working class should always raise its political consciousness in the course of struggle," sum up the experience in leading the struggle-criticism-transformation in the superstructure and win the battle on this front.

ON THE POLICIES OF THE GREAT PROLETARIAN CULTURAL REVOLUTION

In order to continue the revolution in the realm of the superstructure, it is imperative to carry out conscientiously all Chairman Mao's proletarian policies.

Policies for the Great Proletarian Cultural Revolution were early explicitly stipulated in the *Circular* of May 16, 1966 and the *16-Point Decision* of August 1966. The series of Chairman Mao's latest instructions including "serious attention must be paid to policy in the stage of struggle-criticism-transformation in the Great Proletarian Cultural Revolution" have further specified the various policies.

The main question at present is to carry them out to the letter.

The Party's policies, including those towards the intellectuals, the cadres, "the sons and daughters that can be educated" [The sons and daughters of those who have committed crimes or mistakes.—*Translator*], the mass organizations, the struggle against the enemy and the economic policy—all these policies come under the general subject of the correct handling of the two different types of contradictions, those between ourselves and the enemy and those among the people.

The majority or the vast majority of the intellectuals trained in the old type of schools and colleges are able or willing to integrate themselves with the workers, peasants and soldiers. They should be "re-educated" by the workers, peasants and soldiers under the guidance of Chairman Mao's correct line, and encouragement should be given to those who have done well in the integration and to the Red Guards and educated young people who are active in going to the countryside or mountainous areas.

Chairman Mao has taught us many times: "Help more people by educating them and narrow the target of attack" and "carry out Marx's teaching that only by emancipating all mankind can the proletariat achieve its own final emancipation." With regard to people who have made mistakes, stress must be laid on giving them education and re-education, doing patient and careful ideological and political work and truly acting "on the principle of 'learning from past mistakes to avoid future ones' and 'curing the sickness to save the patient,' in order to achieve the twofold objective of clarity in ideology and unity among comrades." With regard to good people who committed the errors characteristic of the capitalist-roader in power but have now raised their political consciousness and gained the understanding of the masses, they should be promptly "liberated," assigned to suitable work and encouraged to go among the masses of the workers and peasants to remold their world outlook. As for those who have made a little progress and became to some extent awakened, we should continue to help them, proceeding from the viewpoint of unity. Chairman Mao has recently pointed out:

> The proletariat is the greatest class in the history of mankind. It is the most powerful revolutionary class ideologically, politically and in strength. It can and must unite the overwhelming majority of people around itself so as to isolate the handful of enemies to the maximum and attack them.

In the struggle against the enemy, we must carry out the policy "make use of contradictions, win over the many, oppose the few and crush our enemies one by one" which Chairman Mao has always advocated. "**Stress should be laid on the weight of evidence and on in-vestigation and study, and it is strictly forbidden to obtain confessions by compulsion and to give them credence.**" We must implement Chair-man Mao's policies of "**leniency towards those who confess their crimes and severe punishment of those who refuse to do so**" and of "**giving a way out.**" We rely mainly on the broad masses of the people in exercis-ing dictatorship over the enemy. As for bad people or suspects ferreted out through investigation in the movement for purifying the class ranks, the policy of "**killing none and not arresting most**" should be applied to all except the active counter-revolutionaries against whom there is conclusive evidence of crimes such as murder, arson or poisoning, and who should be dealt with in accordance with the law.

As for the bourgeois reactionary and academic authorities, we should either criticize them and see, or criticize then and give them work to do, or criticize them and provide them with a proper livelihood. In short, we should criticize their ideology and at the same time give them a way out. To handle this part of the contradictions between ourselves and the enemy in the manner of handling contradictions among the people is beneficial to the consolidation of the dictatorship of the proletariat and to the disintegration of the enemy ranks.

In carrying out the policies of the Party, it is necessary to study the specific conditions of the unit concerned. In places where the revo-lutionary great alliance has not yet been sufficiently consolidated, it is necessary to help the revolutionary masses bring about, in accordance with revolutionary principles, the revolutionary great alliance on the basis of different fields of work, trades and school classes so that they will become united against the enemy. In units where the work of purifying the class ranks has not yet started or has only just started, it is imperative to grasp the work firmly and do it well in accordance with the Party's policies. In units where the purification of the class ranks is by and large completed, it is necessary to take firm hold of other tasks in keeping with Chairman Mao's instructions concerning the various stages of struggle-criticism-transformation. At the same time, it is necessary to pay close attention to new trends in the class struggle. What if the bad people go wild again? Chairman Mao has a well-known saying: "**Thoroughgoing materialists are fearless.**" If the class enemies stir up trouble again, just arouse the masses and strike them down again.

As the *16-Point Decision* indicates, "**The Great Proletarian Cul-tural Revolution is a powerful motive force for the development of the social productive forces in our country.**" Our country has seen good harvests in agricultural production for years running and there is also a thriving situation in industrial production and science and technol-ogy. The enthusiasm of the broad masses of the working people both in revolution and production has soared to unprecedented heights. Many factories, mines and other enterprises have time and again topped their production records, creating all-time highs in production. The technical revolution is making constant progress. The market is flourishing and prices are stable. By the end of 1968 we had redeemed all the national bonds. Our country is now a socialist country with neither internal nor external debts.

"Grasp revolution, promote production"—this principle is absolutely correct. It correctly explains the relationship between revolution and production, between consciousness and matter, between the superstructure and the economic base and between the relations of production and the productive forces. Chairman Mao always teaches us: "Political work is the life-blood of all economic work." Lenin denounced the opportunists who were opposed to approaching problems politically: "Politics cannot but have precedence over economics. To argue differently means forgetting the A B C of Marxism." (Lenin, *Collected Works*, Chinese ed., Vol. 32, p. ¨2.) Lenin again stated: To put politics on a par with economics also means "forgetting the A B C of Marxism." (Ibid.) Politics is the concentrated expression of economics. If we fail to make revolution in the superstructure, fail to arouse the broad masses of the workers and peasants, fail to criticize the revisionist line, fail to expose the handful of renegades, enemy agents, capitalist-roaders in power and counter-revolutionaries and fail to consolidate the leadership of the proletariat, how can we further consolidate the socialist economic base and further develop the socialist productive forces? This is not to replace production by revolution but to use revolution to command production, promote it and lead it forward. We must make investigation and study, and actively and properly solve the many problems of policy in struggle-criticism-transformation on the economic front in accordance with Chairman Mao's general line of "Going all out, aiming high and achieving greater, faster, better and more economical results in building socialism" and in accordance with his great strategic concept "Be prepared against war, be prepared against natural disasters, and do everything for the people" and with the series of principles such as "take agriculture as the foundation and industry as the leading factor." We must bring the revolutionary initiative and creativeness of the people of all nationalities into full play, firmly grasp revolution and energetically promote production and fulfill and overfulfill our plans for developing the national economy. It is certain that the great victory of the Great Proletarian Cultural Revolution will continue to bring about new leaps forward on the economic front and in our cause of socialist construction as a whole.

ON THE FINAL VICTORY OF THE REVOLUTION IN OUR COUNTRY

The victory of the Great Proletarian Cultural Revolution of our country is very great indeed. But we must in no way think that we may

sit back and relax. Chairman Mao pointed out in his talk in October
1968:

> We have won great victory. But the defeated class will still strug-
> gle. These people are sill around and this class still exists. There-
> fore, we cannot speak of final victory. Not even for decades. We
> must not lose our vigilance. According to the Leninist viewpoint,
> the final victory of a socialist country not only requires the efforts
> of the proletariat and the broad masses of the people at home,
> but also involves the victory of the world revolution and the aboli-
> tion of the system of exploitation of man by man on the whole
> globe, upon which all mankind will be emancipated. Therefore, it
> is wrong to speak lightly of the final victory of the revolution in
> our country; it runs counter to Leninism and does not conform to
> facts.

There will be reversals in the class struggle. We must never forget class
struggle and never forget the dictatorship of the proletariat. In the
course of carrying out our policies at present, there still exists the
struggle between the two lines and there is interference from the "Left"
or the Right. It still calls for much effort to accomplish the tasks for
all the stages of struggle-criticism-transformation. We must closely follow Chairman Mao and steadfastly rely on the broad revolutionary
masses to surmount the difficulties and twists and turns on our way
forward and seize still greater victories in the cause of socialism.

ON THE CONSOLIDATION AND BUILDING OF THE PARTY

The victory of the Great Proletarian Cultural Revolution has
provided us with valuable experience on how we should build the Party
under the conditions of the dictatorship of the proletariat. As Chairman Mao has indicated to the Whole Party.

> The Party organization should be composed of the advanced
> elements of the proletariat; it should be a vigorous vanguard
> organization capable of leading the proletariat and the revolu-
> tionary masses in the fight against the class enemy.

Chairman Mao's instruction has determined our political orientation
for consolidating and building the Party.
    The Communist Party of China has been nurtured and built up
by our great leader Chairman Mao. Since its birth in 1921, our Party
has gone through long years of struggle for the seizure of state power
and the consolidation of the dictatorship of the proletariat by armed
force. Led by Chairman Mao, our Party has always stood in the fore-
front of revolutionary wars and struggles. Under the guidance of Chairman Mao's correct line, our Party has, in the face of extremely strong
domestic and foreign enemies and in the most complex circumstances,

led the proletariat and the broad masses of the people of China in adhering to the principle of **maintaining independence and keeping the initiative in our own hands and relying on our own efforts,** in upholding proletarian internationalism and in waging heroic struggles with one stepping into the breach as another fell, and it is only thus that our Party has grown from Communist groups with only a few dozen members at the outset into the great, glorious and correct Party leading the powerful People's Republic of China today. We deeply understand that without the armed struggle of the people, there would not be the Communist Party of China today and there would not be the People's Republic of China today. We must forever bear in mind Chairman Mao's teaching: **"Comrades throughout the Party must never forget this experience for which we have paid in blood."**

The Communist Party of China owes all its achievements to the wise leadership of Chairman Mao and these achievements constitute victories for Mao Tse-tung Thought. For half a century now, in leading the great struggle of the people of all the nationalities of China for accomplishing the new-democratic revolution, in leading China's great struggle for socialist revolution and socialist construction and in the great struggle of the contemporary international communist movement against imperialism, modern revisionism and reactionaries of various countries, Chairman Mao has integrated the universal truth of Marxism-Leninism with the concrete practice of revolution, has inherited, defended and developed Marxism-Leninism in the political, military, economic, cultural and philosophical spheres, and has brought Marxism-Leninism to a higher and completely new stage. Mao Tse-tung Thought is Marxism-Leninism of the era in which imperialism is heading for total collapse and socialism is advancing to world-wide victory. The entire history of our Party has borne out this truth: Departing from the leadership of Chairman Mao and Mao Tse-tung Thought, our Party will suffer setbacks and defeats; following Chairman Mao closely and acting on Mao Tse-tung Thought, our Party will advance and triumph. We must forever remember this lesson. Whoever opposes Chairman Mao, whoever opposes Mao Tse-tung Thought, at any time or under any circumstances, will be condemned and punished by the whole Party and the whole nation.

Discussing the consolidation and building of the Party, Chairman Mao has said:

> A human being has arteries and veins through which the heart makes the blood circulate, and he breathes with his lungs, exhaling carbon dioxide and inhaling fresh oxygen, that is, getting rid of the stale and taking in the fresh. A proletarian party must also get rid of the stale and take in the fresh, for only thus can it be full of vitality. Without eliminating waste matter and absorbing fresh blood the Party has no vigor.

With this vivid analogy, Chairman Mao has expounded the dialectics of inner-Party contradiction. **"The law of contradiction in things, that is, the law of the unity of opposites, is the basic law of materialist dialectics."** Opposition and struggle between the two lines within the Party are a reflection inside the Party of contradictions between classes and between the new and the old in society. If there were no contradictions in the Party and no struggles to resolve them, and if the Party did not get rid of the stale and take in the fresh, the Party's life would come to an end. Chairman Mao's theory on inner-Party contradiction is and will be the fundamental guiding thinking for the consolidation and building of the Party.

The history of the Communist Party of China is one in which Chairman Mao's Marxist-Leninist line combats the Right and "Left" opportunist lines in the Party. Under the leadership of Chairman Mao, our Party defeated Chen Tu-hsiu's Right opportunist line, defeated the "Left" opportunist lines of Ch'ü Ch'iu-pai and Li Li-san, defeated Wang Ming's first "Left" and then Right opportunist lines, defeated Chang Kuo-t'ao's line of splitting the Red Army, defeated the Right opportunist anti-Party bloc of P'eng Teh-huai, Koa Kang, Jao Shu-shih and others and after long years of struggle, has shattered Liu Shao-chi's counterrevolutionary revisionist line. Our Party has consolidated itself, developed and grown in strength precisely in the struggle between the two lines, especially in the struggles to defeat the three renegade cliques of Ch'en Tu-hsiu, Wang Ming and Liu Shao-chi, which did the gravest harm to the Party.

In the new historical period of the dictatorship of the proletariat, the proletariat enforces its dictatorship and exercises its leadership in every field of work through its vanguard the Communist Party. Departing from the dictatorship of the proletariat and from continuing the revolution under the dictatorship of the proletariat, it is impossible to solve correctly the question of Party building, the question of building what kind of Party and how to build it.

Liu Shao-chi's revisionist line on Party building betrayed the very essence of the Marxist-Leninist teaching on the dictatorship of the proletariat and of the Marxist-Leninist theory on Party building. At the crucial moment when China's socialist revolution was deepening and the class struggle was extraordinary acute, Liu Shao-chi had his sinister book *Self-Cultivation* republished and it was precisely his aim to overthrow the dictatorship of the proletariat in our country and restore the dictatorship of the bourgeoisie. When he copied the passage from Lenin on the necessity of the dictatorship of the proletariat, which we quoted earlier in this report, Liu Shao-chi once again deliberately omitted the most important conclusion that **"the dictatorship of the proletariat is essential,"** thereby clearly revealing his own counterrevolutionary features as a renegade to the dictatorship of the proletariat. Moreover, Liu Shao-chi went on spreading such reactionary fallacies as the theory of "the dying out of class struggle," the theory of "docile tools," the theory that "the masses are backward," the theory of "joining the Party in order to climb up," the theory of "inner-Party peace" and the theory of "merging private and public interests" (*i.e.*, "losing a little to gain much"), in a vain attempt to corrupt and disintegrate our Party, so that the more the Party members "cultivated" themselves, the more revisionist they would become and so that the Marxist-Leninist Party would "evolve peacefully" into a revisionist party and the dictatorship of the proletariat into the dictatorship of the bourgeoisie. We should carry on revolutionary mass criticism and repudiation and thoroughly eliminate the pernicious influence of Liu Shao-chi's reactionary fallacies.

The Great Proletarian Cultural Revolution is the most broad and deep-going movement for Party consolidation in the history of our Party. The Party organizations at various levels and the broad masses of Communists have experienced the acute struggle between the two lines, gone through the test in the large-scale class struggle and undergone examination by the revolutionary masses both inside and outside the Party. In this way, the Party members and cadres have faced the world and braved the storm and have raised their class consciousness and their consciousness of the struggle between the two lines. This great revolution tells us: Under the dictatorship of the proletariat, we must educate the masses of Party members on classes, on class struggle, on the struggle between the two lines and on continuing the revolution. We must fight revisionism both inside and outside the Party, clear the Party of renegades, enemy agents and other elements representing the interests of the exploiting classes and admit into the Party the genuine advanced elements of the proletariat who have been tested in the great storm. We must strive to ensure that the leadership of the Party organizations at all levels is truly in the hands of Marxists. We must see to it that the Party members really integrate theory with practice, maintain close ties with the masses and are bold in making criticism and self-criticism. We must see to it that the Party members will always keep to the style of being modest, prudent and free from arrogance and rashness and to the style of arduous struggle and plain living. Only thus will the Party be able to lead the proletariat and the revolutionary masses in carrying the socialist revolution through to the end.

Chairman Mao teaches us:

> Historical experience merits attention. A line or a viewpoint must be explained constantly and repeatedly. It won't do to explain them only to a few people; they must be made known to the broad revolutionary masses.

The study and spread of the basic experience of the Great Proletarian

Cultural Revolution, the study and spread of the history of the struggle between the two lines and the study and spread of Chairman Mao's theory of continuing the revolution under the dictatorship of the proletariat must be conducted not just once but should be repeated every year, every month, every day. Only thus will it be possible for the masses of Party members and the people to criticize and resist erroneous lines and tendencies the moment they emerge, and will it be possible to guarantee that our Party will always forge ahead victoriously along the correct course charted by Chairman Mao.

The revision of the Party Constitution is an important item on the agenda of the Ninth National Congress of the Party. The Central Committee has submitted the draft Party Constitution to the congress for discussion. This draft was worked out jointly by the whole Party and the revolutionary masses throughout the country. Since November 1967 when Chairman Mao proposed that basic Party organizations take part in the revision of the Party Constitution, the Central Committee has received several thousand drafts. On this basis the Enlarged Twelfth Plenary Session of the Eighth Central Committee of the Party drew up the draft Party Constitution, upon which the whole Party, the whole army and the revolutionary masses throughout the country once again held enthusiastic and earnest discussions. It may be said that the draft of the new Party Constitution is the product of the integration of the great leader Chairman Mao's wise leadership with the broad masses; it reflects the will of the whole Party, the whole army and the revolutionary masses throughout the country and gives a vivid demonstration of the democratic centralism and the mass line to which the Party has always adhered. Especially important is the fact that the draft Party Constitution has clearly reaffirmed that Marxism-Leninism-Mao Tse-tung Thought is the theoretical basis guiding the Party's thinking. This is a great victory for the Great Proletarian Cultural Revolution in smashing Liu Shao-chi's revisionist line on Party building, a great victory for Marxism-Leninism-Mao Tse-tung Thought. The Central Committee is convinced that, after the discussion and adoption of the new Party Constitution by the congress, our Party will, in accordance with its provisions, surely be built into a still greater, still more glorious and still more correct Party.

ON CHINA'S RELATIONS WITH FOREIGN COUNTRIES

Now we shall go on specifically to discuss China's relations with foreign countries.

The revolutionary struggles of the proletariat and the oppressed people and nations of the world always support each other. The Albanian Party of Labor and all other genuine fraternal Marxist-Leninist Parties and organizations, the broad masses of the proletariat and revolutionary people throughout the world as well as many friendly countries, organizations and personages have all warmly acclaimed and supported the Great Proletarian Cultural Revolution of our country. On behalf of the great leader Chairman Mao and the Ninth National Congress of the Party, I hereby express our heartfelt thanks to them. We firmly pledge that we the Communist Party of China and the Chinese people are determined to fulfill our proletarian internationalist duty and, together with them, carry through to the end the great struggle against imperialism, modern revisionism and all reaction.

The general trend of the world today is still as Chairman Mao described it: **"The enemy rots with every passing day, while for us things are getting better daily."** On the one hand, the revolutionary movement of the proletariat of the world and of the people of various countries is vigorously surging forward. The armed struggles of the people of southern Vietnam, Laos, Thailand, Burma, Malaya, Indonesia, India, Palestine and other countries and regions in Asia, Africa and Latin America are steadily growing in strength. The truth that **"Political power grows out of the barrel of a gun"** is being grasped by ever broader masses of the oppressed people and nations. An unprecedentedly gigantic revolutionary mass movement has broken out in Japan, Western Europe and North America, the "heartlands" of capitalism. More and more people are awakening. The genuine fraternal Marxist-Leninist Parties and organizations are growing steadily in the course of integrating Marxism-Leninism with the concrete practice of revolution in their own countries. On the other hand, U.S. imperialism and Soviet revisionist social-imperialism are bogged down in political and economic crises, beset with difficulties both at home and abroad and find themselves in an impasse. They collude and at the same time contend with each other in a vain attempt to redivide the world. They act in coordination and work hand in glove in opposing China, opposing communism and opposing the people, in suppressing the national liberation movement and in launching wars of aggression. They scheme against each other and get locked in strife for raw materials, markets, dependencies, important strategic points and spheres of influence. They are both stepping up arms expansion and war preparations, each trying to realize its own ambitions.

Lenin pointed out: Imperialism means war. **". . . imperialist wars are absolutely inevitable under** *such* **an economic system,** *as long as* **private property in the means of production exists."** (Lenin, *Collected Works*, Chinese ed., Vol. 22, p. 182.) Lenin further pointed out: **"Imperialist war is the eve of socialist revolution."** (Lenin, *Collected Works*, Chinese ed., Vol. 25, p. 349.) These scientific theses of Lenin's are by no means out of date.

Chairman Mao has recently pointed out, **"With regard to the question of world war, there are but two possibilities: One is that the**

war will give rise to revolution and the other is that revolution will prevent the war." This is because there are four major contradictions in the world today: The contradiction between the oppressed nations on the one hand and imperialism and social-imperialism on the other; the contradiction between the proletariat and the bourgeoisie in the capitalist and revisionist countries; the contradiction between imperialist and social-imperialist countries and among the imperialist countries; and the contradiction between socialist countries on the one hand and imperialism and social-imperialism on the other. The existence and development of these contradictions are bound to give rise to revolution. According to the historical experience of World War I and World War II, it can be said with certainty that if the imperialists, revisionists and reactionaries should impose a third world war on the people of the world, it would only greatly accelerate the development of these contradictions and help arouse the people of the world to rise in revolution and send the whole pack of imperialists, revisionists and reactionaries to their graves.

Chairman Mao teaches us: "**All reactionaries are paper tigers.**" "**Strategically we should despise all our enemies, but tactically we should take them all seriously.**" This great truth enunciated by Chairman Mao heightens the revolutionary militancy of the people of the whole world and guides us from victory to victory in the struggle against imperialism, revisionism and all reaction.

The nature of U.S. imperialism as a paper tiger has long since been laid bare by the people throughout the world. U.S. imperialism, the most ferocious enemy of the people of the whole world, is going downhill more and more. Since he took office, Nixon has been confronted with a hopeless mess and an insoluble economic crisis, with the strong resistance of the masses of the people at home and throughout the world and with the predicament in which the imperialist countries are disintegrating and the baton of U.S. imperialism is getting less and less effective. Unable to produce any solution to these problems, Nixon, like his predecessors, cannot but continue to play the counterrevolutionary dual tactics, ostensibly assuming a "peace-loving" appearance while in fact engaging in arms expansion and war preparations on a still larger scale. The military expenditures of the United States have been increasing year by year. To date the U.S. imperialists still occupy our territory Taiwan. They have dispatched aggressor troops to many countries and have also set up hundreds upon hundreds of military bases and military installations in different parts of the world. They have made so many airplanes and guns, so many nuclear bombs and guided missiles. What is all this for? To frighten, suppress and slaughter the people and dominate the world. By doing so they make themselves the enemy of the people everywhere and find themselves besieged and battered by the broad masses of the proletariat and the people all over the world, and this will definitely lead to revolutions throughout the world on a still larger scale.

The Soviet revisionist renegade clique is a paper tiger, too. It has revealed its social-imperialist features more and more clearly. When Khrushchev revisionism was just beginning to emerge, our great leader Chairman Mao foresaw what serious harm modern revisionism would do to the cause of world revolution. Chairman Mao led the whole Party in waging resolute struggles in the ideological, theoretical and political spheres, together with the Albanian Party of Labor headed by the great Marxist-Leninist Comrade Enver Hoxha and with the genuine Marxist-Leninists of the world, against modern revisionism with Soviet revisionism as its center. This has enabled the people all over the world to learn gradually in struggle how to distinguish genuine Marxism-Leninism from sham Marxism-Leninism and genuine socialism from sham socialism and brought about the bankruptcy of Khrushchev revisionism. At the same time, Chairman Mao led our Party in resolutely criticizing Liu Shao-chi's revisionist line of capitulation to imperialism, revisionism and reaction and of suppression of revolutionary movements in various countries and in destroying Liu Shao-chi's counterrevolutionary revisionist clique. All this has been done in the fulfilment of our Party's proletarian internationalist duty.

Since Brezhnev came to power, with its baton becoming less and less effective and its difficulties at home and abroad growing more and more serious, the Soviet revisionist renegade clique has been practising social-imperialism and social-fascism more frantically than ever. Internally, it has intensified its suppression of the Soviet people and speeded up the all-round restoration of capitalism. Externally, it has stepped up its collusion with U.S. imperialism and its suppression of the revolutionary struggles of the people of various countries, intensified its control over and its exploitation of various East European countries and the People's Republic of Mongolia, intensified its contention with U.S. imperialism over the Middle East and other regions and intensified its threat of aggression against China. Its dispatch of hundreds of thousands of troops to occupy Czechoslovakia and its armed provocations against China on our territory Chenpao Island are two foul performances staged recently by Soviet revisionism. In order to justify its aggression and plunder, the Soviet revisionist renegade clique trumpets the so-called theory of "limited sovereignty," the theory of "international dictatorship" and the theory of "socialist community." What does all this stuff mean? It means that your sovereignty is "limited," while his is unlimited. You won't obey him? He will exercise "international dictatorship" over you—dictatorship over the people of other countries, in order to form the "socialist community" ruled by the new tsars, that is, colonies of social-imperialism, just like the "New Order of Europe" of Hitler, the "Greater East Asia Co-prosperity

Sphere" of Japanese militarism and the "Free World Community" of the United States. Lenin denounced the renegades of the Second International: **"Socialism in words, imperialism in deeds,** *the growth of opportunism and imperialism."* (Lenin, *Collected Works,* Chinese ed., Vol. 29, p. 458.) This applies perfectly to the Soviet revisionist renegade clique of today which is composed of a handful of capitalist-roaders in power. We firmly believe that the proletariat and the broad masses of the people in the Soviet Union with their glorious revolutionary tradition will surely rise and overthrow this clique consisting of a handful of renegades. As Chairman Mao points out:

> The Soviet Union was the first socialist state and the Communist Party of the Soviet Union was created by Lenin. Although the leadership of the Soviet Party and state has now been usurped by revisionists, I would advise comrades to remain firm in the conviction that the masses of the Soviet people and of Party members and cadres are good, that they desire revolution and that revisionist rule will not last long.

Now that the Soviet government has created the incident of armed encroachment on the Chinese territory Chenpao Island, the Sino-Soviet boundary question has caught the attention of the whole world. Like boundary questions between China and some of her other neighboring countries, the Sino-Soviet bounary question is also one left over by history. As regards these questions, our Party and Government have consistently stood for negotiations through diplomatic channels to reach a fair and reasonable settlement. Pending a settlement, the status quo of the boundary should be maintained and conflicts avoided. Proceeding from this stand, China has satisfactorily and successively settled boundary questions with neighboring countries such as Burma, Nepal, Pakistan, the People's Republic of Mongolia and Afghanistan. Only the boundary questions between the Soviet Union and China and between Indian and China remain unsettled to this day.

The Chinese Government held repeated negotiations with the Indian government on the Sino-Indian boundary question. As the reactionary Indian government had taken over the British imperialist policy of aggression, it insisted that we recognize the illegal "McMahon line" which even the reactionary governments of different periods in old China had not recognized, and moreover, it went a step further and vainly attempted to occupy the Aksai Chin area, which has always been under Chinese jurisdiction, thereby disrupting the Sino-Indian boundary negotiations. This is known to all.

The Sino-Soviet boundary question is the product of tsarist Russian imperialist aggression against China. In the latter half of the nineteenth century when power was not in the hands of the Chinese and Russian people, the tsarist government took imperialist acts of aggression to carve up China, imposed a series of unequal treaties on her, annexed vast expanses of her territory and, moreover, crossed the boundary line stipulated by the unequal treaties, in many places, and occupied still more Chinese territory. This ganster behavior was indignantly condemned by Marx, Engels and Lenin. On September 27, 1920, the Government of Soviets led by the great Lenin solemnly proclaimed: It "declares null and void all the treaties concluded with China by the former Governments of Russia, renounces all seizure of Chinese territory and all Russian concessions in China and restores to China, without any compensation and for ever, all that had been predatorily seized from her by the Tsar's Government and the Russian bourgeoisie." (See *Declaration of the Government of the Russian Socialist Federated Soviet Republic to the Chinese Government.*) Owing to the historical conditions of the time, this proletarian policy of Lenin's was not realized.

As early as August 22 and September 21, 1960, the Chinese Government, proceeding from its consistent stand on boundary questions, twice took the initiative in proposing to the Soviet government that negotiations be held to settle the Sino-Soviet boundary question. In 1964, negotiations between the two sides started in Peking. The treaties relating to the present Sino-Soviet boundary are unequal treaties imposed on the Chinese people by the tsars, but out of the desire to safeguard the revolutionary friendship between the Chinese and Soviet people, we still maintained that these treaties be taken as the basis for the settlement of the boundary question. However, betraying Lenin's proletarian policy and clinging to its new-tsarist social-imperialist stand, the Soviet revisionist renegade clique refused to recognize these treaties as unequal and, moreover, it insisted that China recognize as belonging to the Soviet Union all the Chinese territory which they had occupied or attempted to occupy in violation of the treaties. This great-power chauvinist and social-imperialist stand of the Soviet government led to the disruption of the negotiations.

Since Brezhnev came to power, the Soviet revisionist renegade clique has frenziedly stepped up its disruption of the status quo of the boundary and repeatedly provoked border incidents, shooting and killing our unarmed fishermen and peasants and encroaching upon China's sovereignty. Recently it has gone further and made successive armed intrusions into our territory Chenpao Island. Driven beyond the limits of their forbearance, our frontier guards have fought back in self-defense, dealing the aggressors well-deserved blows and triumphantly safeguarding our sacred territory. In an effort to extricate them from their predicament, Kosygin asked on March 21 to communicate with our leaders by telephone. Immediately on March 22, our Government replied with a memorandum, in which it was made clear that, "In view of the present relations between China and the Soviet Union, it is unsuitable to communicate by telephone. If the Soviet government has anything to say, it is asked to put it forward officially to the Chinese Government through diplomatic channels." On March 29, the Soviet government issued a statement still clinging to its obstinate aggressor stand, while expressing willingness to resume "consultations." Our Government is considering its reply to this.

The foreign policy of our Party and Government is consistent. It is: To develop relations of friendship, mutual assistance and co-operation with socialist countries on the principle of proletarian inter-nationalism; to support and assist the revolutionary struggles of all the oppressed people and nations; to strive for peaceful coexistence with countries having different social systems on the basis of the Five Principles of mutual respect for territorial integrity and sovereignty, mutual non-aggression, non-interference in each other's internal affairs, equality and mutual benefit, and peaceful coexistence, and to oppose the imperialist policies of aggression and war. Our proletarian foreign policy is not based on expediency; it is a policy in which we have long persisted. This is what we did in the past and we will persist in doing the same in the future.

We have always held that the internal affairs of each country should be settled by its own people. The relations between all countries and between all parties, big or small, must be built on the principles of equality and non-interference in each other's internal affairs. To safeguard these Marxist-Leninist principles, the Communist Party of China has waged a long struggle against the sinister great-power chauvinism of the Soviet revisionist renegade clique. This is a fact known to all. The Soviet revisionist renegade clique glibly talks of "fraternal parties" and "fraternal countries," but in fact it regards itself as the patriarchal party, and as the new tsar, who is free to invade and occupy the territory of other countries. They conduct sabotage and subversion against the Chinese Communist Party, the Albanian Party of Labor and other genuine Marxist-Leninist Parties. Moreover, when any party or any country in their so-called "socialist community" hold a slightly different view, they act ferociously and stop at nothing in suppressing, sabotaging and subverting and even sending troops to invade and occupy their so-called "fraternal countries" and kidnapping members of their so-called "fraternal parties." These fascist piratical acts have sealed their doom.

U.S. imperialism and Soviet revisionism are always trying to "isolate" China; this is China's honor. Their rabid opposition to China cannot do us the slightest harm. On the contrary, it serves to further arouse our people's determination to maintain independence and keep the initiative in our own hands, rely on our own efforts and work hard to make our country prosperous and powerful; it serves to prove to the whole world that China has drawn a clear line between herself on the one hand and U.S. imperialism and Soviet revisionism on the other. Today, it is not imperialism, revisionism and reaction but the proletariat and the revolutionary people of all countries that determine the destiny of the world. The genuine Marxist-Leninist Parties and organizations of various countries, which are composed of the advanced elements of the proletariat, are a new rising force that has infinitely broad prospects. The Communist Party of China is determined to unite and fight together with them. We firmly support the Albanian people in their struggle against imperialism and revisionism; we firmly support the Vietnamese people in carrying their war of resistance against U.S. aggression and for national salvation through to the end; we firmly support the revolutionary struggles of the people of Laos, Thailand, Burma, Malaya, Indonesia, India, Palestine and other countries and regions in Asia, Africa and Latin America; we firmly support the proletariat, the students and youth and the masses of the Black people of the United States in their just struggle against the U.S. ruling clique; we firmly support the proletariat and the laboring people of the Soviet Union in their just struggle to overthrow the Soviet revisionist renegade clique; we firmly support the people of Czechoslovakia and other countries in their just struggle against Soviet revisionist social-imperialism; we firmly support the revolutionary struggles of the people of Japan and the West European and Oceanian countries; we firmly support the revolutionary struggles of the people of all countries; and we firmly support all the just struggles of resistance against aggression and oppression by U.S. imperialism and Soviet revisionism. All countries and people subjected to aggression, control, intervention or bullying by U.S. imperialism and Soviet revisionism, unite and form the broadest possible united front and overthrow our common enemies!

On no account must we relax our revolutionary vigilance because of victory or ignore the danger of U.S. imperialism and Soviet revisionism launching a large-scale war of aggression. We must make full preparation, preparation against their launching a big war and against their launching a war at an early date, preparations against their launching a conventional war and against their launching a large-scale nuclear war. **In short, we must be prepared.** Chairman Mao said long ago: **We will not attack unless we are attacked; if we are attacked, we will certainly counterattack.** If they insist on fighting, we will keep them company and fight to the finish. The Chinese revolution won out on the battlefield. Armed with Mao Tse-tung Thought, tempered in the Great Proletarian Cultural Revolution, and with full confidence in victory, the Chinese people in their hundreds of millions, and the Chinese People's Liberation Army are determined to liberate their sacred territory Taiwan and **resolutely, thoroughly, wholly and completely wipe out** all aggressors who dare to come!

Our great leader Chairman Mao points out:

> Working hand in glove, Soviet revisionism and U.S. imperialism
> have done so many foul and evil things that the revolutionary
> people the world over will not let them go unpunished. The
> people of all countries are rising. A new historical period of
> opposing U.S. imperialism and Soviet revisionism has begun.

Whether the war gives rise to revolution or revolution prevents the
war, U.S. imperialism and Soviet revisionism will not last long! Workers
of all countries, unite! Proletarians and oppressed people and nations
of the world, unite! Bury U.S. imperialism, Soviet revisionism and their
lackeys!

THE WHOLE PARTY, THE WHOLE NATION UNITE TO
WIN STILL GREATER VICTORIES

The Ninth National Congress of the Party is being held at an
important moment in the historical development of our Party, at an
important moment in the consolidation and development of the dictatorship of the proletariat in our country and at an important moment
in the development of the international communist movement and
world revolution. Among the delegates to the congress are proletarian
revolutionaries of the older generation and also a large number of
fresh blood. In the previous congresses of our Party there have never
been such great numbers of delegates of Party members from among
the industrial workers, poor and lower-middle peasants, and of women
delegates. Among the delegates from the Party members in the People's
Liberation Army, there are veteran Red Army fighters as well as new
fighters. The delegates of Party members from among Red Guards are
attending a national congress of the Party for the first time. The fact
that so many delegates have come to Peking from all corners of the
country and gathered around the great leader Chairman Mao to discuss
and decide on the affairs of the Party and state signifies that our congress is a congress full of vitality, a congress of unity and a congress of
victory.

Chairman Mao teaches us: **The unification of our country, the
unity of our people and the unity of our various nationalities—these
are the basic guarantees of the sure triumph of our cause.** Through
the Great Proletarian Cultural Revolution our motherland has become
unprecedentedly unified and our people have achieved a great revolutionary unity on an extremely broad scale under the great red banner
of Mao Tse-tung Thought. This great unity is under the leadership
of the Proletariat and is based on the worker-peasant alliance; it embraces all the fraternal nationalities, the patriotic democrats who for

a long time have done useful work for the cause of the revolution and construction of our motherland, the vast numbers of patriotic overseas Chinese and our patriotic compatriots in Hong Kong and Macao, our patriotic compatriots in Taiwan who are oppressed and exploited by the U.S.–Chiang reactionaries, and all those who support socialism and love our socialist motherland. We are convinced that after the present national congress of our Party, the people of all the nationalities of our country will certainly unite still more closely under the leadership of the great leader Chairman Mao and win still greater victories in the struggle against our common enemy and in the cause of building our powerful socialist motherland.

Chairman Mao said in 1962:

> The next 50 to 100 years, beginning from now, will be a great era of radical change in the social system throughout the world, an earth-shaking era without equal in any previous historical period. Living in such an era, we must be prepared to engage in great struggles which will have many features different in form from those of the past.

This magnificent prospect far-sightedly envisioned by Chairman Mao illuminates our path of advance in the days to come and inspire all genuine Marxist-Leninists to fight valiantly for the realization of the grand ideal of communism.

Let the whole Party unite, let the whole nation unite, hold high the great red banner of Mao Tse-tung Thought, **be resolute, fear no sacrifice and surmount ever difficulty to win victory!**

Long live the great victory of the Great Proletarian Cultural Revolution!

Long live the dictatorship of the proletariat!

Long live the Ninth National Congress of the Party!

Long live the great, glorious and correct Communist Party of China!

Long live great Marxism-Leninism-Mao Tse-tung Thought!

Long live our great leader Chairman Mao! A long, long life to Chairman Mao!

AppENdix fOUR

Position Paper Commemorating the Fiftieth Anniversay of the
Communist Party of China, June 1971 [concluding portion].

This essay, according to an eyewitness report, "was in early
July, 1971, a Bible for China. Driver's read it. The girls in the elevator
at Peking read it, between passengers. The radio broadcasts it.
Companions cite it. . . ."*

A review of the fighting course traversed by our Party over the past 50
years confirms this truth: When our Party departs from Chairman
Mao's leadership and goes against Mao Tse-tung Thought and Chairman Mao's line, it suffers setbacks and defeats; when our Party closely
follows Chairman Mao, acts in accordance with Mao Tse-tung Thought
and implements Chairman Mao's line, it advances and triumphs. Comrade Mao Tse-tung's works are the most comprehensive summary of the
theory and practice of the Chinese Communists Party in leading the
revolution and construction. In summing up the historical experience
of our Party, Comrade Mao Tse-tung said in 1939:

> To sum up our eighteen years of experience and our current new
> experience on the basis of our understanding of the unity between
> the theory of Marxism-Leninism and the practice of the Chinese
> revolution, and to spread this experience throughout the Party,
> so that our Party becomes as solid as steel and avoids repeating
> past mistakes—such is our task.

Of the historical experience of our Party summed up by Chairman
Mao, what in particular should the whole Party pay attention to and
study today?

1. It is necessary to adhere to **"the consistent ideological principle
of our Party,"** namely, integrating the universal truth of Marxism-
Leninism with the concrete practice of the Chinese revolution.

---

* Ross Terrill, "The 800,000,000-Report From China," *Atlantic
Monthly*, November 1971, p. 92.

The history of our Party tells us: In his great practice in leading the Chinese revolution, Chairman Mao has always adhered to the world outlook of dialectical and historical materialism and used the Marxist-Leninist stand, viewpoint and method to make thorough investigations and studies of the political and economic status of the various classes in Chinese society and their interrelations, make a concrete analysis of the conditions of our enemies, our friends and ourselves, scientifically sum up positive and negative historical experience and correctly formulate the Party's line and policies; he has thus inherited, defended and developed Marxism-Leninism and led the whole Party, the whole army and the people of the whole country in their triumphant advance. But the divorce of theory and practice and the split between the subjective and the objective are the ideological characteristics of Ch'en Tu-hsiu, Wang Ming, Liu Shao-chi and other sham Marxists. Proceeding from their idealist and metaphysical world outlook, they opposed and distorted dialectical and historical materialism, opposed investigation and study and class analysis, and opposed the unity of theory and practice, either from the Right or from the "Left." They, too, talked about Marxism-Leninism and even pretended to be Marxist theoreticians, but only to bluff and hoodwink worker-peasant cadres and innocent young people, whereas they themselves never intended to act in accordance with Marxism but were always anti-Marxist. Hence their words and deeds inevitably ran counter to the objective laws of social development, to the desires of the masses and to Chairman Mao's revolutionary line which correctly reflects objective laws and the desires of the people, and they were bound to go bankrupt in the practice of revolution. For a time, some of our comrades were unable to distinguish between the correct and incorrect lines because, as far as the subjective factor was concerned, they had not read Marxist-Leninist works or, though having read some, they were unable to apply the fundamental ideological principle stressed time and time again by Comrade Mao Tse-tung in observing and handling problems and remold their subjective world in the process of transforming the objective world. This is a most profound historical lesson all Communist Party members, old and new, must always bear in mind.

In accordance with Chairman Mao's teaching **"Read and study seriously and have a good grasp of Marxism,"** comrades throughout the Party, and primarily senior cadres, are now conscientiously studying works by Marx, Engels, Lenin and Stalin and Chairman Mao's works, and studying the Party's historical experience over the past 50 years and its current new experience. The integration of the cadres' study movement with that of the masses has produced positive results and will continue to do so. We must persist in this. In reading and studying, it is essential to keep to the principle of integrating theory with practice. It is essential to read and study with problems in mind, problems arising in the three great revolutionary movements of class struggle, the struggle for production and scientific experiment, and problems in the Chinese and the world revolution. This means combining reading with investigation and study and with the summing up of experience, combining the study of historical experience with the present-day struggle and the criticism of opportunism in the past with the criticism of modern revisionism. Since countrywide liberation, Chairman Mao has led the whole Party in making a number of criticisms—from the criticism of *The Life of Wu Hsun* and the bourgeois ideology reflected in the study of *The Dream of the Red Chamber*, the criticism of Hu Shih, the Hu Feng counterrevolutionary clique and the bourgeois Rightists to the criticism of the Liu Shao-chi renegade clique; these criticisms have deeply educated the whole Party, army and people. The criticism of modern revisionism with the Soviet revisionist renegade clique at its center conducted by the whole Party under Chairman Mao's leadership and the great polemics on the general line of the international communist movement especially provide most profound and vivid Marxist-Leninist education for the whole Party. The struggle between Marxism-Leninism and modern revisionism is a struggle of principle between the two lines in the international communist movement. Khrushchev, Brezhnev and company are renegades from the proletarian revolution, mad present-day social-imperialists and world storm-troopers opposing China, opposing communism and opposing the people. It is our Party's bounden internationalist duty to continue the exposure of criticism of modern revisionism with Soviet revisionism at its center and carry the struggle through to the end. Comrades throughout the Party must combine the study of Marxism-Leninism with the criticism of modern revisionism in China and abroad, and learn to distinguish between genuine and sham Marxism and acquire a really good grasp of Marxism in the course of struggle.

2. It is necessary to wage inner-Party struggle correctly. Making a correct distinction between the two different types of contradictions—those between ourselves and the enemy and those among the people themselves—and handling them correctly are the fundamental guarantee that the Party will strengthen its unity on the basis of the principles of Marxism-Leninism-Mao Tse-tung Thought and lead the proletariat and the revolutionary masses in defeating the enemy.

It is essential thoroughly to expose the few bourgeois conspirators, careerists, renegades and enemy agents, who have concealed themselves in the Party, and the hidden traitors who have illicit relations with foreign countries. Bad people invariably disguise themselves and resort to conspiracy and double-dealing. But since they are engaged in evildoing, they are bound to expose themselves. For example, the renegade, hidden traitor and scab Liu Shao-chi who had hidden inside the Party for decades was exposed in the end; Wang Ming fled abroad and finally became a "100 percent" traitor and enemy agent.

As for comrades in the Party who have committed errors, they must all be dealt with according to a different principle, namely, **"unity, criticism, unity"** and **"learn from past mistakes to avoid future ones"** and **"cure the sickness to save the patient"** so as to achieve the twofold objective of clarity in ideology and units among comrades. In explaining this principle, Chairman Mao said:

> The mistakes of the past must be exposed without sparing anyone's sensibilities; it is necessary to analyse and criticize what was bad in the past with a scientific attitude so that work in the future will be done more carefully and done better. This is what is meant by "learn from past mistakes to avoid future ones." But our aim in exposing errors and criticizing shortcomings, like that of a doctor curing a sickness, is solely to save the patient and not to doctor him to death.

Chairman Mao once again stressed this principle during the Great Proletarian Cultural Revolution, pointing out:

> Apart from those obstinate anti-Party and anti-socialist elements who have refused to mend their ways after repeated education, people should be allowed to correct their errors and be encouraged to atone for their misdeeds.

This correct principle of Comrade Mao Tse-tung's in handling inner-Party contradictions is different from both the Right opportunist fallacy of "inner-Party peace," which negates contradictions and confuses right and wrong, and the "Left" opportunist fallacy of "ruthless struggle and merciless blows." We should study the historical experience of inner-Party struggle waged under different historical conditions so as to enable our Party to play its leading role as the vanguard of the proletariat still better.

3. Efforts must be made to guard against arrogance. This is of particular importance to a Party which has won great victories, a Party which is in power and leads the people of all nationalities of the country in carrying out the socialist revolution and construction and a Party which shoulders great internationalist obligations to the proletariat and the oppressed people and nations of the world.

Comrade Mao Tse-tung pointed out:

> There have been several occasions in the history of our Party when great conceit manifested itself and we suffered in consequence. The first was in the early half of 1927. The Northern Expeditionary Army had reached Wuhan, and some comrades became so proud and overweening as to forget that the Kuomintang was about to

assault us. The result was the error of the Ch'en Tu-hsiu line, which brought defeat to the revolution. The second occasion was in 1930. Taking advantage of Chiang Kai-shek's large-scale war against Feng Yu-hsiang and Yen Hsi-shan, the Red Army won a number of battles, and again some comrades became proud and overweening. The result was the error of the Li Li-san line, again causing some losses to the revolutionary forces. The third occasion was in 1931. The Red Army had smashed the Kuomintang's third "encirclement and suppression" campaign and, immediately after-wards, faced with the Japanese invasion, the people throughout the country started the stormy and heroic anti-Japanese move-ment; and again some comrades became proud and overweening. The result was an even more serious error in the political line, which cost us about 90 percent of the revolutionary forces that we had built up with so much toil. The fourth occasion was in 1938. The War of Resistance had begun and the united front had been established; and one again some comrades became proud and overweening. As a result they committed an error somewhat similar to the Chen Tu-hsiu line. This time the revolutionary work suf-fered serious damage in those places where the effects of these comrades' erroneous ideas were more especially pronounced. Com-rades throughout the Party should take warning from these in-stances of pride and error.

They should "not repeat the error of becoming conceited at the mo-ment of success."

"Modesty helps one to go forward, whereas conceit makes one lag behind. This is a truth we must always bear in mind."

4. We should follow the theory of two points, not the theory of one point. While paying attention to the main tendency, we should take note of the other tendency which may be covered up. We must take full notice and firmly grasp the principal aspect and at the same time solve one by one the problems arising from the non-principal aspect. We should see the negative as well as the positive aspects of things. We should see the problems that have already arisen and also anticipate problems which are not yet perceived but which may arise.

During the democratic revolution, when our Party formed a united front with the bourgeoisie and alliance became the main trend, Comrade Mao Tse-tung paid attention to opposing the Right tendency of "all alliance and no struggle." When the alliance between our Party and the bourgeoisie broke up and armed struggle became the main form of the revolution, Comrade Mao Tse-tung paid attention to opposing the "Left" tendency of "all struggle and no alliance." On the eve of the countrywide victory of the People's War of Liberation, Chairman Mao foresaw that

there may be some Communists, who were not conquered by enemies with guns and were worthy of the name of heroes for standing up to these enemies, but who cannot withstand sugar-coated bullets; they will be defeated by sugar-coated bullets.

Chairman Mao issued this call to the whole Party: "**The comrades must be helped to remain modest, prudent and free from arrogance and rashness in their style of work. The comrades must be helped to preserve the style of plain living and hard struggle.**"

During the socialist revolution, whenever our attacks on the bourgeoisie and our victories over them become the main trend, Chairman Mao invariably reiterates various proletarian policies and reminds us to remain prudent, help more people through education and narrow the target of attack, unite with all forces that can be united, and prevent and overcome the "Left" tendency running counter to these policies. But when the bourgeoisie launches attacks on us or when our Party encounters temporary difficulties on its way forward or concentrates on correcting certain shortcomings or mistakes in work, Chairman Mao invariably reminds us to remain firm, persist in proletarian leadership, distinguish between the principal and secondary aspects, not to regard everything as positive or to negate everything, to guard against sabotage and counter-attacks by open and hidden enemies and oppose and overcome the Right tendency away from the socialist path. At every crucial moment in history when a certain tendency has developed to such extent as to endanger the cause of the Party, Chairman Mao always firmly steers the course for us with proletarian revolutionary fearlessness against the current.

5. It is necessary to adhere to the mass line. The basic line for all work in our Party is to rely on the masses, have faith in them and fully arouse them, "**from the masses, to the masses,**" "**take the ideas of the masses and concentrate them, then go to the masses, persevere in the ideas and carry them through.**" We adhere to the principle of **maintaining independence and keeping the initiative in our own hands and relying on our own efforts** precisely because we firmly believe that "**the people, and the people alone, are the motive force in the making of world history.**"

Both in the democratic revolution and in the socialist revolution, Comrade Mao Tse-tung has repeatedly stressed the importance of the mass line. He regards perseverance in the mass line as fundamental to perseverance in the dialectical-materialist theory of knowledge, and regards working for the interests of the vast majority of the people of China and the world as a requirement for successors to the revolutionary cause of the proletariat. Chairman Mao has sharply refuted the reactionary viewpoints of such pseudo-Marxists as Ch'en Tu-hsiu, Wang Ming and Liu Shao-chi who slandered and repressed the masses. And he has constantly criticized and corrected the various tendencies in the Party towards keeping aloof from the masses. Chairman Mao has taught us time and again: The relation of the Communist Party to the people is that of fish to water. At no time should a Communist divorce himself from the masses. Today when we have won tremendous victories in the Great Proletarian Cultural Revolution and the ties between the Party and the masses are closer than ever, we should pay still greater attention to going to the masses, showing concern for them, listening attentively to them and consulting with them as matters arise. We should run the May 7 cadre schools well. We should regularly participate in collective productive labor. It is necessary to guard against repeating the mistake of divorcing oneself from the masses. In contradistinction to the type of person who claims to be a "humble little commoner" but is actually a big careerist, we should sincerely learn from the masses while tirelessly educating them in Mao Tse-tung Thought, overcome erroneous tendencies and raise the political consciousness of the people.

Chairman Mao has always showed concern for the unity of all nationalities of the country. Ours is a multinational country; it is essential to ensure good relations between the Han people and the minority nationalities. We should oppose both Han chauvinism and local nationalism, develop the fraternal relations the various nationalities have forged in the revolution and in the struggle to build the motherland, and strengthen the great unity of the people of all nationalities of the country.

6. It is necessary to uphold democratic centralism. Our Party Constitution clearly stipulates that the organizational principle of the Party is democratic centralism, that is, centralism on the basis of democracy and democracy under centralized guidance. Both inside and outside the Party, we must create a political situation in which there are both centralism and democracy, both discipline and freedom, both unity of will and personal ease of mind and liveliness. Our Party is a militant party, and without centralism, discipline and unity of will, it cannot defeat the enemy. But there can be no correct centralism without democracy. Therefore, Comrade Mao Tse-tung always opposes the practice of "what I say counts" and advocates the practice of "letting all people have their say." He opposes telling lies and advocates speaking the truth. He makes it a requirement for successors to the revolutionary cause of the proletariat to be bold in making criticism and self-criticism. We should give play to our Party's traditional democratic style of work, constantly make criticism, uphold the truth and correct mistakes. However, whether in army or in civilian work, our democracy is aimed at consolidating centralism, strengthening discipline and raising militancy, and not the opposite. Party committees at all levels must institute and strengthen the Party committee system, strengthen cen-

tralization and the practice of "many centers," that is, no center, and must achieve unity in thinking, policy, plan, command and action on the basis of Mao Tse-tung Thought and under the leadership of the Central Committee of the Party with Chairman Mao as its leader and Vice-Chairman Lin as its deputy leader.

7. It is necessary to build a powerful people's army. The historical experience of the Party shows that **"without a people's army the people have nothing."** The Chinese People's Liberation Army is a proletarian army created and led by our great leader Chairman Mao and commanded by Vice-Chairman Lin. **"Our principle is that the Party commands the gun, and the gun must never be allowed to command the Party."** Upholding the Marxist-Leninist line, Chairman Mao has defeated sabotage by "Left" and Right opportunism, and as a result, our army has grown in strength and become the pillar of our dictatorship of the proletariat. The world will have no peace as long as there are classes, as long as there is imperialism. The two superpowers, U.S. imperialism and Soviet revisionist social-imperialism, are today contending and colluding with each other and pushing politics of hegemony in a vain attempt to divide the world. Japanese militarism, too, is trying to realize its old fond dream of the "Greater East Asia Co-prosperity Sphere." Therefore on no account must we ever overlook the danger of their aggression and subversion against our motherland. Our principle is: **We will not attack unless we are attacked; if we are attacked, we will certainly counterattack.** We must never for a moment forget preparedness against war. We must at all times be ready to smash aggression and subversion by any imperialism. We are determined to liberate Taiwan. We need not only a powerful army but also a powerful air force and a powerful navy. Not only must we have a powerful regular army, we must also organize the people's militia on a big scale. Thus, should any imperialism dare to invade our country, we will drown it in the vast ocean of people's war.

8. It is necessary to uphold proletarian internationalism. Chairman Mao has always educated the whole Party and the people of the whole country in proletarian internationalism so that they can overcome both "Left" and Right opportunist interferences and correctly handle the relation between the revolution in China and her support and aid to the world revolution.

In its struggles over the past 50 years, the Chinese Communist Party has always enjoyed the support of the world proletariat and the people of all countries, the support of friendly countries and organizations and the support of fraternal Marxist-Leninist Parties and organizations throughout the world. The victories we have won are inseparable from their support. We will be for ever grateful to them and will never forget them. Chairman Mao teaches us:

> According to the Leninist viewpoint, the final victory of a socialist country not only requires the efforts of the proletariat and the broad masses of the people at home, but also involves the victory of the world revolution and the abolition of the system of exploitation of man by man over the whole globe, upon which all mankind will be emancipated.

The fundamental interests of the Chinese proletariat and Chinese people are identical not only with those of the people of Albania, Viet Nam, Laos, Cambodia and Korea and all Asian, African and Latin American countries, but also with those of the people of all countries, including the people of the United States, the Soviet Union and Japan. As Chairman Mao pointed out in his statement of May 20, 1970, "**The danger of a new world war still exists, and the people of all countries must get prepared. But revolution is the main trend in the world today.**" The task of the Chinese Communist Party is: On the one hand, to lead the proletariat and the people of the country in doing a good job in revolution and construction at home; on the other, to exert our greatest efforts to struggle together with the people of all countries to defeat the U.S. aggressors and all their running dogs, oppose the politics of hegemony pushed by the two superpowers and oppose the imperialist policies of aggression and war. This is our principled stand which is firm and unshakable. Although we have achieved some success in our revolution and construction, our country is still comparatively poor and backward. Our contribution to the world revolution is still very small. We must continue our efforts. But even when China becomes a strong socialist country after several decades, we should never become tainted with arrogant great-power chauvinism or big-party chauvinism either. We should always remember Chairman Mao's teaching: "**In our international relations, we Chinese people should get rid of great-power chauvinism resolutely, thoroughly, wholly and completely.**" Every nation, big or small, has its strong and weak points. We should learn from the strong points of the revolutionary people of other countries and always unite with them, fight side by side and win victory together.

Thousands upon thousands of martyrs dedicated their lives to the cause of liberation of the people of China and the world in protracted, arduous struggle. Their revolutionary spirit is forever an inspiration to us. Whatever the difficulties and hardships, nothing can stop our advance.

We are living in the era in which imperialism is heading for total collapse and socialism is advancing to worldwide victory. Compared with the days when the Chinese Communist Party was born 50 years ago, the revolutionary situation throughout the world today is excellent; it is better than ever before. The final destruction of imperialism, revisionism and the reactionaries is not far off.

Unite to win still greater victories!

Long live Marxism-Leninism-Mao Tse-tung Thought!

Long live the great, glorious and correct Communist Party of China!

Long live the victory of Chairman Mao's proletarian revolutionary line!

Long live the great leader Chairman Mao! A long, long life to Chairman Mao!

Appendix five

Chiang Ching's Speech on the Revolution in Peking Opera, July 1964.

The following speech was made by Mao Tse-tung's wife at a forum
attended by theatrical artists and workers participating in a festival of
Peking Opera on contemporary themes. In her speech, Chiang Ching
developed the "guiding principles of Chairman Mao on this question,"
according to Hsinhua news release on May 9, 1967.

I offer you my congratulations on this festival, for which you have
worked so hard. This is the first campaign in the revolution of Peking
Opera. It has achieved promising results and will have a relatively
far-reaching influence.

Peking Opera on revolutionary contemporary themes has now
been staged. But do we all look at it in the same way? I don't think
we can say so yet.

We must have unshakable confidence in the staging of Peking
Operas on revolutionary contemporary themes. It is inconceivable that,
in our socialist country led by the Chinese Communist Party, the domi-
nant position on the stage is not occupied by the workers, peasants and
soldiers, who are the real creators of history and the true masters of
our country. We must create literature and art which protect our socialist economic base. When we are not clear about our orientation, we
must try our best to find the right orientation. Here I would like to
give two groups of figures for your reference. These figures strike me
as shocking.

Here is the first group: according to a rough estimate, there are
3,000 theatrical troupes in the country (not including amateur troupes
and unlicensed companies). Of these, around 90 are professional modern
drama companies, 80-odd are cultural troupes, and the rest, over 2,800,
are companies staging various kinds of operas. Our operatic stage is
occupied by emperors and kings, generals and ministers, scholars and
beauties, and, on top of these, ghosts and monsters! As for those 90
modern drama companies, they don't necessarily all depict the workers,
peasants and soldiers either. They, too, lay stress on staging full-length
plays, foreign plays and plays on ancient themes. Therefore we can say

that the modern drama stage is also occupied by ancient Chinese and foreign figures. Theatres are places in which to educate the people, but now the stage is dominated by emperors and kings, generals and ministers, scholars and beauties—by feudal and bourgeois stuff. This state of affairs cannot serve to protect our economic base but will undermine it.

Here is the second group of figures: there are well over 600 million workers, peasants and soldiers in our country, whereas there is only a handful of landlords, rich peasants, counterrevolutionaries, bad elements, Rightists and bourgeois elements. Are we to serve this handful, or the well over 600 million? This question calls for consideration not only by Communists but also by all those literary and art workers who are patriotic. The grain we eat is grown by the peasants, the clothes we wear and the houses we live in are made by the workers, and the People's Liberation Army stands guard at the fronts of national defense for us and yet we do not portray them. May I ask which class stand you artists take? And where is the artists' "conscience" you always talk about?

For Peking Opera to present revolutionary contemporary themes will not be all plain sailing, there will be reverses; but if you consider carefully the two groups of figures I have mentioned above, there may be no reverses, or at least fewer of them. Even if there are reverses, it won't matter, because history always goes forward on a zigzag course but its wheels can never be made to turn backwards. It is our view that opera on revolutionary contemporary themes must reflect real life in the 15 years since the founding of our Chinese People's Republic, and that images of contemporary revolutionary heroes must be created on our operatic stage. This is our foremost task. This is not to say that we don't want historical operas. Revolutionary historical operas have formed no small proportion of the program of the present festival. Historical operas portraying the life and struggles of the people before our Party came into being are also needed. Moreover, we need to foster some pacesetters, to produce some historical operas which are really written from the standpoint of historical materialism and which can make the ancient serve the present. Of course, we should take up historical operas only on the condition that the carrying out of the main task (that of portraying contemporary life and creating images of workers, peasants and soldiers) is not impeded. This is not to say that we don't want any traditional operas either. Except for those about ghosts and those extolling capitulation and betrayal, good traditional operas can all be staged. But these traditional operas will have no audience worth mentioning unless they are earnestly re-edited and revised. I have made systematic visits to theatres for more than two years and my observation of both actors and audiences led me to this conclusion. In the future, the editing and revising of traditional operas is necessary, but this work should not replace our foremost task.

I will next discuss the question of where to make a start.

I think scripts are the crux of the matter. If you have only directors and actors and no scripts there is nothing to be directed or acted. People say that scripts form the basis of theatrical productions. I think that is quite true. Therefore attention must be devoted to creative writing.

In the last few years the writing of new plays has lagged far behind real life. This is even more true in the writing of libretti for Peking Opera. Playwrights are few and they lack experience of life, so it is only natural that good scripts are not being written. The key to tackling the problem of creative writing is the formation of a three-way combination of the leadership, the professional theatrical artists and the masses. Recently, I studied the way in which the play *Great Wall Along the Southern Sea* was produced and I found that they did it exactly like this. First the leadership set the theme. Then the playwrights went three times to acquire experience of life, even taking part in a military operation to round up enemy spies. When the script was written, many leading members of the Kwangchow (Canton) military command took part in discussions on it, and after it had been rehearsed, opinions were widely canvassed and revisions made. In this way, as a result of constantly asking for opinions and constantly making revisions they succeeded in turning out in a fairly short time a good topical play reflecting a real life struggle.

In the Shanghai Municipal Party Committee it was Comrade Ko Ching-shih who personally took a firm grasp on this problem of creative writing. All localities must appoint competent cadres to handle the question of creative writing.

It will be difficult for some time yet to create libretti directly for Peking Opera. Nevertheless, people have to be appointed right now to do the job. They must first be given some special training and then go out to get some experience of life. They can begin by writing something short and gradually go on to full-length operas. Short works, if well written, are also very valuable.

In creative writing, new forces must be cultivated. Send them out into the world and in three to five years they will blossom and bear fruit.

Another good way to get scripts is by adaptation.

Theatrical items for adaptation must be carefully chosen. First, we must see whether or not they are good politically and secondly whether or not they suit the conditions of the company concerned. Serious analysis of the original must be made when adapting it, its good points must be affirmed and not changed, while its weak points must be made good. In adapting for Peking Opera attention must be paid to two main questions: on the one hand the adaptations must be in keeping with the characteristics of Peking Opera, having singing and acrobatics, and words which fit the rhyme schemes of Peking Opera singing. The language used must be that of Peking Opera. Otherwise, the performers will not be able to sing. On the other hand, excessive concessions should not be made to the performers. An opera must have a clear-cut theme with a tightly knit structure and characters that stand out. There should be no digression or slowing down of the action to afford all the principal performers good parts.

Peking Opera uses artistic exaggeration. At the same time, it has always depicted ancient times and people belonging to those times. Therefore, it is comparatively easy for Peking Opera to portray negative characters and there are some people who like this. On the other hand, it is very difficult to create positive characters, and yet we must create advanced revolutionary heroes. In the original version of the opera *Taking the Bandits' Stronghold* produced by the Shanghai troupe the negative characters were blatant, while the positive characters were quite colorless. Since the leadership attended to this question personally, this opera has been definitely improved. Now, the scene about the Taoist Ting Ho has been cut. The part of the bandit leader, Eagle, basically has not been altered (the actor who plays the part acts very well), but since the roles of Yang Tzu-jung and Shao Chien-po have been made prominent, the negative characters by comparison have paled. I heard that there are different views on this opera. Debates can be conducted on this subject. You must consider which side you stand on, the side of the positive or the negative characters. I heard that there are still people who oppose writing about positive characters. This is wrong. Good people are always the vast majority. This is true not only in our socialist countries but even in imperialist countries, where the vast majority are laboring people. In revisionist countries, the revisionists are still only a minority. We should place the emphasis on creating artistic images of advanced revolutionaries so as to educate and inspire the people and lead them forward. Our purpose in producing operas on contemporary revolutionary themes is mainly to extol the positive characters. The opera *Little Heroic Sisters on the Grassland* performed by the Peking Opera Troupe of the Inner Mongolian Art Theatre is very good. The librettists' revolutionary feeling was inspired by the advanced deeds of the two little heroines and this opera was written. The middle section of the opera is very moving, but because the librettists still lack experience of real life, worked in haste and had no time for careful polishing, the opening and closing scenes are not so good. As it is now, it looks like a fine painting placed in a crude old frame. There is another point which merits attention: a Peking Opera has been written for our children. In short, this opera has a firm foundation and is good. I hope that the writers will go back to experience the life of the people and do their best to perfect the script. In my opinion we should treasure the fruits of our labor, and shouldn't scrap them lightly. Some comrades are unwilling to revise their works, but this prevents them from making comparatively big achievements. In this respect, the Shanghai artists have set us a good example. Because they have been willing to polish their scripts over and over again, they have made *Taking the Bandits' Stronghold* the success it is today. All the items in the repertory of the present festival should be given further polishing when you go back. The items which have stood up well in the festival should not be knocked down lightly.

In conclusion, I hope that all of you will make the effort to learn one another's items so that audiences throughout the country will be able to see this festival's achievements.

Appendix six

Commentary and Reports on problems of Industrial Pollution, 1971

Editorial Commentary, 5 February 1971

This is one of the first of a series of editorial commentaries on problems of industrial pollution, published in **Peking Review** (February 5, 1971).

Studying and applying Chairman Mao's brilliant philosophical thinking in a living way and breaking with metaphysics, staff members and workers on China's industrial front are going all out for multi-purpose use, thus opening up broad prospects for developing industry with greater, faster, better and more economical results.

Turning "Waste" Into Something Valuable

Chairman Mao has taught us:

> In given conditions, each of the two opposing aspects of a contradiction invariably transforms itself into its opposite as a result of the struggle between them. Here, the conditions are essential. Without the given conditions, neither of the two contradictory aspects can transform itself into its opposite.

According to this teaching, what is "waste" and what is valuable are the unity of opposites in a thing. In given conditions, "waste" can be transformed into what is valuable and the useless into the useful. Revolutionary staff members and workers on the industrial front have studied and mastered this dialectical relationship. Their subjective dynamic role unreined, they have gone all out for comprehensive use and devoted themselves to turning "waste matter" into useful wealth.

Tail gases belching from the chimney of a Shanghai oil refinery used to foul the air. These gases have been transferred to a nearby chemical plant via a 2-kilometer-long channel set up by the workers who analysed, separated and purified them, obtaining ethylene, propylene and butane from this noxious exhaust. After being synthesized, the gases were transformed into many kinds of chemical materials. They were then delivered to Shanghai's textile mills, plastic and pharmaceutical factories and machine-building plants, which processed them into light, abrasion-resistant and anti-moisture artificial wool, dacron, capron and other synthetic fiber goods, as well as various plastic goods needed for industry and the people's livelihood, insecticides, medicines and medical equipment.

A sugar-cane chemical plant in Kwangtung Province had to spend a hundred thousand yuan annually to ship pulverized cinders, filtered mud and pyrite slag and dump them into the sea. Now it can change them into raw materials for making cinder bricks, cement, carbon steel and pig iron. Since last year, just by making use of these wastes alone, it has created wealth worth hundreds of thousands of yuan for the state. In the spirit of the Foolish Old Man who removed the mountains, workers in a Shanghai steel plant produced well over 1,500 tons of iron and steel by comprehensive use of the steel slag that had piled up as high as three stories.

The revolutionary committee of a Peking chemical plant fully mobilized the masses to completely explode the myth about the electronics industry. Through their own labor and indigenous methods, they used a large amount of the plant's tail gases to make polycrystal silicon, an important material for the electronics industry, in a matter of 37 days. This has opened up broad vistas for developing China's electronics industry. Comprehensive utilization of agricultural and sideline products by many small chemical plants set up in the rural areas of Kiangsu and other provinces has enabled them to use cotton seed hulls, corncobs, rice husks, sugar-cane residue and castor oil to produce alcohol, furfural, acetic acid, acetone, glucose, antibiotics and other chemical products.

Making What is Harmful Beneficial

Pollution of the environment is not only unhealthy to people, it is destructive to nature. It destroys crops, creates countless hazards for animal and fish life and is unbalancing nature. What to do about the garbage of industrial production is a big question all over the world, particularly in the capitalist world where profits get priority. In China this problem is now being tackled. Industry is at work to control pollution and re-cycle waste materials.

Large amounts of waste acids, liquid and gases were emitted from Shanghai's metallurgical, chemical, electroplating, dyeing and printing and paper-making enterprises. The revolutionary staff members and workers went about dealing with the waste acids and gases with a will. Their all-out efforts for comprehensive utilization turned what had been harmful into something beneficial.

By making an all-round and dialectical analysis of the copper, nickel and acids found in various waste liquids, workers at a small plant realized that the harmful could be made beneficial. Through decomposition, they created wealth amounting to more than 1.7 million yuan for the state last year. The copper oxide obtained from such "industrial rubbish" as waste liquids meets the demand for pigment in the country's enamel industry.

The big amount of daily waste gases and liquids emitted from a factory had damaged 700 *mu* of farmland every year and caused a loss of 50,000 yuan in income from farming there. Collecting and utilizing the waste gases and liquids, the workers obtained a lot of valuable resources, enabling the factory to acquire an additional income of 3 million yuan each year. Moreover, they have done away with the big destructive factor causing great harm to farmland and the people's health.

Making One Thing Serve Many Purposes

Through practice in production, the workers' understanding of the need to fully tap the potential of material resources has deepened step by step and in many respects they have made one thing serve many purposes.

In addition to producing sugar in which sugar-cane was the chief raw material, the Kiangmen Sugar-cane Chemical Plant in Kwangtung Province has made comprehensive use of waste sugar-cane residue and liquids to make more than ten kinds of light industrial and chemical products. These include pulp board, glazed and wrapping paper, furfural, cementing material, alcohol, yeast and "702" farm chemical made from waste sugar-cane residue and other wastes. Formerly, this plant was in operation half a year and lay idle for the other half. This situation now has been completely reversed. Cutting across the limits set, it has changed into a multi-producing factory making light industrial products such as sugar, paper and artificial fiber pulp as well as steel, iron, chemicals, medicines, building materials and polycrystal silicon.

On the basis of constantly summing up practical experience, workers have made new advances in recent years in comprehensively using pigs. From bristles, they extract protein fiber which is used as textile material and obtained glue and lard from pig bones which, when ground to powder, become potassium fertilizer used in helping crops grow. When made into a powder, pig blood can be used as an industrial material. From the visceral organs of pigs and their glands and throat-bones, medicines such as bile acid and chondroitin are manufactured. Brain lipoid can also be obtained from pig brains, each kilogram worth several thousand yuan.

Turning the Old Into the New

An important aspect in multi-purpose use, turning the old into the new reflects the proletariat's and other working people's fine quality of working hard and living simply and their practice of being industrious and frugal. As a result, it becomes possible to make the maximum use of material resources.

Alongside the rapid growth of industry and agriculture, large quantities of new machines, equipment, tools and packing boxes or containers are needed. All things gradually become old or damaged in the course of use. This is the natural law of the development of things. After an all-round analysis of damaged equipment, workers have become aware of the fact that something that is damaged is bad in one respect but this does not mean everything about it is bad. After being repaired or restored, old or damaged equipment becomes greatly changed and very serviceable.

There is nothing final about the boundaries between industries. With the development of production techniques and the state's growing demands, existing enterprises are bound to continuously make new products and increase varieties, thereby transforming themselves from enterprises making one product into ones turning out a number of products. The viewpoint that one enterprise should only produce one kind of product does not conform to the objective law of the development of production.

Multi-purpose use is the objective law of production development. Materialist dialectics holds that all of nature's resources can be put to multi-purpose use. The history of mankind's production is one in which man uses natural resources under different modes of production and in varying degrees and extent. The objective possibilities for using resources know no limits. Man's cognition of nature, which constantly develops from the realm of necessity to the realm of freedom, also has no limits. Things in the world exist that are still unknown and unused, but there is nothing that is beyond knowledge and cannot be used. **"Socialism has liberated not only the working people and the means of production from the old society, but also the vast world of nature which the old society could not make use of."** The incomparable superiority of our socialist system offers the most favorable conditions and immeasurable prospects for the multi-purpose use of natural resources. The Great Proletarian Cultural Revolution has greatly promoted the revolutionization of people's thinking and mobilized the masses' potentially inexhaustible socialist enthusiasm and creativeness. The use of natural resources on an increasingly deeper and wider scale will make even bigger contributions to national construction and the people's livelihood.

RADIO BROADCAST

[Text] Tientsin, April 30, 1971 (HSINHUA) —Workers, cadres and technical personnel in North China's important industrial city of Tientsin have achieved big successes in the multi-purpose use of industrial waste. This movement is guided by the party organizations and revolutionary committees at all levels.

Statistics to hand show that 70 chemical, light industrial, textile, metallurgical, building material and commercial units and local industries devised 190 kinds of multi-purpose uses up to last March. Over 46 percent are in serial-production. They have provided the state with 35,000 tons of chemicals and chemical products, 170 million medicinal tablets and 500 tons of non-ferrous metals. They have smelted 2,500 tons of iron and steel from scraps and saved 1,000 tons of grain for industrial use. The city has recovered 35,000 tons of waste acid, equal to the annual production of a medium-sized sulphuric acid plant. It has produced 60 million bricks by utilizing waste heat and gas, 4,000 tons of cement from water quenched slag and other waste materials and irrigated 13,330 hectares of farmland with sewage water. Polycryzstalline silicon, cadmium, titanium, manganese, coagulants and other important products have been extracted.

Tientsin factories made some achievements in multi-purpose use before the Great Proletarian Cultural Revolution. But, the renegade, hidden traitor and scab Liu Shao-chi and his agents spread idealist metaphysics, pushed the counterrevolutionary revisionist line, insisted on a minute division of labor and advocated "putting profit in command." This held back the multi-purpose use of industrial waste.

The city's cadres and workers made a living study and application of Mao Tse-tung Thought, roundly criticized Liu Shao-chi's counterrevolutionary revisionist line and repudiated various kinds of erroneous ideas last year to encourage the multi-purpose use of industrial waste.

People used to think metaphysically that waste consisted of unusable things. The workers and cadres studied Chairman Mao's philosophic thinking and came to understand that "every thing divides into two" and that waste materials can be transformed into useful things.

The Tientsin insecticide plant used to find it very difficult to deal with its sewage water, waste gas and slag. It stored the smelly and poisonous waste of ethyl sulfide from hydroxyethyl sulfide in boxes in the open air. The boxes rotted and the ethyl sulfide was lost. This wasted ten to twenty thousand yuan annually. After the workers studied Chairman Mao's philosophic works, they used materialist dialectics to analyze the properties of ethyl sulfide. They finally produced a highly effective anodyne. Now the plant has seven projects for multi-purpose use of 80 percent of the plant's waste. They produce 2.5 million yuan of value every year. The Tientsin pharmaceutical works used its waste liquid to trail-produce fodder containing tetracyclin, sodium acetate, potassium iodide, amonia water, plasma substitute and other products.

The cadres and workers in the Tientsin factories and workshops recognize that the multi-purpose use of industrial waste is of great importance in production and involves a deep-going ideological revolutionization. Only when the thinking of the people is revolutionized, is it possible to make good use of industrial waste.

A chemical works in Tientsin used to discharge 1,000 tons of waste liquid daily. Some of the cadres wanted to ask for a large government investment to build a modern recovery system. The workers criticized this idea of blind faith in big and foreign projects, which can be traced back to Liu Shao-chi's influence. The workers set to work themselves. They dug ditches and laid pipes to lead the waste liquid into a reservoir where it is filtered before being used. The problem of recovering useful material from waste liquid was thus quickly solved. This was a profound education to leading cadres in the factory. They mobilized the workers to start a mass drive for other multi-purpose utilization. In less than one month, they recovered 109 tons of chemical products with a total value of 240,000 yuan.

Workers and staff members at the Tientsin winery have fostered the concept that a socialist enterprise should make full use of things to serve the people. This followed criticism of the revisionist fallacy spread by Liu Shao-chi and his agents that "the purpose of a winery is to turn out wine to make big profit." The leading cadres went to the workshops and teams to carry out experiments with the masses. They made polycrystalline silicon from recovered waste gas and insecticide and artificial ice from waste liquid and residue.

Tientsin's industrial enterprises cooperated to investigate possible multi-purpose use of material, breaking through the rigid division of labor between different trades. They are using the waste gas, liquid and residue from chemical works to make iron and steel or grow polycrystalline silicon and extract chromium, cadmium and lithium. They also use residue from food-processing and other light industry factories to produce yeast, perrlycin, tetracyclin and other medical [supplies]. Bringing their wisdom into full play, the workers and revolutionary technicians strive to develop new techniques and processes to make the fullest use of material and create more wealth for the country. The Chinku winery extracts a medical material and makes three insecticides and a wine from residue. Workers of the Tientsin sulphuric acid works have tried out a new process for making acid and steel.

Appendix SEVEN

Diplomatic Notes on Sino-Soviet Border Disputes

NOTE OF PROTEST FROM THE MINISTRY OF FOREIGN AFFAIRS OF THE PEOPLE'S REPUBLIC OF CHINA TO THE SOVIET EMBASSY IN CHINA

(March 2, 1969)

Embassy of the U.S.S.R. in China:

On the morning of March 2, 1969, Soviet frontier guards intruded into the area of Chenpao Island, Heilungkiang Province, China, and killed and wounded many Chinese frontier guards by opening fire on them, thus creating an extremely grave border armed conflict. Against this, the Ministry of Foreign Affairs of the People's Republic of China is instructed to lodge the strongest protest with the Soviet Government.

At 09:17 hours on March 2, large numbers of fully armed soldiers, together with four armored vehicles and cars, sent out by the Soviet frontier authorities, flagrantly intruded into the area of Chenpao Island which is indisputable Chinese territory, carried out blatant provocations against the Chinese frontier guards on normal patrol duty and were the first to open cannon and gun fire, killing and wounding many Chinese frontier guards. The Chinese frontier guards were compelled to fight back in self-defense when they reached the end of their forbearance after their repeated warnings to the Soviet frontier guards had produced no effect. This grave incident of bloodshed was entirely and solely created by the Soviet authorities. It is another grave new crime perpetrated by the Soviet authorities which have long been deliberately encroaching upon China's territory, carrying out armed provocations and creating ceaseless incidents of bloodshed.

The Chinese Government firmly demands that the Soviet Government punish the culprits of this incident and immediately stop its encroachment upon China's territory and its armed provocations, and reserves the right to demand compensation from the Soviet side for all the losses suffered by the Chinese side. The Chinese Government once again sternly warns the Soviet Government: China's sacred territory brooks no violation; if you should wilfully cling to your reckless course and continue to provoke armed conflicts along the Sino-Soviet border, you will certainly receive resolute counter-blows from the Chinese people; and it is the Soviet Government that must bear full responsibility for all the grave consequences arising therefrom.

Ministry of Foreign Affairs of
the People's Republic of China

Peking, March 2, 1969

NOTE OF PROTEST FROM THE EMBASSY OF THE PEOPLE'S REPUBLIC OF CHINA IN THE SOVIET UNION TO THE MINISTRY OF FOREIGN AFFAIRS OF THE U.S.S.R.

(March 11, 1969)

Ministry of Foreign Affairs of the U.S.S.R.:

At 15:00 hours on March 10, 1969, when a driver of the Chinese Embassy who was on a mission drove his car to building No. 93, Lenin Street, a group of Soviet ruffians wrested open the door of the embassy car, broke into it and forcibly took away 20 packs of letters and materials which the Embassy addressed to foreign correspondents in Moscow. This piratical incident of flagrant robbery is another new grave anti-China provocation which is wholly the making of the Soviet authorities.

Meanwhile, the Soviet authorities have since March 7 organized despicable anti-China demonstrations before the Chinese Embassy, in which they flagrantly directed ruffians to inflict serious damage on the embassy premises and garage, smash several hundred panes of door and window glass and the glass of all the Embassy's news picture display cases and smear large stretches of the walls of the embassy premises, causing heavy losses to the Embassy. It should be pointed out that Soviet ruffians are still carrying on these savage destructive activities.

After carrying out armed provocations on Chinese territory, Chenpao Island, the Soviet authorities have become insensate in whipping up anti-China hysteria throughout the country. Grossly trampling upon the principles of international law, the Soviet authorities have gone so far as to direct ruffians to violate a diplomatic car of the Chinese Embassy, brazenly take away by force letters and materials and raid and damage the diplomatic mission of the People's Republic of China. The Chinese Embassy hereby lodges a strong protest with the Soviet authorities against these barefaced fascist outrages and demands that they severely punish the culprits, return the seized documents, compensate for all the losses suffered by the Chinese Embassy, immediately stop their unbridled anti-China criminal activities and guarantee against the recurrence of similar incidents.

The Soviet authorities must be held fully responsible for their above-mentioned fresh crime against China. In rabidly opposing China, the Soviet authorities are lifting a rock only to drop it on their own feet. All their anti-China schemes are doomed to utter bankruptcy.

Embassy of the People's Republic of China in the Soviet Union

Moscow, March 11, 1969

NOTE OF PROTEST FROM THE EMBASSY OF THE PEOPLE'S REPUBLIC OF CHINA IN THE SOVIET UNION TO THE MINISTRY OF FOREIGN AFFAIRS OF THE U.S.S.R.

(March 12, 1969)

Ministry of Foreign Affairs of the U.S.S.R.:

With a view to supporting the rabid anti-China hysteria they have whipped up at home, the Soviet authorities are resorting to every possible means in repeatedly directing ruffians to use fascist violence against personnel of the Chinese Embassy going out on official missions. Ignoring the Chinese Embassy's strong protest against Soviet ruffians attacking and ransacking a diplomatic car of the Embassy on March 10, the Soviet authorities have further organized ruffians to brazenly insult and beat up the Embassy's working personnel.

On March 12, when working personnel of the Chinese Embassy went to the residence of foreign correspondents at No. 7, Kutuzov Street on an official mission, a group of Soviet ruffians waiting there in advance all of a sudden peremptorily and unwarrantedly interfered in the embassy working personnel's official functions under the direction of special agents, beating them up with fists and using violence to push them down from the fifth floor. These ruffians, some carrying iron clubs in hand and others striking with their fists and feet, intimidated and abused the embassy personnel in every possible way, thus seriously endangering the personal safety of the embassy working personnel and hampering and disrupting the normal functioning of the Chinese Embassy. It must be pointed out that these ruffians declared outright that they were acting on behalf of the Soviet Government and that the Soviet policemen on the spot, far from stopping the outrage of the Soviet ruffians, took a direct part in this anti-China provocation. The Chinese Embassy hereby lodges a strong protest with the Soviet authorities against these increasingly unbridled fascist outrages and demands that they punish the culprits and put an immediate end to these grave criminal activities. The Soviet authorities will never succeed in their attempt to save themselves from their ill fate by engineering anti-China fascist outrages, but this will only accelerate their complete doom.

Embassy of the People's Republic
of China in the Soviet Union

Moscow, March 12, 1969

Appendix Eight

Policy Commentary on Japanese "Militarism" by "People's
Daily Commentator," June 16, 1971.

The reactionary Sato government of Japan recently made public a
so-called "Draft of the Fourth Military Defense Build-up Plan" after
long and careful premeditation. This is a blueprint of the Japanese
reactionaries to step up arms expansion and war preparations. It fully
reveals the ambition of the reviving Japanese militarism to carry out
aggression and expansion abroad with increased tempo. After the publication of the draft of the arms expansion plan, Japanese military
bigwigs Nakasone and his ilk came out to camouflage it in every way
and did their utmost to justify the stepped-up revival of Japanese militarism. However, the more they tried to conceal the crime, the more
they revealed it.

The draft of Japan's fourth arms expansion plan stipulates that
Japan's direct military expenditure for 1972–76 will total 5,800,000
million yen (equivalent to more than 16,000 million U.S. dollars), more
than double the comparable figure in the third arms expansion plan
and exceeding the grand total of direct military expenditures of the
previous three arms expansion plans by some 5,000 million U.S. dollars.
Judging from Japan's actual capacity at present, she needs less than five
years to fulfil the targets set forth in the draft of the fourth arms expansion plan. More than once the plan stresses that Japan's military
strength "should maintain its flexibility to deal with the change of the
situation" and that it should change with the changing of "the international situation, the progress of science and technology and other
important factors." This paves the way for the further acceleration of
the tempo of the arms expansion in future.

By putting forth such a huge arms expansion plan and speeding
up the tempo of arms expansion by every possible means, the Sato
government aims at "killing two birds with one stone." That is to make
preparations for unleashing a war of aggression so as to lord it over in
Asia and at the same time to meet the needs of the Japanese Zaibatsus
to stimulate arms production as a way out for the Japanese economy

which is plagued by overproduction. The publication of the draft of the fourth arms expansion plan shows once again that the lopsided development and vicious expansion of the Japanese economy will inevitably lead to the militarization of Japan's national economy and expansion abroad, and that economic expansion is bound to lead to military expansion, and an "economic power" will surely become a "military power." The pretension of Sato, Nakasone and their ilk that Japan "will not become a military power" is a confession rather than a denial of their designs.

The fourth arms expansion plan is obviously aimed at stepping up expansion abroad and preparing for an aggressive war. Sato, Nakasone and their like, however, present it under the label of so-called "purely defense-oriented preparedness," alleging that the purpose of their arms expansion is "to cope with aggression by localized warfare involving conventional weapons." The reason for them to unscrupulously resort to such a trickery is that Japanese militarism has long become notorious and the present revival of Japanese militarism in particular has aroused vigilance and resolute opposition among the people of Japan and other Asian countries. In such circumstances, the cunning Japanese reactionaries are trying their utmost to paint Japan in the image of "a peaceful country" in an attempt to mislead the Japanese people and world opinion so that they may engage in arms expansion and war preparations still more unbridledly.

What a "purely defense-oriented preparedness!" It is nothing but a refurbishing of the so-called "self-existence, self-defense" advocated by Hideki Tojo in the past. Sato openly clamored that Korea "was essential to Japan's own security" and that China's Taiwan "was also a most important factor for the security of Japan." Nakasone even flagrantly included China's sacred territory Tiaoyu and other islands in "the scope of Japanese defense," declaring that Japan will use military force to "defend" these islands. They called this place the "life line" of Japan and that place the "sphere of Japanese life." They asserted frenziedly that "the meaning of national boundary in the past no longer exists" and that "the scope of Japanese defense will expand rapidly." In other words, "the scope of Japanese defense" includes not only Korea, China's Taiwan, the Philippines and Indochina, but also the Indian Ocean and the Arabian Gulf in West Asia. The fourth arms expansion plan also brazenly calls for the "maintenance of air supremacy and control of the sea to the necessary degree" in areas around Japan. Turning things upside down, it describes the People of China, Korea, Viet Nam and other countries in Asia as a threat to Japan, while on the other hand, it raises a hue and cry about "preventing aggression before it happens" and "ruling out aggression in its early stage." This trick of a thief crying "stop thief!" clearly shows that the spearhead of aggression of the Japanese reactionaries is directed against the people of Korea, China and other Asian countries. "Defense" on their lips is a synonym of aggression.

The Japanese reactionaries have admitted long ago that through the implementation of the fourth and fifth arms expansion plans they would bring about a "big leap" in Japan's military strength and greatly strengthen Japan's "tactical offensive capability" and "strategic offensive capability." The fourth arms expansion plan stipulates that while raising the "mobility" of the army, stress must be laid on increasing the strength of the navy and air force, expanding enormously such equipment as F-4EJ Phantoms, tanker aircraft, amphibian tanks, large-sized frigates carrying helicopters. According to the fourth arms expansion plan, expenditure for the study of military technology will be increased most swiftly for the purpose of reinforcing Japan's military offensive capability. But how can the Japanese reactionaries fool others by describing these military equipment as "defensive" and acting as if they were in "strategic defense"?

Sato, Nakasone and their ilk spoke of preparing to fight a limited local war involving conventional weapons, but in reality, they are making preparations for launching an aggressive war on a large scale. Since the Japanese reactionaries have a big appetite for expansion abroad, directing their spearhead of aggression against Korea, China, Indochina and other Asian countries, how can the war, once unleashed by them, be a "limited war"? History shows that the Japanese militarists used to camouflage their insatiable ambitions for aggression with the smokescreen of "not enlarging" the war. Forty years ago, when they created the "September 18" incident in aggression on northeast China, they declared that they would "not enlarge the incident." But not long afterwards, they unleashed an all-round aggressive war against China. Furthermore, an all-round war can also be fought with conventional weapons. Was it not Japanese militarism which provoked a large-scale Pacific war through its naval and air attacks on the Pearl Harbor 30 years ago?

It must also be pointed out that the Japanese reactionaries have long prepared for nuclear armaments. They have worked with the United States in the production of enriched uranium so that nuclear weapons can be manufactured at any time. The so-called "three-point non-nuclear principle" loudly advertised in the fourth arms expansion plan is nothing but a smokescreen. Once Japanese militarism embarks on the old path of unleashing an aggressive war, it may fight a conventional as well as a nuclear war.

The difference between today's Japanese militarism and that of pre-war days is that it is tied to the U.S. war chariot. The publication of Japan's draft fourth arms expansion plan is precisely aimed at meeting the needs of the "Nixon doctrine." To retrieve itself from its failure, U.S. imperialism is eager to use Japanese militarism as its shock force in aggression in Asia, while the Japanese reactionaries are trying their utmost to step up the revival of militarism and renew the fond dream of a "Greater East Asia Co-prosperity Sphere" by relying on the influence of U.S. imperialism. The fourth arms expansion plan calls for "adhering to the Japan-U.S. security system," and Sato and his ilk openly clamored for "a greater Japanese role in helping to keep world order and solve international conflicts." All this shows that the Japanese reactionaries are continuing to follow the U.S. imperialist policies of aggression and war, and energetically serve the criminal scheme of the "Nixon doctrine" in "using Asians to fight Asians."

Another vicious aim of the Japanese reactionaries in stepping up arms expansion is to maintain their domestic fascist rule and intensify their bloody suppression of the Japanese people. In the fourth arms expansion plan, the Japanese reactionaries raved about the need to cope with so-called "indirect aggression," and "to control the situation, regain security as soon as possible." This bares their criminal intention to intensify counter-revolutionary violence for stamping out the revolutionary struggle of the Japanese people.

Our great leader Chairman Mao points out: **"Japan is a great nation." "The Japanese people have a bright future."** Today, the Japanese people are more awakened than ever before and will never allow the U.S.-Japanese reactionaries to push the Japanese nation into the abyss of disaster once again. At the same time, the Asian situation has undergone a basic change and the Asian people's revolutionary force is stronger than ever before. The criminal plan of the U.S.-Japanese reactionaries to step up the revival of Japanese militarism is being strongly opposed by the people of Japan, Korea, China, the three Indochinese countries and other Asian countries. Should Japanese militarism dare to provoke a new war of aggression in Asia, it will only suffer another defeat—a more disastrous defeat than the previous one.

Appendix Nine

Biodata of Party Leadership in the Ninth Central Committee, 1969

A. FULL MEMBERS

MAO TSE-TUNG

Experience: Chairman, Eighth Central Committee; Chairman, Military Commission, CC; a founding member.

LIN PIAO

Experience: Vice-Chairman, Eighth CCP Central Committee; First Vice-Chairman, Military Commission, CC; Vice-Chairman, National Defense Committee, State Council; Vice-Premier and concurrently Minister of National Defense, State Council.

Status: military (First Front Army; Fourth Field Army), purged in 1971.

CHANG CHIH-MING

Experience: Political Commissar, General Rear Service (Logistics) Department.

Status: military (First Front Army; Fourth Field Army).

CHANG CHUN-CHIAO

Experience: Deputy Director, Central Cultural Revolution Group; Chairman, Shanghai Municipal Revolutionary Committee.

Status: revolutionary leading cadre.

CHANG FU-HENG

Experience: unknown.

Status: peasant/worker.

CHANG FU-KUEI

Experience: a responsible man of the Tungfanghung Brigade, Kaochun Commune, Wenteng *hsien*; a responsible man of the Poor And Middle-Lower Peasants Rebel General Headquarters in Shantung; Member, Standing Committee, Shantung Provincial Revolutionary Committee.

Status: representative of mass organizations.

CHANG HENG-YUN

Experience: a worker of the Lanhsi Section of Machine, Bureau of Lanchow Railway.

Status: representative of mass organizations.

CHANG KUO-HUA
Experience: Chairman, Szechwan Provincial Revolutionary Committee; First Political Commissar, Chengtu Military Region.
Status: military (First Front Army; 115th Division; Second Field Army).

CHANG TA-CHIH
Experience: Alternate Member, Eighth Central Committee; Commander, Lanchow Military Region.
Status: military (Red Army in Northern Shensi; 120th Division; First Field Army).

CHANG TI-HSUEH
Experience: First Secretary, Hupei Provincial Party Committee and concurrently Governor of Hupei Province; Vice-Chairman, Hupei Provincial Revolutionary Committee.
Status: revolutionary leading cadre.

CHANG TIEN-YUN
Experience: Vice-Political-Commissar, General Rear Service (Logistics) Department.
Status: military (115th Division; Fourth Field Army).

CHANG TSAI-CHIEN
Experience: Deputy Commander, Nanking Military Region.
Status: military (Fourth Front Army; 129th Division; Fourth Field Army).

CHANG TING-CHENG
Experience: Member, Eighth Central Committee; Procurator General, Supreme people's Procuratorate.
Status: revolutionary leading cadre.

CHANG YI-HSIANG
Experience: Commander, Railway Engineer Headquarters.
Status: military (First Front Army; New Fourth Army; Third Field Army).

CHANG YUN-I
Experience: Member, Eighth Central Committee; Member, Standing Committee, Military Commission, CC; Secretary, Control Commission, CC.
Status: military (First Front Army; New Fourth Army; Third Field Army).

CHEN CHI-HAN
Experience: Alternate Member, Eighth Central Committee; Director, Military Control Section, Higher Military Academy.
Status: military (First Front Army; Fourth Field Army).

CHEN HSI-LIEN
Experience: Alternate Member, Eighth Central Committee; Chair-

man, Liaoning Provincial Revolutionary Committee; Commander, Shenyang Military Region.

Status: military (Fourth Front Army; 129th Division; Second Field Army).

CHEN HSIEN-JUI

Experience: Vice-Political-Commissar, Peking Military Region.

Status: military (Fourth Front Army; 129th Division; the Army Corps Directly Under Control of the Central Government).

CHEN KANG

Experience: Vice-Chairman, Yunnan Provincial Revolutionary Committee; Commander, Kunming Military Region.

Status: military (Fourth Front Army; 129th Division; Second Field Army).

CHEN PO-TA

Experience: Member, Eighth Central Committee; Member, Standing Committee, Politburo, CC; Chief, Central Cultural Revolution Group, CCP; Vice-President, Chinese Academy of Sciences.

Status: revolutionary leading cadre.

CHEN SHIH-CHU

Experience: Commander, Engineer Headquarters.

Status: military (First Front Army; 120 Division; Third Field Army).

CHEN YI

Experience: Member, Eighth Central Committee; Member, Politburo; Vice-Chairman, National Defense Council; Vice-Premier, State Council; Minister, Ministry of Foreign Affairs and concurrently Director, Staff Office For Foreign Affairs; Vice-Chairman, Military Commission, CC.

Status: revolutionary leading cadre.

CHEN YU

Experience: Member, Eighth Central Committee; Secretary, Central-South CCP-CC Regional Bureau; Governor, Kwangtung Province; Vice Chairman, Kwangtung Provincial Revolutionary Committee.

Status: revolutionary leading cadre.

CHEN YUN

Experience: Member, Eighth Central Committee; Member, Standing Committee, Politburo; Vice-Premier, State Council.

Status: revolutionary leading cadre.

CHEN YUNG-KUEI

Experience: Secretary, Party Branch at Ta-tsai Brigade, Shi-yang; Chairman, Shi-yang *hsien* Revolutionary Committee; Vice-Chairman, Shansi Provincial Revolutionary Committee.

Status: representative of mass organizations.

CHENG SHIH-CHING
Experience: Chairman, Kiangsi Provincial Revolutionary Committee; Political Commissar, Kiangsi Provincial Military Committee.
Status: military (Fourth Front Army; Fourth Field Army).

CHEN WEI-SHAN
Experience: Vice-Chairman, Peking Municipal Revolutionary Committee; Acting Commander, Peking Military Region.
Status: military (Fourth Front Army; the Army Corps Directly Under Control of the Central Committee).

CHI TENG-KUEI
Experience: Alternate Secretary, Honan Provincial Party Committee; Vice-Chairman, Honan Provincial Revolutionary Committee.
Status: revolutionary leading cadre.

CHIANG CHING (f.)
Experience: First Deputy Director, Central Cultural Revolution Group, CCP.
Status: revolutionary leading cadre (Mao Tse-tung's wife).

CHIANG HSIEN-YUAN
Experience: Deputy Commander, Kwangchow Military Region.
Status: military (First Front Army; Fourth Field Army).

CHIANG LI-YIN
Experience: unknown.
Status: representative of mass organizations (a worker of Machine Section, Bureau of Fuchow Railway).

CHIANG YUNG-HUI
Experience: Chief of Staff, Shenyang Military Region.
Status: military (First Front Army; Fourth Field Army).

CHIEN CHIH-KUANG
Experience: Minister, Ministry of Textile Industry, State Council.
Status: revolutionary leading cadre.

CHIU CHUANG-CHENG
Experience: Minister, Fifth Ministry of Machine Building, State Council.
Status: revolutionary leading cadre.

CHIU HUI-TSO
Experience: Deputy Chief, General Staff Department and concurrently Director, General Rear Service Department.
Status: military (First Front Army; Fourth Field Army).

CHIU KUO-KUANG
Experience: Vice-Chairman, Kwangtung Provincial Revolutionary Committee; Deputy Commander, Kwangchow Military Region.
Status: military (First Front Army; Fourth Field Army).

CHOU CHIEN-JEN

Experience: Governor, Chekiang Province; Vice-Chairman, Third National People's Congress; Vice-Chairman, Chekiang Provincial Revolutionary Committee.

Status: revolutionary leading cadre.

CHOU CHIH-PING

Experience: Vice-Minister, Ministry of Metallurgical Industry, State Council.

Status: revolutionary leading cadre.

CHOU EN-LAI

Experience: Member, Eighth Central Committee; Member, Standing Committee, Politburo; Premier, State Council; Chairman, Fourth Chinese People's Political Consultative Conference.

Status: revolutionary leading cadre.

CHOU HSING

Experence: Governor, Yunnan Province; Vice-Chairman, Yunnan Provincial Revolutionary Committee.

Status: revolutionary leading cadre.

CHU TEH

Experience: Member, Eighth Central Committee; Member, Standing Committee, Politburo, CC; Chairman, Third National People's Congress.

Status: revolutionary leading cadre.

FAN WEN-LAN

Experience: Alternate Member, Eighth Central Committee; Director, Institute of Modern Historical Research, Chinese Academy of Sciences.

Status: revolutionary leading cadre.

HAN HSIEN-CHU

Experience: Alternate Member, Eighth Central Committee; Chairman, Fukien Provincial Revolutionary Committee; Deputy Chief, General Staff Department and concurrently Commander, Fuchow Military Region.

Status: military (Fourth Front Army; 115th Division; Fourth Field Army).

HSIA PANG-YIN

Experience: Member, Standing Committee, Hupei Provincial Revolutionary Committee; a responsible man of Hupei Provincial Workers' Congress; a worker of Hanyang Steel Rolling Plant.

Status: representative of mass organizations.

HSIAO CHING-KUANG

Experience: Member, Eighth Central Committee; Vice-Minister, Ministry of National Defense; Commander, Navy Headquarters.

Status: military (First Front Army; Fourth Field Army).

HSIEH CHIA-HSIANG

Experience: Member, Szechwan Provincial Revolutionary Committee; Vice-Political-Commissar, Chengtu Military Region.
Status: military (Fourth Field Army).

HSIEH FU-CHIH

Experience: Member, Eighth Central Committee; Alternate Member, Politburo; Vice-Premier, State Council; Director, Staff Office For Internal Affairs; Minister, Ministry of Public Security; Commander and concurrently Political Commissar, Public Security Forces Headquarters; Chairman, Peking Municipal Revolutionary Committee.
Status: military.

HSIEH HSUEH-KUNG

Experience: First Secretary, Tientsin Municipal Party Committee; Chairman, Tientsin Municipal Revolutionary Committee.
Status: revolutionary leading cadre.

HSIEN HENG-HAN

Experience: Chairman, Kansu Provincial Revolutionary Committee; Political Commissar, Lanchow Military Region.
Status: military (Second Front Army; 120th Division; First Field Army).

HSU CHING-HSIEN

Experience: Vice-Chairman, Shanghai Municipal Revolutionary Committee.
Status: representative of mass organizations.

HSU HAI-TUNG

Experience: Member, Eighth Central Committee; Member, Standing Committee, Military Commission, CC.
Status: military (Fourth Front Army; 115th Division; New Fourth Army).

HSU HSIANG-CHIEN

Experience: Member, Eighth Central Committee; Member, Politburo; Vice-Chairman, Military Commission, CC; Vice-Chairman, National Defense Council, State Council.
Status: military (Fourth Front Army).

HSU SHIH-YU

Experience: member, Eighth Central Committee; Secretary, East China CCP-CC Regional Bureau; Vice-Minister, Ministry of National Defense, State Council; Chairman, Kiangsu Provincial Revolutionary Committee; Commander, Nanking Military Region.
Status: military (Fourth Front Army; Third Field Army).

HU CHI-TSUNG

Experience: Vice-Governor, Kansu Province; Secretary, Kansu

Provincial Party Committee; Vice-Chairman, Kansu Provincial Revolutionary Committee.
Status: revolutionary leading cadre.

HUA KUO-FENG
Experience: Secretary, Hunan Provincial Party Committee; Vice-Chairman, Hunan Provincial Revolutionary Committee.
Status: revolutionary leading cadre.

HUANG CHEN
Experience: Ambassador to France.
Status: revolutionary leading cadre.

HUANG YUNG-SHENG
Experience: Member, Eighth Central Committee; Chief, General Staff Department; Chairman, Kwangtung Provincial Revolutionary Committee.
Status: military (First Front Army; 115th Division; Fourth Field Army).

JAO HSING-LI
Experience: Vice-Chairman, Hupei Provincial Revolutionary Committee; Chairman, Hsihsui *hsien* Revolutionary Committee.
Status: representative of mass organizations.

JEN SSU-CHUNG
Experience: Member, Standing Committee, Kwangtung Provincial Revolutionary Committee; Vice-Political-Commissar, Kwangchow Military Region.
Status: military (115th Division; Fourth Field Army).

KANG SHENG
Experience: Member, Eighth Central Committee; Member, Standing Committee, Politburo; Advisor, Central Cultural Revolution Group; Vice-Chairman, Third National People's Congress.
Status: revolutionary leading cadre.

KAO WEI-SUNG
Experience: Vice-Political-Commissar, Lanchow Military Region.
Status: military (Red Army in Northern Shensi; First Field Army).

KENG PIAO
Experience: Ambassador to Burma; Ambassador to Albania.
Status: revolutionary leading cadre.

KUANG JEN-NUNG
Experience: Director, Civil Aviation General Administration Bureau, State Council; Deputy Commander, Air Force Headquarters.
Status: military (New Fourth Army; Third Field Army).

KUNG SHIH-CHUAN
Experience: First Vice-Chairman, Kwantung Provincial Revolu-

tionary Committee; Third Political Commissar, Kwangchow Military Region.

Status: military (First Front Army; Fourth Field Army).

KUO MO-JO

Experience: Chairman, Third National People's Congress; President, Chinese Academy of Sciences.

Status: revolutionary leading cadre.

LAI CHI-FA

Experience: Minister, Ministry of Building Materials, State Council.

Status: revolutionary leading cadre.

LI CHEN

Experience: Director, Political Department, Shenyang Military Region.

Status: military (Fourth Front Army; Second Field Army).

LI CHIANG

Experience: Vice-Minister, Ministry of Foreign Trade; Vice-Chairman, Foreign Trade And Economic Council.

Status: revolutionary leading cadre.

LI FU-CHUN

Experience: Member, Eighth Central Committee; Member, Standing Committee, Politburo, CC; Vice-Premier, State Council and concurrently Chairman, State Planning Commission.

Status: revolutionary leading cadre.

LI HSIEN-NIEN

Experience: Member, Eighth Central Committee; Member, Politburo, CC; Vice-Premier, State Council; Director, Staff Office For Finance And Trade; Minister, Ministry of Finance.

Status: revolutionary leading cadre.

LI HSUEH-FENG

Experience: Member, Eighth Central Committee; Alternate Member, Politburo, CC; First Secretary, North China CCP-CC Regional Bureau; Vice-Chairman, Third People's National Congress; Chairman, Hopei Provincial Revolutional Committee.

Status: revolutionary leading cadre.

LI JUI-SHAN

Experience: Secretary, Hunan Provincial Party Committee; Chairman, Shensi Provincial Revolutionary Committee.

Status: revolutionary leading cadre.

LI SHUI-CHING

Experience: Commander, Tsinan Military Region.

Status: military (First Front Army; 115th Division; the Army Corps Directly Under Control of the Central Government).

LI SHUN-TA

Experience: Member, Standing Committee, Shansi Provincial Revolutionary Committee; Chairman, Pingshun *hsien* Revolutionary Committee; Commander, Hsikou Brigade, Pingshun *hsien*.

Status: representative of mass organizations.

LI SSU-KUANG

Experience: Minister, Ministry of Geology; Vice-Chairman, Fourth Chinese People's Political Consultative Conference; President, Chinese Academy of Sciences.

Status: revolutionary leading cadre.

LI SU-WEN (f.)

Experience: Vice-Chairman, Shenyang City Revolutionary Committee.

Status: representative of mass organizations (a worker of Hoping Subsidiary Food Store).

LI TA-CHANG

Experience: Alternate Member, Eighth Central Committee; Governor, Szechwan Province; Secretary, Southwest CCP-CC Regional Bureau; Vice-Chairman, Szechwan Provincial Revolutionary Committee.

Status: revolutionary leading cadre.

LI TEH-SHENG

Experience: Chairman, Anhwei Provincial Revolutionary Committee; Commander, Anhwei Provincial Military District.

Status: military (Fourth Front Army; Second Field Army).

LI TIEN-YU

Experience: Deputy Chief, General Staff Department, Ministry of National Defense.

Status: military (First Front Army; 115th Division; Fourth Field Army).

LI TSO-PENG

Experience: First Political Commissar, Navy Headquarters.

Status: military (First Front Army; 115th Division; Fourth Field Army).

LIANG HSING-CHU

Experience: Vice-Chairman, Szechwan Provincial Revolutionary Committee; Commander, Chengtu Military Region.

Status: military (First Front Army; 115th Division; Fourth Field Army).

LIU CHIEH-TING

Experience: Secretary, I-pin Party Branch Committee, Szechwan; Vice-Chairman, Szechwan Provincial Revolutionary Committee.

Status: revolutionary leading cadre.

LIU CHIEU-HSUN
Experience: Alternate Member, Eighth Central Committee; First Secretary, Honan Provincial Party Committee; Secretary, Central-South CCP-CC Regional Bureau; Chairman, Honan Provincial Revolutionary Committee.
Status: revolutionary leading cadre.

LIU CHUN-YI
Experience: Member, Standing Committee, Kwangtung Provincial Revolutionary Committee; Chairman, Kwangtung Provincial Workers' Congress.
Status: representative of mass organizations.

LIU FENG
Experience: Vice-Chairman, Hupei Provincial Revolutionary Committee; Political Commissar, Wuhan Military Region.
Status: military (Fourth Front Army; 129th Division; Chungyuan Field Army; Second Field Army).

LIU HSI-CHANG
Experience: Member, Standing Committee, Peking Municipal Revolutionary Committee; Chief, Hard Core Section, Peking Municipal Workers' Congress; a worker of Kwanghua Lumber Mill.
Status: representative of mass organizations.

LIU HSIEN-CHUAN
Experience: Chairman, Tsinghai Provincial Revolutionary Committee; Political Commissar, Air Force Headquarters.
Status: military (First Front Army; 115th Division; Fourth Field Army).

LIU HSING-YUAN
Experience: Second Political Commissar; Kwangchow Military Region.
Status: military (First Front Army; Fourth Field Army).

LIU KE-PING
Experience: Member, Eighth Central Committee; Vice-Governor, Shansi Province; Chairman, Shansi Provincial Revolutionary Committee.
Status: revolutionary leading cadre.

LIU PO-CHENG
Experience: Member, Eighth Central Committee; Member, Politburo, CC; Vice-Chairman, Military Commission, CC; Vice-Chairman, National Defense Council; Vice-Chairman, Third National People's Congress.
Status: military (First Front Army; Second Field Army).

LIU SHENG-TIEN
Experience: Vice-Chairman, Liaoning Provincial Revolutionary

Committee; Chairman, Suiyuan Commune Revolutionary Committee, Yingkou.

Status: representative of mass organizations.

LIU TZU-HOU

Experience: Alternate Member, Eighth Central Committee; First Secretary, Hupei Provincial Party Committee; Governor, Hupei Province; First Vice-Chairman, Hopei Provincial Revolutionary Committee.

Status: revolutionary leading cadre.

LIU WEI

Experience: Vice-Minister, Second Ministry of Machine Building.

Status: revolutionary leading cadre.

LU JUI-LIN

Experience: Vice-Chairman, Yunnan Provincial Revolutionary Committee; Deputy Commander, Kunming Military Region.

Status: military (First Front Army; Second Field Army).

LU TIEN-CHI

Experience: a miner of Chaochuang Coal Mines in Shantung.

Status: representative of mass organizations.

LU YU-LAN (f.)

Experience: Secretary, Party Branch, of the Shanku Brigade, Tung-liu, Linhsi *hsien*; Member, Standing Committee, Hopei Provincial Revolutionary Committee.

Status: representative of mass organizations.

LUNG SHU-CHIN

Experience: Chairman, Sinkiang Autonomous Region Revolutionary Committee; Commander, Sinkiang Autonomous Region Military District.

Status: military (First Front Army; 115th Division; Fourth Field Army).

MA FU-CHUAN

Experience: a worker of No. 1 State Cotton Mill at Shih-chia-chuang.

Status: revolutionary leading cadre.

MO HSIEN-YAO

Experience: Member, Standing Committee, Chekiang Provincial Revolutionary Committee; a responsible man of Chekiang Provincial Peasants' Congress.

Status: representative of mass organizations.

NAN PING

Experience: Chairman, Chekiang Provincial Revolutionary Committee; Political Commissar, Chekiang Provincial Military District.

Status: military (New Fourth Army; Third Field Army).

NI CHIH-FU
Experience: A Worker Engineer, Peking First Machine Building Plant.
Status: representative of mass organizations.

NIEH JUNG-CHEN
Experience: Member, Eighth Central Committee; Member, Politburo; Vice-Chairman, Military Commission, CC; Vice-Chairman, National Defense Council, State Council; Vice-Premier and concurrently Chairman, Scientific And Technological Commission, State Council.
Status: military (First Front Army; 115th Division).

NIEN CHI-JUNG
Experience: Vice-Chairman, Kansu Provincial Revolutionary Committee; Commander, Red Flag Militia Company, Ho Chia Chuang.
Status: representative of mass organizations.

PAN FU-SHENG
Experience: Alternate Member, Eighth Central Committee; First Secretary, Heilungkiang Provincial Party Committee; Chairman, Heilungkiang Provincial Revolutionary Committee.
Status: revolutionary leading cadre.

PAN SHIH-KAO
Experience: a miner of Anyuan Coal Mines, Kiangsi.
Status: representative of mass organizations.

PAO-JIH LE-TAI (f.)
Experience: Member, Inner-Mongolia Autonomous Region Revolutionary Committee; Chairman, Wu-shen-tai Commune Revolutionary Committee, Wu-shen-chi, Inner-Mongolia.
Status: representative of mass organizations.

PENG SHAO-HUI
Experience: Deputy Chief, General Staff Department.
Status: military (First Front Army; 120th Division; First Field Army).

PI TING-CHUN
Experience: Vice-Chairman, Fukien Provincial Revolutionary Committee; Deputy Commander, Fuchow Military Region.
Status: military (Fourth Front Army; 129th Division; Chungyuan Field Army; Third Field Army).

SAI FU-TIN
Experience: Alternate Member, Eighth Central Committee; Chairman, Sinkiang Autonomous Region People's Committee; Vice-Chairman, Sinkiang Autonomous Region Revolutionary Committee; Deputy Commander, Sinkiang Autonomous Region Military District.
Status: revolutionary leading cadre.

SHEN MAO-KUNG

Experience: Member, Standing Committee, Hunan Provincial Revolutionary Committee; Director, Chairman, Honan Provincial Workers' Congress.

Status: representative of mass organizations.

SU CHING

Experience: Deputy Director, Operation Department.

Status: military (First Front Army; Fourth Field Army).

SU YU

Experience: Member, Eighth Central Committee; Member, Standing Committee, Military Commission, CC; Vice-Minister, Ministry of National Defense.

Status: military (First Front Army; New Fourth Army; Third Field Army).

TAN FU-JEN

Experience: Chairman, Yunnan Provincial Revolutionary Committee; Political Commissar, Kunming Military Region.

Status: military (Second Front Army; Fourth Field Army).

TANG CHI-SHAN

Experience: Member, Standing Committee, Honan Provincial Revolutionary Committee; a responsible man of Honan Provincial Workers' Congress.

Status: representative of mass organizations (a railway worker).

TANG CHUNG-FU

Experience: Member, Standing Committee; Hunan Provincial Revolutionary Committee; a responsible man of Hunan Provincial Workers' Congress; a worker of Shukuang Electronic Plant at Changsha.

Status: representative of mass organizations.

TENG HAI-CHING

Experience: Chairman, Inner-Mongolia Autonomous Region Revolutionary Committee; Deputy Commander, Peking Military Region and concurrently Commander, Inner-Mongolia Autonomous Region Military District.

Status: military (First Front Army; New Fourth Army; Third Field Army).

TENG TAI-YUAN

Experience: Member, Eighth Central Committee; Vice-Chairman, Fourth Chinese People's Political Consultative Conference.

Status: revolutionary leading cadre.

TENG TZU-HUI

Experience: Member, Eighth Central Committee; Vice-Chairman, Fourth Chinese People's Political Consultative Conference.

Status: revolutionary leading cadre.

TENG YING-CHOA (f.)

Experience: Member, Eighth Central Committee; Second Secretary, Women's Work Committee; Deputy Director, All-China Women's Association.

Status: revolutionary leading cadre (Chou En-lai's wife).

TIEN HUA-KUEI

Experience: Secretary, Party Branch at the Huang Shan Brigade, Polo *hsien*; Vice-Chairman, Kwangtung Provincial Revolutionary Committee.

Status: representative of mass organizations.

TIEN PAO

Experience: Alternate Member, Eighth Central Committee; Vice-Chairman, Szechwan Provincial Revolutionary Committee; Vice-Governor, Szechwan Province.

Status: revolutionary leading cadre.

TING SHENG

Experience: Deputy Commander, Kwangchow Military Region.

Status: military (First Front Army; Fourth Field Army).

TSAI CHANG (f.)

Experience: Member, Eighth Central Committee; Director, Women's Work Department, CCP; Chairman, All-China Women's Association.

Status: revolutionary leading cadre (Li Fu-chun's wife).

TSAI HSIEH-PIN

Experience: Member, Standing Committee, Szechwan Provincial Revolutionary Committee.

Status: representative of mass organizations (a peasant).

TSAI SHU-MEI (f.)

Experience: Member, Standing Committee, Tientsin Municipal Revolutionary Committee; a worker of Tientsin Textile No. 4 Plant.

Status: representative of mass organizations.

TSAO LI-HUAI

Experience: Deputy Commander, Air Force Headquarters.

Status: military (First Front Army; Fourth Field Army).

TSAO YI-OU (f.)

Experience: unknown.

Status: revolutionary leading cadre (Kang Sheng's wife).

TSENG KUO-HUA

Experience: Deputy Commander, Air Force Headquarters.

Status: military (First Front Army; 115th Division; Fourth Field Army).

TSENG SHAN
Experience: Member, Eighth Central Committee; Minister, Ministry of Internal Affairs.
Status: revolutionary leading cadre.

TSENG SHAO-SHAN
Experience: Political Commissar, Shenyang Military Region.
Status: military (Fourth Front Army; Second Field Army).

TSENG SSU-YU
Experience: Chairman, Hupei Provincial Revolutionary Committee; Commander, Wuhan Military Region.
Status: military (First Front Army; 115th Division; the Army Corps Directly Under Control of the Central Government).

TSUNG HSI-YUN
Experience: Member, Kirin Provincial Revolutionary Committee; Chief, Core Section, Kirin Provincial Workers' Congress.
Status: representative of mass organizations (a miner).

TU PING
Experience: Political Commissar, Nanking Military Region.
Status: military (First Front Army; 129th Division; Fourth Field Army).

TUNG MING-HUI
Experience: a responsible man of Huhehot Peasants' Congress, Inner-Mongolia.
Status: representative of mass organizations.

TUNG PI-WU
Experience: Member, Eighth Central Committee; Member, Politburo; Vice-Chairman, People's Republic of China.
Status: revolutionary leading cadre.

WANG CHAO-CHU
Experience: a worker engineer, the Public Work Department for building of the Nanking Yangtze River Bridge.
Status: representative of mass organizations.

WANG CHEN
Experience: Member, Eighth Central Committee; Minister of State Farms And Land Reclamation, State Council.
Status: revolutionary leading cadre.

WANG CHIN-HSI
Experience: a worker and Vice-Chairman of the Taching Oil Field Revolutionary Committee.
Status: representative of mass organizations.

WANG HSIAO-YU
Experience: Chairman, Shantung Provincial Revolutionary Committee; Vice-Mayor of Tsingtao.
Status: revolutionary leading cadre.

WANG HSIN-TING

Experience: Deputy Chief, General Staff Department.

Status: military (Fourth Front Army; 129th Division; the Army Corps Directly Under Control of the Central Government).

WANG HSIU-CHEN (f.)

Experience: Member, Standing Committee, Shanghai Municipal Revolutionary Committee; a worker of No. 30 State Cotton Mill.

Status: representative of mass organizations.

WANG HUAI-HSIANG

Experience: Chairman, Kirin Provincial Revolutionary Committee; Political Commissar, Kirin Provincial Military District.

Status: military (First Front Army; Second Field Army).

WANG HUI-CHIU

Experience: Deputy Political Commissar, Air Force Headquarters.

Status: military (Fourth Front Army; Chungyuan Field Army; Second Field Army).

WANG HUNG-KUN

Experience: Second Political Commissar, Navy Headquarters.

Status: military (Fourth Front Army; the 129th Division; Second Field Army).

WANG HUNG-WEN

Experience: Vice-Chairman, Shanghai Municipal Revolutionary Committee; a responsible man of the Shanghai Workers Headquarters; worker of No. 17 State Cotton Mill.

Status: representative of mass organizations.

WANG KUO-FAN

Experience: Member, Standing Committee, Hopei Provincial Revolutionary Committee; Secretary, Party Branch at the Shih-pu Brigade, Chien-ming Commune, Chunhua *hsien*.

Status: representative of mass organizations.

WANG PAI-TAN

Experience: unknown.

Status: worker/peasant.

WANG PING-CHANG

Experience: Minister of Seventh Ministry of Machine Building; Vice-Chairman, Scientific And Technological Commission; Deputy Commander, Air Force Headquarters.

Status: military (First Front Army; 151st Division; the Army Corps Directly Under Control of the Central Government).

WANG-SHOU-TAO

Experience: Member, Eighth Central Committee; Secretary, Central-South CCP-CC Regional Bureau; Vice-Chairman, Kwangtung Provincial Revolutionary Committee.

Status: revolutionary leading cadre.

WANG SHU-SHENG

Experience: Member, Eighth Central Committee; Vice-Minister of National Defense, State Council.

Status: military (Fourth Front Army; Chungyuan Field Army; Fourth Field Army).

WANG TUNG-HSING

Experience: Vice-Minister, Ministry of Public Security, State Council; Director, Administrative (Staff) Office, CCP.

Status: revolutionary leading cadre.

WEI FENG-YING (f.)

Experience: Vice-Chairman, Liaoning Provincial Revolutionary Committee; a responsible person in the Liaoning Provincial Workers' Congress; a worker of a machine building plant in Manchuria.

Status: representative of mass organizations.

WEI KUO-CHING

Experience: Member, Eighth Central Committee; First Secretary, Kwangsi Provincial Party Committee and concurrently Chairman, Kwangsi Provincial People's Committee, Chairman, Kwangsi Provincial Revolutionary Committee; First Political Commissar, Kwangchow Military Region.

Status: revolutionary leading cadre.

WEI PING-KUEI

Experience: Vice-Chairman, Anshan City Revolutionary Committee; a worker of the Anshan Steel and Iron Company.

Status: representative of mass organization.

WEN YU-CHENG

Experience: Deputy Chief, General Staff Department and concurrently Commander, Peking Garrison District.

Status: military (Fourth Front Army; 115th Division; Fourth Field Army).

WU FA-HSIEN

Experience: Deputy Chief, General Staff Department and concurrently Commander, Air Force Headquarters.

Status: military (First Front Army; 115th Division, Fourth Field Army).

WU JUI-LIN

Experience: Deputy Commander, Navy Headquarters.

Status: military (First Front Army; Fourth Field Army).

WU KUEI-HSIEN (f.)

Experience: Member, Shensi Provincial Revolutionary Committee; worker of the Northwest State No. 1 Cotton Mill.

Status: representative of mass organizations.

WU TA-SHENG

Experience: Vice-Chairman, Kiangsu Provincial Revolutionary Committee; responsible man of Nanking Military Region.

Status: military.

WU TAO

Experience: Chairman, Inner-Mongolia Autonomous Region Revolutionary Committee; Political Commissar, Inner-Mongolia Autonomous Region Military District.

Status: military (First Front Army; the Army Corps Directly Under Control of the Central Government).

WU TEH

Experience: Member, Eighth Central Committee; Second Secretary, Peking Municipal Party Committee and concurrently the Acting Mayor of Peking; Chairman, Peking Municipal Revolutionary Committee.

Status: revolutionary leading cadre.

YANG CHUN-FU

Experience: Secretary, Liaoning Provincial Party Committee; First Secretary, Shenyang City Party Committee; Vice-Chairman, Liaoning Provincial Revolutionary Committee.

Status: revolutionary leading cadre.

YANG FU-CHEN (f.)

Experience: Member, Standing Committee, Shanghai Municipal Revolutionary Committee; a worker of State No. 1 Cotton Mill.

Status: representative of mass organizations.

YANG TEH-CHIH

Experience: Member, Eighth Central Committee; First Vice-Chairman, Shantung Provincial Revolutionary Committee; Commander, Tsinan Military Region.

Status: military (First Front Army; 115th Division; the Army Corps Directly Under Control of the Central Government).

YAO WEN-YUAN

Experience: Member, Central Cultural Revolution Group; Vice-Chairman, Shanghai Municipal Revolutionary Committee.

Status: revolutionary leading cadre.

YEH CHIEN-YING

Experience: Member, Eighth Central Committee; Member, Politburo, CC; Vice-Chairman, Military Commission, CC; Vice-Chairman, National Defense Council.

Status: military (First Front Army).

YEH CHUN (f.)

Experience: Member, Administrative Section, Military Commission, CC.

Status: military (Lin Piao's wife).

YU CHIU-LI

Experience: Vice-Chairman, State Planning Commission; Minister, Ministry of Petroleum Industry, State Council.
Status: revolutionary leading cadre.

YU SANG

Experience: Vice-Minister of Public Security, State Council.
Status: revolutionary leading cadre.

YUAN SHENG-PING

Experience: Shantung Provincial Revolutionary Committee; Political Commissar, Tsinan Military Region.
Status: military (First Front Army; 115th Division; Fourth Field Army).

B. ALTERNATE MEMBERS

CHANG CHI-HUI

Experience: Commander, First Division, Air Force.
Status: military (Fourth Field Army).

CHANG CHIANG-LIN

Experience: First Vice-Chairman, Tsinghai Provincial Revolutionary Committee; Commander, Tsinghai Provincial Military District.
Status: military.

CHANG HSI-TING (f.)

Experience: Secretary, Yipin City Party Committee, Szechwan Province; Vice-Chairman, Szechwan Provincial Revolutionary Committee.
Status: revolutionary leading cadre (Liu Chieh-ping's wife).

CHANG HSIU-CHUAN

Experience: Vice-Political-Commissar, Navy Headquarters.
Status: military (First Front Army; 115th Division; Fourth Field Army).

CHANG JIH-CHING

Experience: Vice-Chairman, Shansi Provincial Revolutionary Committee; Second Political Commissar, Shansi Provincial Military District.
Status: military (New Fourth Army; Third Field Army).

CHANG LING-PIN

Experience: Deputy Director, General Rear Services Department, Ministry of National Defense.
Status: military (First Front Army; Third Field Army).

CHANG SHIH-CHUNG

Experience: Vice-Chairman, New China News Agency Revolutionary Committee; a responsible person of the Workers Propaganda Group, Peking College of Petroleum.

Status: representative of mass organizations (a worker).

CHANG SSU-CHOU

Experience: Secretary, Party Branch at the Mienfeng People's Commune, Chienyang *hsien,* Szechwan Province; Vice- Chairman, Szechwan Provincial Revolutionary Committee.

Status: representative of mass organizations.

CHANG YEN-CHENG

Experience: unknown.

Status: unknown.

CHANG YING TSAI

Experience: Commander, 39th Division, 13th Army.

Status: military (129th Division; Second Field Army).

CHAO CHI-MIN

Experience: Deputy Commander, Navy Headquarters.

Status: military (New Fourth Army; Third Field Army).

CHAO FENG

Experience: a responsible person of the 6003rd Army Unit.

Status: military (Third Field Army).

CHAO HSING-YUAN

Experience: Commander, 118th Division, 40th Army.

Status: military (Fourth Field Army).

CHEN HO-FA

Experience: unknown.

Status: peasant/worker.

CHEN HUA-TANG

Experience: Vice-Chairman, National Defense Scientific Committee.

Status: military (New Fourth Army; Third Field Army).

CHEN JEN-CHI

Experience: political commissar of an artillery unit.

Status: military (First Front Army; Fourth Field Army).

CHEN KAN-FENG

Experience: Member, Standing Committee, Shanghai Municipal Revolutionary Committee; Chairman, Shanghai Tungchi University Revolutionary Committee.

Status: representative of mass organizations.

CHEN LI-YUN

Experience: First Vice-Chairman, Chekiang Provincial Revolutionary Committee; Political Commissar, 7350th Air Force Unit.

Status: military.

CHENG SAN-SHENG

Experience: Vice-Chairman, Tientsin Municipal Revolutionary Committee; Commander, Tientsin Garrison District.

Status: military (the Army Corps Directly Under Control of the Central Government).

CHIANG PAO-TI (f.)

Experience: unknown.

Status: peasant/worker.

CHIAO LIN-YI

Experience: First Secretary, Canton City Party Committee; Vice-Chairman, Canton City Revolutionary Committee.

Status: revolutionary leading cadre.

CHIEN HSUEH-SEN

Experience: Vice-Chairman, National Defense Scientific and Technological Committee; Director, Institute of Mechanics, Chinese Academy of Sciences.

Status: revolutionary leading cadre (a missile expert).

CHILINWANGTAN

Experience: Vice-Chairman, Tiching Tibetan Autonomous *chou* Revolutionary Committee, Yunnan Province.

Status: representative of mass organizations (hero of the militia).

CHIN TSU-MIN

Experience: a worker at the Shanghai Electronic Engineering Plant.

Status: representative of mass organizations.

CHU KUANG-YA

Experience: Vice-Chairman, National Defense Scientific Committee.

Status: revolutionary leading cadre (a scientist).

FAN HSIAO-CHU (f.)

Experience: Vice-Chairman, Hsiuhsui *husien* Revolutionary Committee, Kiangsi Province.

Status: representative of mass organizations.

FAN TEH-LING

Experience: a worker at Kailuan Coal Mines, Hopei Province.

Status: representative of mass organizations.

FANG I

Experience: Alternate Member, Eighth Central Committee; Deputy Director, Staff Office for Foreign Affairs, State Council; Chairman, Economic Relations with Foreign Countries Commission, State Council.

Status: revolutionary leading cadre.

FANG MING

Experience: Chairman, Wuhan City Revolutionary Committee; Commander, Wuhan Garrison District.

Status: military (Fourth Front Army; Second Field Army).

FENG CHAN-WU
Experience: unknown.
Status: peasant/worker.

FU CHUAN-TSO
Experience: Commander of the Air Force units in the Wuhan Military Region.
Status: military (Second Field Army).

HAN YING
Experience: unknown.
Status: peasant/worker.

HSIEH CHIA-TANG
Experince: Member, Standing Committee, Szechwan Provincial Revolutionary Committee; a worker at the Chengtu Machine Building Plant.
Status: representative of mass organizations.

HSIEH WANG-CHUN (f.)
Experience: unknown.
Status: peasant/worker.

HSU CHIH
Experience: Chairman, Tukou City Revolutionary Committee; Vice-Chairman, Szechwan Provincial Revolutionary Committee; Vice-Minister of Metallurgical Industry, State Council.
Status: revolutionary leading cadre.

HU LIANG-TSAI
Experience: Chairman, Tukou City Revolutionary Committee; Vice-Chairman, Szechwan Provincial Revolutionary Committee; Vice-Minister of Metallurgical Industry, State Council.
Status: revolutionary leading cadre.

HU LIANG-TSAI
Experience: Vice-Chairman, Sinkiang-Uighur Autonomous Region Revolutionary Committee; a responsible person of the Workers Congress.
Status: representative of mass organizations.

HU WEI
Experience: Vice-Chairman, Shensi Provincial Revolutionary Committee; Commander of the 21st Army.
Status: military (First Front Army; New Fourth Army; Third Field Army).

HUA LIN-SEN
Experience: unknown.
Status: unknown.

HUANG CHENG-LIEN
Experience: unknown.
Status: unknown.

HUANG CHIH-YUNG
Experience: Political Commissar, Amor Headquarters.
Status: military (First Front Army; Fourth Field Army).

HUANG JUNG-HAI
Experience: Vice-Chairman, Kwangtung Provincial Revolutionary Committee; Chairman, Canton City Revolutionary Committee; Commander, Kwangtung Provincial Military District.
Status: military (First Front Army; 115th Division; Fourth Field Army).

HUANG TSO-CHEN
Experience: General Secretary, Peking Municipal Revolutionary Committee; Vice-Political-Commissar, Peking Military Region and concurrently Second Political Commissar, Peking Garrison District.
Status: military (the Army Corps Directly Under Control of the Central Government).

HUANG WEN-MING
Experience: political commissar of a signal troop unit.
Status: military (First Front Army).

JOUTZUTUERHTI
Experience: unknown.
Status: representative of mass organizations (a peasant in Sinkiang).

JUAN PO-SHENG
Experience: Secretary, Kirin Provincial Party Committee; Vice-Chairman, Kirin Provincial Revolutionary Committee.
Status: revolutionary leading cadre.

KANG CHIEN-MIN
Experience: Chairman, Ninghsia *Hui* Autonomous District Revolutionary Committee; Vice-Political-Commissar, Lanchow Military Region.
Status: military (First Field Army).

KENG CHI-CHANG
Experience: Chairman, Hsinhsiang District Revolutionary Committee; Vice-Chairman, Honan Provincial Revolutionary Committee.
Status: revolutionary leading cadre.

KUO HUNG-CHIEH
Experience: unknown.
Status: peasant/worker.

KUO YU-FENG
Experience: a commander of the PLA troop unit stationed at Port

Arthur and Dairen; Chief, Military Control Section, United Front Work Department, CCP.

Status: military (the Army Corps Directly Under Control of the Central Government).

LAN JUNG-YU

Experience: Vice-Governor, Fukien Province; Vice-Chairman, Fukien Provincial Revolutionary Committee.

Status: revolutionary leading cadre.

LAN YI-NUNG

Experience: Member, Standing Committee, Szechwan Provincial Revolutionary Committee; Chairman, Chunking City Revolutionary Committee; Political Commissar, 54th Army.

Status: military (Fourth Field Army).

LI HUA-MIN

Experience: Deputy Commander, Wuhan Military Region.

Status: military (Fourth Field Army).

LI LI

Experience: Governor, Kueichow Province; Vice-Chairman, Kueichow Provincial Revolutionary Committee.

Status: revolutionary leading cadre.

LI SHOU-LIN

Experience: Member, Standing Committee, Shensi Provincial Revolutionary Committee.

Status: representative of mass organizations (a peasant).

LI SHU-MAO

Experience: Member, Standing Committee, Kansu Provincial Revolutionary Committee; Deputy Commander, Lanchow Military Region.

Status: military (First Front Army; First Field Army).

LI TING-SHAN

Experience: Chairman, Kuangchi *hsien* Revolutionary Committee, Hupei Province.

Status: revolutionary leading cadre.

LI TSAI-HAN

Experience: Chairman, Kweichow Provincial Revolutionary Committee; Political Commissar, Kweichow Provincial Military District.

Status: military.

LI YUAN

Experience: Chairman, Hunan Provincial Revolutionary Committee; Commander 47th Army.

Status: military (Fourth Field Army).

LI YUEH-SUNG

Experience: Chairman, Peking Textile Plant.

Status: representative of mass organizations (a worker).

LIANG CHIN-TANG

Experience: Member, Standing Committee, Kwangtung Provincial Revolutionary Committee; a responsible person of the Workers Congress in Kwangtung; a worker of the Canton Electronic Engineering Plant.

Status: representative of mass organizations.

LIU CHEN-HUA

Experience: political commissar of an Army unit.

Status: military (Fourth Field Army).

LIU CHUN-CHIAO

Experience: unknown.

Status: representative of mass organizations (a peasant at Changteh *hsien*).

LIU HAO-TIEN

Experience: Political Commissar, East China Fleet.

Status: military (New Fourth Army; Third Field Army).

LIU HSI-YAO

Experience: Vice-Chairman, Scientific and Technological Commission, State Council.

Status: revolutionary leading cadre.

LO CHUN-TI (f.)

Experience: a peasant of Sha *hsien*, Fukien Province.

Status: representative of mass organizations.

LO HSI-KANG

Experience: Member, Standing Committee, Kweichow Provincial Revolutionary Committee; a responsible person of the Workers Congress; a worker of Kweiyang Power Plant.

Status: representative of mass organizations.

LO YUAN-FA

Experience: Commander, Air Force Headquarters.

Status: military (First Front Army; 115th Division; First Field Army).

LU HO

Experience: Secretary, Party Branch at Taiping Brigade, Kannan *hsien*; Member, Heilungkiang Provincial Revolutionary Committee; Vice-Chairman, Nenkiang District Revolutionary Committee.

Status: representative of mass organizations.

LU TA-TUNG

Experience: Secretary, Chungking City Party Committee; Member, Standing Committee, Szechwan Provincial Revolutionary Committee; Vice-Chairman, Chungking City Revolutionary Committee.

Status: revolutionary leading cadre.

LU TSUN-CHIEH (f.)

Experience: a peasant member of the Red Star Brigade, Sungto Commune, Hachu *tu* Autonomous *hsien*, Tsinghai.

Status: representative of mass organizations.

LUNG KUANG-CHIEN

Experience: Member, Standing Committee, Tsinghai Provincial Revolutionary Committee; a responsible person of the Tsinghai 818 Joint Committee (a mass organization).

Status: representative of mass organizations.

MA TIEN-SHUI

Experience: Secretary, Shanghai Municipal Party Committee; Vice-Chairman, Shanghai Municipal Revolutionary Committee.

Status: revolutionary leading cadre.

NIEH YUAN-TZU (f.)

Experience: Chief, Core Section, the Capital Colleges and Universities Red Guards Congress; Vice-Chairman, Peking Municipal Revolutionary Committee.

Status: representative of mass organizations.

PAN MEI-YING (f.)

Experience: unknown.

Status: unknown.

PEI CHOU-YU

Experience: Vice-Chairman, Sinkiang Uighur Autonomous Region Revolutionary Committee; Vice-Political-Commissar, Sinkiang Autonomous Region Military District and concurrently Second Political Commissar, the Production and Construction Army Corps.

Status: military (First Front Army; First Field Army).

PENG CHUNG

Experience: Secretary, Kiangsu Provincial Party Committee; Vice-Chairman, Kiangsu Provincial Revolutionary Committee.

Status: revolutionary leading cadre.

PENG KUEI-HO

Experience: unknown.

Status: peasant/worker.

SHIH SHAO-HUA

Experience: Deputy Director, *New China News Agency*; President, China Photo Association.

Status: revolutionary leading cadre.

SHU CHI-CHENG

Experience: (honored as an Air Force Combat Hero).

Status: military.

SUNG SHUANG-LAI

Experience: Vice-Political-Commissar, 63rd Army.

Status: military (First Front Army; the Army Corps Directly Under Control of the Central Government).

TA LO

Experience: Vice-Chairman, Tsinghai Provincial Revolutionary Committee.

Status: representative of mass organizations.

TAN CHI-LUNG

Experience: Alternate Member, Eighth Central Committee; CCP; First Secretary, Shantung Provincial Party Committee.

Status: revolutionary leading cadre.

TANG LIANG

Experience: Alternate Member, Eighth Central Committee, CCP; Political Commissar, Nanking Military Region.

Status: military (First Front Army; 129th Division; Third Field Army).

TANG LIN

Experience: Member, Standing Committee, Fukien Provincial Revolutionary Committee; Commander, the 28th Army.

Status: military (New Fourth Army; Third Field Army).

TENG HUA

Experience: Member, Eighth Central Committee; Vice-Governor, Szechwan Province.

Status: revolutionary leading cadre.

TSEN KUO-JUNG

Experience: a worker of the Liuchow Steel and Iron Plant, Kwangsi.

Status: representative of mass organizations.

TSENG YUNG-YA

Experience: Chairman, Tibet Autonomous Region Revolutionary Committee; Commander, Tibet Autonomous Region Military District.

Status: military (First Front Army; Fourth Field Army).

TSUI HAI-LUNG

Experience: Chairman, Yenpien *Korean* Autonomous *chou* Revolutionary Committee; Vice-Political-Commissar, Yenpien Military Subdistrict.

Status: military.

TSUI HSIU-FAN

Experience: Vice-Chairman, Liaoning Provincial Revolutionary Committee.

Status: representative of mass organizations (a locomotive operator).

WANG CHIA-TAO

Experience: Vice-Chairman, Heilungkiang Provincial Revolution-

ary Committee; Commander, Heilungkiang Provincial Military District.
Status: military (Third Field Army).

WANG CHIH-CHIANG
Experience: Vice-Chairman, Ninghsia *Hui* Autonomous Region People's Committee; Vice-Chairman, Ninghsia *Hui* Autonomous Region Revolutionary Committee.
Status: revolutionary leading cadre.

WANG EN-MAO
Experience: Member, Eighth Central Committee; First Secretary, Sinkiang Uighur Autonomous Region Party Committee; Vice-Chairman, Sinkiang Uighur Autonomous Region Revolutionary Committee; Commander and concurrently Political Commissar, Sinkiang Autonomous Region Military District.
Status: revolutionary leading cadre.

WANG HSIN
Experience: Second Political Commissar, Honan Provincial Military District; Vice-Chairman, Honan Provincial Revolutionary Committee.
Status: military (Fourth Front Army; Second Field Army).

WANG KUANG-LIN
Experience: unknown.
Status: representative of mass organizations (a steel and iron worker).

WANG LIU-SHENG
Experience: Director, Political Department, Nanking Military Region.
Status: military (New Fourth Army; Third Field Army).

WANG TI
Experience: Vice-Chairman, Yangchuan Coal Mines Revolutionary Committee, Shansi Province.
Status: representative of mass organizations.

WANG WEI-KUO
Experience: Member, Standing Committee, Shanghai Municipal Revolutionary Committee; responsible person of Air Force units stationed in Shanghai.
Status: military.

WEI TSU-CHEN
Experience: a responsible person of a Navy unit.
Status: military (Fourth Field Army).

WEN HSIANG-LAN (f.)
Experience: Member, Standing Committee, Honan Provincial Revolutionary Committee.
Status: representative of mass organizations (a peasant).

WU CHIN-CHUAN
Experience: Vice-Chairman, Hunan Provincial Workers Congress.
Status: representative of mass organizations.

WU CHUN-JEN
Experience: Deputy Commander, Kwangchow Military Region.
Status: military (First Front Army; Fourth Field Army).

YANG CHUN-SHENG
Experience: Deputy Commander, Second Artillery Headquarters.
Status: military (First Front Army; 115th Division; Second Field Army).

WU CHUNG
Experience: Deputy Commander, Peking Garrison District.
Status: military (First Front Army; 115th Division; Second Field Army).

YANG HUAN-MIN
Experience: Deputy Commander, Air Force Unit, Lanchow Military Region; Vice-Chairman, Shensi Provincial Revolutionary Committee.
Status: military (Fourth Field Army).

YANG TSUNG (f.)
Experience: Vice-Director, "Leaping Forward" Commune, Chia-cha *hsien*, Shannan Special District, Tibet.
Status: representative of mass organizations.

YAO LIEN-WEI
Experience: unknown.
Status: peasant/worker.

YEN CHUNG-CHUAN
Experience: Vice-Chairman, Kwangtung Provincial Revolutionary Committee; Chief of Staff, Canton Military Region.
Status: military (the Red Army in northern Shensi).

YI YAO-TSAI
Experience: a responsible person of the North Sea Fleet.
Status: military (the Army Corps Directly Under Control of the Central Government).

YU TAI-CHUNG
Experience: commander of an infantry corps.
Status: military (Second Field Army).

Appendix TEN

Resource Information Guide on the People's Republic of China

Today it is possible to travel and study in China. To apply for a visa, write to an embassy of the People's Republic of China. The nearest one for Americans is in Canada: Chinese Embassy, Juliana Apartments, 12th Floor, 100 Bronson Avenue, Ottawa 4, Ontario, Canada. Americans may also apply through China Travel Service (H.K.) Ltd., Yu To Sang Building, Queen's Road, Central, Hong Kong.

For entry into China, a smallpox vaccination certificate is required. A yellow book issued by the World Health Organization is acceptable. Travelers arriving from South Asia, Southeast Asia, Hong Kong and Macao must have a valid cholera innoculation certificate. If a traveler comes from or through an area where yellow fever is prevalent, he must have a yellow fever immunization certificate.

Recent experience indicates that the Chinese prefer students or persons associated with Committee of Concerned Asian Scholars, an organization with open membership for those who oppose the Vietnam War. The Chinese also welcome Blacks or other minority students.

For those who cannot go to China, the main information sources are located at the major centers for Chinese studies at various American university cities: Berkeley, Palo Alto, Seattle, Los Angeles, Ann Arbor, Cambridge, Honolulu, etc.

The U.S. government is also a main source of information on China.

The U.S. Consulate-General, Hong Kong, publishes the following materials:

Survey of China Mainland Press (daily)
Current Background: Extracts from China Mainland Press (weekly)
Current Scene (biweekly)
Problems of Chinese Communism (monthly): by U.S.I.A.
Rand Corporation Publications (individual authorship, although under U.S. contract): published in Santa Monica, California.
U.S. Joint Publications Research Service: under Department of Commerce.

Daily Report, Foreign Radio Broadcasts

Other important English Language Periodicals:
Asian Affairs (Tokyo, semiannual)
Asian Survey (Berkeley, monthly)
Biographical Service (Hong Kong, monthly)
China News Analysis (Hong Kong, weekly)
China Report (New Delhi, bimonthly)
China Quarterly (London)
China Trade Report (Hong Kong, monthly)
Eastern Horizon (Hong Kong, monthly)
Far Eastern Economic Review (Hong Kong, monthly)
Issues and Studies (Taipei, monthly)

For further details of these publications, consult *Contemporary China:*
A Research Guide Peter Berton and Eugene Wu (Stanford, Hoover Institution Press, 1967); also
Bibliography of Asian Studies, September, (published by Association of Asian Studies, Ann Arbor, Michigan).

Books and magazines from China are available from China Books and Periodicals, San Francisco; or China Publications, New York.

Index